Rise of the Brao

New Perspectives
in Southeast Asian Studies

RISE OF THE BRAO

ETHNIC MINORITIES
IN NORTHEASTERN CAMBODIA
DURING VIETNAMESE OCCUPATION

IAN G. BAIRD

THE UNIVERSITY OF WISCONSIN PRESS

Publication of this book has been made possible,
in part, through support from the Anonymous Fund
of the College of Letters and Science at the University
of Wisconsin–Madison.

The University of Wisconsin Press
728 State Street, Suite 443
Madison, Wisconsin 53706
uwpress.wisc.edu

Gray's Inn House, 127 Clerkenwell Road
London EC1R 5DB, United Kingdom
eurospanbookstore.com

Names: Baird, Ian (Ian G.), author.
Title: Rise of the Brao: ethnic minorities in northeastern Cambodia
    during Vietnamese occupation / Ian G. Baird.
Other titles: New perspectives in Southeast Asian studies.
Description: Madison, Wisconsin: The University of Wisconsin
    Press, [2020] | Series: New perspectives in Southeast Asian
    studies | Includes bibliographical references and index. |
Identifiers: LCCN 2019014806 | ISBN 9780299326104 (cloth)
Subjects: LCSH: Brao (Southeast Asian people)—Cambodia—History.
    | Cambodia—History—1979-
Classification: LCC DS554.46.B78 B35 2020 | DDC 959.6/0049593—dc23
LC record available at https://lccn.loc.gov/2019014806

Contents

Contents

PART 3

Preface

This book is largely based on oral histories collected by me through in-person interviews, many of them conducted over many hours, over many meetings, and through many experiences working and conducting research in Ratanakiri Province, and to a lesser extent Stung Treng Province, since 1995 (Figures 1 and 2). I first visited northeastern Cambodia to conduct research in support of nongovernmental organizations (NGOs) in Ratanakiri Province (Baird et al. 1996). In 2000, I started to learn about the recent political history of the Brao, and I decided to conduct my master's research in geography on the social aspects of wood resin tree management in three Brao villages in Taveng District, Ratanakiri Province (Baird 2003, 2009c). It was then that I met a number of key Brao leaders from the People's Republic of Kampuchea (PRK) period and learned to speak Brao. After completing my master's degree in 2003, I immediately started my doctoral studies in geography at the University of British Columbia, in Vancouver, Canada. I conducted an ethnohistory of the Brao, applying a critical postcolonial theoretical framework for conceptualizing how the Brao have perceived outsider interventions into their lives as various forms of colonialism, rather than simply considering the French Indochina period, from 1893 to 1954, to be the only "colonial" period to have affected them (Baird 2008).

Apart from relying on my experiences working with the Brao and people from other ethnic groups living in the Sesan River basin and information I collected more generally during my previous master's and doctoral studies, I conducted a series of more specific interviews with ethnic minorities from Ratanakiri Province (mainly Brao but also some ethnic Kreung, Tampuon, and ethnic Lao people) at about the time period that is the focus of this book. Thus, between 2009 and 2017 I frequently visited Ratanakiri and Stung Treng Provinces and met key individuals involved in the events and period of interest to me. In total, I have conducted well over one hundred interviews, including many with key leaders, especially Bou Thang, Soy Keo, Kham Toeung, Thang

Ngon, Dop Khamchoeung, Kham Sai, Yoep Vanson, Kham Phai, Kreng Siengnoi, Bui Yung, Dam Chanty, and others. These names may not mean much to most readers, but these people were key leaders who I hope to give some voice. Virtually all of the interviews were conducted by me in either Brao or Lao languages without the use of a translator. I speak basic Khmer, but none of my research informants are first-language Khmer speakers, so even if I did speak Khmer well, it would still have been preferable to conduct interviews in either Brao or Lao. Most interviews were conducted in Brao.

While fluent in Brao and Lao, I recognize the constraints of my own positionality as a white male Canadian now working as a faculty member in geography at the University of Wisconsin–Madison. I believe, however, that the close relations I developed with my informants over many years have been crucial for facilitating my research.

I had a small portable scanner with me as I traveled to conduct interviews so that I could scan photographs and other documents that I encountered during my research. I thank the late Grant Evans, an important anthropologist and historian of Laos and mainland Southeast Asia more generally, for inspiring me to adopt this method, although at the time he employed it to study Lao royalty, portable scanners were much larger and bulkier than they are today. Thus, I was able to scan photographs in places with no electricity, which proved useful in a number of Brao villages over the years.

I recognize that there are important limitations associated with making use of oral histories. People forget things or tend to overstate some memories while deemphasizing others. This shift can occur both intentionally and unintentionally, but the point is that we cannot expect memories of events that occurred thirty, forty, or even fifty years ago to be stagnant or fully "accurate." Some informants even purposefully lie or focus on the events that make them look good and others look bad. Memory is never external to politics and thus shifts with politics. Indeed, many scholars have pointed out that oral histories are often more important for understanding how people understand the past than they are for documenting exact events that occurred long ago (Fentress and Wickman 1992).

However, what does one do when there is only limited written documentation regarding particular events, or when the documentation that does exist does not include the voices of the main people involved? This is the case for this project. Thus, my interviews necessarily had to have two broad purposes. One was to better understand the meanings that people put on past events, and the other was to gather information to try—albeit necessarily imperfectly—to piece together some of the historical information that has never before been written down. For marginalized peoples, the ones who do not typically write down their histories, or have their histories recorded by others, oral histories are indeed necessary, even if they are imperfect.

My reliance on oral histories does not, however, mean that I have been inattentive to making use of the limited written documentation available. It is crucial to recognize that written sources are few, as much of the documentation has not been archived, especially in northeastern Cambodia. Therefore, I do include what I could access, especially translated Vietnamese-language materials and some media sources, but this material only makes a limited contribution to the overall study, although it does feature prominently in some of the chapters.

Most stories, like the one that follows, simply fade into history unrecorded and are eventually forgotten after those who experienced it pass away. The hope is that this book can serve to record important history, especially for the ethnic minorities this book focuses on, and also provide some idea about how this history has affected the perspectives of many Brao people in northeastern Cambodia today. It is also intended to convey a marginal but important history of ethnic minorities in northeastern Cambodia more generally.

Acknowledgments

Thanks to all the Cambodians who assisted me with this project, in particular Yoep Vanson, who served as my research assistant at times. His assistance was crucial for making contact and gaining the trust of many of those interviewed. Thanks also to Bou Thang for providing many long and detailed interviews and for encouraging others to allow me to interview them. The political capital that he employed made it much easier for me to conduct this research. Thanks to all the people who shared their experiences during interviews, both in Cambodia and Laos. Thanks also to those who allowed me to scan and use their photographs in this book. I am thankful to Merle Pribbenow for translating important documents from Vietnamese to English, to Hồng Đình for correcting Vietnamese-language names, and to Sochea Pheap and his colleagues (coordinated by Peter Swift) for translating much of Bou Thang's two books from Khmer to English. Thanks also to Stephen Heder and Ben Kiernan for providing valuable research materials; and to Stephen Heder, Kosal Path, Michael Vickery, Peter Starr, Sara Colm, W. Nathan Green, and Katherine Bowie for providing useful comments on earlier drafts. Thanks also for the recommendations provided by the two official reviewers, one of whom has identified himself as Stephen Heder. Thanks also to Gwen Walker for her assistance. Finally, thank you to my wife, Monsiri, and my sons, Ben and Khen, for giving me the space and time required to conduct the research that eventually allowed me to write, revise, and finally complete this book.

Abbreviations

ARVN	Army of the Republic of Vietnam (South Vietnam)
ASEAN	Association of Southeast Asian Nations
CIA	Central Intelligence Agency of the United States
CPP	Cambodian People's Party
FANK	Forces Armées Nationales Khmères
FARK	Forces Armées Royales Khmères
FBIS	Foreign Broadcast Information Service
FULRO	Front Uni de Lutte des Races Opprimées (United Front for the Liberation of Oppressed Races)
FUNCINPEC	Front Uni National pour un Cambodge Indépendant, Neutre, Pacifique, et Coopératif
FUNK	Front Uni National du Kampuchea
KPNLF	Khmer People's National Liberation Front
Lao PDR	Lao People's Democratic Republic (or Laos)
NADK	National Army of Democratic Kampuchea (Khmer Rouge) (established in late 1979)
NGO	nongovernmental organization
NTFP	non-timber forest products
PAVN	People's Army of Vietnam
PRAK	People's Revolutionary Army of Kampuchea (under the PRK government) (or Cambodian People's Armed Forces
PRK	People's Republic of Kampuchea
PRPK	People's Revolutionary Party of Kampuchea
SRV	Socialist Republic of Vietnam
UFNSK	United Front for the National Salvation of Kampuchea
UNHCR	United Nations High Commission on Refugees
UNTAC	United Nations Transitional Authority in Cambodia
VODK	The Voice of Democratic Kampuchea (radio)
VVA	Vietnamese Voluntary Army
WPK	Workers' Party of Kampuchea

Glossary

Brao Amba	One of the Brao subgroups in Ratanakiri who historically came from present-day Taveng District, Ratanakiri Province.
Brao Tanap	One of the Brao subgroups in Ratanakiri Province who are presently frequently referred to as Kreung.
Bunong	One of the Austroasiastic language-speaking ethnic groups in northeastern Cambodia, mainly in Mondulkiri Province, who are often referred to as Phnong, a term also used by Khmer people to refer pejoratively to ethnic minority uplanders more generally.
Jarai	One of the Austronesian language-speaking ethnic groups in Ratanakiri Province and adjacent parts of the Central Highlands of Vietnam.
Kachok	One of the Austronesian language-speaking ethnic groups in Ratanakiri Province.
Kavet	One of the Brao subgroups in Ratanakiri Province who historically came from present-day Kok Lak Commune, Voeunsai District, Ratanakiri Province.
Khmer Hanoi	Cambodian Communists who regrouped to North Vietnam in 1954 after the Geneva Accords.
Khmer Kandal	Sihanouk-era designation for majority Khmer people in Cambodia.
Khmer Kraom	Sihanouk-era designation for ethnic Khmer people from present-day Vietnam.
Khmer Loeu	Sihanouk-era designation for upland minorities in Cambodia.
Khmer Rouge	Informal name for Democratic Kampuchea.
Kinh	Ethnic Vietnamese.
Kreung	One of the Brao subgroups in Ratanakiri Province.
Lun	One of the Brao subgroups in Ratanakiri Province who tend to live near large rivers.

Tampuon   One of the Austroasiatic language-speaking ethnic
              groups in Ratanakiri Province.

Rise of the Brao

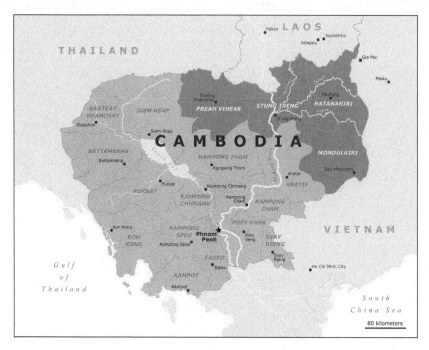

Figure 1. Northeastern Cambodia, 2019 (Ellie Milligan and Meghan Kelly, Cart Lab, Department of Geography, University of Wisconsin–Madison)

Figure 2. Northeastern Cambodia, 1990s (Ellie Milligan and Meghan Kelly, Cart Lab, Department of Geography, University of Wisconsin–Madison)

Introduction

The Golden Age of the Brao of Northeastern Cambodia

It was 2000, and my ethnic Brao friend, Yoep Vanson, was accompanying me to meet the leaders of some remote Brao villages in Taveng District, Ratanakiri Province, where I planned to conduct graduate field research (Figure 2). The Brao are a western Bahnaric language-speaking upland ethnic minority found in the southernmost part of Laos and the northeasternmost part of Cambodia and are historically marginalized within lowlander-dominated city states, kingdoms, and nation-states. When we arrived in Trabok Village—which at the time was located adjacent to the Trabok stream, in the Sesan River basin—I was introduced to Thang Ngon, an elderly man, dressed humbly like other poor people in the village, but clearly highly respected within his community. He was the former secretary of Mondulkiri's Provincial Party Committee, and I soon learned that like others in the community, he was also an active swidden cultivator. A few days later we visited another nearby Brao village, although this one was located adjacent to the Sesan River. There I was introduced to another important elderly Brao man, Veng Khoun, who was previously secretary of Preah Vihear Province's Party Committee and chairman of the province's People's Committee. At that time, I also reflected on another elderly Brao man I had met in Taveng a few years earlier, Kham Toeung, who was the former vice-chairman of Stung Treng Province's People's Committee. I ended up spending considerable amounts of time with all three of these men, as well as other Brao leaders. I wondered why so many rural ethnic Brao people had come to hold senior positions in government, as none were fully fluent in Khmer nor had any of the three received more than a few years of formal education.

Through interviewing Brao leaders and others, and speaking with people from other ethnic minority groups in northeastern Cambodia, what began to emerge was what I call a "peripheral" or "marginal" history: a different perspective on the past, in particular on the Vietnamese occupation period. Crucially, when the Vietnamese entered Cambodia in late 1978, many Brao and other minorities from the northeast were elevated to positions of authority. Viewed from their perspective on the margins, the People's Republic of Kampuchea (PRK) period of Vietnamese occupation, between 1979 and 1989, was a golden age, the first and only time in their history when they played a significant role in the life of the nation.

After the Vietnamese withdrew from Cambodia in 1989, the role of the Brao and other ethnic minorities from the northeast rapidly declined due to their relatively lower levels of formal education, but also because of their lack of upper-level Khmer-based political networks. By the time I met them in the mid-1990s and early 2000s, they had largely retired and returned to their home villages in Taveng District, but they still had much to say about their experiences.

The Golden Age of the Brao of Northeastern Cambodia

The Brao were not a prominent ethnic group in Cambodia, or even northeastern Cambodia, prior to the rise of the Khmer Rouge, which is best known for starving and killing about 1.8 million people between April 1975 and the first few days of 1979. However, a series of events transpired that would propel the Brao to what many of them now consider to be their "golden age." As with the other ethnic minorities of Ratanakiri, most Brao joined the Khmer Rouge in the 1960s. The northeast was "liberated" by the Khmer Rouge in 1970, although the region was heavily bombarded by the US Air Force until 1973. Once the bombing was over, the Khmer Rouge began to more fully implement their draconian policies. They also became increasingly negative toward the Vietnamese, and those who were close to them, including some Brao. This radical shift eventually led to tensions between the Khmer Rouge and the Brao, causing all the Brao in Taveng and some other ethnic minorities from other parts of the Sesan River basin in Ratanakiri Province

4

to flee to Vietnam and Laos as political refugees in 1975. When the Vietnamese decided to remove the Khmer Rouge from power, many of these political refugees joined them. Once the Khmer Rouge had been defeated, the Vietnamese did not trust those who had worked under the Khmer Rouge, and so they appointed a number of former political refugees in Vietnam and Laos to leadership positions in the PRK government, in the military at the central level, and in all senior positions in the four northeasternmost provinces: Ratanakiri, Stung Treng, Mondulkiri, and Preah Vihear. This sudden rise to power was surprising considering that most Brao were effectively illiterate and only spoke a limited amount of Khmer. It helps explain why the period of Vietnamese occupation of Cambodia during the PRK period in the 1980s can be considered the golden age for the Brao because it was a time when they held power like never before, and not since.

The Vietnamese military "invasion" or "liberation" of Cambodia—depending on one's viewpoint—that precipitated the rise to power of the Brao began on December 22, 1978.[1] The arrival of approximately 150,000 Vietnamese soldiers, and later large numbers of specialist advisors from Vietnam, marked a major juncture in the histories of Cambodia and Vietnam. It was also an important period in Asian history, one that also greatly affected China, Thailand, and many other countries in Asia and around the world.

Initially, a Vietnam government spokesperson claimed that Democratic Kampuchea (the Khmer Rouge) had not been toppled by the People's Army of Vietnam (PAVN) but by the United Front for the National Salvation of Kampuchea (UFNSK), a newly established Cambodian revolutionary organization linked to the Communist Party of Kampuchea, which traced its origins back to 1951 when the Indochina Communist Party set up a committee to establish the party (Heder 2004). Indeed, the leader of the UFNSK, Heng Samrin, greatly downplayed the role of the Vietnamese when he announced the liberation of the country on January 7, 1979 (Deth 2011).

It soon became clear to most international observers, however, that PAVN were the main military force behind the toppling of the Khmer Rouge regime (Deth 2011). Thus, the Socialist Republic of Vietnam (SRV) began encountering strong criticisms from the international community, including members of the Association of Southeast Asian Nations (ASEAN) (ASEAN 1979);[2] the People's Republic of China, the main backer of the Khmer Rouge; the United States; and many other western countries. On January 9, 1979, Vietnam officially recognized the Revolutionary Council of the People's Republic of Kampuchea as the legal representative of Cambodia. Laos, the Soviet Union, the Democratic Republic of Germany, Hungary, Poland, Bulgaria, Cuba, Mongolia, Afghanistan, Nicaragua, and Ethiopia promptly did the same (Bou Thang 1993). India, however, was the only noncommunist country to explicitly recognize Cambodia's new government. The Khmer Rouge maintained control over the United Nations seat for Cambodia (Deth 2011), and some notable Cambodia-watchers, such as William Shawcross, generally agreed with the rhetoric of the opposition to the Vietnamese occupation of Cambodia and went as far as to suggest that the PRK period was worse than during the Khmer Rouge period (Shawcross 1984). His position, however, was heavily critiqued by Ben Kiernan (1986) and Michael Vickery (1989).

Most Cambodians were undoubtedly deeply relieved to see the brutal Khmer Rouge regime rapidly removed from power, and its leadership, including "Brother #1," Pol Pot,[3] forced to regroup along the Cambodia-Thailand border, far from where most Cambodians lived. As one Cambodian civil servant later explained: "At that time [January 1979], we were as if submerged under water. Someone came to us and held out a stick for us. We did not think at that time about who was holding the stick. We only knew that we needed to grasp the stick or we would die" (quoted in Tully 2005, 216).

Any sense of relief or even exuberance does, however, not appear to have lasted long. Large numbers of Cambodians—ethnic Khmers in particular—soon lost any enthusiasm that they might have initially had for the Vietnamese voluntary soldiers and the new PRK regime; some feared that their country had come under the neocolonial domination of the Vietnamese. Much anti-Vietnamese propaganda sponsored by the political resistance to the PRK government, including the Khmer Rouge and other groups, as well as many governments and much of the international media. Moreover, it upset many ethnic Khmers to learn of an influx of large numbers of Vietnamese soldiers and advisors into the country. In addition, there was initially no scheduled withdrawal date set, which left many concerned about when, if ever, the Vietnamese would depart. Still more, the takeover of Cambodia was a violation of international law, even if it arguably saved countless lives. In March 1979, once the PRK was established, the new Vietnam-installed government tried to legitimize the arrangement between the PRK and the SRV by signing a twenty-five-year "Treaty of Peace, Friendship and Cooperation" (Slocomb 2003). This formality allowed the PRK government to officially request assistance from Vietnam to ensure its national defense, but it did not convince most of the world that the PRK was actually acting independently from Vietnam.

Importantly, as Sok Udom Deth (2011, 4) has pointed out, the Vietnamese have long been regarded by most Cambodians as their "traditional enemies." Michael Vickery (2010) discussed concerns that many Khmers have long held that Vietnam wants to annex part or all of Cambodia. Frank Smith (1989, 31) also concluded that Khmer peasants have "long-standing traditions of, if not hatred, at least distaste for and distrust of the Vietnamese." Even Norodom Sihanouk, the former king of Cambodia, acknowledged that it is true that "from time immemorial the Vietnamese and the Khmers have been mortal enemies" (Vu 2014, 9). While it is also the case that Khmers and Vietnamese have cooperated at various times over history, the animosity that many Khmers have for Vietnamese probably influenced many, including Ea Meng-Try (1981), to assume that the goal of the Vietnamese in 1979 was to displace and assimilate the Khmer people into a new colony dominated by Vietnamese. The journalist Henry Kamm (1998, 183) put it this way, "The Cambodian puppet regime was not admired but was accepted as a burden Cambodians had to bear. They accepted the view that the Vietnamese Army was their only protection against the return of Pol Pot."

The Political Situation in Cambodia during the PRK Period

The socialist character of Cambodia's "democracy" allowed by the PRK, after the removal of the Khmer Rouge from power, did not permit multiparty electoral contestation (Sorpong 2000), but it was at least more democratic than the previous anti-Vietnamese racist Khmer Rouge regime (Evans and Rowley 1984; Vickery 1984; Sorpong 2000). At times there were serious abuses of power, and the rights and freedoms included in the 1981 constitution were generally not fully respected (Sorpong 2000). Indeed, it must be acknowledged that, "[Since] coming to power in 1979, the government . . . has imprisoned thousands of persons for taking part in violent or non-violent activities on behalf of the Khmer Rouge or the non-communist opposition" (Lawyers Committee for Human Rights 1992, quoted by Sorpong 2000, 68).

Although criticisms of human rights abuses proliferated by the PRK government during the 1980s were certainly exaggerated by those who opposed the PRK (Sorpong 2000), it is nevertheless true that there were arbitrary arrests, and that those arrested were frequently subjected to intensive interrogation and torture, especially by the Vietnamese-established military intelligence unit called T-6. Moreover, individuals were sometimes imprisoned without having a chance to defend themselves in a court of law (Sorpong 2000). On the whole, however, the Vietnamese undertook self-critical measures to investigate such abuses and in some cases disciplined those Vietnamese cadres who had acted inappropriately (Anh 2015).

It remains unclear exactly how many Vietnamese soldiers stayed in Cambodia between 1979 and 1989. Ea Meng-Try (1981) reported that the number increased to 200,000 by the end of 1979, and that it reached 250,000 by 1981, but these numbers seem far from certain.[4] The PRK Ministry of Foreign Affairs (1985) claimed there were 180,000 Vietnamese troops in Cambodia in 1979, but according to Vickery (1989) the number declined to 150,000 in 1982, and was apparently down to 100,000 by 1988. Gottesman (2002) reported that 180,000 Vietnamese troops were stationed in Cambodia, but without considering changes in the number of troops over time, while Carney (1986) claimed that there were 100,000 in Cambodia in 1982. Dũng (1995) claimed that the number was closer to 200,000, but also without providing a specific year. Since Bou Thang was minister of defense for Cambodia between 1982 and late 1985, I queried him about this. His answer was telling. He said, "I never asked." Surprised by this response, I asked him why not, as he was the PRK's minister of defense. Was that not something that he should have known? He referred to Pen Sovan, saying that the former prime minster asked too many questions, and that he did not want to make the same mistake.[5] Indeed, Pen Sovan was arrested and imprisoned in Vietnam in 1981 until after the end of the PRK period, a topic addressed later in the chapter.

During the 1980s, as time passed and the Vietnamese continued to play a major role in the governance of Cambodia, fears that the Vietnamese would never leave increased, and claims that Cambodia was being "Vietnamized" intensified (Beijing in Cambodian to Kampuchea 1983; VODK 1986; Deth 2011). Therefore, when the Vietnamese soldiers officially withdrew from Cambodia in September 1989 (Tomoda 1997;

Slocomb 2003; Gottesman 2002)[6], many Cambodians were happy to see them go.[7] Kamm (1998, 156) wrote that, "In 1989 the last Vietnamese troops crossed the border toward home, to the immense relief of the Cambodian and Vietnamese peoples."

Others, however, feared that the Vietnamese departure might lead to the return to power of the murderous Khmer Rouge (Gottesman 2002; Bekaert 1998; Kamm 1998). Indicative of this, Bou Thang, the most important ethnic minority leader from northeastern Cambodia during the PRK period, told me that when the Vietnamese departed from Cambodia, the PRK leadership informed the Vietnamese that they would ask them to return if the Cambodian military started losing the civil war.[8] Even so, many Vietnamese were undoubtedly happy to leave Cambodia, as living conditions had been poor. Moreover, Cambodia was a dangerous place. Pribbenow (2006) estimated that between 30,000 and 55,000 Vietnamese soldiers and civilians were killed in Cambodia between 1977 and 1989, while Dũng (1995) claimed that 100,000 Vietnamese were killed or wounded, including the 60,000 that were announced as being killed. The number of Cambodians who died during the civil war of the 1980s was, however, potentially higher.

Indicative of the mood of the population nationally, when the first largely free-and-fair election occurred under the supervision of the United Nations Transitional Authority in Cambodia (UNTAC) in May 1993, the Front Uni National pour un Cambodge Indépendant, Neutre, Pacifique, et Coopératif (FUNCINPEC), the political party led by Prince Norodom Sihanouk's son,[9] Prince Norodom Ranariddh, received more votes than any other political party (Conboy 2013; Bekaert 1998). Clearly, the late 1950s and 1960s—when Prince Norodom Sihanouk dominated Cambodian politics—were looked upon rather favorably by many Cambodians, even if the Sihanouk era had its own dark side, which extended to the northeast (see, for example, Meyer 1979; Short 2004; Baird 2008).

The 1980s, however, appear to represent—at least in mainstream Khmer narratives—a dark period in Cambodian history (see, also, Gottesman 2002), not dark in the same way the Khmer Rouge period had been, but dark in the sense that many believed that Cambodia had lost its independence to Vietnam. If most Khmer did not show much gratitude toward the Vietnamese at the time of the "occupation," time and reflection has apparently not resulted in increased appreciation of the

Vietnamese for saving them from the Khmer Rouge. If anything, it would appear that a large number of Cambodians are less grateful to the Vietnamese than ever.

Framing the Book

This study is best framed in relation to ethnic studies, and particularly the study of ethnic minorities from northeastern Cambodia. It is an ethnohistory, one that emphasizes the important political events that influenced the ethnic Brao Amba, and to a lesser extent the Tampuon, Kreung, Lun, Jarai, and ethnic Lao peoples from Ratanakiri Province and Stung Treng Province to a lesser extent. Gerald Hickey tried to do something similar for the southern part of the Central Highlands of Vietnam, where he considered the multiethnic circumstances, although without focusing on any one ethnic group (Hickey 1982a, 1982b), as I do here.

The first researchers to explicitly study the peoples of this relatively remote part of mainland Southeast Asia were French agents of colonialism, one being Captain Pierre Cupet, who was part of the famous Pavie Mission, which spearheaded French efforts to expand its territorial control up the Mekong River basin. He produced detailed documentation of his 1891 investigations of the ethnic groups, including the Brao, which he encountered in what are now Ratanakiri and Stung Treng Provinces (Cupet 1998 [1891]). Then between 1909 and 1911, Henri Maître, a French explorer, conducted a detailed study of parts of northeastern Cambodia and southern Laos, including areas inhabited by Brao (Maître 1912). Others made more modest contributions to understanding these peoples, including Henri Klein (1912), who published a study about the area known as Mounlapoumok Province at the time, and which is now the northern part of Ratanakiri Province. Henri Bruel (1916) also produced a study of Stung Treng, but with less focus on the Brao. Pierre Bitard (1952a, 1952b), however, conducted specific research regarding the Brao in the Voeunsai area near the end of the French colonial period. These initial studies largely treated the Brao as static and essentialized research subjects, with single and inflexible identities, not as changing peoples or as agents of their own change.

The only dedicated research in Brao areas of northeastern Cambodia following Cambodia's independence from France in 1954, and prior to the rise of the Khmer Rouge in the late 1960s, was conducted by

Jacqueline Matras, a French anthropologist and a student of Georges Condominas. Condominas wrote the well-known 1957 book *We Have Eaten the Forest*, which dealt with the culture and livelihoods of ethnic Mnong (Bunong) peoples in parts of the Central Highlands of Vietnam (Condominas 1977 [1957]). Between 1966 and 1968, Matras conducted ethnographic research about the spatial organization of the Brao, focusing her structural study on one Brao village in Ratanakiri Province (Matras-Troubetzkoy 1975, 1983). Although Matras certainly did not have the same explicit colonial objective as the French researchers that preceded her, her study of the way that the Brao spatially organize their lives only superficially considered the impacts of the land grabbing for rubber plantation development that had displaced a number of Brao communities. Nor did she explicitly discuss her own positionality or relationship with the French plantation managers. Moreover, politics were not central to her research, and the people she studied were not recognized as political agents whose positionality, alliances, and understandings were constantly shifting. Individual agency was not acknowledged or discussed. Charles Meyer (1979), on the other hand, studied the development circumstances in northeastern Cambodia in the 1960s. He did not do the type of detailed on-the-ground field research that Matras did, but he was more attentive and critical of the politics of development in northeastern Cambodia. In this study, I attempt to be sensitive to ethnic group culture as well as politics and individual agency. Indeed, maintaining this balance is key to this study.

No dedicated academic research appears to have been conducted in northeastern Cambodia for a twenty-five-year period between around 1968 and 1992. Armed conflict between the Khmer Rouge and the Norodom Sihanouk–led government began in 1968, and by mid-1970 the Khmer Rouge had taken full control of the northeast, after Lon Nol, who had just disposed Sihanouk in a coup d'état, decided—on the advice of the US government—to withdraw all its troops from the northeast so that the area could become a free-fire zone (Sutsakhan 1978; Baird 2008). Not surprisingly, it was impossible for foreigners to conduct research in northeastern Cambodia at this time. Nor was it possible to do studies in Cambodia after the Khmer Rouge took control of Phnom Penh, the capital city, in April 1975. Also research could not be done in northeastern Cambodia between when the Vietnamese ousted the Khmer Rouge from power in late 1978 and when the Vietnamese withdrew from Cambodia near the end of the 1980s.

Since the early 1990s, however, a number of scholarly studies focused on ethnic groups and ethnicity issues have been conducted in northeastern Cambodia, particularly by anthropologists, geographers, linguists, and historians (Keller 2001; Keller et al. 2008; Baird 2003, 2008, 2009c; Bourdier 2006; Guérin 2003, 2008; Uk 2016; Padwe forthcoming). There have also been important studies conducted for development agencies (e.g., White 1995; Colm 1996; Ironside and Baird 2003; Ironside 2009). Much of this recent research, both by scholars and NGO researchers, has been especially influenced by postmodernism and poststructuralism (Foucault 1978) and has generally been much more attentive to ethnic change and individual agency than previous studies. Identities are no longer seen as singular, stagnant, and unchanging; neither are they viewed as being tied only to particular ethnic groups. Instead, identities are recognized to be multiple, flexible, and constantly in flux (Ong 1999), an understanding that allows me to conceptualize my research as not being related simply to a single ethnic group or ethnic subgroup, the Brao Amba, but involving other identities and ethnic groups, such as the Tampuon, Kreung, Lun, Kavet, Jarai, and ethnic Lao. Thus, I have chosen not to draw firm lines between ethnic groups and people who self-identify as belonging to these groups, as identities and languages used by different groups, subgroups, and individuals suggest much more group diversity and individual agency than early studies of the region and its peoples acknowledged.

When writing about upland ethnic minorities like those at the center here, it might seem tempting to adopt a framing in line with James Scott's *The Art of Not Governing: An Anarchist History of Upland Southeast Asia* (2009), as he sees upland peoples as having anarchist agency through deliberately trying to avoid being controlled by states. This framing, while capturing some aspects of upland-lowland relations, is problematic because it tends to underestimate the ways that highland ethnic minorities frequently engaged with lowlanders, even before World War II. That is, uplanders did not only seek to be free of lowland influences but also frequently went to considerable efforts to obtain prestigious titles and positions of power through establishing relations with lowland leaders or otherwise cooperated with lowland states in ways that seriously challenge Scott's "non-state peoples" framework. Thus, Scott has tended to open up opportunities for one type of agency—an anarchist type—while at the same time suppressing another, relations between upland and lowland peoples. Indeed, various scholars have pointed to the need for a more nuanced and balanced approach to understanding upland-lowland relations (Lee 2015; Baird 2013b; Jonsson 2010, 2012), one that I also adopt here.

In line with recent scholarly interest in the rise of the concept of indigeneity in Southeast Asia, including Cambodia, my research is also informed by new understandings regarding Indigenous self-determination and agency and the politics surrounding the concept of indigeneity in Cambodia (Baird 2011a, 2013a, 2016b, 2019; Padwe 2013; Milne 2013; Keating 2013; Swift 2013). While the modern concept of "Indigenous peoples" had not yet been conceived in Cambodia during the period that this book is focused on, lessons learned from research about the adoption of indigeneity, its uneven movement across space, and its internalization and hybridization are important for conceptualizing this research and ethnic studies scholarship more generally.

Through adopting a flexible and nuanced ethnic studies framing, I have been able to put ethnic perspectives and the marginalized histories of the Brao at the forefront of my work without overly essentializing ethnic and other identities of the people I write about. This nonessentializing positionality helps to explain why people from the same ethnic groups and subgroups sometimes saw things in very different ways and followed substantially different political paths. In the past, there has been a tendency to either ignore or confuse ethnic classifications, thus rendering them unimportant, or, on the other hand, elevate ethnicity to where all individual ideas and actions are incorrectly attributed to ethnic group membership. This orientation led to a sort of ethnicity fetishization. Thus, the goal here is to not overly privilege ethnic group membership but also to not ignore it. Ethnicity is often important but needs to be contextualized; ethnicity alone is never sufficient to understand people's actions and political alliances.

The Ethnic Minority View of the Demise of Pen Sovan in Northeastern Cambodia

The ethnic minorities of northeastern Cambodia often saw things differently from other Cambodians. The story of the demise of Pen Sovan is useful for demonstrating this divergence. In late 1981, Pen Sovan, the ethnic Khmer first prime minister of the PRK, was arrested and sent to prison in Vietnam, where he would linger in jail until finally being released and allowed to return to Cambodia in 1991. The arrest of Pen Sovan was arguably the most important political change that occurred during the PRK period. Early on in my discussions with Bou Thang, a key character in this book, he refused to say much about the sensitive issue of Pen Sovan's arrest, even though he certainly knew what happened, since he was in the Politburo at the time. Finally, in 2017, he told me that the reason that Pen Sovan was arrested was because "he spoke too much."[10] Presumably, Pen Sovan had been too critical of his Cambodian and Vietnamese colleagues. This view generally fits with Deth's (2011) contention that Pen Sovan was imprisoned for disagreeing with the presence of illegal Vietnamese immigrants and wanting to improve relations with the Soviet Union. Similarly, Gottesman (2002, 121) claims that Pen Sovan was arrested for irritating the chief Vietnamese advisor to the UFNSK, Lê Đức Thọ, a theoretician and member of the Vietnamese Politburo who is best known for negotiating the peace agreement with Henry Kissinger that ended the war with the United States.[11]

Because an official explanation for Pen Sovan's arrest was not provided, many rumors circulated regarding the reasons for his dramatic fall from power.[12] Ethnic minority views usefully illustrate the particular perspectives of many in northeastern Cambodia, and the agency of individuals. For example, Khamphan Thivong—an ethnic Lao former vice-chairman of Stung Treng's provincial People's Committee—told me that Pen Sovan was arrested because the Vietnamese wanted to convince the Khmer Rouge to surrender rather than endorse too much military conflict, whereas Pen Sovan supported a stronger line against the Khmer Rouge.[13] Yoep Vanson and Kham Sai, two ethnic Brao leaders from Taveng District, Ratanakiri Province, informed me that Pen Sovan wanted to marry the daughter of the Vietnamese leader, Phạm Văn Đồng, even though Pen Sovan was already married. They believe this led to Pen Sovan's arrest in Ho Chi Minh City. They believe that Pen Sovan was a womanizer and not loyal to the Vietnamese.[14] However, Kham Sai also stated that the Vietnamese were upset when they allegedly overheard Pen Sovan say that he thought the Vietnamese were staying too long in Cambodia, and that they were not giving the Cambodians enough control over the governance of their own country. In addition, Kham Sai told me that Pen Sovan was overheard stating that he feared that the Vietnamese would not return to Vietnam, which was a politically dangerous thing to say.[15]

There are other stories. Dop Khamchoeung from Bang Koet Village, a Brao former Mondulkiri PRK military leader, told me, quite unbelievably, that he had heard that Pen Sovan was arrested because he wanted to sell Cambodian land to the French, while the Khmer Rouge's Ieng Sary wanted to sell land to China.[16] Probably the most interesting thing that Kham Sai told me, however, was that Pen Sovan was especially concerned that the Vietnamese would not return to Vietnam, since he did not agree with the pro ethnic minority policies being promoted by the Vietnamese.[17]

Regardless of whether such sentiments reflect reality or not, many minorities from the northeast viewed the Vietnamese policies there during the 1979 to 1989 period as pro ethnic minority. Indeed, Bou Thang (1993) wrote that Article 5 of the 1981 constitution of the PRK stated that, "Every ethnic minority person in the People's Republic of Kampuchea has equal freedom." Article 30 also stated that all Cambodian citizens "are equal before the law and have the same rights and duties, irrespective of their sex, religious belief or race" (quoted in Sorpong 2000, 64). Bou Thang also emphasizes that the PRK Party and State strongly supported ethnic minorities.[18] For example, in November 1984, a nationwide cadre congress approved policies considered to be pro ethnic minority, with the aim of pushing for equality between the ethnic minorities and Khmers, including ensuring that ethnic minorities were well represented in government. Various other measures were also taken in 1985 and 1986 to promote ethnic minorities, and a strong focus was put on developing and modernizing the northeast (Bou Thang 1993).

The statements of ethnic minorities from northeastern Cambodia help explain why many imagine the Vietnamese occupation period as a kind of "golden age," even if the majority of people in Cambodia have a very different view and do not consider that period to be anything like a golden age.

The Mainstream Cambodian View of Vietnamese Occupation

Indicative of the tensions associated with the PRK period, in many parts of Cambodia there is no longer much enthusiasm for January 7, the official holiday that commemorates the 1979 Vietnamese forces' "liberation" of Cambodia from the Khmer Rouge, even if the ruling Cambodian People's Party (CPP) continues to organize celebrations throughout the country in recognition of their victory. Although the CPP has called January 7 a "second birthday" for the Cambodian people (Deth 2011), there has long been fierce debate as to whether January 7 represents the liberation of Cambodia or its "invasion" (Berman 1996; Gottesman 2002, ix; Deth 2009, 2011). January 7 was not celebrated as a national holiday for four years, between 1992 and 1995, but on January 5, 1996, "Victory Day" was reintroduced as a national holiday (Ker 1996), although this has been strongly opposed by the political opposition in Cambodia. Khmer racism toward Vietnamese Cambodians, and Vietnamese more generally, remains rife in Cambodia, and this racism is believed to be partially linked to various stories in the early 1990s about Vietnam trying to gain control of large parts of Cambodia's territory, especially along the border with Vietnam (Leonard 1996). Vietnam is frequently seen as gradually eating away territory along the border with Cambodia (Kimkong Heng and Sovinda Po 2017), something that my research in northeastern Cambodia also suggests (see chapter 5).

Opposition politicians have linked January 7 and April 17, 1975, the day that the Khmer Rouge took control of Phnom Penh. There have also been criticisms that Vietnam protracted the occupation of Cambodia to exploit Cambodia's natural resources, including forests and fisheries, and also rice production through state policies. These were coupled with concerns about illegal Vietnamese immigration (Deth 2011).

Indicating the bizarre and convoluted nature of the debate, members of the political opposition in Cambodia have sometimes tried to link the Khmer Rouge to Vietnam, even though the Khmer Rouge and Vietnam became increasingly hostile to each other beginning around 1973 (Meas 2012). There are, however, various reasons why many Khmer appear so unappreciative of the human and material "sacrifices" the Vietnamese military, government, and people made to "free" Cambodia from the clutches of the Khmer Rouge and keep the Khmer Rouge from returning to power throughout the 1980s. Some have been alluded to previously, but it is worth summarizing them again here. First, the government that replaced the Khmer Rouge was itself, at least initially and ideologically, committed to watered-down socialism, following the Vietnamese/Soviet Union model. This included the adoption of at least some cooperatives (Gottesman 2002; Slocomb 2003). The UFNSK presented itself politically as the heir to the 1970–1975 revolution, arguing that the "Pol Pot–Iang Sary clique"[19] had prevented the revolution from moving ahead as originally envisioned (Vickery 1984). Considering the radical variety of Maoism that the Khmer Rouge had imposed, it should be of little surprise that most people were not enthusiastic about socialism by the time the Vietnamese gained control of most of Cambodia (Gottesman 2002). The recent past had important implications for how politics was organized in Cambodia after 1979, as will be elaborated on later in the book. But in line with this, Michael Vickery (1984) has already argued that despite the propaganda, nothing really "socialist" was implemented in the early years after the arrival of the Vietnamese. Moreover, others have pointed out that living conditions for most Cambodians did improve, especially during the late 1980s (Gottesman 2002; Kamm 1998). Still, life remained very hard for much of the population of Cambodia throughout the PRK period. This was due to the continuing civil war, the centralized socialist economic system imposed on the people, and because of the political and widespread international and United Nations–supported economic sanctions put on Cambodia throughout the Vietnamese occupation period, which did not make it easy to improve living conditions for most Cambodians (Vickery 1984, 1989; Chanda 1986; Mysliwiec 1988; Bekaert 1997).

It would appear that the main obstacle to most Khmers fully acknowledging and appreciating the crucial support provided by Vietnam in the 1980s, and the sacrifices of so many Vietnamese who went to Cambodia during this period (Gottesman 2002), can be found in the past. Long before the Vietnamese soldiers crossed the border and came into Cambodia in late 1978, most Khmers already held deep feelings of suspicion and even animosity toward their ethnic Kinh (Vietnamese) neighbors to the east, and social memories and oral and written histories (i.e., Khin 2002) of many Khmer people, ones that have transformed the way space is understood, and have thus created "political landscapes" (Baird 2014). This deep-set animosity to the Vietnamese is indicated by the policies and practices of both the Lon Nol government between 1970 and 1975, and the Democratic Kampuchea government from 1975 to the first few days of 1979. Despite being at the opposite ends of the political ideological spectrum and being deeply hostile to each other, these governments had two key things in common: they were both strongly anti-Vietnamese and both supported massacres of ethnic Kinh in Cambodia (Short 2004; Gottesman 2002; Vickery 1984).

These feelings of hostility toward the Vietnamese are connected to Khmer identity construction and the sense that many Khmers have that Cambodia reached its pinnacle during the Angkor period in the thirteenth and fourteenth centuries. From then, the Khmer have frequently seen themselves as having fallen into decline beginning in the fifteenth century (Chandler 1996). Since then the "Khmer nation" is often imagined as having been in almost constant decline, which coincided with the aggressive expansion of Vietnamese territorial control to the south, where they became dominant over territory previously controlled by the Cham Kingdom, before moving into areas further south populated by the Khmers. While the Siamese and the Lao gained influence over many regions to the north and west that were under Khmer control during the Angkor period, the loss of the Mekong delta, or Kampuchea Kraom (lower Cambodia) as most Khmer refer to the area today, to Vietnamese southern expansion beginning in the seventeenth century, appears to be the most deeply troubling loss related to present-day Khmer identity construction (Chandler 1996; Edwards 2007; Kimkong Heng and Sovinda Po 2017).

Thus, when Vietnamese tanks rolled across the border into Cambodia in late December 1978, many Cambodians did not see a liberating army that was going to bring an end to one of the darkest periods of Cambodian history. Instead, they saw a continuation of the Vietnamese colonial advancement into Cambodia that had already been occurring for centuries. Many were predisposed to believe that the Vietnamese occupation forces were a bigger threat than even the brutality of the Khmer Rouge. For some, Vietnamese dominance even represented the potential end of the Khmer people, the Khmer race, and the Cambodian nation (see Chanda 1986). Indeed, tensions between Vietnamese and Cambodians have often emerged. Berman (1996) described anti-Vietnamese discrimination in Cambodia as being common. Indicative of this, in 1996, one Khmer student who purportedly supported Cambodia's ethnic minorities told me when I asked if Vietnamese living in Cambodia were "ethnic minorities": "The Vietnamese are not ethnic minorities, they are the ethnic majority." Some remembered stories about how the Vietnamese, during the Nguyễn dynasty in the nineteenth century, had briefly imposed their will on the Khmer, including forcing Khmer officials to dress as Vietnamese (Khin 2002). Cambodia was also divided into provinces connected to the Nguyễn administration, subjected to Vietnamese taxes, and forced to be labor for canal and drainage projects in the Mekong delta, at the same time as Vietnamese farmers, who were only answerable to Vietnamese laws and authorities, settled in Cambodia (Gottesman 2002).

Some also recall how most of the key bureaucrats during the French colonial period in Cambodia were Vietnamese brought in to assist in administering the country (Gottesman 2002). For many Khmers, the Vietnamese had not come with the intention of ousting the Khmer Rouge, but to complete their colonization of Cambodia (see, for example, Ea Meng-Try 1981), with the expected result being the total obliteration of the Khmer nation. Many also feared that the Vietnamese would re-create colonial France's "Indochina Federation," a state that would include the original territories of French Indochina, including Vietnam, Laos, and Cambodia (Chanda 1986; Ea Meng-Try 1981). Many Khmers did not doubt that if the Indochinese Federation was recreated, it would be dominated by the Vietnamese, and that over time, Cambodia—and the Khmer people more generally—would cease to exist altogether. Some feared that Cambodia would end up just like Laos, which they believed had already come under full Vietnamese control (see Chanda 1986, 48, 54; Ea Meng-Try 1981, 222–223).

Many Vietnamese must have recognized what they were up against when they decided to push into Cambodia in late 1978, but the aggressive nature of the Khmer Rouge's rhetoric against Vietnam, and especially the Khmer Rouge's cross-border violent attacks into Vietnam's Gialai-Kontum, Daklak, Dong Thap, Tay Ninh, An Giang, and Kien Giang Provinces, which left thousands of civilians, including women, children, and the elderly slaughtered, forced their hand. Indeed, between May 1975 and December 1978, the Khmer Rouge reportedly killed 5,000 people, injured 50,000, and took 20,000 men back to Cambodia for execution (Liên 2013; Son 2016), although Vickery (1989) put the figure at 30,000 casualties for just a two-year period between January 1977 and January 1979. Whatever the actual number might be, by late 1978 the Vietnamese felt that they had few options but to remove the Khmer Rouge from power (Vickery 2010).

The objective of this book is not to entirely challenge the mainstream perceptions of most Cambodians regarding the PRK period or even to suggest that the Khmer people should be more grateful of the Vietnamese for liberating them from the Khmer Rouge, even if some non-Cambodian observers tend to think that Khmers should be more appreciative of the Vietnamese (see, for example, Vickery 1984; Evans and

Rowley 1984; Fawthrop and Jarvis 2004). I too have some sympathy for this view. But the feelings and critical impressions of those Khmers who have a negative impression regarding the role of Vietnamese in Cambodia are potentially as legitimate as the views already highlighted. I am not trying to tell the story of all Cambodians, or even most of them. Rather, I am interested in the experiences and views of a particular small group of Cambodians, largely ethnic Brao people, and other aligned minorities whose experiences associated with the occupation of Cambodia by the Vietnamese had a dramatically different perspective, as many became key figures in the Vietnam-installed PRK government. The perspectives presented here regarding the PRK period are unique and so far have not been well documented in either popular or academic literature, and they are generally not well-known, even in Cambodia, including among those academics who have spent years living and working in the country. Yet, it is a history that is more significant for Cambodia as a nation than many recognize, since large numbers of minorities ended up in leadership positions during the PRK period, and thus their stories need to be told. The picture I present here may not be supported by all ethnic Khmers, either inside or outside of Cambodia, but hopefully I will be able to appropriately convey the views of the people who are the focus of this book.

Focusing on the Brao and other ethnic minorities, this book represents an effort to present histories from the peripheries or histories of people living in marginal parts of nation-states. These peripheral or marginal histories, as I refer to them, are actually often much less marginal than might be imagined. They are only marginal because they have not been well reported on or documented, not because they have been insignificant. While ultimately it will be important for northeasterners to write their own histories, at this point there are not any Brao doing that. I will, therefore, try to interpret some Brao history here. Moreover, some of the elders who I interviewed have since passed away, including key people such as Khom Toeng, Veng Khoun, Kreng Siengnoi, Heng Khamvan, and most recently Bou Thang and Soy Keo.

The book is organized into three parts, moving from a chronological approach to themed chapters and then back to chronology again. Part 1, which encompasses chapters one to three, considers the period leading up to Vietnam's occupation of Cambodia, including the period when the Brao first joined the Khmer Rouge in the 1950s and 1960s, the tensions between Brao leaders and the Khmer Rouge that led the Brao to flee to Vietnam and Laos as political refugees, and finally the events that eventually resulted in the Vietnamese entering Cambodia to bring down the Khmer Rouge. Part 2 of the book is organized thematically, as it is focused on the 1979 to 1989 PRK period. Chapter 4 considers how the PRK government, particularly in northeastern Cambodia, was established following the ouster of the Khmer Rouge from power in 1979. Chapter 5 examines how northeastern Cambodia gradually developed during the PRK period. Chapter 6 investigates important issues related to security and the military in northeastern Cambodia during the PRK period. Chapter 7 considers the relations between northeasterners and Vietnamese during the PRK period, as well as the trips that Brao and other ethnic minorities from the northeast took to Vietnam, Laos, and Eastern Europe during the PRK period. Part 3 returns to a chronological approach and serves as a sort of epilogue to the PRK period, the main focus of this book. Chapter 8 briefly considers what happened after the Vietnamese military withdrew from Cambodia, and how the Brao and other ethnic minorities in northeastern Cambodia think about the PRK period. The final chapter provides concluding remarks.

Ultimately I want to convey a view of the PRK period—between 1979 and 1989—that is more complex and nuanced than has been previously conveyed through presenting information about the circumstances of many highlanders who now live mainly in Ratanakiri and Stung Treng Provinces in northeastern Cambodia, particularly different subgroups of the Brao. While ethnic divisions are crucial in northeastern Cambodia and need to be taken seriously, it is often the case that political differences trump ethnic ones. Thus a nuanced understanding of events is required, one that takes ethnic differences seriously but does not essentialize them in ways that tend to ignore important political differences that transcended ethnicity. For example, some accounts have tended to essentialize based on ethnicity, without adequately considering political differences, such as LeBar et al. (1964), Condominas (1977 [1957]), Matras-Troubetzkoy (1983), Schliesinger (1998), and others, and on the other hand, many political accounts of conflict in the region, such as Osborne (1973), Chanda (1986), Vickery (2007), have tended to overemphasize national differences and have underappreciated local histories and in-country ethnic differences. In this book, I try to find the right balance between these two extremes.

While it would not be possible, or particularly useful, to provide all the details of the circumstances that eventually led the Brao ethnic group to arguably become the biggest "winners" of the Vietnamese "liberation" of Cambodia, I try to present a broad overview of what happened because these events are crucial for developing more nuanced and regional perspectives of the PRK period. Voices outside of mainstream Cambodia have, unfortunately, been too frequently omitted from the official record (see Baird 2009d). One important goal of this book is to help see Cambodia from more of a regional perspective. Indeed, most of the histories of Cambodia have focused on the national scale, which often results in Phnom Penh and other centers such as Angkor in Siem Reap being the main focus of inquiry (Osborne 1973; Forest 1980; Kiernan and Boua 1982; Vickery 1984, 2007; Chanda 1986; Heder and Ledgerwood 1995; Chandler 1996; Gottesman 2002; Slocomb 2003; Short 2004; Tully 2005; Hansen 2007; Edwards 2007; Kiernan 2008; Jacobson 2008; Conboy 2013; Mertha 2014), but with the notable exception of Guérin (2003, 2008), who focuses on the uplands of northeastern Cambodia during the French colonial period. The overall central-level focus should, however, not come as a surprise considering the dearth of literature on various aspects of Cambodia, thus making central-level investigations the early priority. There is also generally more documentation to support such studies. While these works have made important scholarly contributions, we need to start paying more attention to particular geographical areas in Cambodia, whether provinces, districts, communes, or regions, defined in various ways. This book discusses places outside of Stung Treng and Ratanakiri Provinces, in the most northeastern part of Cambodia, but my regional focus is on that part of the country. In making this decision, I challenge others to also think of histories in Cambodia from regional perspectives.

It is similarly important to look at histories in Cambodia from different ethnic perspectives, including from documentation where available, as so far ethnically Khmer people have been the focus of almost all of the histories written about Cambodia. This focus is not surprising, as the Khmers constitute a large majority of the country's population. Other groups, such as the ethnic Vietnamese, Cham, Chinese, Thai, and Lao, make up much smaller proportions, with upland minorities constituting about 1 to 2 percent of the national population (Ironside 2009). Yet it seems important to understand the various perspectives of people who come from different places and belong to different ethnic groups.

PART 1

The Brao and Their
Early Involvement
in the Khmer Rouge

The Brao—the main ethnic group dealt with in this book—encompasses peoples who largely live in present-day Attapeu and Champasak Provinces in southern Laos and in Ratanakiri and Stung Treng Provinces in northeastern Cambodia. Attapeu and Champasak are the southernmost provinces in Laos and the only two adjacent to Cambodia. The Brao were historically mainly found in upland areas of the easternmost part of these provinces, particularly in the Sekong River basin in Phou Vong District, Attapeu Province, where all the villages are majority Brao. xThe district is adjacent to both Cambodia and Vietnam. In northeastern Cambodia, in Stung Treng and Ratanakiri Provinces, the Brao are also mainly found in upland areas, in the Sesan River basin, where they dominate Taveng and O Chum Districts. Ratanakiri is adjacent to both Laos and Vietnam.

The Brao speak various dialects of a western Bahnaric Austroasiatic language broadly known as Brao (Keller et al. 2008). Linguistically, the Brao include those who now categorize themselves as belonging to one of nine different subgroups,[1] although these peoples have widely differing senses of belonging in relation to the label "Brao," and the boundaries between them are sometimes fuzzy. There are at least 65,000 Brao globally, of which more than half live in northeastern Cambodia, with a smaller number residing in southern Laos. Just one Brao village is located in the Central Highlands of Vietnam. Most of those referred to here are ethnically Brao Amba, one of the Brao subgroups, and when the term "Brao" is evoked in this book, it can be assumed to refer to this group unless otherwise specified. Other Brao subgroups found in Cambodia are, however, also frequently referred to, including the Kreung, Kavet, Lun, and Brao Tanap (Baird 2008).

Although the Brao are particularly significant for this history, various other ethnic groups in northeastern Cambodia also play important roles, particularly the Tampuon, Jarai, and ethnic Lao. The Tampuon speak a central Bahnaric language that is not mutually intelligible with Brao, the ethnic Lao speak a Tai-Kadai language unlike any of the Austroasiatic languages spoken in Cambodia, and the Jarai speak an Austronesian language that is similar to Cham language but very different from Brao. All are important ethnic groups in the Sesan River basin of Ratanakiri Province. Most people who belong to these ethnic groups do not, however, figure particularly prominently here, with the exception of the Tampuon from Kachoan Village in Voeunsai District, Ratanakiri Province, a small number of Jarai from O Yadao District, and some ethnic Lao people from Ratanakiri and Stung Treng Provinces.

So, how did so many Brao and some other ethnic minorities in northeastern Cambodia become involved with the communist movement that was to become Democratic Kampuchea or the Khmer Rouge? Not surprisingly, there was not a single reason, nor is there an easy answer to this question, but the foundations of an answer can be located at the beginning of the 1960s when large numbers of Brao people living in the mountains north of the Sesan River were forcibly resettled in the lowlands adjacent to the Sesan River, with the goal of Khmerization through forcing them to attend Khmer language schools. Soon the large number of people concentrated together faced serious food shortages, which led most to return to the mountains where they could more easily make a living. The people also became disenchanted with the government because of its efforts to establish a large rubber plantation in the central part of Ratanakiri Province beginning in the early 1960s. Because of plantation development, a number of communities lost their ancestral lands and were forced to resettle elsewhere. Not surprisingly, this seriously upset many people because they had no option but to move and received no compensation for their losses. Moreover, due to a lack of labor, ethnic minorities from various parts of Ratanakiri Province were forced to work on the plantation. They were paid for their labor, but most would have preferred to work for themselves. Thus the establishment of the rubber plantation was a major catalyst for villager dissent and eventually violent resistance.

With the emergence of resistance to resettlement to the lowlands and forced Khmerization, as well as to the establishment of the large rubber plantation, the government of Cambodia did not respond well. The military frequently used indiscriminate brute force against those they believed to be against them, resulting in violence against people who were actually opposed to them but also mistakenly against others who were not. Some were shot and villages were burnt to the ground, thus leaving no option for many but to join the only group willing to support them, the Khmer Rouge. Thus, in 1968 and 1969, over a relatively short period of time, resistance against the government of Cambodia in Ratanakiri Province rapidly expanded, along with the ranks of the Khmer Rouge, as most of the ethnic minorities in the northeast joined the revolution.

In 1970, as the Khmer Rouge gained more and more power, a large number of Cambodians who had been in North Vietnam studying since leaving Cambodia in 1954 returned to Cambodia. During the same year, Lon Nol launched a successful coup d'état against Norodom Sihanouk. On the advice of the United States, Lon Nol withdrew all the remaining government forces from the northeast to allow the US Air Force to escalate bombing of the region, which was designated as a "free-fire zone." But despite this aerial bombardment, the Khmer Rouge were able to consolidate control.

Thus many Brao and other ethnic minorities in Ratanakiri Province were drawn into conflict with the government. Particular things happened that taxed the patience of the Brao and others and eventually drew many into the communist revolution. Others, however, did not embrace communism and left Ratanakiri Province. Crucially, people in northeastern Cambodia often thought of identities in terms of ethnic group membership. It is also, however, true that people from the same ethnic group sometimes established different political alliances, with some aligning with the Khmer Rouge and others siding with noncommunists. Thus we need to be attentive to ethnic issues, but we also need to avoid essentializing based on ethnicity.

Taking a Step Back

In the early 1950s the First Indochina War was escalating, particularly in Vietnam, but also in Laos and Cambodia. Up until the end of the 1940s the Vietnamese communists operating in Laos and

Cambodia had largely been unsuccessful in encouraging locals to join them (Heder 2004; Engelbert 2004; Goscha 2005). However, after totally revamping their recruiting strategy in the late 1940s, including encouraging Vietnamese operatives to "go native," Vietnamese recruiting improved in the uplands, even if no minority recruits had yet to be admitted into the party. In the late 1940s and early 1950s most served as porters, guides, messengers, trail blazers, and intelligence gatherers (Baird 2008; Goscha 2005; Engelbert 2004).

The People's Revolutionary Party of Kampuchea (PRPK) was officially formed in September 1951 (Chanda 1986; Vickery 1984; Heder 2004), with 1,800 members who had previously been members of the Indochina Communist Party in Cambodia. However, most were Cambodian-born ethnic Vietnamese, with just 150 being considered to be true "Khmers" (Chanda 1986; Heder 2004). In any case, in 1952 a "Government of National Resistance" was declared with Sơn Ngọc Minh (also known as Achan Mien)[2] as president (Vickery 1984).[3] By 1954, however, Siev Heng allegedly began betraying the party and its supporters to the Sihanouk government as a secret informant, and in 1959 he openly defected. Siev Heng revealed secrets about the party that proved to be devastating (Vickery 1984; Short 2004). Indeed, information provided to officials led to the apprehension of a large number of communist operatives and supporters. The party was in shambles.

After the defeat of the French at Dien Bien Phu, in northern Vietnam, in 1954, the first Geneva Accord brought an end to French rule in Indochina, including in Cambodia. By then some Brao and members of other highland ethnic groups in the northeast had become heavily involved in the communist struggle. The Vietnamese communists, however, did not push for an independent territory where the Cambodian communists could regroup and organize, as was the case for Laos and Vietnam. This strategy probably emerged because of geography; there were no parts of Cambodia that were adjacent to communist Vietnam, just noncommunist Vietnam in the south.[4] These circumstances would later result in considerable resentment among the ethnic Khmer leadership of the Khmer Rouge, including Pol Pot (Short 2004). Therefore, whereas communists from southern Laos traveled to organize in the provinces of Houaphanh and Phongsaly in northern Laos in 1954, Cambodian communists did not have a sanctuary in Cambodia. Instead, thousands ended up traveling to study in Hanoi, Vietnam's capital city (Chanda 1986). They would later become known as the Khmer

Hanoi.[5] By all accounts, most of those who went to Hanoi from north-eastern Cambodia were ethnically Lao; only a few were from other ethnic groups.

Significantly, however, one of those who made the trip was a young ethnic Tampuon man from Kachoan Village in Voeunsai (in present-day Ratanakiri Province), adjacent to the Sesan River. His name was Bou Thang, and he joined the communists on April 14, 1954, following the Viet Minh's second attack on Voeunsai. Bou Thang was recruited by the respected revolutionary named Kon.[6] Another ethnic minority youth, Soy Keo, who lived in the nearby ethnic Kachok Village of Kaoh Pheak (although he is half Kreung and half Tampuon) was recruited into the revolution in 1954, just a few months after his teenage friend Bou Thang. Soy Keo and Bou Thang traveled together by foot with many others. There were apparently about one hundred Cambodia-born insurgents from Ratanakiri who made the trip to North Vietnam. Interestingly, Bou Thang thought of himself as Tampuon and Lao when he was young, as there were virtually no ethnic Khmer living near where he was brought up. However, once he arrived in Hanoi in 1954, he started feeling for the first time that he was Cambodian. Apparently the first Khmer he spoke with was none other than Sơn Ngọc Minh, although he only knew a few words at the time. Boua Chuong, an ethnic Lao revolutionary from Ratanakiri Province, mainly translated for him.[7] There were not any Brao among the regroupees, but there were thirty ethnic minorities in total, including some Kreung, Tampuon, and Jarai, and many ethnic Lao.[8]

Bou Thang and Soy Keo both received "advanced" military training in Vietnam. Bou Thang studied in Nghe An. Soy Keo initially studied medicine in Hai Duong but later switched over to military studies. In 1962, they both received military training at Bac Ninh.[9] In 1968, they also supported their North Vietnamese comrades through participating in the Tet Offensive, traveling as far south as Hue.[10]

The Sihanouk Era

During the French period I used to have to do fifteen days of corvée labor a year. The French only rarely came to the villages; they mainly stayed in Stung Treng and Voeunsai, but when they did come to our village they would shake everyone's hands and give us big bags of salt, tobacco, and sometimes also clothes, such as short pants. The Khmers were much more brutal than the French ever were. (Brao villager from Taveng District, 2002)

Norodom Sihanouk's Sangkum Reastr Niyum (People's Socialist Community) government was established and took control of newly "independent" Cambodia in 1955. This change in government had especially important social and spatial implications for the Brao and other ethnic minorities in northeastern Cambodia. According to Charles Meyer (1979)—one of Sihanouk's advisors during the Sangkum period—Khmer officials of newly independent Cambodia were shocked and disappointed when they visited the northeast and found that mainly non–Khmer-language-speaking peoples lived in the remote region. The situation differed from Laos, where officials were more familiar with ethnic minorities because they make up a much greater proportion of the population there. In addition, Sihanouk and many of his Khmer colleagues were already concerned that Cambodia's larger neighbors, particularly Vietnam, could gradually "consume the country." Thus the new Cambodian government focused on building up the Khmer nation (Burchett 1970). Khmer nationalism emerged not only in response to French colonialism but was also socially constructed in the context of historical pressures put on the Khmer by the Thai and Vietnamese (Grabowsky 1997).

Soon, the Khmers began enforcing their cultural norms on the highlanders. Initially, it was just relatively small things. For example, Brao men had to cut their hair short. But soon the government started promoting more substantial changes related to language use, culture, religion, and livelihood practices. Encouraging spatial change was a crucial part of the new government's plan. Charles Meyer (1979) described government efforts as a form of colonization in which the economic role of the highlanders, or their rights to remain settled on their ancestral lands, were not recognized. But the Cambodia media generally applauded the government's efforts, and in 1962 a *Cambodia Daily* article stated, in relation to government work in the northeast, that "Until now, poverty seemed irremediable. Today, hope is reborn" (quoted in Bourdier 2006, 177). Development discourses justified government interventions in the highlands, much as the "civilizing mission" of the French had justified the colonialism that preceded it. Ethnic politics was undoubtedly crucial, as the ways people saw what was happening were often dependent of one's ethnic lens.

Figure 3. Northeastern Cambodia, 1959 (Meghan Kelly, Cart Lab, Department of Geography, University of Wisconsin–Madison)

Big Changes in Ratanakiri Province

During the late 1950s and 1960s, the Sangkum government promoted the "Khmerization" of the northeast through what it called "a broad civic action program," handing over responsibility for its implementation to the military, the Forces Armées Royales Khmères (FARK) (US Library of Congress 2006). Promoting the migration of ethnic Khmer groups of families to the northeast, so as to colonize the territories of the highlands and ensure that they would remain firmly linked to Cambodia, was an important part of this program (Guérin

31

2003). Khmer immigration into the region was especially promoted beginning in 1958, a decision that was inspired by similar efforts to promote Vietnamese immigration to the highlands on the other side of the border, in Daklak and Kontum Provinces (Meyer 1979; see also Hardy 2003). While many of these Khmer settlers returned to southern parts of Cambodia after becoming ill and failing to find the conditions for settlement suitable,[11] some stayed.

In addition, the FARK promoted what it called "military colonists." This colonialization process involved encouraging ethnic Khmer soldiers and officers from lowland areas to retire in the northeast. Those who took up the offer received three years of salary, a house on a 2,400 square meter piece of land, and five hectares of good agriculture land and the means to cultivate it. Thus, at great expense to the state, three hundred Khmer families migrated into four villages in the Lebansiek (present-day Banlung) area. While some were able to farm the land and even establish private rubber plantations, the military did little to promote a smallholder model of rubber production, such as had been developed in Malaysia or Thailand (Meyer 1979). As Meyer (1979, 687) put it, "[T]he military leaders . . . were immensely incompetent."

Sihanouk insisted on the use of education as a means for rapid Khmerization of the ethnic minority population, along with the regular presence of health care services (Meyer 1979), and by June 1957, education was already seen as key to the government's "civilizing" efforts. The idea, as quoted by Meyer (1979, 685–686), was to "gather the Phnongs [a pejorative for highlanders]—make them feel the need to learn how to speak, read and write Khmer—teach them how to get dressed—teach them how to work." Classic forms of modernization were expected to bring about the dramatic loss of cultural identity. The government wanted the highlanders to exchange their traditional dwellings for Khmer ones, their traditional clothing for Khmer attire, and their languages for Khmer. They expected the Brao and others to convert from animism to Theravada Buddhism.

Creating Khmer-friendly places in the unhospitable northeast was seen as important. Ethnic Khmer teachers from the south were recruited to educate non-Khmer peoples about Khmer language and culture. As reported by the US Library of Congress (2006, 2),

> The goals of this program were to educate the Khmer Loeu [upland Khmer], to teach them Khmer, and eventually to assimilate

them into the mainstream of Cambodian society. There was some effort at resettlement; in other cases, civil servants went out to live with individual Khmer Loeu groups to teach their members Khmer ways. Schools were provided for some Khmer Loeu communities; and in each large village, a resident government representative disseminated information and encouraged the Khmer Loeu to learn the lowland Khmer way of life. Civil servants sent to work among the Khmer Loeu often viewed the assignment as a kind of punishment.

The measures adopted for changing the Brao Amba and Kavet (two Brao subgroups) were particularly drastic, as these people were located to the north between the Sesan River and the border with Laos, and thus were viewed with particular suspicion. They were told to prepare to move in 1958,[12] and in 1959 a large number of ethnic Brao Amba people living in fifteen communities in present-day Taveng District were forced to move down from the mountains. A new two-kilometer-long village was established along the north bank of the Sesan River. As part of the same program, Brao from Tanaich, Siang Sai, and Hamawk Villages were ordered to study in another school downstream along the Sesan River at the mouth of the Hamawk stream in present-day Taveng Kraom Commune. They were told to reorganize into linear villages. Children from Phayang and Ke Kuang Villages came down to study, although most parents did not come with them. The Kavet people from present-day Siempang District were forced into similar villages adjacent to the Sekong River.

Among the first important instructions from the Sangkum government for northeastern Cambodia—dated 1958—were to improve and extend the road system to make the region more accessible. This order was particularly inspired by strategic need: to enable the rapid deployment of military units if necessary (Meyer 1979). It was, in fact, during this period that the highlanders in northeastern Cambodia began political activities against the government, such as organizing meetings and recruiting members, but these activities were limited and were not carried out in all areas.

The ethnic Khmer teachers sent to work in the schools had little or no experience in the northeast, and most had never encountered ethnic minorities. Thus, like other settlers sent to the northeast, they generally did not easily adapt; the diseases and evil spirits thought to be common in the region were of great concern. Many were scared of the magic that highlanders were believed to possess and returned to where they came from. Others, however, stuck with their efforts to help build the nation. Those who persisted were often strongly influenced by nationalist sentiments. The schools and the associated resettled villages were, however, both ill-conceived and poorly implemented, as there was little concern regarding how the people would feed themselves. Initially, there was forest nearby, where people could do swidden agriculture, but within a couple of years people needed to move farther away to find suitable land for agriculture (Baird 2008).

In May 1959, the Sangkum government combined Mounlapoumok Province and Lumphat District of Stung Treng Province to create Ratanakiri Province (Figure 3). Sihanouk found it convenient to mold history to fit his vision of Cambodia's highlands. He emphasized that Ratanakiri and Mondulkiri had been Cambodian since the "dawn of time," and that they had the same rights as other provinces (Baird 2008). Charles Meyer (1979) believed that he was probably sincere in his sentiments but that the contemptuous and patronizing way in which he viewed the local population was easily recognizable and unbecoming. The new Ratanakiri Province was put under military leadership with the army eager to exploit its rich natural resources (Meyer 1979). The Sangkum government Khmer nationalist policies followed the logic of the French administration that preceded it, except that the Khmer were favored in ways that the French did not envision. Yet overall, Sihanouk's plans fit well with the "civilizing mission" of the hinterlands that the French colonialists had promoted. They were just more ardent in their zeal to implement it.

By 1964, however, all of the schools north of the Sesan River had been abandoned. The Brao were fed up with the Sangkum government's policies and moved back into the mountains to the north and east. Many only returned half way back to where they previously lived, near the Lao border, as it was too far for them to move all their possessions in one year. As one Kavet elder put it, "It was during this period that people began to enter the revolution in large numbers."[13] Sihanouk's soldiers initially tried to follow the Kavet into the mountains to the north, but they encountered large numbers of punji stick traps on the paths that impeded their movement and resulted in them turning back (Baird 2008).

Reorganizing the Villages

Reorganizing village spaces was crucial to the Sangkum government's civilization efforts in Ratanakiri, and as Ruohomaki (2003, 80) has stated, "In order to better control the population, it [the government] favored highland villages to be arranged in parallel lines along roads, according to typical lowland patterns." As one elder from Bang Koet Village explained, "We always had circular villages until the Sihanouk period." Having linear villages was seen as both practical and symbolically significant. It provided easier access to outsiders into villages via roads and was supposed to be better suited for long-term habitation and make it easier for parcels of private lands to be allotted for perennial fruit tree cultivation. The linear shape symbolized openness to the outside and a willingness to integrate into Cambodia (Baird 2008).

The Sangkum government also implemented other measures fundamentally designed to reorganize Brao space. For example, some of the Brao Tanap villages in western Ratanakiri Province were coerced into resettling to areas where officials expected that the highlanders could be converted from being swidden cultivators to becoming lowland wet-rice farmers. A 1964 editorial in the review *Cambodge aujourd'hui* described swidden agriculture in the northeast as "wasteful agriculture" (quoted in Bourdier 2006, 176), a view that was prevalent among much of Khmer urban society. This view, however, went against the local proverb: "Growing lowland rice paddy produces only rice, but doing swidden agriculture produces all kinds of crops" (Bou Thang 1993, 314).

The Khmer Rouge Period: The Early Years

After independence in 1954 and the migration of many Cambodian communists to Hanoi, the communist movement in Cambodia was very weak and suffered from various crackdowns and other setbacks at the hands of the Norodom Sihanouk government. During this period, some Vietnamese Communists began operating in northeast Cambodia, and more Brao decided to join the revolution, although armed struggle was still out of the question. Yoep (Brao, Bong Village),

Lao Nyai[14] (Brao, Trabok Village), Jawel (Brao, Soin Village), Bun (Brao, Paroe Thom Village), and Veng Khoun (Brao, Bang Koet Village) were the first five to reenter the forests in 1959.[15] Yoep was forced to take the rest of his family to the forest in 1960, fearing government reprisals. Bun was the first leader at the Drayak Lapong base. In 1961, the whole Brao village of Jarong Laik (now integrated into Leang Veng Village) fled to stay near the Laos-Cambodia border, and in 1962, Bun Mi, Kham Toeung, and Moi Choem returned to the forests again. Many other Brao also began to join the communists. These early revolutionaries were mainly assigned to provide intelligence to the leaders and increase their grassroots networks (Colm 1996). Between 1957 and 1963, these early revolutionaries only studied and used Lao writing. Illustrative of the times, To Bioe (Brao, Soin Village), who was still a teenager, became a member of the mobile unit (*Kong Chalat*), and went with these early leaders to help translate from Khmer to Lao language.[16] However, after 1964, the revolutionary northeasterners started to learn Khmer.[17]

During the 1960s the in-country elements of the communist leadership could do little (Heder 2004). Moreover, the United States gradually scaled up its support for the repression of communists in the region. It was at this time that the Cambodian Communists decided to change their name to the Workers' Party of Kampuchea (WPK). In particular, they wanted to ensure that Cambodian revolutionaries had an equal status to Vietnamese revolutionaries in the Vietnam Workers' Party. The WPK put these in order of lowest to highest class: the working class, the peasantry, the petit bourgeoisie, the bourgeoisie, and the feudalists. The highlanders of the northeast were considered to have excellent potential as revolutionaries, as they were mostly all considered peasants. Moreover, many had serious grievances with the Cambodian Sangkum government, resulting in generally strong support for the revolution (Baird 2008).

In 1961, Lon Nol's military detained the leader of the WPK, a Khmer named Tou Samouth, who died in custody. Tou Samouth's downfall had a number of important implications. First, it decreased the links between the WPK and the Vietnam Worker's Party. Second, it demonstrated to the WPK leadership that it was impossible to cooperate with the Sangkum government. The loss of Tou also opened up the leadership of the WPK to returning students from France, of which Pol Pot was the leader (Heder 2004; Short 2004). Nevertheless, in about 1962 the ex-Indochina Communist Party began reactivating revolutionary cells in Cambodia from the First Indochina War. The Brao veteran cadres, Bun Mi and Moi Choem, led the recruitment drive in Voeunsai. Minorities, and especially the Brao, were the main group targeted, since the WPK did not want to attract attention by entering into urban centers where ethnic Khmers lived (Baird 2008). In 1963, Kham Chan and Thang Ngon from Trabok Village entered the revolution and went to stay in the forest. It was also during this period that the first American bombs fell on Cambodia soil, as the Army of the Republic of Vietnam (ARVN) (South Vietnam) began targeting Viet Cong bases along the Vietnam-Cambodia border (Baird 2008). Still, bombing was quite limited compared to what was to come years later.

In 1963, a decision was made by the leadership of the WPK to send 90 percent of the membership of the Party Central Committee to the countryside. All its energies were to be put into mobilizing peasant resistance against the government, to the dissatisfaction of Vietnamese and Chinese communists, who continued to support Sihanouk's neutralist position (Heder 2004).

During the same year, the Sangkum government cracked down on rebels in Voeunsai District, killing three ethnic Lao men from Fang Village. Nevertheless, many Brao from Taveng became increasingly receptive to communist propaganda, and by 1964, the movement had expanded significantly in Brao areas. Many of the Brao and Kavet living north of the Sesan River returned to the bamboo forests in the mountains where they had originally come from. However, most were still only armed with crossbows and bush-knives, and they also employed punji stick pitfalls. Still, the forests were thick and difficult to pass, so retreating there was often sufficient to discourage government forces from following (Colm 1996).

Rubber Plantations

In the late 1950s, the Sangkum government decided to establish a large commercial rubber plantation in Ratanakiri Province. The government was convinced of the desirability of applying classical methods of western capitalist economic growth through creating large agro-industrial companies, expropriating the best land from the people, and exploiting local labor to develop the companies' interests. These government efforts, which can be considered to be equivalent to what Karl Marx called "primitive accumulation" (Marx 1976), and what

David Harvey (2003) has more recently referred to as "accumulation by dispossession," had devastating impacts on the local ethnic minorities and made efforts by the communists to gain allies among northeasterners increasingly easy (Baird 2008). Others have also written about more recent rubber plantation development by Vietnamese companies in Brao-populated areas of southern Laos (Baird 2011b; Kenney-Lazar 2012).

The initial push for the expansion of large French-owned rubber plantations into Indochina began during the French colonial period (Guérin 2008). The French thought that the soils along the Lao-Cambodia frontier were suitable for cultivating rubber, but it was not until Cambodian independence that serious steps were taken to develop rubber plantations there. An 8,000-hectare land concession was finally granted by the central government to the Preah Sihanouk State Rubber Plantation Company, a government-owned company, for rubber plantation development in Ratanakiri (Colm 1996). Most rubber planting occurred between 1961 and 1967. Five hundred hectares were planted in 1961, and by 1966, 2,200 hectares had been sowed, mainly near the military post at Lebansiek. The goal was to further expand to 3,700 hectares by 1969, and to have the whole 8,000 hectares planted by 1980, although that did not happen. Although the plantation was state owned, many villagers thought it was French, as a French company was hired by the Cambodian government to manage operations (Meyer 1979).

Apart from the main plantation, Khmer officials and senior military commanders established smaller rubber plantations. The ethnic Khmer Lumphat-based governor of Ratanakiri at the time, Ong Nhot, had his own private one-hundred-hectare rubber plantation. Not surprisingly, the expropriation of large amounts of land by the state, government officials, and settlers from the south displaced and greatly upset the land's original occupants, the Brao to the west and the Tampuon to the east. No compensation was given to the original land owners. They were simply forced to uproot themselves and move (Baird 2008). The Brao Tanap villages directly affected by losing all of their land to the rubber plantation were Kanchaign, Tang Kap, Panteung, Chet, Taong, and Tuh.[18] Other villages, such as Kantriang, were partially displaced. According to those who remember being relocated, the French got a truck from the rubber company and used it to move the people to the edges of the plantation, where they were dumped and expected to re-establish themselves. Those who resisted expropriation of their lands for the plantation or providing labor for the plantations faced military detachments sent to discipline them by "plundering, raping and killing," as Meyer (1979, 686) put it. Apart from losing land, there were other restrictions. If a highlander's cow damaged any rubber seedlings, the owner of the cow would be fined. The same happened if pigs and chickens caused damage. The people were upset with the plantations from the beginning, but most did not dare oppose the Cambodian military and the French-managed company (Baird 2008).

While the rubber plantations in the center of Ratanakiri only covered part of the red-soiled Plateau, they directly affected the whole province. One of the immediate problems that the development of rubber plantations faced in Ratanakiri was a lack of labor (Whitaker et al. 1973), as the state plantation alone required a continuous labor force of more than one thousand workers (Meyer 1979). The local highlanders were not initially interested in working on the plantations and the government found it difficult to convince Khmers from other parts of the country to migrate to Ratanakiri, therefore it was deemed necessary to force locals, including those who had been removed from their land, to "participate" in the development of rubber. In other words, a form of corvée labor was reinstated with the highlanders having to spend time working on the plantations whether they wanted to or not. They were paid for their labor, but declining to participate was not an option. According to one Brao elder, people from all ethnic groups worked at the plantation. For some, the plantations became a source of employment, especially in the rainy season when villagers needed income to buy rice (Mallow 2002), but the domineering style of the Khmer managers at the rubber plantations made many highlanders bitter. A Kreung elder reported that people from his village, Kok Poi, had to work for fifteen-day periods. Men were paid fifteen lien a day for their work, while women got ten lien a day.[19] They also received rice and fish paste (*prahok* in Khmer and Brao) when they worked. According to an ethnic Kavet elder who, as a young man, twice traveled from north of the Sesan River south to work on the plantations, the district government of Voeunsai would send representatives to the villages to demand that all able-bodied men rotate as laborers on the rubber plantations. Those who refused were threatened with being fined a pig and a jar of rice beer. Therefore, groups of twenty to thirty Kavet would travel to the rubber plantations where they would work for between ten days and over a month. Economically, there were other problems (Baird 2008).

39

Rather than encouraging the local population to cultivate food to supply the work force of the plantation, the managers continued to be almost totally dependent on supplies from Phnom Penh over 550 kilometers away. This dependence on Phnom Penh was not economical, as transport costs were high (Meyer 1979), and it also failed to benefit the local population.

The importance of the labor issue in mobilizing anti-government sentiments has sometimes been underestimated in comparison to the land issue, but labor issues were crucial for many highlanders. As one Kavet put it, "If we had not been forced to work on the rubber plantations, there would not have been a revolution. It might have happened eventually, but it would have taken much longer to begin. We did not lose any land, but we were still upset" (Baird 2008, 229). Not surprisingly, the development of rubber plantations in Ratanakiri, along with those in central Cambodia, would become centers for mobilizing opposition to the Sangkum government (Colm 1996; Chandler 1991), as presented in the next section.

Resistance Begins

In 1964, the first serious clashes between Khmer settlers and highlanders erupted in Ratanakiri Province, spurring some highlanders to join the underground communist revolution and the government to become increasingly wary of the highlanders. The conflict was associated with the rubber plantations, as Khmers were employed in managerial roles, while the highlanders were forced to do most of the hard labor. The Khmers looked down on and discriminated against the highlanders, and this contributed to violent highlander resistance, which was initially put down by the FARK (Baird 2008).

In April 1964, Norodom Sihanouk traveled to Ratanakiri to try to calm the situation. He suggested that Son Sen, a Khmer Rouge leader, was behind the upheaval. Sihanouk ordered a crackdown on communists in the northeast, with Nai Kong (equivalent to district chief) Yoot leading the way in Brao Amba areas in the Sesan basin.[20] Indeed, not all Brao Amba were pro-communist. After using other Brao informants, Nai Kong Yoot ordered his soldiers to arrest suspected Brao and ethnic Lao communists, including Toon and Thook (Trabok Village), Jem Yen and Lat (Viengchan Village), Chao and Blem (Bang Koet Village), and Choeua (ethnic Lao, Pong Village), along with the others. All were imprisoned in Lumphat, the provincial capital. The prisoners were transferred by Sip Koet, the ethnic Khmer responsible for the provincial FARK military. He was said to have been vicious, and over the next seven months Toon, Thook, and Choeua died in captivity. However, five Brao and an ethnic Lao man were able to make a nighttime escape from prison just five days before they were to be executed. The group fled to the Cambodian Communist base in the Trabok stream basin (Baird 2008).

By 1965, the Vietnamese were developing an extension of the Ho Chi Minh Trail in Laos. Known as the Sihanouk Trail, it extended from Laos through the Dragon's Tail in the triborder area of Cambodia. The Vietnamese began to operate out of safe bases in northern Ratanakiri Province. PAVN's 559 Group dominated the triborder area with an estimated 15,000 soldiers and 7,000 porters under its command. The Vietnamese's largest base in the triborder region was on Hill 875. PAVN forces there were part of the B-3 Front (Colm 1996). The Brao came into most contact with Post 32, located on Ya Kra Mountain, which the Brao considered to be a place with powerful spirits and thus avoided (Baird 2008).

During a Khmer Rouge Central Committee meeting in September or October 1966, it was secretly decided to change the name of the WPK to the Communist Party of Kampuchea (Office of the Co-Investigating Judges 2010; Liên 2013), probably to even more clearly separate themselves from the Vietnamese revolutionaries. However, the decision was not implemented until 1971 (Heder 2004). The Cambodian Communist headquarters, Office 100, was located in the forest in northeast Ratanakiri Province (Office of the Co-Investigating Judges 2010), along the Drayak and Lapong streams, tributaries of the Trabok stream, itself a tributary of the Sesan River, an area populated exclusively by Brao people. This move was historic because it made the Cambodian Communists independent of the Vietnamese, even though PAVN bases remained nearby. Office 102, specifically for the northeast zone office, was located nearby and was run by the zone secretary, a French-educated Khmer named Ieng Sary (Office of the Co-Investigating Judges 2010). It is also likely that the Cambodian communists wanted to create a rear base for future operations. Bun Mi was the Brao leader and became party secretary of the 55 *Kaw* District of Taveng, which was in Sector 3.[21] He was also the deputy military chief of Sector 3, with Kham Sai as the chief.[22]

The Cambodian communist base at Drayak and Lapong streams was not far from the Vietnamese, who were spread out in the forest in the Ya Kra mountains area, near the Dragon's Tail, where the borders of Cambodia, Laos, and Vietnam converge, but PAVN and Cambodian communists reportedly had only limited interactions despite their close geographical proximity. The Cambodian communists were allowed to use the Vietnamese hospital as its base, but that was reportedly the extent of support offered by the Vietnamese. In any case, PAVN was not providing any weapons or other supplies to the Cambodian communists during this period, as they wanted to retain good relations with the Sihanouk government. The Vietnamese were, however, under strict orders to treat the communists and local people respectfully, and the Vietnamese always paid for food supplies, like chickens, that they bought from Brao villagers in the area. In 1966, for example, the Vietnamese had very limited food supplies and often bought food from the Brao (Baird 2008).

During the same year, the Cambodian communists decided to separate their forces into two groups, one of which would continue to operate in the northeast while the other would work to the south. Ieng Sary, who had already been in the northeast for years, was put in charge of the northeast.[23] Between August 1966 and June 1967, Ieng Sary actively recruited ethnic minorities in the northeast, especially Ratanakiri Province, as they fit well with the movements' class struggle ideology because they could be defined as "base people." However, it is likely that the success of the movement's recruiting in the northeast had much less to do with Ieng Sary than the Brao people and other ethnic minorities who had already entered the movement and were actively supporting the cause. The message coming from the Cambodian party was appealing, as it addressed the oppression and discrimination that had long been a source of resentment for highlanders (Baird 2008). Recruiting efforts received an additional boost in early 1967, when Lon Nol ordered the forced collection of rice from rural areas to generate revenue (Heder 2004).

In February 1967, a local protest march (*dong he batokam*) was organized at Voeunsai, with logistical support from the Khmer Rouge. Ethnic Lao villagers from Phnom Kok (Brao and Lao), Kalan Thom, and Kalan Toich were the main instigators of the protest. However, Sihanouk's police responded violently, and six people were killed when the unarmed protesters were fired upon. Other Kavet from Kok Lak and villagers from other ethnic Lao villages on the south side of the Sesan River were also preparing to protest at the time but were late in getting organized. Once the shooting began, the others dared not proceed (Baird 2008).

The Brao leader, Kham Toeung, met Pol Pot in Ratanakiri Province in the forest in 1967. Ieng Sary had arrived a little before him. Kham Toeung was very impressed with Pol Pot and how he maintained good relations with villagers he was trying to recruit. As Kham Toeung explained, "Everyone believed in him."[24] Many people had faith in Pol Pot and in his professed emancipatory efforts for the benefit of poor highlanders and other peasant classes (Baird 2008).

These successes in generating rural support was not, however, welcomed by other communists in the region. The Chinese communists continued to support Sihanouk and did not have much interest in the Cambodian party, and the Democratic Republic of Vietnam, more than ever, wanted to keep Sihanouk happy to maintain their sanctuaries in the northeast (Heder 2004). Thus, the Cambodian party was largely forced to "go it alone."

In mid-1967, the Sangkum government scaled up its suppression of supporters of the communist movement who were rebelling in Battambang in northwestern Cambodia. Village supporters of the communists were surrounded and massacred, villages were burnt down, and bounties were paid for the severed heads of dissidents. Indeed, the movement was brutally suppressed, resulting in the communist leadership increasing its emphasis on establishing a strong military structure so that it could defend rebelling peasants in ways it was unable to do in Battambang (Heder 2004). This shift in strategy would have a huge impact on events in the northeast.

In mid-1967, the movement gained more favor among the communist leadership in China, as Sihanouk cracked down on Chinese embassy-supported Red Guard–type activities by Chinese residents of Cambodia, enraging the Chinese government and bringing diplomatic relations between Cambodia and China to their lowest levels in years (Heder 1979).

In November 1967, parts of the Ho Chi Minh Trail were extended into present-day Taveng District. PAVN closed in on and prepared to overrun Dak To District, Kontum Province, on the Vietnamese side of the triborder area. The Khmer Rouge ensured that their rearguard was well secured on the Lao and Cambodia sides of the border. Even after taking Dak To, PAVN maintained its main base in the northeastern tip of Cambodia. Sihanouk also became increasingly concerned about PAVN's use of Cambodian territory in the northeast, but his FARK military was too weak to do much about it. It had only 9,000 troops in the Vietnam-Cambodia border area, whereas PAVN and the Cambodian communists had at least 20,000 combined, with the vast majority being Vietnamese. All Sihanouk could do was announce that he did not object to limited American attacks against PAVN troops that they were in "hot pursuit" of inside Cambodia (Baird 2008).

This was a particularly difficult decision for Sihanouk, especially considering the influence that Cambodian Sarin Chhak's 1965 dissertation, which was published in French in 1966 as the book *Les Frontières du Cambodge* [The borders of Cambodia], had had on Sihanouk and other Cambodian elites of his era. Crucially, Chhak promoted an irredentist view of Cambodia's borderlands, arguing that parts of southern Laos, the Central Highlands of Vietnam, the Mekong delta in Vietnam, and parts of northeastern Thailand rightfully belonged to Cambodia. Indeed, Chhak's work actually appealed to Cambodian leaders across the political spectrum and not only influenced Sihanouk's Sangkum government, but also Lon Nol's Republic of Cambodia regime, which followed, and especially Pol Pot's Democratic Kampuchea, which became especially strongly irredentist, in a way that would eventually lead to its downfall in 1979.

In the 1960s, Norodom Sihanouk invented the term "Khmer Rouge" to describe the communist movement in Cambodia. His intent in using the term was to criticize and mock the communists publicly. It was at this point that the Cambodian party prepared to launch its armed struggle against the Sihanouk government. At the same time, PAVN troops increasingly moved into the triborder region and the relationship between Sihanouk and the Democratic Republic of Vietnam soured. At the same time, the North Vietnamese strongly objected to the Khmer Rouge launching military campaigns against the Sihanouk government. As before, they did not want to anger Sihanouk, fearing that he might stop turning a blind eye to the PAVN's use of Cambodian territory for supply lines and sanctuaries. In fact, heavy air bombardment along the Ho Chi Minh Trail in 1966 and 1967 had made the PAVN's sanctuaries in Cambodia more important than ever. While the Cambodian party was ready for armed resistance against Sihanouk, the Vietnam Worker's Party wanted to maintain good relations with the

Sangkum government. Both sides saw the other as being selfish (Heder 2004).

Resistance Increases

In the beginning of 1968, the Khmer Rouge leadership began to seriously deviate from the Vietnam Worker's Party position vis-à-vis the Sihanouk regime. On January 17, 1968, the party's long-awaited military campaign against Sangkum began, with their first attack against a military post in Battambang in northwestern Cambodia. But the Khmer Rouge was on its own at this point, as relations between China and Sihanouk had improved from their low point in 1967, and China had even sent a large amount of military aid to Lon Nol. Nobody wanted the Khmer Rouge to attack the Cambodian government, except for the Cambodian communists themselves (Heder 2004). Despite a lack of international communist support, the revolution had some successes in the northwest in 1968, although almost everywhere else FARK initially crushed the Khmer Rouge (Baird 2008).

In early 1968, the Kreung of Poi Commune, in Ratanakiri Province, began to more seriously rise up against the Sangkum government after Vietnamese and Lao agents convinced them to join the revolution (Colm 1996; Mallow 2002). As time passed, more and more people joined them. As Kham Chan, the Brao former general from Trabok Village explained, "By 1968 all the people were in the forests." The ethnic minorities had to mainly rely on crossbows and punji stick pitfalls to fight. Since the Vietnamese did not agree with the Khmer Rouge's armed struggle, they did not assist them in developing their military capabilities (Baird 2008).

In early 1968, when the government was still in control of much of the countryside in the northeast, Sihanouk and Lon Nol visited Ratanakiri. Sihanouk announced that dissidents had failed to win over the local population and predicted their demise. He tried to convince the highlanders that the development activities organized by the state were for their benefit. In a speech he delivered in Bokeo on February 1, he criticized people for using "poisonous roots" to kill the schoolmasters in the school. "If you persist with this foolishness in the future, I will be forced to punish you; that is, I will authorize planes to come to bomb your villages," he warned (*Phnom Penh Domestic Service* 1968a). Following Sihanouk's visit, a crackdown in the province was initiated and involved arresting and killing suspected communists and threatening the party's base on the Drayak and Lapong streams. Air attacks also began on Khmer Rouge bases throughout the nation. In one incident, Nai Kong Yoot's soldiers caught and killed a group of thirty to forty Vietnamese communists in Taveng. The Sihanouk government increased FARK's strength in the northeast (Baird 2008).

In mid-February, Sihanouk admitted that Khmer Loeu had opposed forced resettlement that would allow them "to enjoy the social achievements that *Sangkum* offers" (cited by Colm 1996, 27). However, Sihanouk clearly misunderstood the situation in the highlands, as even with the knowledge of the unpopularity of his Khmerization efforts, he said that subversion was not the main problem. Instead, he reasoned that the main obstacle was underpopulation. He argued that what the region needed was the development of roads and the movement of large numbers of Khmer settlers from the south (Colm 1996). This perspective was, in fact, in line with earlier policy (Baird 2008). It appears that he had learned little from past abusive government policies and that he was only able to see things from the perspective of privileged elite Khmers in Phnom Penh.

The Khmer Rouge launched its first military operations in the northeast at the end of March 1968. FARK hit back hard, resulting in large numbers of killings and arrests (Colm 1996). Sihanouk himself argued that the Sangkum regime must be "pitiless" in dealing with its enemies (Heder 1979). But if anything, this helped mobilize highlander support for the communists, and by August, Sihanouk acknowledged that the movement covered half of Ratanakiri and Mondulkiri Provinces. Sihanouk ordered that insurgents be shot without trial; and many were (Colm 1996). Villagers started cutting large areas of small rubber trees down during the night. The Tampuon village of Patang, which had been displaced by the plantation, was angry about the rubber and was the first to take this action. Later others followed, although not all villages resisted. The French manager of the rubber concession fled from Ratanakiri as the security situation deteriorated (Baird 2008). There was also considerable dissatisfaction with the actions of soldiers based at the Lebansiek military post near present-day Banlung. In one incident, a soldier raped a young Tampuon woman studying at the Khmer language school near the post. A few days later, angry villagers took revenge with crossbows. Without any warning, three soldiers were hit, which had the additional effect of scaring other soldiers, as they did not know where the arrows had come from. Nor could they see their assailants, since the highlanders were hiding in the nearby bushes when they launched the attack (Baird 2008).

In Bokham and Bokeo, protests against livestock appropriation by the government also erupted, while in Voeunsai there were protests against taxes on boats, fish, and livestock. The FARK brutally repressed these uprisings. Villages were burnt, and several hundred people were killed. However, these actions backfired, as the government simply chased the people into the arms of the awaiting Khmer Rouge, whose ranks rapidly expanded (Baird 2008).

In early 1968, insurgents in the northeast, led by Bun Mi and Bun Chan (Brao, Phao Village) attacked Post Lo on the Sesan River near the mouth of the Palang stream, forcing most of the thirty soldiers there to flee in disarray to Post Kot at Bokham. The soldiers were mainly Khmer but some were Brao and ethnic Lao. Nai Kong Yoot was apprehended by Brao revolutionaries and killed in his village, which was located across the river from Post Lo. Other Brao communists wanted vengeance for the crackdown he orchestrated against them earlier. After Nai Kong Yoot was killed, a group of soldiers came up the Sesan River in a boat with a large gun on it. They told all the villagers they could find to go to Voeunsai but most fled to the forest. Only the Brao from Hamawk Village followed their orders. An attack was also orchestrated by communists against Post Kot, but there were over one hundred soldiers there and the post did not fall (Baird 2008).

By the end of March, armed resistance had increased in Voeunsai, and many government troops fled the area. Therefore, when the district town finally fell, the insurgents were only able to obtain a few weapons. Nevertheless, by the end of March, most of the roads in Ratanakiri had been cut off by rebel activities. Still, the Cambodian communists had few arms, although when PAVN soldiers were short on food, they sometimes traded guns and ammunition for rice and produce, but only on a small scale. The Cambodian communists pressed on, while Sihanouk considered the revolutionaries in the northeast to be agents of Lao communists or minority secessionists under foreign pay. In fact, the Cambodian communists had very good relations with the communists in Laos (Baird 2008), but they were certainly not under their control. Sihanouk, however, found it convenient to link the Vietnamese and Cambodian communists, and he chose to make no distinctions between Pol Pot's activities and those of the PAVN. This rhetoric resulted in

increased tensions between the Cambodian and Vietnamese communists (Heder 2004).

On April 13, 1968, Sihanouk recorded a special message to the nation, in which he stated that while there were problems in various provinces in the country, the situation was particularly grave in Ratanakiri
because:

> a number of Khmer Loeu [upland Khmers] have connived with
> foreigners—that is, the Vietnamese and Laotians who have mis-
> treated us and wanted our territory . . . saying that the region be-
> longs to neither the Khmer Kandal [central Khmers] or Cambo-
> dia. . . . That is not all. They have advocated war to expel Khmer
> Kandal and Khmer Kraom from Ratanakiri and to forbid these
> Khmer to live there. . . . At present, many groups of Phnong
> [pejorative for Khmer Loeu] have stopped cooperating with the
> Khmer Kandal under the pretext that they [Phnong] are not Khmer
> and must, therefore, expel the Khmer from their territory. (*Phnom
> Penh Domestic Service* 1968b)

In May 1968, Sihanouk traveled to the northeast again, where he tried
to explain his policy with regards to captured communist cadre. Speaking specifically about operations in Ratanakiri, he said,

> they gave rifles to the Khmer Loeu and ordered them to fire on
> the national forces. . . . I could not allow this and took stringent
> measures which resulted in the annihilation of 180 and the capture
> of 30 ringleaders, who were shot subsequently. . . . I do not care if
> I am sent to hell, . . . And I will submit the pertinent documents to
> the devil himself. (quoted in Heder 1979, 14)

Later Sihanouk also acknowledged that he himself had given the orders
to execute those fighting against the Sangkum government (Heder 1979).

Kreung elders from Dong Krapu Village in Ratanakiri explained
how they became engulfed in the revolution. In fact, the community
had no intention of entering the revolution in 1968, and because the
deputy commune chief lived in the village, communist propaganda
had not yet reached there. However, things suddenly changed when
FARK soldiers showed up and the commanding officer used a pistol to
unexpectedly shoot the welcoming ethnic Kreung deputy commune

chief, Jrim, in the face, killing him instantly. He had apparently been incorrectly accused of being a communist sympathizer. After Jrim's death, the soldiers went on a rampage. They shot at the communal house where most of the villagers had gathered, killing eleven people. "Blood was flowing like water under the *rong* [communal house in the village]," explained one man. The FARK soldiers then massacred all the chickens, pigs, and water buffaloes they could find and also burned down all the houses in the village, forcing those who survived to flee into the forest. One elder said, "We did not have any plans to enter the revolution but we had to flee, and only the communists were there to help us. So we joined them." Thus the heavy-handed tactics of Sihanouk did not have the desired effect. Rather than suppressing the Cambodian communists, it was drawing more and more people into the movement.

Soon after, new Kreung communists started turning the roads built to improve security against their new enemies. Groups of ten or so men were organized to ambush FARK soldiers. The groups were poorly armed, with usually just one rifle. The rest carried traditional hunting crossbows. When a truck carrying soldiers traveled along the road between Lebansiek and Voeunsai, the man with the gun shot out the tire of the vehicle. Then, when the vehicle stopped, and soldiers came out from the back, the others would fire their deadly crossbows while remaining concealed in the surrounding forest. In one case, a group of thirty Kreung attacked a group of about fifty FARK soldiers traveling along the road. About fifteen soldiers were killed with crossbow arrows. One of the scariest things for the Khmers was not being able to see their enemy or hear where the crossbow shots were coming from. Kreung people rarely died in these attacks. In other cases, pits were dug along roads at night, and camouflaged with banana leaves on top. When trucks or jeeps came along the road the next day, they would fall into the pits and then be attacked by an onslaught of crossbow-wielding highlanders. Many soldiers died or were injured in these attacks (Baird 2008).

In April 1969, Sihanouk made another visit to Ratanakiri, but by this time the security situation was very poor and FARK soldiers were largely restricted to their base posts due to increasing ambushes by the growing Khmer Rouge movement (Colm 1996). Sihanouk became enraged when the Khmer Rouge cadre successfully convinced highlanders in the province to largely boycott a showing of a film that was aired during the trip. After returning to Phnom Penh, Sihanouk and his lead-ing FARK General, Lon Nol, heavily criticized the Vietnamese for the support they were providing for the growing communist movement in the northeast. Fighting between government and Khmer Rouge troops increased after Sihanouk's visit. By October, the government estimated that there were 40,000 PAVN troops in the northeast, compared to just 1,500 Khmer Rouge fighters. PAVN had bases in many Brao areas, the most important being in the Dragon's Tail in Taveng, where the 2nd Division directed operations, along with operations in adjacent parts of the Central Highlands of Vietnam (Colm 1996).

By November 1969, the government became increasingly concerned that the PAVN in Ratanakiri, along with the Khmer Rouge, were re-sponsible for the increasing pressure being put on local authorities and the FARK (Sutsakhan 1978). In fact, Khmer Rouge attacks were occur-ring without the involvement or even the blessing of the Democratic Republic of Vietnam, but in any case, the FARK high command autho-rized Operation Test VC/NVA (North Vietnam Army), to locate and determine the size of the PAVN bases and sanctuaries in Ratanakiri. Lieutenant General Sak Sutsakhan was put in charge of the mission and remained commander of military operations in Ratanakiri until March 11, 1970, when he was called to Phnom Penh in preparation for the Lon Nol coup d'état a week later (Sutsakhan 1978). During the over four-month period that the operation continued, FARK launched operations against communist positions in Bokeo, Lumphat, and Siempang. How-ever, they were largely unsuccessful, as PAVN chose to not engage them in battle because they were under orders to avoid direct military conflict. According to Sutsakhan (1978, 63, 66), "They [the PAVN] were content to leave the fighting for the moment to their auxiliary troops, the dissident Khmer Loeu. These auxiliaries were used either to slow the advance of FARK units or to divert them from the main centers of VC/NVA strength." In fact, it seems unlikely that the Khmer Rouge highlanders and the PAVN were not working as close together as Sutsa-khan believed, as by that time the Khmer Rouge had gained consider-able strength—especially in the northeast—and their ranks had grown to 4,000 regular soldiers and 50,000 local militiamen nationwide.

On March 6–7, 1970, Lon Nol visited Ratanakiri for the last time. He went to Lebansiek and even traveled to Taveng by helicopter to inspect the local military post there. He paid 2,000 riel to each of the twenty families that moved near the post. He also considered a plan for creating a new province, which he hoped would help prevent "expansionist de-signs of neighboring countries" (*Phnom Penh Domestic Service* 1970), but this plan would never materialize.

The CIA Brao at Kong My

Although a large portion of the Brao in northeastern Cambodia sympathized with the Khmer Rouge and joined them in fighting against the Cambodian government, especially beginning in 1968, there were, however, a smaller number of Cambodian Brao who sided with the US Central Intelligence Agency (CIA). Ya Ha, the chief of Kok Lak Commune, in Voeunsai District, Ratanakiri, and his chief military man, Ya Heum, led their Kavet followers, particularly the in-habitants of Phya Vong Village, to flee to southern Laos in 1966, after they were extracted from a natural mountain field known as Treng Tih in Brao (Viel Thom in Khmer) by four or five American helicopters. Once in Laos they joined other pro-American Brao from Laos who had established a five-kilometer by five-kilometer mountain stronghold in southeastern Attapeu Province near the borders of both Cambodia and Vietnam at place called Kong My (Baird 2010d).

All the Brao Amba from Savanbao, Tambouan Roeng, and Ke Kuang Villages—and also some from Phayang and Phya Vang Villages—were extracted from the Cambodia side of the border by American helicopters as well, as were Kavet from Vongvilai Tai, Kan Teung, La Meuay (Tih), Phya Vong, Phathainy, and Viangkham. In early 1968, the Kavet from La Meuay Village were taken away by other Brao soldiers from Kong My. They all traveled back to Kong My by foot, although it was not easy. Many of the male Brao young men who fled to Kong My from Cambodia ended up becoming Road Watchers, who were paid directly by CIA case officers based in Laos and were sent on missions to moni-tor and disrupt activities along the Ho Chi Minh Trail (Baird 2010d).

Although most of Attapeu Province was under communist control by the late 1960s, the CIA continued to support road watching opera-tions out of Kong My until the Vientiane Agreement in 1973 led to a ceasefire, the creation of a coalition government with both communist and noncommunist representation, and the gradual withdrawal of the CIA from Laos. However, Kong My remained under nominal noncom-munist control until the central government came under Pathet Lao communist control and the former CIA-supported Brao soldiers at

Kong My finally came down from the stronghold and surrendered on June 1, 1975 (Baird 2010d). Some Brao who stayed at Kong My eventually made their way back to Cambodia, while others settled permanently in Laos.

Lon Nol Takes Control

The political orientation of Cambodia changed drastically on March 18, 1970, when Lon Nol and Sirik Matak orchestrated a parliamentary takeover of the government from Norodom Sihanouk when he was out of the country in Moscow. The new government immediately escalated its actions against the presence of Vietnamese communist forces in Cambodia. The United States took advantage of the situation to attack those forces and thereafter provided military aid to support the war against both the Vietnamese and Cambodian communists. Lon Nol renamed the Cambodian army, Forces Armées Nationales Khmères (FANK). Sihanouk, who based himself in China immediately after the coup d'état, lent his popular support to the Front Uni National du Kampuchéa (FUNK) (Renaksey Ruop Ruom Cheat Kampuchea), which was established in Beijing on March 23, 1970.[25] It included forces loyal to Sihanouk, Cambodian communists aligned with Vietnam, domestic Khmer Rouge, and some intellectuals. However, the domestic Khmer Rouge retained real control inside Cambodia, although Sihanouk's strong image among the local population was used for recruiting (Bou Thang 1993).

In early 1970, after Sihanouk's fall, the Lon Nol government's efforts to convince the Kreung to return from the forests were centered at Post Poi, in present-day O Chum District. Rice was sent to people who remained in their villages, but ethnic Khmer soldiers responsible for distributing it kept most for themselves. Thus, it was supposed to be a positive public relations move, but ended up backfiring (Mallow 2002). People continued to flee to the forests in large numbers. Soon after, Post Poi was attacked by a group of forty guerillas. According to one former Khmer Rouge soldier who participated in the battle, five bazooka blasts were fired into the main military barracks of the government troops. Most of the thirty mainly ethnic Khmer FANK soldiers were killed. The rebels were also able to seize a large cache of arms. After Post Poi fell, the twelve soldiers at Post Dao Hom deserted. Soon after, Lebansiek was attacked; it took three days and three nights of fighting before the major military post was overrun (Baird 2008).

As the FANK's situation deteriorated, government soldiers prepared to abandon Post Kot. But the FANK made one last attempt to reinforce troops there. Ninety soldiers were sent up the Sesan River from Stung Treng by boat. However, they were forced to stop for the night near Chuay Village, in Ratanakiri Province, and that evening they were ambushed by a group of Kreung villagers from Chuay. It started with a soldier suddenly being hit with a crossbow arrow as he crossed the Sesan River to get firewood. A bomb was thrown at the boat, and shooting began. Some soldiers were wounded and killed; there were apparently no Kreung casualties. After the incident, the soldiers dared not travel farther upriver, and the next morning they returned to Stung Treng. Soon after, Post Kot was abandoned (Baird 2008).

The Evacuation of the Northeast by FANK

By the end of March 1970, FANK attempted to withdraw two infantry battalions and one engineer battalion from Ratanakiri by road. However, PAVN launched military attacks on the FANK on March 29, shocking and isolating large concentrations of FANK troops in Ratanakiri and Kratie. Thus, in April 1970, plans began to be developed with the United States and ARVN to evacuate the remaining FANK troops and their dependents from the northeast, as well as a large number of highlanders, about 9,000 people in total (US Library of Congress 2006). The United States took the lead in organizing the operation (Sutsakhan 1978), called Binh Tay 4, in which the FANK conceded almost a quarter of the country's land area to the Khmer Rouge (US Library of Congress 2006).

According to *Hanoi VNA* (1970), between June 24 and 26, 1970, FUNK troops either killed or wounded nearly one hundred FANK and ARVN troops in the Lebansiek and Bokeo areas, including destroying six vehicles. This attack apparently forced the rapid withdrawal of the area, which began on June 27. A large number of noncommunist highlanders, including many Brao Tanap and Kreung, and also others who had been digging for gems in Bokeo, were evacuated by Air America to Pleiku, Vietnam. Air America shuttled all those who could get to the planes quick enough without advance notice, regardless of whether they were soldiers, civilian officials, or highlanders. Six large Air America transport planes, probably C-123 providers, were used to ferry about one thousand people from the airstrip at Bokeo (east of present-day Banlung) to Pleiku over a three-day period. All the commune chiefs, village headmen, and others who feared the communists and wanted to leave were directed to gather at Bokeo (Baird 2008). The last stage of the evacuation was carried out according to plan. However, several military units far from the meeting point, such as those at Voeunsai, Stung Treng, and Siempang, could not be reached. These bases were overrun soon after (Sutsakhan 1978). A Kreung elder from Kok Poi Village said that it took a total of three days for the large American transport planes to evacuate all who wanted to leave the area. One elder reported that he was actually on the stairs to go up into the plane, but decided not to go, as his wife and children had not arrived in time, and he did not want to leave without them. Although most of the ethnic minorities sided with the communists, the government still had some highland supporters. People were not simply making decisions on ethnic lines but had varying viewpoints and political alliances. In any case, this marked the full liberation of Ratanakiri Province (Baird 2008). The FANK evacuation from Ratanakiri was critical for the Khmer Rouge, as it provided them with a more secure base area for training and recruiting (Colm 1996).

Later, the evacuees from Ratanakiri traveled to Saigon for a period before continuing onto Phnom Penh, where most stayed temporarily at the Phnom Penh "Music School." Charles Keller conducted the first detailed linguistic studies with the Brao from November 1974 to March 1975 at Pailin (see Keller 1976), where they had gone to dig for gems. The first Brao man to meet Keller in Pailin told him that he was "*Meo*" (a pejorative for ethnic Hmong), apparently thinking that such an identity might please Keller. Later, after some discussion in Khmer language, the man acknowledged that he was actually Brao (Baird 2008). Keller estimated that there were approximately five hundred Brao or Kreung people in Pailin, in northwestern Cambodia, at the time, as well as some people from other highland groups in the northeast, such as Tampuon.[26] After 1979, many of these Kreung ended up in refugee camps along the border in Thailand, where Keller again came into contact with them. In 1982, he met many at Khao I Dang refugee camp near Aranyaprathet, in eastern Thailand. Later many became refugees in the United States, where about ninety Kreung in twenty families live today.[27]

Conflict Continues

Daily bombing of Cambodia by the US Air Force began in 1968, but it was not acknowledged by the US government until it was revealed by the media after 1970 (Colm 1996; Shawcross 1979; Conboy and Bowra 1989). In March 1969, the Nixon administration authorized secret bombing operations in Cambodia, apparently with approval from Sihanouk. These bombing operations started small, but gradually increased to B-52 carpet-bombing raids (Colm 1996). While Sihanouk initially publically protested against these operations in Cambodia, he also wanted to improve relations with the United States, which he was able to do by mid-1969, when the United States recognized Cambodia's frontiers and reestablished diplomatic relations with Cambodia (Heder 2004). However, FANK's abandonment of the northeast especially opened it up for more intensive US aerial bombing, since the US Air Force no longer had to be concerned about any potential impacts on "friendlies." Khmer Rouge bases were moved around to avoid being targeted, but it was still a difficult time. The communists controlled the land but not the air. Richard Nixon, the president of the United States, and Henry Kissinger, the secretary of state, maintained that the areas bombed were largely unpopulated and that only communist troops— legitimate targets—were there. For example, when Kissinger was confirmed by the US Senate as secretary of state in 1973, he declared that, "It was not a bombing of Cambodia, but it was a bombing of North Vietnamese in Cambodia" (quoted in Shawcross 1979, 28). He was either not aware of, or found it convenient to ignore, the Brao civilians and other highlanders who populated the area.

One Kreung man from Chuay Village, a community situated along the Sesan River in present-day Taveng District, said, "During the bombing period we couldn't live in our villages. The villages were empty. We couldn't do swidden agriculture or live in our houses. We had to hide in the forests. We were running around like monkeys. We didn't even have any clothes to wear. Some forest areas were totally leveled. There was no forest. Everything changed" (Baird 2008, 235). Jyao Dawl, a Brao Amba man from Bang Koet Village, reported that five or six people died due to US aerial bombardment. However, most were protected by hiding in pits that they dug for protection. Ethnic Lao villagers reported that leaflets were dropped on Voeunsai Village, warning villagers to stay away from the Sesan River and big roads, in order to avoid being bombed on. There were three divisions of PAVN soldiers scattered around in the vicinity of the Lapong stream, near the Vietnamese border. One of those was mainly used for defensive purposes, whereas the other two were deployed to attack the enemy.[28] Although few highlanders allied with the Khmer Rouge died as a direct result of the bombing, the fear and trauma of always having to hide from bombs greatly affected them emotionally. People had to abandon their villages and live in the forest. It was also very difficult to farm, which resulted in food security problems (Baird 2008).

Apart from the bombing, on May 1, 1970, 30,000 American and 40,000 ARVN troops swept through northeastern Cambodia. A Brao man based in the Drayak stream area recalled the attack, "When the Americans and Vietnamese were dropped into the area we had to go to the mountains, as the lowlands were full of American soldiers. They stayed two months and there was heavy fighting the whole time. We had to stay in pits for most of the time."[29] An elderly Kreung man from nearby Chuay Village remembered seeing what he described as "thousands of US soldiers" parachuting into Cambodia near the Sesan River and the Vietnamese border. A Brao Amba man also recalled, "We had to flee to the mountains, as there were so many American soldiers in the lowlands. The fighting was fierce but the Americans could not defeat the Vietnamese [PAVN] and retreated."[30] The war had fully arrived in the northeast.

Although the FANK withdrew regular troops from the northeast soon after they were formed, they continued to send special operations forces into the northeast, including from southern Laos and the Central Highlands of Vietnam. These included both Brao and ethnic Khmer forces trained by the CIA in southern Laos, including at Kong My in Attapeu Province (see the section "The CIA Brao at Kong My") (Conboy 1995; Baird 2010d).

Apart from the communist/noncommunist conflict, by September 1970, tensions between the Khmer Rouge and PAVN, two communist groups, increased in the northeast, resulting in some clashes (Baird 2008). Ney Sarann—known as Ya—told an ethnic Jarai revolutionary in 1970 that the Khmer Rouge and the Vietnamese communists must wait to see how their relationship developed. Ya said that the two groups needed to remain separate and equal, and that if equality was not maintained, armed conflict would ensue. The Jarai man recalled one incident that indicated why Ya felt this way. In 1968–69 the Khmer Rouge

and the Vietnamese Communists had been conducting military operations together, and they jointly overran some government posts in Bokeo
District, Ratanakiri Province. Bad feelings emerged, however, when the
spoils of the operation were divided up. The Vietnamese apparently
took all the small guns, leaving the Khmer Rouge with the big guns.
The problem was that the guns left for the Khmer Rouge were too big to
move. Similarly, the Vietnamese took all the small gas containers, while
the large gas containers were left for the Khmer Rouge. Again, they
were too large to transport. Finally, the already prepared gun powder
was taken by the Vietnamese, while the unprepared gun powder was
left for the Cambodians. Ya and the key Khmer Rouge leader, Son Sen,[31]
were intensely unhappy.[32] Mistrust of the Vietnamese was increasing
among the Khmer Rouge.

The Return of the Khmer Hanoi from Vietnam

On May 1, 1970, Bou Thang and Soy Keo—and many
other Khmer Hanoi—started the three-month journey by foot along the
Ho Chi Minh Trail from North Vietnam. They moved during the rainy
season when aerial bombardment was less of a concern and arrived in
Cambodia in August after an arduous journey.[33] Later, in 1972, as revolutionary forces gained increasing support in Cambodia, a larger number of repatriating communists made the same trip. Although over
1,000 of the 1,500 Khmer 1954 regroupees who had originally traveled
to Hanoi came back to Cambodia in the early 1970s (Encyclopedia of
World Biography 2004), only a few dozen survived the 1970s. According
to Vickery (1984), 822 of those who returned were party members. Most,
however, were either put into dangerous frontline positions where they
died in combat or were purged and killed by the Khmer Rouge (Heder
2004; Chandler 1996). Valuable human resources were sacrificed due to
concerns about the Khmer Hanoi being too pro-Vietnamese.

According to Kham Toeung, Pol Pot was immediately wary of these
Cambodians because they had spent many years in Vietnam. In 1970,
he told the Brao, Kham Toeung, "This group is not going to command
us."[34] Ya also secretly told the ethnic Jarai revolutionary, Bui Yung, that
the returning Khmer Hanoi needed to be carefully watched and that
they would not be given high positions. Many were put in lower positions in the villages and communes. Initially, however, the former regroupees did not understand how much suspicion was directed toward

them.[35] Bou Thang claims that in reality some people with particular skills that the zone needed were given higher positions. Indeed, he is a good example, as he had military skills that the zone needed. Bou Thang mentioned that some people had studied overly obscure subjects, and that as a result their skills were not useful to the Khmer Rouge. He thought that the Vietnamese had made mistakes in assessing what subjects many Khmer Hanoi should have usefully studied. As he explained it, "Many studied at an overly high level."[36]

After returning from Vietnam in 1970, Bou Thang became the military leader in Sector 1 (*Tambon*) of the northeast zone, which encompassed present-day O Yadao District in Ratanakiri Province, near the border with Vietnam. Later he was made deputy head of the Khmer Rouge military in the northeast zone, with Son Sen as leader.[37] Soy Keo, on the other hand, was assigned to set up Company 703, which was the first northeastern Khmer Rouge military unit. The company was initially based in Poi Commune, O Chum District, Ratanakiri Province, with Soy Keo as military head and Chan (Tampuon, Sida Commune) as chief of politics. Later Company 703 relocated to what is now Koun Moum District, Ratanakiri Province. During that period, Son Sen was chief of staff of the northeast zone (*Phum Pheak*) military. Later in 1973, Ya took up the top position, secretary of northeastern zone party committee (Bou Thang 1993). Bun Mi (Brao, Savanbao Village) was Ya's deputy, and he was also the district chief in Taveng. Thong Dam (ethnic Lao, Kalan Village) was head of the committee for helping the northeastern zone, called *Kho 32*. His deputies were Bou Thang (politics) and Thang Samai (ethnic Lao, Pong Village). Soy Keo mainly worked on recruiting new soldiers. He also worked with Bou Thang to do political training. They were key people at the beginning, moving around between different heavily forested areas. Soy Keo's group of largely ethnic minority combatants was involved in providing security to Norodom Sihanouk when he traveled from China and visited liberated parts of northern Cambodia in 1973. "Sihanouk trusted the minorities more than soldiers from his own group," claimed Soy Keo during a 2009 interview in Phnom Penh. According to Soy Keo, other senior Khmer Rouge, including Son Sen, Ya, and Vong also used ethnic minority soldiers to guard them. Soy Keo also claimed that minorities were asked to wash the clothes of Son Sen's wife after she bloodied them during menstruation. He claimed that ethnic Khmer people would have refused the chore, but ethnic minorities did whatever they were asked. "They were taken advantage of," claimed Soy Keo,[38] indicating that while some people in the same ethnic groups made very different political decisions, ethnic issues were also still important to those in the northeast.

Later, Company 703 expanded to be the size of two companies. Di Thin (Tampuon, Patang Commune) was put in charge of the new company, numbered 704. Both companies were sent via Kratie to participate in the Chenla I military campaign,[39] along with Company 515. After overrunning parts of western Kampong Cham Province, they continued on to Kampong Thom and then Siem Reap, where they became based. According to Soy Keo, his soldiers were highly motivated, but about forty died in heavy combat.[40] When in Siem Reap, Companies 703 and 704 were elevated to battalions.[41] In 2017, Soy Keo commented that while he is just one year older than Bou Thang, and has long been his very close friend and colleague, it was he who ended up fighting on the battlefield, including at Chenla II, not Bou Thang, who was never personally involved in any serious fighting. Still, Soy Keo acknowledges that Bou Thang was always one level above him in seniority.[42]

While the return to Cambodia of Bou Thang and Soy Keo was important, the key revolutionary leader in Ratanakiri Province was Bun Mi, who had emerged as the Brao leader of the revolution in Ratanakiri during the 1960s when others, such as Bou Thang and Soy Keo, were in Vietnam. According to Kham Phai, a senior Brao military leader during the PRK period and afterward, "Bun Mi knew the history of the revolution best. He knew about everyone who was involved and where different battles had occurred. He knew much more than Bou Thang and Soy Keo, as they had been away in Vietnam. Bun Mi really knew a lot and was the most respected leader. Only after Bun Mi's demise did Bou Thang replace him."[43]

The Administrative Reorganization of Northeastern Cambodia by the Khmer Rouge

In the mid-1970s, the Khmer Rouge moved their national headquarters from the northeast to the border between Kampong Cham and Kampong Thom Provinces (Office of the Co-Investigating Judges 2010). The relocation occurred around the same time that the Khmer Rouge gained full control over the northeast zone. The Khmer Rouge administratively reorganized the region to fit with their vision for the future. The zone was divided into five sectors, or *tambon* (also called *ta*). Under each Sector were districts (*srok*), communes (*khum*), and villages (*phum*). The zone's headquarters was in the forest at the end of Rai stream, in present-day Sesan District, Stung Treng Province, about twenty kilometers north of the Sesan River. Sector 1 included present-day O Yadao and Bokeo Districts and Sida Commune in Ratanakiri Province. Sector 2 encompassed the southern parts of presentday Voeunsai and O Chum Districts, as well as the north side of presentday Bokeo District, in Ratanakiri Province. Sector 3 consisted of present-day Kok Lak Commune, part of Voeunsai District, and all of Taveng District. Sector 4 included present-day Siempang District, Stung Treng Province, and Sector 5 constituted southern Ratanakiri Province and Mondulkiri Province. In addition, individual communes were coded by number. For example, O Yadao was coded 52, O Chum was 52 *Lo*, and Voeunsai was 52 *To*. Similarly, Sida was 54 while Bokeo was 54 *To*.[44] In 1972, the headquarters of the northeast zone was moved to near Srekor Village,[45] on the south side of the Sesan River in presentday Sesan District, Stung Treng Province. The area was secure, and it was easier to go down to Kratie via boat from there. It was also easier to contact Preah Vihear from there.[46]

Ny Kan, an ethnic Khmer Kraom, was the first head of Sector 3, which included three districts: (1) 55 *Kaw*, covering what is now Taveng District. It was led by Bun Mi. (2) 55 *Kho*, covering what now encompasses present-day Kok Lak and Kopong communes in Voeunsai District. It was led by Buo Khav (ethnic Kavet).[47] (3) 55 *Ko*, which now encompasses much of Voeunsai District (apart from Kok Lak Commune). It was led by Kham Phuy (ethnic Lao, Mai Village).[48]

By the end of 1970, the communist-led armed forces in Cambodia apparently numbered 15,000. Because Lon Nol's government was firmly against any Vietnamese communist presence in Cambodia, the Democratic Republic of Vietnam altered its position and lent its support to the Khmer Rouge. PAVN also helped weaken Lon Nol's forces, winning a number of back-breaking battles. By late 1971, PAVN felt confident in the Khmer Rouge's ability to take on FANK's remaining forces (Conboy and Bowra 1989), and the Khmer Rouge's control over the northeast had been consolidated. Therefore, highlanders in the special forces began fighting for the Khmer Rouge in other parts of Cambodia, including the south. These operations continued around the country between 1972 and 1975 (Colm 1996). Cities and towns also started to empty (Baird 2008). Kham Toeung reported in 1986 that cooperatives began to be established in 1972. Collectivization began and individuals were only allowed to keep one plate and one spoon.[49]

In January 1973, the Paris and Vientiane Peace Agreements that were supposed to end the war in Vietnam and Laos were signed, but the Khmer Rouge boycotted the talks, despite Vietnamese recommendations to the contrary. Thus, war continued in Cambodia. In early February 1973, the US Air Force stepped up aerial assaults, with 250,000 tons of bombs being dropped on Cambodia on a daily basis over a 140-day period (Kiernan and Bou 1982). One of the goals was to build a wall of fire around Phnom Penh. Attacks in the northeast also continued on a daily basis. These actions provided Lon Nol's regime with some more time. However, on August 15, 1973, by which time the bulk of the PAVN had withdrawn from Cambodia (Conboy and Bowra 1989), the US Congress decided to only sanction military aid and unarmed reconnaissance flights over Cambodia. This decision ended the bombing (Colm 1996).

Conclusion

Many Brao and other ethnic minorities in Ratanakiri Province supported the Vietnamese in fighting against the French before 1954, and in the 1960s many joined the Khmer Rouge, largely due to problems associated with forced resettlement and schooling in the lowlands, and later because of land grabbing and being forced to be laborers on the large rubber plantation being developed in the center of Ratanakiri Province. However, it is crucial to not view the Brao and other ethnic minorities as having a singular point of view or political perspective, as not all chose to become aligned with the Vietnamese and later the Khmer Rouge. Some sided with the government of Cambodia and the US CIA, while others, like Nai Kong Yoot, ended up being killed by other pro-Khmer Rouge Brao. Still others were evacuated by helicopter to Kong My, a CIA-supported base in southern Laos. The United States also evacuated some Kreung supporters to Pleiku in the Central Highlands of Vietnam. All these circumstances and different political positions indicate that ethnicity is not sufficient to understand why different people from the same ethnic groups ended up on different sides of the conflict. Political preferences are crucial and differ widely, even among relatively small ethnic groups such as the Brao.

We now turn to considering how the Khmer Rouge became more and more draconian in their policies, and also increasingly anti-Vietnamese, especially after the bombing stopped in 1973. In particular, we examine the chain of events that eventually led to virtually all of the Brao of present-day Taveng District to turn against the Khmer Rouge and flee to Vietnam and Laos between 1973 and 1975, along with some Tampuon, Kreung, Jarai, and ethnic Lao people from the Sesan River basin in Ratanakiri Province. Those who were farther away had to stay with the Khmer Rouge and endure Pol Pot's warped communist experiment, as geography was the key to who ended up leaving Cambodia and who had to stay with the Khmer Rouge once the country was fully under their control in April 1975.

Brao Discontent
with the Khmer Rouge and
Their Exodus from Cambodia
to Vietnam and Laos

After the US bombing of Cambodia ended in August 1973, relative peace came to the northeast, and the Khmer Rouge had the opportunity to begin consolidating power and seriously implementing their radical political agenda, as they were in control of the northeast. They had already begun promoting sedentary wet-rice agriculture in 1971, and had also generally restricted religious practices, including animism, since that time. But in 1973, even more dramatic changes were ordered. Markets were closed to stop private commerce. The Khmer Rouge also more strongly enforced a ban on highland religious practices. They confiscated cows, elephants, clay beer jars, and highly valued gongs for playing music important for rituals. Those who opposed the new policies were often accused as being *Yuan* (a term that became increasing a pejorative for Vietnamese) or being allied with America's CIA. Some were executed in the forest, and a climate of fear developed (Colm 1996). The town of Stung Treng was largely emptied in 1973, with its population being sent to open up wet-rice paddy in new cooperatives in lowland forested areas in Ratanakiri Province (Baird 2008).

It is hard to assess exactly why Pol Pot's policy of enmity toward Vietnam became so virulent, although a number of factors have already been mentioned. Apart from those, Hanoi's support for Prince Norodom Sihanouk angered the Khmer Rouge. In April 1970, when Vietnam's Party First Secretary Lê Duẩn proposed the establishment of a combined military force that would have included the Khmer Rouge and forces supporting the prince, Pol Pot, who was in Hanoi on a stop-over, bluntly rejected the idea. Vietnam's support for Sihanouk not only made Pol Pot unhappy but also offended many Khmer Hanoi living in Vietnam. Following his exile from Cambodia in 1970, Sihanouk traveled to Vietnam to celebrate the Tet Vietnamese New Year every year. To keep Sihanouk happy, the Khmer Hanoi living in Hanoi were "invited" to leave the city and go out to the provinces. According to Ngo Dien, the Vietnamese Ambassador to Cambodia between 1979 and 1991, "Whenever there was talk about this, the eyes of the late Prime Minister, Chan Si, a regrouped cadre [Khmer Hanoi] who had close ties with Vietnam, would fill with tears and he would criticize us [the Vietnamese] for paying too little heed to Cambodian communists while over-valuing the Prince" (Huy Đức 2012a, 145).

The events and circumstances that led most of the Brao and other ethnic minorities in northeastern Cambodia to join the Khmer Rouge have already been described. Here the focus is on the series of events that led a small group of Brao to flee to Vietnam in 1973, and a much larger group to flee to Vietnam and Laos in 1975, ironically at around the same time as Phnom Penh was about to fall to the Khmer Rouge. Although some Brao were among the earliest and strongest supporters of the Khmer Rouge, they gradually became disillusioned and disenchanted with the Khmer Rouge's increasingly strict and draconian policies. In the end, however, it was a conflict between the Khmer Rouge and a key Brao leader from Taveng, Bun Mi, that would eventually lead to most of the Brao living in the Sesan River basin, as well as some Tampuon, Kreung, Jarai, and ethnic Lao people, fleeing to Vietnam and Laos, where they became political refugees.

Brao Discontent with the Khmer Rouge

In the 1960s, and even in the beginning of the 1970s, the Khmer Rouge in Ratanakiri Province were not ideologically strict (Colm 1996). However, beginning in around 1973, the Communist Party of Kampuchea central leadership began issuing more draconian orders. For example, Kham Toeung, the ethnic Brao Amba deputy chief of Taveng Kraom Commune in the early 1970s, received an order in 1973 for people to eat communally. From that point onward the Brao people in his community would eat communally when outside officials visited, but once they left they would return to eating as families, just as they had in the past. Kham Toeung also altered orders such as "Don't eat until you are full" to "Eat until you are full." He received orders as early as 1968 to 1969 to stop religious practices but also ignored them.[1] He became increasingly wary, especially when Pol Pot labeled all those in Taveng Loeu Commune as "a CIA group, a Vietnamese network."[2] Kham Toeung personally asked Pol Pot why he was so negative about the Vietnamese, reminding him that they all worked together in the Indochinese Communist Party from 1930 to 1951. Pol Pot replied, "No . . . If we have solidarity [with the Vietnamese], we lose our soul. We can't. We rely on our own strength." Kham Toeung remained silent, but he did not agree.[3]

According to Kham Toeung, his quiet resistance (cf. Scott 1985) against radical Khmer Rouge orders from the center was soon being compounded by more serious problems related to growing Khmer Rouge hatred for anyone connected with Vietnam. Many Brao had fought with or had otherwise supported Vietnamese communists against the French during the First Indochina War and had already spent considerable periods with Vietnamese communists. Still, anyone perceived to be pro-Vietnamese became a target for paranoid Khmer Rouge purges (Baird 2008).

In July 1973, Ya, the northeast zone leader, visited Taveng Kraom Commune and stayed for two weeks. He asked Kham Toeung to go to study in Stung Treng, but he was wary and declined, stating, "I dare not go. . . . You go." Then in September, Ya returned to Taveng Kraom Commune. He again invited Kham Toeung to go to study, but he still dared not accept the offer. But twelve others did, including Thang Ngon, Kham Sai, Kham Len, and Kham Toeu (Brao, Savanbao Village), a relative of Bun Mi. They studied for a month and returned with salt, cloth, medicine, and other items.[4]

In November 1973, the Brao Amba village of Bong, which had a population of just seventy-four people and was led by Kreng Siengnoi, became the first community in the northeast to flee from Cambodia to Vietnam. Kreng Siengnoi and Yoep Vanson explained that they were driven to make the move due to purges against two people a few months before they fled. Bunchon was killed because the Khmer Rouge said he received a gun from the Vietnamese, which was apparently not true. The second person killed was Kreng Siengnoi's younger brother, Kreng Eat, who was killed after being accused of a social discretion with a woman. Kreng Eat was studying Lao writing with Kreng Siengnoi at around the time Kreng Eat and Bunchon were arrested and taken to the district center at Lalay stream. They were killed one or two weeks later.[5] Bong villagers initially fled to stay with Brao relatives in Hala Troo Village, which was adjacent to the Dak Mi River, in Dak Jala Commune, Dak To District, Kontum Province. They stayed there four years before joining refugees that fled to Gia Poc two years after they had (see the section "Fleeing to Vietnam and Laos"). Kham Khoeun (ethnic Lao, Pong Village) emphasized, in 2017, that resistance against the Khmer Rouge started with the Brao in Taveng,[6] although it is also true that resistance by some Thais in Koh Kong also began early.

According to Yoep Sat, who was part of the group from Bong Village, once in Vietnam the people initially conducted swidden cultivation just as they previously had in Cambodia. During the first year in Vietnam, in late 1974, the Vietnamese government provided the refugees with some rice so that they had something to eat between then and when they harvested their first crop of rice almost a year later. At that time they were still living close to the border.[7]

I learned the story of the main exodus of Brao from Taveng by way of a number of people, but especially via long interviews conducted in 2002 with Veng Khoun, whose revolutionary name was Bun Yot, and in 2009 with Kham Sai. Both played key roles, although their stories did not entirely align. As they explained, in early 1973 the Khmer Rouge began criticizing Bun Mi, the head of 55 *Kaw*, and Kham Sai, the military leader of Sector 3. The sector leadership, particularly its head, Ny Kan, allegedly accused both Bun Mi and Kham Sai of contacting Vietnamese soldiers. According to Veng Khoun and Kham Sai, Ny Kan wanted to kill Bun Mi. He apparently first intended to do this at the sector's main military office near the Lalay stream in 55 *Ko*, after Bun Mi had completed a week of training there. Bun Mi did not have a gun with him and was not allowed to go anywhere during the training, so it initially seemed like a viable plan. At the same time, Kham Sai was staying at the old sector headquarters, also near the Lalay stream, but three days later he too was sent to stay with Bun Mi at the military office. Kham Sai's arrival apparently led Ny Kan to hesitate and decide not to follow through with the first plan to kill Bun Mi, as there were many soldiers from Taveng there, and Ny Kan was apparently afraid that the plan would not succeed.[8] However, Bui Yung believes that initially Ny Kan did not plan to kill Bun Mi, and that he simply tried to persuade him to step down from his position as head of 55 *Kaw* due to what he believed were nerve problems associated with a gunshot injury that he had sustained in 1968. When Bun Mi objected, Ny Kan probably decided to kill him due to his insubordinance.[9]

In any case, a second plan was devised, and Bun Mi, Kham Sai, and the others were ordered to join a meeting about economics at the new sector headquarters, which was also near the Lalay stream. Some of the group at the sector military office, including Kham Sai, traveled by boat along the Lalay stream to the new sector headquarters. Bun Mi walked. Veng Khoun was also present, as were the committee members from all the districts and communes in the sector. More than one hundred people were there, so it became too risky to kill Bun Mi during the meeting. However, three days after the meeting ended, Kham Sai was sent to 55 *Kaw* with sixty soldiers. The plan was to isolate Bun Mi from Kham Sai and his troops so that he could be easily targeted.[10]

The day after Kham Sai left with the soldiers, one of Ny Kan's personal couriers, Ya Choi, a 55 *Kho* Brao soldier from Hin Lat Village, was sent to kill Bun Mi. Choi, however, did not like Ny Kan, and did not want to follow through with the order. Therefore, he informed Bun Mi that Ny Kan thought that Bun Mi was crazy and that Choi had been sent to kill him. Bun Mi believed Choi, and Choi encouraged Bun Mi to escape by swimming underwater across the Lalay stream when he was bathing, and then to run back to 55 *Kaw* from there. Bun Mi followed Choi's suggestion, and Choi reported to Ny Kan that he was unable to complete the mission because Bun Mi had escaped when taking a bath.[11]

After Bun Mi had returned safely to Taveng Loeu Commune, he met with Kham Sai, Kham Toeung, Moeng Chuon (Brao, Paroe Touich Village), and Hai He (Brao, Paroe Touich Village) for two days to decide how to proceed. Kham Sai came to realize that his life was also in danger. It was determined that there was no way to resolve the problem locally. Therefore, in March 1973, Bun Mi and Kham Sai led sixty soldiers (two small companies), three medics,[12] five officials, including Kham Toeung, and five women north to Laos via the Khampha stream, intending to make contact with the Khmer Rouge leadership from there. All were Brao. They hoped that they could resolve the problem with Ny Kan by going over his head.[13] Although Rathie (2019, 216) claimed that Bun Mi "led an aborted uprising," this was not actually the case.

Soon after Bun Mi and the others departed for the Lao border, Ny Kan came up the Sesan River to Taveng Loeu Commune and met with Veng Khoun, who was one of the committee leaders there. Ny Kan noticed that the government officials who had gone with Bun Mi were missing and asked Veng Khoun where they were. Khoun made up a story on the spot, claiming that they did not want to stay with him because Veng Khoun had a girlfriend, and they did not approve of such behavior because he was married. Ny Kan apparently believed the story and returned to the sector center on the Lalay stream. But before he left he told Veng Khoun that Bun Mi was crazy and that he had "eaten American medicine." He ordered Veng Khoun to apprehend him when he returned.[14]

Bun Mi and his soldiers arrived at the border and crossed three kilometers into Laos, where they set up camp near Kreut Village in Xaysettha District, Attapeu Province. Xieng Mai, a Brao man living there, was a Lao Party member and a relative of Bun Mi. He agreed to assist in making contact with government officials in Xaysettha District. Bun Mi asked permission, through Xieng Mai, to take refuge in Laos. The Pathet Lao District officials were, however, not initially willing to grant him permission. They sent a message for Veng Khoun to go to the border to explain the situation to them because they knew him well. Once Veng Khoun received the message, he immediately walked to the border, telling his wife that if anyone came looking for him, she was to tell them that he had gone to the forest for fifteen days to collect rattan. Thus, in April 1973, Veng Khoun traveled to the border with two officials and four soldiers (including Dop Khamchoeung and Jareng, Kham Sai's father); all were Brao. Once Veng Khoun arrived, Bun Mi, Kham Sai, Kham Toeung, and a few soldiers joined him at Xaysettha District center to talk with the district's ethnic Lao Party secretary/district chief, Mr. Khamtanh and other Lao officials. After the meeting, Khamtanh went with the Brao leaders from Cambodia to Kreut Village to meet with the rest of the group.[15] His Vietnamese advisor, known by the Lao name Khamdeng, arranged for rice to be given to the Brao from Cambodia.[16] They prepared a Lao language report to send to the provincial and central government authorities to inform them of the situation. Kham Sai and other leaders believed that the zone leadership, based in what is now Stung Treng, including the zone leader, Ya, probably did not know of Ny Kan's plan to kill Bun Mi and Kham Sai. Therefore, Kham Sai asked the Xaysettha District officials to contact the zone leadership and inform them of the circumstances. Bun Mi hoped that they would intervene and rectify the problem. As requested, the Lao officials sent a report to the Khmer Rouge zone leadership, informing them that there were seventy-one people on the border who were seeking political asylum and claiming that their superior wanted to kill them.[17] Although the Lao were not fully convinced that Bun Mi and Kham Sai's group was really in danger, they allowed Bun Mi to stay in Laos temporarily, but said that since Veng Khoun had not been accused of any wrongdoing, he should return to Taveng Loeu Commune. Four Lao soldiers were sent with him to learn more about the circumstances.[18]

Upon returning, Veng Khoun heard from his wife that Chan Deng, the ethnic Lao chief of Voeunsai District (55 Ko), and one of the founding members of the Indochina Communist Party in northeastern Cambodia, had come looking for Khoun when he was gone. Khoun's wife told Chan Deng the story that had been prepared in advance, and Chan Deng returned to Voeunsai, leaving a message with Khoun's wife that he would come back later. The day after Khoun arrived at his house, Buo Khav, the Kavet District chief of Kok Lak (55 Kho), arrived from Voeunsai at Veng Khoun's house instead of Chan Deng. Buo Khav suspected that the missing soldiers and officials must have fled with Bun Mi, and he encouraged Veng Khoun to convince them to return. He said that nobody would be punished. Buo Khav then returned to Voeunsai, but he told Veng Khoun just before leaving that the Khmer Rouge zone leadership would come to see him about the missing officials and soldiers before long.[19]

Resolving the Rift with the Khmer Rouge?

Once it was reported to the Lao officials in Attapeu that the Khmer Rouge leadership had given authority to the zone to negotiate a resolution to the conflict, they ordered all seventy-one of the asylum seekers—including Bun Mi and Kham Sai—to return to Cambodia to join the negotiations. The group cautiously complied, but they were still wary and thus on their return they camped in the forest near the headquarters of 55 Kaw, so as not to overly expose themselves.[20]

Sure enough, three days later a high-level leader of the zone came up the Sesan River with three soldiers and a large boat full of supplies. The boat was moored near the mouth of the Khampha (Amba) stream, a large tributary of the Sesan River. Veng Khoun claimed the leader was the deputy chief, a Khmer named Um Neng, who was mainly known by his revolutionary names Vong and Vy. Other Brao claim that it was the zone leader himself, Ney Sarann or Ya,[21] who led the group that came to Taveng.[22] In any case, one of the leaders arrived at the Taveng Kraom government office. Once there, Veng Khoun was sent for in Taveng Loeu Commune. He brought a letter from Bun Mi and delivered it to the zone leader. Khoun was afraid when he went to see the zone leader, so he organized thirty soldiers to accompany him for protection. Although the zone leader only had three soldiers with him, Veng Khoun's thirty men were poised in case more of the zone leader's soldiers arrived from the south. It was tense.[23]

According to Veng Khoun, Bun Mi's letter explained that Ny Kan had plotted to kill him for no reason. The zone leader apparently openly cried after reading Bun Mi's words, and he promised that he would not punish Bun Mi or anyone else in 55 *Kaw*. After further discussion, he gave sixteen rolls of black cloth, sixteen sacks of salt, and three large packs of tobacco to Veng Khoun and his men. Veng Khoun then returned to Taveng Loeu to inform Bun Mi of the zone leader's response. They met at his house, which was heavily guarded by Veng Khoun's soldiers. Some landmines were also laid in case Khmer Rouge soldiers from elsewhere tried a surprise attack. Bun Mi agreed to return with Veng Khoun to meet the zone leader at Taveng Kraom. Six missing officials (including Bun Mi, Veng Khoun, Kham Toeung, and Jareng) and ten missing soldiers (including Kham Sai and Kham Toeu) went to meet the zone leader. They arrived at Taveng Kraom at 10:00 the next morning. The zone leader was waiting, and warmly hugged Bun Mi and Kham Sai. At 2:00 pm the meeting began. After three days of discussions, the zone leader informed Veng Khoun and Bun Mi that he would transfer Ny Kan and make Bun Mi the new chief of Sector 3. Thang Ngon replaced Bun Mi as the head of 55 *Kaw*, with Kham Chan as his deputy. Kham Sai would become the military leader of both Sector 3 and 55 *Kaw*. The zone leader then returned to his headquarters in Stung Treng, asking Bun Mi to distribute all the supplies in the 55 *Kaw* commune.[24] Eight months after it started, the conflict appeared to have been resolved. Bun Mi continued to stay at 55 *Kaw*, even though the sector headquarters was to the west near the Lalay stream, as Bun Mi was too wary to stay at the sector headquarters. Ny Kan was also transferred in early 1974 as promised.[25] It is not clear, however, whether he was transferred to Siempang of Kampong Som.

In late 1973, Veng Khoun was called, possibly along with Bun Mi, to Vietnam by the Vietnamese military general who he knew as "Ong Binh" (probably Lieutenant General Phan Bình, the commander of the PAVN's 3rd Division). After Bong Village had fled to Vietnam in November 1973, the remaining Brao Amba in Taveng District became increasingly dissatisfied with the Khmer Rouge. They too were ready to flee to Laos and Vietnam.[26] Veng Khoun claimed that at that time the Vietnamese still did not believe that the Khmer Rouge were so negative toward the Vietnamese. Therefore, they were unwilling to give permission to the Brao from 55 Kaw to cross into Vietnam. Veng Khoun suggested that the Vietnamese send an intelligence officer back with him to confirm the truth. General Binh assigned a man named Heeo, who was dark-skinned like a Khmer and could speak some Brao. Heeo quietly blended in at 55 Kaw. He observed what was happening there, including the anti-Vietnamese propaganda that was being spread by the Communist Party of Kampuchea zone leadership. In early 1974, Heeo also observed three Kavet people being killed near the Lalay stream after they were accused of being Vietnamese spies. The victims were led to the forest where they were forced to dig their own graves before being murdered.[27]

Veng Khoun and Heeo then returned to a secret PAVN base near the Drayak stream and from there Heeo traveled to Vietnam to report to General Binh. Veng Khoun was still one of the leaders of Taveng Loeu Commune, while Kham Toeung, Jawel, and Kham Foeung (Brao, Tambouan Roeng Village) were responsible for Taveng Kraom Commune. Kreng Siengnoi had been responsible for Trabok Commune in 1973, along with Yoep, before fleeing to Vietnam in late 1973. There had been three communes in Taveng District, or 55 Kaw. But once Trabok Commune had fled to Vietnam, only two remained.[28]

In July 1974, a letter came for Bun Mi and Veng Khoun, inviting them to meet at the zone headquarters in present-day Sesan District, Stung Treng Province. They went as requested. They were supposed to study for five days, but according to Veng Khoun they only ended up staying two or three. At the meeting, it was vaguely stated that 55 Kaw had been in contact with the Vietnamese. But later, outside the meeting, the story was conveyed to Bun Mi more clearly. He was told that all the officials and soldiers at 55 Kaw were to be killed for being traitors, and that the villagers there were then going to be moved to Preah Vihear Province and replaced with villagers from there, so that the Cambodian population near the border would be loyal. Bun Mi and Veng Khoun heard that at the end of the training they were going to be arrested. Therefore, according to Veng Khoun, he and Bun Mi forced an ethnic Chinese man with a motorized boat to take them back up the Sesan River at night to *55 Kaw*. The soldiers who were guarding the area did not try to apprehend them, as they were the former soldiers of Bun Mi. Bun Mi had made his second daring escape to Taveng. According to Veng Khoun, he and Bun Mi informed all the villages along the Sesan River in Voeunsai to prepare to flee to Laos on their way back to *55 Kaw*. However, Veng Khoun told me that only the ethnic Tampuon villagers of Kachoan were able to prepare in time. Most other villagers in Voeunsai District were too slow.[29]

Kham Sai conveyed a somewhat different story. He claimed that Veng Khoun did not attend the meeting at the zone center with Bun Mi, and that Bun Mi went by himself with two soldiers. Kham Sai also claimed that Bun Mi did not escape from the meeting, but that instead, the zone leadership actually sent Bun Mi back to *55 Kaw* by boat after the five-day meeting ended. According to Kham Sai, people along the Sesan River were not told to prepare to travel to Vietnam and Laos during the return trip. He claimed that once Bun Mi returned to *55 Kaw*, he organized a major meeting of all the village and commune leaders in the district. Kham Sai claimed that two cows were killed, and after three days of discussions it was agreed that they would flee to Laos and Vietnam. Kham Sai claimed that once the decision was made, Bun Mi began informing others living along the Sesan of the plan, including the veteran revolutionaries, Thang Bai in Kachoan Commune[30] and Moi Choem in Kapong Commune. Bun Mi apparently also wanted to inform the Kreung people, including its leader Kham Sanit, in Poi Commune, but when Kham Sai tried to go there, Bong, one of the Khmer Rouge leaders, tried to apprehend him. Kham Sai was able to evade arrest, but he could not send word about the plan to escape to those in Poi Commune.[31]

Fleeing to Vietnam and Laos

According to Bou Thang (1993), Thang Bai assigned two mutual relatives from Kachoan Village to contact Bun Mi to coordinate the plan to flee Cambodia for Vietnam and Laos. In turn, Thang Bai told Bou Thang about the plan when they met at the center of the

Brao commune of Kapong.[32] Around this time, they heard that Thong Dam had been arrested in Voeunsai, and Kham Mon and Bun Thang—both former Khmer Hanoi—had been killed in Siempang (Bou Thang 1993).

In 1974, Bou Thang began having serious reservations about the Khmer Rouge leadership in the northeast.[33] In December he left Kachoan to prepare to flee to Vietnam. Bou Thang's reasons for leaving the Khmer Rouge were that 1) he did not think Pol Pot's plan made sense, 2) he did not want to kill people, and 3) he was ready to support a new way in Cambodia.[34] Later, Bou Thang told me that they fled in 1975 because they did not want Brao killing Brao and Tampuon killing Tampuon.[35] Indeed, people from the same ethnic groups were taking different sides.

In late 1974, Soy Keo returned to Voeunsai from Siem Reap for a few days leave. The Khmer Rouge were planning to send Battalion 703 to the border with Laos and Regiment 515 to the Vietnam border to keep the Vietnamese out of Cambodia (Bou Thang 1993). Bou Thang was, however, concerned that these troops might be used to prevent people from the northeast from escaping because tensions were already high. The points to be blocked were the Stung Treng border with Laos, the Lalay-Trabok border with Laos and Vietnam, and the O Yadao border with Vietnam.[36]

When Soy Keo was in Voeunsai, Heng Khamvan, an ethnic Lao soldier with the Khmer Rouge, tried to convince him to flee to Vietnam with them. According to Soy Keo, "If I had returned [from Voeunsai] to Stung Treng, I would have been killed."[37] Bun Mi and Thang Bai also helped to convince Soy Keo to join them. At first Soy Keo did not agree, but eventually he was persuaded, especially after hearing of Bun Mi's own difficulties with Ny Kan.[38] Soy Keo later claimed that Bou Thang and Thang Bai played the most important roles in convincing him not to return to command Battalion 703.[39] Even before then, however, he had already become concerned about Pol Pot's behavior. For example, at one point Pol Pot arrived at a meeting lying in a hammock carried by Vietnamese soldiers. Soy Keo was surprised when Pol Pot got out of the hammock without showing any gratitude, or even a word of thanks, to the Vietnamese who had carried him. In another case, Pol Pot ordered guerillas under Soy Keo's command to attack some Vietnamese boats on a river. Soy Keo went to check the situation and found that they were not ARVN troops but PAVN troops. He informed Pol Pot, who responded that they should be attacked anyway. This news shocked Soy Keo and caused him to question Pol Pot like never before (Vũ 1979). According to Bou Thang, once Soy Keo became fully convinced that breaking away totally from the Khmer Rouge was the right decision, he went with Bun Mi to discuss the situation with the Vietnamese based in Cambodia, near Lapong and Lapi streams, tributaries of the Trabok stream near the border with Vietnam.[40] Initially, the Vietnamese were not willing to fully support them.[41]

Dop Khamchoeung began staying on the border with Laos and Cambodia in 1974. He commanded the Khmer Rouge's northeastern border military, which was based in the Dragon's Tail of Cambodia near the borders with both Vietnam and Laos. He had about seventy men under his command, all of whom were Brao. There was a camp adjacent to the Lao border, called Ma Mong, and another at a place called Mek, which was adjacent to the border with Vietnam. Khamchoeung's men were divided between the two posts, which were about ten kilometers away from each other. Khamchoeung did not know about the plan to flee when Jareng called him to come down to the Sesan River to meet. Once he learned of the plan, he went to see Bou Thang and Soy Keo. He brazenly asked them if they would give up land to Vietnam. Bou Thang responded by lecturing him, explaining that Vietnam did not want to take land from Cambodia. Khamchoeung did not return to the border posts but instead prepared to escape together with other Brao.[42]

After initially leaving Kachoan Village for a few months, Bou Thang returned slightly before the exodus to get his brother, Bou Lam,[43] and a number of other people. Since by the time Bou Thang arrived, Bou Lam had already cut the trees in his swidden field. Therefore, Bou Thang believes that the villagers fled in around February 1975. It might have been March. According to Bou Thang, they initially moved to Lapeung stream, where they stayed a few days. At that point all the leaders were there, including Kham Len, Veng Khoun, Kham Toeung, Kham Sai, and others.[44]

Phuy Bunyok—the niece of Thang Bai, who was the older brother of her father, Kham Phuy—was less than ten years old when most of the inhabitants of Kachoan fled to Vietnam. She was old enough to carry a small carrying basket on her back. Bou Thang had already fled into the forest to hide with ten or so other people. They stayed near the Trabok stream and obtained rice to eat from nearby villagers.[45]

Around the same time as the people from Kachoan were beginning to make their move toward the border, the zone leadership became aware of the plan and ordered three battalions of soldiers to rush to the border to prevent the people from fleeing. One battalion was under the command of a Khmer named Kong Deng. The second was led by another Khmer named Bian. The third was headed by a Kreung named Phoi. Kong Deng was sent to the Cambodia-Laos border. Bian was sent to the Cambodia-Vietnam border. Phoi was sent to the Cambodia-Vietnam border at Phatam. Kong Deng's group arrived at the Cambodia-Laos border in March 1975, and his soldiers ended up fighting with some of those trying to flee.[46]

The main group of villagers fled Kachoan Village at night, although it took many hours for them all to depart. Beginning at 10 pm, they started crossing the Sesan River from their village on the south side of the river, but they only had two old boats to transport the people, so they had to make many trips to shuttle everyone across. According to Bou Thang (1993), only three or four people could fit in each boat. Therefore, some of the people swam across the river to speed up the process. It was almost dawn by the time everyone had crossed over. They left behind all their domestic animals, including water buffaloes, cattle, pigs, and chickens. The villagers were able to escape by claiming that they were conducting their annual village ritual at that time. They lied to the Khmer Rouge soldiers and sacrificed a large pig to make the ruse believable. They claimed that, following tradition, their village would be need to be taboo and thus off limits to all outsiders for two days. That would give the villagers a good head start in case soldiers tried to follow them, which they did.[47]

The escape plan was well executed, but it was only the very beginning of the trip. The people from Kachoan and those from various other villages in the area came together at the Tamawk forest. From there, the consolidated group met with the Brao villagers who were coming together to the east. They then walked for almost three months, stopping for days at various points along the way. They were monitoring the situation as they gradually moved toward Vietnam.[48] Some joined the group later and so spent a considerably shorter period of time making the trip. For example, Kham Sana (Kreung, Phak Nam Village), who had been a Khmer Rouge district-level soldier in Voeunsai since 1969, claimed that he departed on the journey on April 4, 1975,[49] which is much later than others. In any case, when they reached Tuk and Lapeung streams, the group was attacked by the pursuing Khmer Rouge soldiers (Bou Thang 1993). Two people who could not escape are believed to have been killed. One was an old woman and the other was a fifteen-year-old boy. It is uncertain how they died, but both disappeared at the time the Khmer Rouge were shooting at them. Later, another man also mysteriously disappeared along the way. In any case, Thang Bai found the group and helped guide them to the Dragon's Tail, near the borders with Laos and Vietnam. They ate rice that they brought with them during the first part of the journey. Once the rice was finished, they dug tubers that Vietnamese soldiers had planted on the Cambodian side of the border earlier in the year before Vietnam was unified. Therefore, there was plenty for them to eat. The group finally crossed into Vietnam at Tangao Mountain.[50]

Not long before the Tampuon from Kachoan Village fled, the Brao planning to flee also started to get rid of their livestock in preparation for escaping. However, they were closer to the border than those from Kachoan, and so they did not have to travel as far. Some animals were sold to the PAVN's 3rd Division, but the Vietnamese did not provide much support, apart from a little advice.[51]

Bun Mi organized all the Brao villages so that they met about five kilometers up the Khampha stream from its confluence with the Sesan River. Moi Choem separately organized the Brao in Kopong Commune.[52] For the ethnic Lao villages in Voeunsai District, like Fang and Pong Villages, and the Kreung villages of Phak Nam and Khuan, only some males came together to make the trip. The women and children were left in the villages.[53] Crucially, Thao Sim (Kreung, Phak Nam Village, and Soy Keo's brother-in-law), who led the military in O Chum (55 *Taw*), and Kham Sanit did not only lead thirty soldiers to join the large group after Soy Keo contacted them, but they were able to escape with their guns as well.[54] Mong Then (Kreung, Kalai 3 Village) was one of those who fled with him.[55] However, like those from Kachoan Village, everyone from the Brao and Kreung communities in Taveng fled, leaving empty villages behind.[56]

Finally, in March 1975, once the villagers had gathered near the Khampha stream, the whole group, which by then made up thousands of people, began to slowly make their way to the Vietnam border. They started their journey during the night.[57] Some were not able to join the group. Dam Jyun (Kreung, Phak Nam Village), for example, had helped to prepare people to flee for a number of months prior to the exodus, but by the time he was ready to go, Kong Deng's soldiers had blocked his way, so he had to stay in Cambodia for the whole Khmer Rouge period. Although some Khmer Rouge apparently suspected that he had been involved in organizing the exodus, there was no evidence, so he somehow survived.[58]

Although those fleeing were initially together, when they came to the Drayak stream, the group split into two, as the Brao from Taveng mainly wanted to go directly to Laos, while the other group was intent on reaching Vietnam. Bou Thang, Soy Keo, Bun Mi, Thang Bai, and Kham Len led the smaller group going to Vietnam, while Veng Khoun, Kham Toeung, and Kham Sai led the group going to Laos. The larger group initially traveled north to a place called Arayak, which is not far from the Lao border. They stayed there for about a month but could not find a way to easily cross the high mountains in the area. Kong Deng's forces at Lapeung stream tried to intercept them near the Drayak stream and attacked them one afternoon.[59] There was a fire fight and one Khmer Rouge soldier was killed and one Brao resister was injured. At about 3 pm, Kong Deng's forces were able to capture sixty Brao villagers along the trail near Tuk stream. It was almost dark, so Kong Deng's soldiers stopped and ate dinner. Some guarded the villagers. Others went north to try to apprehend other villagers from Tambouan Roeng Village. At 9 pm, Kham Sai's two small battalions of soldiers, commanded by Moeng Chuon and Chim, arrived at Tuk stream and started shooting at Kong Deng's soldiers. They fought for one night and two days. Six of Kong Deng's soldiers were reportedly killed in an hour. Others were injured. Kong Deng apparently stepped on a landmine and lost a foot. Finally, Kong Deng's forces retreated with the captured villagers.[60] The next day, Kong Deng's troops tried to retreat further, but Kham Sai's forces attacked them. After twenty minutes of fighting, Kong Deng's troops retreated to the south, and the villagers escaped to the north with Kham Sai's troops. The civilians went first, and the soldiers protected them from behind. It took Kham Sai's group two days to double back to Gia Gom[61]—which is located between seven and eight kilometers from the border with Vietnam, still in Cambodia.

The other group of hundreds of people took about a month to reach the border with Vietnam, but they did not encounter any zone troops along the way.[62] Near Drayak and Lapeung streams, where a PAVN base was located, some villagers traded domestic animals for guns, and because PAVN forces were in the process of relocating to Vietnam, they even gave some old guns to the escapees for free, as well as some land-mines that they no longer needed.[63]

When everyone in both groups had arrived at the border with Viet-nam, they met with Vietnamese officials.[64] A group of Brao leaders, in-cluding Lao Nyai, Bun Mi, Kham Len, Kham Toeung, and Thang Ngon negotiated with the Vietnamese to allow some of the group to cross into Vietnam near Gia Ho, which is about six kilometers north of Gia Gom, but in Vietnam. By that time Heeo had already reported all that he had heard when he was secretly with Veng Khoun in Sector 3. Thus, they were allowed to enter Vietnam. However, many Brao were still intent on going to Laos, not Vietnam, as most Brao spoke Lao more fluently than Vietnamese, and some Brao had relatives in Laos. Others wanted to return to their villages in Cambodia. Therefore, after staying seven days on the border with Vietnam, it was decided that the group would divide into two. According to Bou Thang, the people who made it to Gia Gom/Gia Ho were actually separated into four subgroups.[65] Each group wanted to go to a different place. The first group decided to enter Vietnam and eventually ended up at Gia Poc. The second group, which was initially part of the first group, and only separated later, also entered Vietnam, but went to cut trees in the reservoir of the Yali Falls Dam. The third group, which included 2,999 people, continued on to Laos,[66] and the fourth voluntarily returned to Cambodia to face the Khmer Rouge (Bou Thang 1993; Institute of Military History 2010).

Bun Mi, Kham Sai, Bou Thang, Soy Keo, Ma Ranchai, Lao Nyai, Kham Len, and Thang Ngon led the group that crossed into Vietnam. The Vietnamese required everyone entering Vietnam to disarm at the border.[67] They were short of food so reluctantly asked the Vietnamese for some cassava to eat. Some of the refugees also went fishing and traded fish for tobacco and vegetables, including eggplants and chilies (Bou Thang 1993). Bou Thang (1993, 2011) wrote that he arrived to Viet-nam on May 8, 1975.

Kong (Kreung, Tiem Loeu Village) led the two hundred young men who went to work, albeit for low wages, to cut trees down in the reser-voir area at the future site of the Yali Falls Dam. They did that work until 1977, when they were brought back to Gia Poc.[68] It is sadly ironic that the refugees were forced to work on a hydropower project that would later, beginning in the late 1990s, result in significant social and environmental downstream impacts along the Sesan River in north-eastern Cambodia (Wyatt and Baird 2007).

According to Kham Sai, the villagers in the first group stayed twenty kilometers inside Vietnam for the first two nights. Bun Mi then sent Kham Sai, along with Dop Khamchoeung, Kham Phai (Brao, Paroe Touich Village), Japang (Brao Trabok Village), Jyao Dawl, and Aroe (Brao) back to provide security for the group continuing on to Laos.[69] Kham Sai's soldiers helped carry some sick people. Two people died on the way, Veng Khoun's mother and his younger sister. During the trip, three villagers were also shot and killed by Kong Deng's soldiers near Arung and Trabok streams. Another was shot at Khampha stream.[70] According to Kham Toeung, five people died during the trip: one soldier and four civilians.[71] The group of 2,999 people finally arrived at the Lao border, but they were initially told to wait there, while three of the ten Lao soldiers guarding the border went to obtain permission for the group to enter Laos. The chief of Xaysettha District returned with the soldiers. He agreed to allow the group to enter Laos, provided that they give up their guns, which they did.[72] Kham Toeung claimed that he arrived at Gia Gom on May 5, 1975, and that he arrived in Xaysettha District, Attapeu Province, on May 25[73] or May 28, 1975.[74] In any case, much of the travel had taken place after Phnom Penh had fallen to the Khmer Rouge on April 17.

Once the group traveling to Laos was safe, Kham Sai returned to Vietnam.[75] Later, the Brao from Kapong Commune, led by Moi Choem, who had not prepared in time for the main groups, walked directly to the Lao border.[76] Later, Thang Bai also took some ethnic Lao villagers to Laos with him, but his own Tampuon people mainly stayed in Vietnam because the terrain there was more suitable for swidden cultivation.[77] Kham Sai later returned to Laos a second time, along with Kham Khoeun, to help Kham Khoeun's family relocate from Laos to Vietnam.[78]

The fourth group, which was made up of between eighty and one hundred ethnic Lao people, mainly from Fang Village in Voeunsai District, decided to return to Cambodia and face the Khmer Rouge. Many had left their wives and children at home and missed them. They also felt less comfortable in the uplands compared to many of the highlanders who had fled with them. Some were arrested and killed by the Khmer Rouge upon their return; others somehow survived.[79]

The Jarai Who Fled

A few other groups of people near the border in Ratana-kiri Province also fled to Vietnam, including villagers from the ethnic Jarai communities of Triel and Lam. They traveled from what is now O Yadao District, Ratanakiri Province to Ia Pnon Commune, Duc Co District, Gialai-Kontum (now Gialai) Province in 1975 (*Tuoi Tre News* 2015).

Bui Yung (Jarai, Yang Commune) is one Jarai man from O Yadao District in Ratanakiri who fled to Vietnam in 1975 and would later take up a senior position in the government in Ratanakiri Province in 1979. He joined the communist revolution in 1957, and became a full party member in 1969. In 1970, he was given responsibility for commune-level commerce in District 21. He mainly traded cassava, sesame, rice, and domestic animals with the PAVN's Military Region 5. In 1974, he became seriously concerned about the increasingly radical nature of orders issued by the Khmer Rouge. Later, he realized that Bun Mi and others were preparing to escape to Vietnam even though they did not have any direct communications. In May 1975—not long after Bun Mi, Bou Thang, Soy Keo, and others fled to Vietnam—Bui Yung decided to do the same. Initially, he organized fifty of the fifty-five families, or 190 people, in Chai Village, Talao Commune, where he was living, to escape with him to Vietnam. The only five families he did not contact were headed by Khmer Rouge officials who he felt were "hard headed" and would therefore not be receptive to his plan. He dared not approach them.[80] Again, we can see how politics differed even among people from the same ethnic group.

The group successfully left the village without the other five families knowing, but the escape plan did not go as smoothly as anticipated. Initially, when they were in the forest, some of the group were sent to collect some rice supplies that they had previously hidden in the forest, and when they were gone, the deputy chief of the district, Hwet, himself Jarai, and some of his men caught up with them about ten kilometers from the village. The escapees only had five guns between them, so they decided not to fight. Instead, Bui Yung told Hwet that the group was leaving because 1) they did not like the fact that all possessions had been made communal property, 2) they did not like it that they were not allowed to follow their traditional rituals, including playing gongs, and 3) they did not like that trading with the Vietnamese had been banned by the Khmer Rouge. Indeed, no contact with the Vietnamese was allowed. In addition, he mentioned that they did not like it that lazy people could live off the hard work of others; and sometimes even accuse the hard workers of being rich. Finally, he said that he had planned to report what was happening to the district officials and to try to convince the people not to leave, but that he had been unable to find the leadership, and so had left with the group. He planned to return and report on the situation later. Hwet seemed satisfied with the explanation, and told Bui Yung to try to get the people to return. But at the time the people were scattered in the forest, and Bui Yung told Hwet that it would take two or three days to gather the villagers and bring them back.[81]

In preparation for the escape, but unknown to Hwet, Bui Yung had already communicated with the military in Vietnam, and they had agreed to fire some shots in the air to scare the Khmer Rouge away. They did exactly that, which gave the group additional time to flee. But the group encountered other problems during their journey. They planned to go to the north and join Bun Mi's group, but some PAVN soldiers that they met on the way inadvertently gave them wrong directions, so they became lost. By this time the group was short on food, so forty people were sent to a nearby PAVN base to try to get some rice and cassava to eat. The Vietnamese said they would give them all the food they desired if they allowed two young unmarried women in the group to be their "wives." The two women objected so no food was acquired.[82]

The group walked to the southeast and came to the Sa Thay River. Everyone crossed it except for two families who were determined to go to the north because they had relatives on the Vietnamese side of the border in that area. The rest of the group met some Jarai villagers from the Vietnamese side of the border, including some of Bui Yung's wife's relatives, and twenty of them had guns and went with some of his group to help transport supplies they needed. In the meantime, a group of forty well-armed Khmer Rouge soldiers arrived on the other side of the river, intending to take the villagers back with them. Bui Yung crossed back over the river and told the soldiers that the group was simply trying to find a new place to establish a village inside Cambodia, and he told the soldiers that if they crossed the river, the villagers would become frightened and flee into the forest. He said that it would be more effective for him to return by himself to gather the villagers and bring them back. The soldiers believed him and allowed Bui Yung to cross back over the river by himself. Soon after, the twenty Vietnamese Jarai returned with rice to eat.[83]

After everyone ate in the forest, the whole group had a meeting. They were still in Cambodian territory,[84] but they were near the border with Vietnam. During the meeting, the group was informed that if they entered Vietnam they would face more restrictions on cutting bamboo and conducting swidden agriculture compared to in Cambodia. Once the group heard this, some decided that they did not want to go to Vietnam. In the end, only sixteen of the remaining forty-eight families, including Bui Yung's family, continued to Vietnam. They arrived in Tang, a Jarai Village in Vietnam. The sixteen families fled ten kilometers from the village into the forest to hide. However, when the threat subsided, they returned to the Tang Village, B12 (Y.A.) Commune, Sepa District, Gialai-Kontum Province. They lived there for the next three years. The Vietnamese officials would not tell them where Bun Mi's group had gone so they were not able to make contact.[85]

Settling in Laos

Prior to settling the refugees from Laos into villages, Khamtanh, the District Chief of Xaysettha District, organized a special meeting. All the village chiefs were invited. The difficult political situation in Cambodia was described and finally it was agreed by everyone that they should settle the refugees from Cambodia in preexisting villages.[86] The strategy was to integrate them into existing communities in the district. The larger the village, the more refugees they would be expected to host. Interestingly, the Brao refugees requested not to be sent to ethnic Lao villages. Initially, the Brao from Laos looked after the refugees without receiving any government support.[87] However, some ethnic Tampuon, Kreung, and Lao refugees were settled in ethnic Lao villages. For example, sixteen ethnic minority families from Cambodia were settled in Saisy Village, Xaysettha District. Later, over ten other families moved to Saisy because there was more potential for opening up paddy land there than in the initial villages where they were settled, Fang Deng, Khan Mak Kong, and Phoxai.[88]

Veng Khoun, along with over 200 Brao families, settled in Keng Makkheua Village near the Xexou River in Xaysettha District. There was plenty of land to do swidden cultivation there, and some refugees also developed small pieces of lowland rice paddy land.[89] Others stayed

82

in Siang Chai Village, where there was also plenty of land for swidden cultivation. People there were also encouraged to cultivate lowland paddy land, but because they did not have water buffaloes to till the fields, most ended up only cultivating small plots of wet-rice paddy land.[90] Another village where Brao refugees stayed was Kreut—Xieng Mai's village—where one former refugee interviewed focused on developing lowland rice paddy land, while also doing some swidden cultivation.[91] Another informant stayed at Done Khene Village, where thirty Brao families from Cambodia took refuge. He only did swidden agriculture.[92]

According to United Nations High Commission on Refugees (UNHCR) statistics, a total of 10,400 Cambodians fled to Laos as refugees in 1975 (United Nations 1990), of which less than half were probably Brao. The rest were ethnic Lao and Khmers who entered Laos from Stung Treng Province to the west. For example, 400 ethnic Lao people from Nachantha Village, in Siempang District, Stung Treng Province, tried to flee to Laos in 1974 after some people from the village were killed by the Khmer Rouge. Although seventy were unsuccessful and were captured by the Khmer Rouge, most made it to Laos.[93]

The vast majority of people who made it to Laos as refugees dared not return to Cambodia for many years. Two years of rice aid was eventually provided by the Lao government, as well as some salt and cloth for making clothing. The refugees also received blankets and agricultural tools such as knives and spades. However, there were initially no international organizations involved.[94]

Most of those who made it to Laos were sorry to have left Cambodia, but they were happy to be safe from the Khmer Rouge. Kham Toeung, however, remained concerned about his siblings, who he had left behind. Therefore, later in 1975, he decided to return to Cambodia with twelve others to try to bring his siblings to Laos. However, his group was apprehended along the way. Kham Toeung's hands were bound and he went without food for eighteen days. Later he was sent to do hard labor to build dams, canals, and houses. Finally, he was assigned to make plows and harrows. He was told to make fifteen a day or he would be killed. Finally, he was able to fight back, escape, and return to Laos. Kham Toeung told Ben Kiernan, "As I tell you this I want to cry." None of the twelve others who went to Laos with him survived.[95]

In Saisy Village, the headman allocated one refugee family to move in with a responsible Lao family. The refugees initially ate with their host families and also helped work their fields. The village also allocated land for the refugees to open up new paddy. From the beginning, it was orally agreed that the refugees could farm the land, but that they would have to return it to the village when they left. The refugees initially did swidden on the land, and then gradually converted it to lowland paddy. Later, the Lao government allocated one water buffalo to each refugee family for plowing these newly created fields. At that time, buffaloes were cheap, costing just 300 to 400 Lao kip each. The refugees in Saisy had done lowland paddy farming before in Cambodia, and so they had no problem opening up the new paddy land or farming it. According to the former village headman of Saisy, the refugees and their hosts got along well. "They did their own rituals, but they also joined our village ceremonies to show solidarity," he commented. He claimed that there were not any serious conflicts or other cultural problems, and that all the refugees could speak Lao well, so communication was easy. After about a year living with their host families, the refugees started building their own small houses. They were quite industrious, and within just a few years they were largely able to feed themselves.[96] The Brao from Laos also apparently had few problems with the Brao refugees from Cambodia.[97]

Settling in Vietnam

In Vietnam, the refugees from Cambodia initially camped out at Gia Ho, a temporary site very close to the border. It was not a very good location, as security was not strong there, and to make matters worse, the soils were rocky and not desirable for agriculture. Therefore, in mid-May they moved from Gia Ho to Gia Lae and then to the Sa Thay River. Some people made money helping to transport supplies for PAVN (Bou Thang 1993).

The 1,943 people who remained in Vietnam were initially expected by the Vietnamese government to integrate into already established villages along the border, as was the case in Laos. However, the refugees did not like the idea. They wanted to stay together.[98]

Each of the original villages was given one hundred kilograms of rice, regardless of the number of inhabitants. Food was scarce soon after crossing the border. In September 1975, when the group moved farther into Vietnam, the Vietnamese government disarmed them.[99] In December 1975, after having done swidden agriculture near the Sa

Thay River for a season, Bun Mi, Bou Thang, Boua Chuong, Kham Chan, Kham Phai, Kham Len, and Soy Keo met with Vietnamese officials. They said that whether they stayed in Vietnam, Laos, or Cambodia, they did not want to remain in a precarious and unsafe border situation.[100] Bou Thang had identified an appropriate place to settle, an area with many swidden fallows, but where no other people were living. It was proposed that the people move there.[101] Therefore, in January 1976, the group resettled at Gia Poc, in Sa Thay District, Gialai-Kontum Province, where they would remain for the next few years. It took a day to walk from Gia Gom to Gia Poc. Kreng Siengnoi's group also moved from Dak Jala Commune, Dak To District, to Gia Poc.[102] Bou Thang told me that he thought that it would be a good location because the landscape reminded him of Cambodia, and it was near the Sa Thay River.[103] Before moving to Gia Poc, a small group of mainly ethnic Tampuon and Kreung people, led by Kham Loeua (Kreung, Tiem Loeu Village) decided to move to Laos instead of staying in Vietnam.[104]

Those who moved to Gia Poc included people from the original villages of Trabok, Sieng Sai, Paroe, Tambouan Roeng, Taveng, Tangaich, Chuay, Dook, Kachoan, and Bong (incorrectly named Yorn by the Vietnamese). Boua Chuong was the first commune chief at Gia Poc, even though he was ethnic Lao from Kalan Village. However, in 1976, Bou Thang was elected to replace him. Bun Mi and Soy Keo were appointed as his deputies, and Kham Len became a member of the Committee for Managing the Gia Poc Camp. Bou Thang was assigned ten bodyguards for security (Bou Thang 1993). However, according to Kham Phai, "Bun Mi was still the real leader at Gia Poc, as he had long been based in the northeast. The Vietnamese knew Bun Mi the best and he was the one that they first contacted when they wanted to organize a military force to fight against the Khmer Rouge."[105]

Villagers at Gia Poc were given some rice support from the Vietnamese government, as well as some salt, cassava, clothing, and other supplies specifically reserved for the military, thus preventing hunger. Many people were quite happy to be located at Gia Poc, as they felt relatively free and secure there; and they were also able to begin engaging in relatively prosperous swidden agriculture (Bou Thang 1993). There was plenty of land for doing swidden cultivation, but there were no flat areas suitable for developing lowland rice paddy.[106]

A health care center and a new area for marketing agricultural products were established at Gia Poc. Later, provincial authorities helped the villagers sell some of their agricultural products. The defenses at Gia Poc were also improved, and a small rice mill and a sewing machine were eventually bought for the residents. Bou Thang purchased a transistor radio to keep up with current events, and the Vietnamese military occasionally brought him newspapers to read (Bou Thang 1993).

There were no other communities near Gia Poc except for four ethnic Jarai villages (Kateng, Ya Re, Shop, and Rop), but the closest of those villages was still twenty kilometers away. The Jarai from these communities sometimes visited Gia Poc, and because there were typically three or four people in each Brao village who could speak Jarai, they were able to communicate. A few adult Jarai also knew some Brao. Neither the Brao nor the Jarai spoke much Vietnamese.[107]

The people at Gia Poc were expected to follow the Vietnamese policy related to "three goods and three cleans." Essentially, the three goods necessitated that the people be 1) unified in following Vietnamese law, 2) pushed to increase agricultural production to ensure that hunger is prevented, and 3) encouraged to ensure that security was maintained. The three cleans required that the people 1) keep the villages and commune clean, 2) maintain good household cleanliness, and 3) eat hygienically (Bou Thang 1993).

Although some ethnic Lao people from Fang Village went to Laos, the majority stayed in Vietnam. A few ethnic Lao from Voeunhoi, Hat Po, and Pong Villages (three to ten people from each village) also stayed at Gia Poc. The Lao at Gia Poc decided to stay in Vietnam rather than go to Laos because they wanted to be near Bou Thang and Soy Keo, who they considered to be their leaders.[108]

It took these refugees just two years, both in Laos and Vietnam, before they were granted citizenship in each country, something that would be hard to imagine today. Dop Khamchoeung, Kham Chan, and Teng (Brao) (a younger man who spoke Vietnamese)[109] had to inquire at PAVN's Military Region 5 headquarters in Danang before citizenship was granted. Bou Thang and Soy Keo did not dare approach the Vietnamese about this potentially sensitive topic, but Dop Khamchoeung was eventually successful.[110]

One problem that those in Vietnam faced was, however, that the Vietnamese did not accept the Cambodian practice of using one's father's name as one's family name. Therefore, many had to change their names in Vietnam. For example, Yoep Son, Yoep's son, had to take up a new last name, and thus became known as Vanson. Similarly, Kreut Sim became Thao Sim.[111]

Although the Cambodian refugees in Vietnam had been disarmed, Dop Khamchoeung—who was a bit rougher around the edges than most Brao—was able to convince the Vietnamese to let him keep three rifles. He told them that he did not want them to shoot people but to hunt wild pigs because there were many near Gia Poc. The Vietnamese apparently asked him if he would shoot Khmer Rouge if he saw them. He said he would, which satisfied them, and so they gave him the guns, along with three clusters of 800 bullets each. Nobody else was apparently able to negotiate to keep guns. In fact, Khamchoeung shot a large number of wild pigs, often two or three each day. There were many fallow swidden fields in the area, but few people, which created almost perfect conditions for an explosion in the wild pig population.[112]

The Khmer Rouge sent three companies of troops to attack the Gia Poc-based rebels, but two PAVN battalions (370 and 378) were assigned to guard the border, so the Khmer Rouge dared not attack. They came up a second time, but again dared not take on the larger Vietnamese force. Khamchoeung is convinced that if the Khmer Rouge had had the opportunity, they would have attacked Gia Poc and killed everyone.[113]

When at Gia Poc, the Vietnamese military asked the soldiers to help improve security in the area. Therefore, Kham Sai and Jalee, who were commune-level soldiers by that time, captured seven and later another twenty members of the Front Uni de Lutte des Races Opprimées (FULRO) on two separate occasions. The Brao shot above the heads of the dissidents, and they lay down and surrendered almost immediately. The dissidents only had about one gun for every ten people, and they only had wild food that they collected in the forest to eat. They were mostly ethnic Jarai, but a few were ethnic Kinh.[114] The Brao who apprehended the FULRO dissidents were rewarded with sets of notebooks and pens. The Brao at Gia Poc also shot two FULRO dissidents, although Gia Poc was never attacked by FULRO. According to Dop Khamchoeung, "The Brao helped the Vietnamese protect the border. FULRO wanted to take part of Vietnam's land and give it to Thailand." He thought that the politics of the day was very confusing, with Cambodians aligning with Vietnamese, and Vietnamese aligning with Thais.[115] The people at Gia Poc did not seem to sympathize with FULRO, even though they were also ethnic minorities fighting for freedom. Again, political divisions were often more important than ethnic affiliations.

After being based at Gia Poc for a period, in 1977, a school was established for children to study Vietnamese. The first group of students graduated grade one, and went on to study grade two in 1978. By 1979, there were students in grades one through three. Eventually there were more than one hundred students attending the school. Phuy Bunyok, Thang Bai's niece, was one of those who graduated from grade three, although at the end of 1979, she would return to Cambodia.[116] The Khmer Rouge made no mention in the media of those who fled; nor did the Vietnamese.

Those Who Remained—the Beginning of a New Era

As already mentioned, Phnom Penh fell to the Khmer Rouge on April 17, 1975, at the same time as the Sector 3 refugees were on their way to Vietnam and Laos. Pol Pot declared victory, and in January 1976, Democratic Kampuchea was established, as was the Revolutionary Army of Kampuchea; it was year zero—the beginning of a new era. More cities and towns were evacuated, including Phnom Penh. Plans were also made to suppress money. But not everyone in the higher echelons of the party agreed with Pol Pot's vision, and there was lively debate regarding how best to proceed. Ya—the head of the northeast zone—was apparently in favor of a softer policy than what Pol Pot envisioned.[117] Ya was generally considered more moderate than other Khmer Rouge leaders (Colm 1996), but when Lat Vansao met Ya in the mid-1970s, he thought he was actually quite hard-headed.[118] However, Kham Toeung claimed that Ya was a good man. "He did not kill people," he claimed.[119] In any case, the leadership of Democratic Kampuchea was clearly ready to move ahead with radical change.

Although the focus here is on the people who fled to Vietnam and Laos in the mid-1970s—not those who stayed in Cambodia during the main Khmer Rouge period, between April 1975 and January 1979—it seems necessary to at least generally present the circumstances of the highlanders, and particularly the Brao, who remained in northeastern Cambodia during this period. The highlanders of the northeast—due to their designation as "base people" (*prachachon mulethan*) or "full rights persons" (*prachachon penh sith*)—were subject to less extreme treatment than those in other classes (Colm 1996).[120] Pol Pot suggested that people living near the country's frontier with Laos should be relocated to the interior. He was undoubtedly concerned that others would flee to Laos and Vietnam. However, only some were moved to other parts of the country (Baird 2008).

The Khmer Rouge became stricter in their radical policy implementation. For example, they increasingly encouraged the highlanders to not use their own languages (see Mallow 2002). Illustrative of this, a Kavet man said that during meetings in the cooperative where he lived in Stung Treng, Khmer had to be used, although Brao could still be used at home (Baird 2008).

Many Kavet gained leadership positions in the Khmer Rouge, and large numbers of people were killed at cooperatives where the Kavet were in charge, such as Ou Ranong in Siempang District. The Kavet were understood to be straight, honest, and able to unquestioningly follow tough orders. They were also often considered fierce. Other highlanders were also entrusted with leadership positions in highland areas, including some Jarai who became the bodyguards of Pol Pot and were feared, and some Tampuon who gained various leadership positions. However, Khmer people dominated the top positions, even if highlanders were generally more trusted than Khmers (Colm 1996).

The Khmer Rouge also became increasingly strict about banning all kinds of religious practices. Ceremonial jars and gongs were confiscated with even more determination than before. Much like the Sangkum government, the Khmer Rouge wanted to Khmerize the people in some ways and de-Khmerize them in others. For example, they banned highlander clothing, such as colorful decorations on their clothes, and highlander jewelry, including necklaces and wrist and ankle bracelets (Colm 1996). They also detraditionalized and pushed for assimilation, but with more determination than the Sangkum government. They rejected highlander taboos. For example, in 1974, they forced a group of Kavet to climb the sacred mountains of Haling-Halang, a place where hunting and collecting forest products is prohibited or greatly restricted by custom, and where the spirits only tolerate Brao language being spoken (Baird 2013c). The Kavet in the group told the Khmer not to talk, and they burned candles and chanted to appease the powerful mountain spirits (Baird 2008). The Khmer Rouge did not speak of a multinational Kampuchean society, instead focusing on the defense of the "Kampuchean race" (*Phnom Penh Domestic Service* 1978d). The Khmer Rouge also dismantled and restructured the spatial organization of the landscape.

To give the *Angkor* (a name inherited from the Khmer Rouge) at the top as much power and control as possible, zone commands were emphasized. For example, in the 1960s, Kratie/Mondulkiri, Ratanakiri, and Stung Treng were combined in a new northeast zone (Baird 2008).

From 1975 to 1976, cooperatives were organized, some with about 1,000 people[121] (Colm 1996; Colm and Sim 2008), and everybody had to move to one of the cooperatives. One of those was in a lowland paddy field area north of the Sesan River and upriver from the mouth of the Trabok stream. Some Kreung were sent to cooperatives in what would later become Koun Moum District, in Ratanakiri Province. Another cooperative was located at the ethnic Lao village of Srekor, on the southern banks of the Sesan River in Stung Treng Province, the Khmer Rouge's northeast zone center (see Figure 4).

Although there were fewer long-distance population movements in the northeast than in some other parts of Cambodia during the main 1975 to late 1978 Democratic Kampuchea period, and most cooperatives consisted of people from the same or similar ethnic groups, many people were moved around the province, and some were also relocated out of the province to faraway places to the south. The cooperatives set up in northeastern Cambodia were divided into groups of thirty people. Groups of youth fifteen years old or older were organized into mobile work brigades, or *Kong Chalat*, which traveled around to work on special projects like large-scale forest clearance and dam building (Colm 1996). Those eleven years old and above were organized as *Kong Koma*. Most people had to give up swidden agriculture to concentrate on lowland wet-rice cultivation. People had to give up all private property and were left with just a bowl, a spoon, and minimal clothing. Rice rations were reduced substantially, with each person getting approximately sixty-two grams of rice per day, as compared to 250 grams per day between 1973–1975, and over twice that amount before the war began (Colm 1996). There were no specified rations prior to 1973.

In that the Khmer Rouge wanted to wipe the slate clean, they strove to maintain total control over peoples' lives. In August 1976, the Khmer Rouge adopted a four-year plan, which included ambitious objectives for rice production. Double rice cropping was an important part of the plan, and large numbers of irrigation projects were initiated, using the labor of those in the cooperatives (Colm 1996). Colm (1996) reported that in Ratanakiri Province about sixty irrigation projects were constructed during the Khmer Rouge period. Some worked well, others

Figure 4. Northeastern Cambodia, 1975 (Meghan Kelly, Cart Lab, Department of Geography, University of Wisconsin–Madison)

never functioned properly. Some were designed to take advantage of hilly terrain, but most were poorly conceived. By the end of 1978, about 7,000 hectares of lowland paddy was under cultivation in Ratanakiri (Baird 2008).

Indicative of the total social and spatial control that the Khmer Rouge had over the general population, in 1978, the Communist Party of Kampuchea were eager to rapidly increase the population of Cambodia, allegedly so as to have two million soldiers to fight against the Vietnamese. To boost the birth rate, mass weddings were not only organized, but newlywed cadres were required to consummate their marriages in long wooden "love houses." Sihanouk wrote about the matter in a letter written in 2006, stating that the couples were ordered to "make love like industrial machines." In one case in Ratanakiri Province couples were given three to seven days to make love (Thet and Kinetz 2006, 16).

Conclusion

The Brao and many other ethnic minorities in northeastern Cambodia—including some of the earliest and strongest supporters of the Khmer Rouge—gradually turned against Pol Pot and the Khmer Rouge in the early 1970s. They became skeptical because the Khmer Rouge gradually adopted stricter policies, including enforcing communal eating and banning various highland animist religious practices. Crucially, the Khmer Rouge also became increasingly anti-Vietnamese, which troubled many Brao who had previously worked closely with the Vietnamese when fighting the French. However, it was the conflict with Bun Mi—a key Brao revolutionary leader in Ratanakiri Province— that ultimately caused so many former supporters of the Khmer Rouge to turn against them.

The Brao from Bong Village were the first to flee to Vietnam in 1973, after two members of their group were accused of being pro-Vietnamese and killed. Bun Mi and other Brao also tried to flee to Laos, but they were eventually convinced to return and mend their ways with the Khmer Rouge zone leadership, which they did. The conflict was resolved temporarily, but the mutual distrust was still simmering. Finally, as the Khmer Rouge was preparing to arrest and kill Bun Mi, he decided with other leaders to flee the country. Indeed, they had already demonstrated to the Vietnamese that the Khmer Rouge was very strongly against them. Geography was crucial for determining who fled and who stayed, with those closer to the border and farther away from Khmer Rouge strongholds being able to receive information about the plan for them to join the group of decenters. Thousands fled, including virtually all of the Brao Amba from Taveng, but also some Tampuon, Kreung, Lun, and ethnic Lao. It was a long hard journey through thick forests and mountainous terrain, and Khmer Rouge units attacked them along the way, but they eventually made it to the border with Vietnam, ironically not long after Phnom Penh had fallen to the Khmer Rouge. But individual agency again proved important when the dissidents arrived at the border. Some wanted to take refuge in the Central Highlands of Vietnam, while others preferred to continue on to Attapeu Province, in southern Laos. The circumstances for the political refugees differed considerably depending on whether they settled in Vietnam or in Laos. In Vietnam, the refugees were able to establish a brand new commune for themselves at Gia Poc. In Laos, they were broken up into family groups and settled into existing villages in Attapeu Province, with most of the Brao being settled in ethnic Brao communities.

Meanwhile, back in Cambodia, Democratic Kampuchea was celebrating their takeover of the country in April 1975. The situation for those who were left behind worsened, with many ethnic minorities from the northeast being moved from their villages to join cooperatives focused on lowland rice cultivation because swidden agriculture was not part of Pol Pot's plan for developing Cambodia's agricultural potential. The Khmer Rouge also generally became more and more draconian in their creation and implementation of policy, and the situation for the people became increasingly dire, including for all of the Kavet and most of the Kreung, Tampuon, Jarai, and ethnic Lao people who had not fled to Vietnam and Laos. We can see, once again, how the particular circumstances and geography of the region left those who had fled and those who were left behind divided, even though people on both sides belonged to the same ethnic groups, and most on both sides were strong supporters of communism.

We now turn to considering what happened to the refugees who fled from northeastern Cambodia and settled in Vietnam and Laos, including how conflict increased along the Cambodia-Vietnam border, but also how tensions arose in Phnom Penh, Hanoi, and Beijing, ones that eventually led the Vietnamese to begin, in mid-1977, organizing the refugees in Vietnam in preparation for attacking the Khmer Rouge, and eventually to the establishment of the UFNSK, with the goal of fighting back against the Khmer Rouge.

The Deterioration of
Vietnam-Cambodia Relations,
Preparations in Vietnam, and
the Attack on the Khmer Rouge

Beginning immediately after the Khmer Rouge entered and gained control of Phnom Penh, on April 17, 1975, Pol Pot's forces adopted an aggressive position along the border with Vietnam. They organized attacks deep into Vietnam and massacred ethnic Kinh citizens of Vietnam. The Vietnamese were generally weary from many years of fighting other Vietnamese and the Americans and initially tried to prevent such incidents from escalating into more serious confrontation. The Khmer Rouge leadership also initially blamed particular military units for localized excesses. Over time, however, it became increasingly clear that the Khmer Rouge were intent on challenging the legitimacy of the border to attempt to gain back lost territories, inspired by Sarin Chhak's (1966) book.

Escalating border conflicts led the government of Vietnam, in 1977, to approach the ethnic minority refugees from Cambodia who had fled to the Central Highlands of Vietnam in 1975, and propose to militarily organize them to fight against the Khmer Rouge. Eventually, after the Vietnamese military had already started training the Brao and other ethnic minorities from northeastern Cambodia, the UFNSK was established in 1978, not long before the government of Vietnam came to the conclusion that there was no chance of resolving the border conflict with the Khmer Rouge, and that the only way forward would be to oust Pol Pot from power. As preparations were being made for the attack, some Brao traveled from Laos to join other UFNSK troops in Vietnam.

The military force, which attacked Cambodia on December 25, 1978, was easily able to overpower the Khmer Rouge, which quickly retreated toward the Cambodia-Thailand border. While the ethnic minority UFNSK were part of the attack force, Vietnam's PAVN did almost all of the actual fighting, with the Brao forces following behind them at a generally safe distance. The number of UFNSK troops deployed was highly exaggerated for political purposes, and the Vietnamese went to great efforts to preserve the small number of mainly Brao troops so that they could help govern the country once the Khmer Rouge had been removed from power.

The Deterioration of Vietnam-Cambodia Relations

As has been well-documented elsewhere, the relationship between the Khmer Rouge and the Vietnamese deteriorated rapidly in the mid-1970s (Chanda 1986; Becker 1998). Indeed, according to the Vietnamese, just one day after Phnom Penh fell to Democratic Kampuchea, the Khmer Rouge deployed troops along the Vietnam border. Seoun, the ethnic Khmer commander, and a son-in-law of Ta Mok, the notorious commander of the Khmer Rouge Army, allegedly told his troops, "We must attack Vietnam because eighteen of our provinces, including Prey Nokor (Saigon), are there [inside Vietnam]." On April 19, the Vietnamese reported that another of Ta Mok's son-in-laws had ordered the Khmer Rouge Navy to land troops on small islands in the Gulf of Thailand and to attack Phu Quoc Island. Then on May 1, the Khmer Rouge started attacking and harassing many places along the border, from Tay Ninh down to Ha Tien. In early May, more Khmer Rouge attacks occurred against Vietnamese islands. On June 2, Nguyễn Van Linh, representing the Vietnamese Communist Party [Lao Dong Party], traveled to Phnom Penh to meet with Pol Pot. The two men already knew each other, and Pol Pot claimed that, "This painful bloody conflict occurred because our Cambodian army did not know the geography." In mid-June, PAVN forces were, however, able to capture a large number of Khmer Rouge prisoners of war and retake the islands that had been attacked, although the Vietnamese agreed to give Hon Troc

Island to Cambodia in August 1975 (Huy Đức 2012a, 134–135). However, the Vietnamese also initiated attacks into Cambodia in 1975–1976 in response to the Khmer Rouge attacks.[1]

In April 1976, Cambodia and Vietnam agreed to hold a summit meeting to try to resolve the border issues. However, negotiations achieved virtually no results. Nevertheless, on May 23, in a letter sent to the Politburo of the Vietnamese Communist Party, Nuon Chea (Brother #2 in the Khmer Rouge) used friendly words, stating, "The work of our two delegations has achieved great success that has strengthened and expanded the spirit of combat solidarity between us. . . . Our two delegations understand and sympathize with one another and both delegations are extremely sincere in their spirit of combat friendship and revolutionary brotherhood" (Huy Đức 2012a, 136). It was initially proposed that negotiations would occur in Hanoi, and there was even talk of sending a helicopter to Gia Poc to take leaders there to Hanoi for talks. However, it appears that the proposal was simply a ploy, as soon after the Khmer Rouge increased their attacks along the border with Vietnam. Negotiations were canceled.[2] The contradictions that were evident led to considerable debate in Vietnam, as it was unclear how much unity actually existed among the Khmer Rouge leadership. Some believed that Pol Pot and Ieng Sary were part of one faction, while Nuon Chea and others led another. According to the Vietnamese, the fact that Nuon Chea's language was generally much more favorable to the Vietnamese contributed to considerable confusion (Dũng 1995). That was probably Nuon Chea's intention.

Beginning in December 1975, the Khmer Rouge conducted a series of hostile actions farther north, penetrating more than ten kilometers into Vietnam's Gialai-Kontum Province near the Sa Thay River. However, Phnom Penh continued to claim that these actions were just the result of "misunderstandings at the local level." Indeed, according to Ngo Dien, despite evidence of tremendous atrocities along the border, even up to 1978, some senior Vietnamese politicians, such as Central Committee member, Phạm Hai Xô, believed that these crimes might actually have been the result of decisions by local leaders (Huy Đức 2012a, 136). After so many years of war, Vietnam was not eager to escalate conflict and certainly had no desire to enter into a war against the Khmer Rouge (Pribbenow 2006; Chanda 1986). This lack of interest in instigating conflict may have been why the Vietnamese were so slow to fully recognize the full nature of the atrocities being committed along the border. The Vietnamese were probably also concerned about upsetting China, which was politically close to the Khmer Rouge.

Not surprisingly, China took a keen interest in Vietnam-Cambodia border issues. Thus, in the spring of 1977, China issued a four-point proposal for a negotiated settlement related to the Cambodia-Vietnam border dispute. They offered to mediate the conflict (Pao-Min 1985). However, this proposal did not develop into anything. Moreover, tensions between China and Vietnam increased (Pao-Min 1985), especially after the northeastern Cambodian border provinces completely cut off contact with Vietnam border provinces between January and March 1977. Then the situation deteriorated even further, with all contact between Cambodian and Vietnamese provinces being severed between March and May 1977. More Khmer Rouge attacks into Vietnam followed (Dũng 1995).

Beginning to Organize Revolution

According to Bou Thang, in 1976, Soy Keo accidentally met Lieutenant Colonel Phan Thanh Vân, a PAVN officer, when Soy Keo was taking his child to the hospital in the district center of Dak To. Phan Thanh Vân was already familiar with Kachoan Village in Voeunsai District, as he had previously spent time in Cambodia, so the two immediately hit it off. Later, in November 1976, Phan Thanh Vân visited Gia Poc, met Bou Thang and Soy Keo, and learned more about why the group had fled from the Khmer Rouge. Phan Thanh Vân was sympathetic and in December 1976 he helped set up a meeting between Bou Thang and the Gialai-Kontum provincial party secretary. The goal was to provide more information to Vietnamese leaders about the circumstances in Cambodia (Bou Thang 1993).

In March 1977, a group of delegates led by Phi Hùng, from the foreign relationship section of the Communist Party of Vietnam, came to visit Bou Thang at Gia Poc. A major working at the office of security defense and a number of Vietnamese military officers were included in the delegation. Bou Thang provided details about the circumstances in Cambodia while the delegates took careful notes. Eventually they asked Bou Thang what should be done. Bou Thang declined to answer (Bou Thang 1993), instead hoping that the delegates would draw their own conclusions. Later in the same month, Vietnamese officials contacted Kham Sai and told him that due to the massacres of Vietnamese people along the border by the Khmer Rouge, the Vietnamese wanted to assemble an army to attack the Khmer Rouge.[3]

In early 1977, Lieutenant Colonel Trần Tiến Cung, a veteran who had fought against the French in the 1940s, and the commander of the intelligence unit Group 11 based in Danang, was ordered to travel to Hanoi to meet the minister of defense of the SRV (Son 2012; Cung 2011). Cung was initially surprised by the order, as he previously only reported to Lieutenant General Phan Bình, the director of Department 2 of PAVN; so he wondered why he was being asked to report directly to the minister. At the ministry, Cung was led by Deputy Minister of Defense Lieutenant General Trần Văn Quang to meet with Four-star General Văn Tiến Dũng, a member of the Politburo and also the chief of the general staff of PAVN. Not following the usual protocol, General Dũng asked about Cung's family and the education of his children (Son 2016; Cung 2011). Then he said, "Today the Ministry has invited you here to discuss a very important matter. You will have to have a firm understanding of the thinking of the Politburo and of the Central Military Party Committee to carry out this assignment properly" (Son 2016). After explaining the general Khmer Rouge crisis and the atrocities the Khmer Rouge were committing in Cambodia and along the border in Vietnam, Dũng explained that there were forces opposed to the Khmer Rouge that had taken refuge in Vietnam. He reportedly stated, "It is now our responsibility to support and assist these forces so that they can liberate their nation from the threat of genocide and rebuild the spirit of solidarity and friendship between the Vietnamese and Cambodian peoples" (Son 2016). Cung was then ordered to go to Gia Poc to 1) support the dissident forces to grow food and to provide Cambodian cadres with additional political and military training, 2) build up the area to be the base for the dissidents from northeastern Cambodia, and 3) develop military forces there, hopefully to the level of one full division. Soon after, Cung started on his mission (Son 2016).

Lieutenant General Phan Bình gave Cung a vehicle to use and assigned Khang Sarin, a Cambodian who had been a captain assigned to the Son Tay City Military Unit, to translate for him.[4] Cung returned to Danang to report on his orders to Major General Đoàn Khuê, the commander of Military Region 5. After receiving approval to proceed, his group traveled to Sa Thay District, where they met the district party secretary and chairman of the District People's Committee. They finally arrived at Gia Poc on May 20, 1977, after traveling on a poor quality and treacherous road across the Ngoc Rinh Pass. They met Bou Thang and Soy Keo inside a twenty-square meter bamboo hut with a temporary tin roof, which was the group's headquarters (Son 2016; Cung 2011). Cung spent four days studying the general situation at Gia Poc, where he believed about 200 dissidents were living, but it was initially hard to arrange for a working meeting with Gia Poc's leadership. This challenge was, he learned later, because many of the Cambodians were afraid that the Vietnamese might send them back to Cambodia, since the SRV government was still maintaining diplomatic relations with the Khmer Rouge (Cung 2011). Cung later admitted in his memoirs, however, that at the time he knew almost nothing about the Cambodians he was assigned to work with (Cung 2011). Finally, Cung informed Bou Thang and other leaders that the dissidents would not be sent back to the Khmer Rouge. Indeed, the Vietnamese intended to support the refugees, making Gia Poc the headquarters for operations in northeastern Cambodia (Son 2016; Cung 2011; Bou Thang 1993).

Cung and the northeastern Cambodian dissidents then turned to thinking about the name of the new group. Someone suggested the "Northeastern Cambodia Revolutionary Organization." Another person proposed the "Insurrection Committee of the Five Provinces of Northeastern Cambodia." In the end, however, it was agreed that the group would temporarily be called the "Northeastern Cambodia Insurrection Committee." Once this decision had been made, Cung left Gia Poc, informing the Cambodians that he would be back in two weeks (Son 2016). Upon returning to Danang, Cung reported to Lt. General Trần Văn Quang and Lt. General Phan Bình, who approved with Cung's progress (Son 2016).

As promised, Lt. Col. Cung returned to Gia Poc in June 1977. The people were much happier to see him the second time he visited. Bou Thang told Cung that he had reported to all the people at Gia Poc about their previous discussions, and that all but one ethnic group leader had provided him with concrete positive responses (Son 2016). According to Bou Thang, that leader was Boua Chuong, who was doing swidden relatively far away from the commune center and was showing little interest in politics and retaking Cambodia.[5] He might have also been unhappy about having been replaced as commune chief by Bou Thang. In any case, Cung met with the leaders of Gia Poc, and they indicated support for the plan to overthrow the Khmer Rouge (Son 2016). In reality, however, a number of people at Gia Poc did not support the plan.

Many were afraid that they would be killed in combat.[6] Nevertheless, in around June 1977, the Cambodians at Gia Poc organized a conference to elect a Standing Committee [Current Affairs Committee] for the Northeastern Cambodia Insurrection Committee. It consisted of Bun Mi, Bou Thang and Soy Keo, with Bun Mi serving as Chairman (Son 2016).

In June and July 1977 Cung and Khang Sarin traveled regularly between Danang and Gia Poc, to consolidate the northeastern forces and improve their spirit for fighting (Son 2016). Cung brought small gifts with him each time he visited, to gradually build relations with the Cambodian minorities. These included clothes, salt, soap and even underwear for the women. Cung gradually came to know the people at Gia Poc well (Cung 2011).

According to Brao informants now living in Ratanakiri, the Vietnamese began actively recruiting them in mid-1977. Thirty people based in Gia Poc were the first to join. According to some of them, the only requirement was that the recruits had to have "good hearts" (be committed to the cause). A basic medical check-up was also performed, but according to one of the early recruits, that mainly consisted of checking if the men's penises were normal.[7] Training at Gia Poc began on July 7, 1977 (symbolically important, as it was 7/7/77),[8] a date that is easy to verify because some Brao in Ratanakiri Province have the date tattooed to their bodies.[9] However, guns were not distributed to trainees until about a year later,[10] when serious training actually began. In any case, the Brao living at Gia Poc represented the vast majority of those trained.[11] According to Bou Thang, there were only a little over 100 pre-1975 soldiers based at Gia Poc,[12] and there were about 100 Vietnamese assigned to support them. Of those, there were four key Vietnamese technical military trainers, two of which were named Yung and Re.[13] They had someone to translate from Vietnamese to Khmer, but in reality most recruits could not speak Khmer much better than they could speak Vietnamese. Training took place four days a week, from 7–11 am, and then from 2–4 pm.[14]

In October 1977, an order came from Hanoi for Lt. Col. Cung to accompany the Northeastern Standing Committee to Danang to participate in a secret inaugural ceremony. Bun Mi, Bou Thang and Soy Keo stayed at the home of Mrs. Trần Thị Diên, Cung's older sister, who was the Chief Justice of the Danang City People's Court. Because the visit was top secret, Group 11 assigned two female captains to cook and clean for the group. To avoid any suspicions, neighbors were told that the visitors were from the Central Highlands of Vietnam (Son 2016). At that time Bun Mi was still the official leader of the refugees from northeastern Cambodia, and it was at this meeting that the serious problems between the Vietnamese and the Khmer Rouge were clearly articulated. Since Bun Mi spoke little Vietnamese, Bou Thang and Soy Keo translated for him. It was at this time that Bun Mi's ability to talk began to become seriously impaired. However, Bou Thang and Soy Keo still wanted Bun Mi to be their leader, so they protected him from being criticized for his declining mental health.[15]

During the ten days they were in Danang, Bou Thang asked for assistance to meet other resistance leaders in the south. He also specifically requested help liberating Cambodia from the Khmer Rouge, including providing training and military hardware, support for establishing a clandestine rebel radio broadcasting station, and assistance in informing other countries about the abuses committed by Democratic Kampuchea. General Trần Văn Quang reportedly agreed to support all these requests (Bou Thang 1993; Son 2016).

Once back in Gia Poc, Cung informed Bou Thang and his colleagues that five military units would need to be established, one each for the provinces of Ratanakiri, Stung Treng, Mondulkiri, Preah Vihear and Kratie. However, there were insufficient people at Gia Poc to populate all five units. Therefore, efforts needed to be made to recruit Cambodian refugees in Laos. Bou Thang sent two messengers through the forest to inform Thang Bai in Laos of the plans that were rapidly developing in Vietnam (Son 2016; Bou 1993). Efforts were also made to improve the living conditions at Gia Poc, so that they would be prepared to accept incoming recruits from Laos (Son 2016).

Initially Vietnamese leaders hoped that they would not have to directly militarily intervene in Cambodia. Instead, they tried to subversively promote internal changes in the leadership of the Khmer Rouge, although it is hard to know the extent that this was actually pursued. Certainly the Khmer Rouge believed that it was happening throughout the country, and this justified various purges of the government and the military up until late 1978 (Short 2004).

Tensions Rise

As time passed, the Khmer Rouge increased the severity of attacks into Vietnam, and ramped up anti-Vietnamese rhetoric, including speaking out about re-conquering Kampuchea Kraom and Saigon[16] (Vickery 1984), although Stephen Heder claims that such a policy has never been proven.[17] In any case, considering the complicated situation, the Vietnam's Party Secretariat decided to form a "Provisional Sub-Committee to Study the Cambodia Problem," which was called "77 Team" for short. The head of this Sub-Committee was Trần Văn Bách, the Chief d' Cabinet of the Office of Vietnam's Central Committee. In January 1978, 77 Team released its findings and recommendations, heavily criticizing the Khmer Rouge. They made the following assertion:

> The policy of our Party toward the Cambodian problem should be . . . To resolutely and ferociously fight back by striking strong blows of annihilation against any Cambodian forces that conduct armed provocations, harass us, violate our borders, or massacre our people. We must coordinate the military, political, and diplomatic struggles to defeat the enemy, we must block and defeat any and all external plots, and we must steadfastly protect and preserve the spirit of solidarity and friendship between the Vietnamese and Cambodian peoples. (Dũng 1995, 12)

However, tensions had already escalated by the time this recommendation was made. Not surprisingly, the Khmer Rouge was angered and on the last day of 1977, Phnom Penh radio announced that Democratic Kampuchea had temporarily severed diplomatic relations with Vietnam, accusing its neighbor of "ferocious and barbarous aggression" (quoted in Kamm 1998, 148; Vu 2014, 24). Between November 5, 1977, and January 5, 1978, PAVN conducted a large-scale campaign involving a total of eight divisions. Their goal was to attack the Khmer Rouge, drive them away from the border, and pursue them into Cambodia. They penetrated 20 to 30 kilometers deep into the country in some places (Anh 2015). PAVN wanted to control a 450-kilometer strip along the border to demonstrate Vietnam's military superiority to the Khmer Rouge (Pao-Min 1985).

On January 6, 1978, the same day that Vietnamese forces withdrew from Cambodia, Phnom Penh released a statement accusing Hanoi of trying to establish an Indochina Federation (Pao-Min 1985; Dũng 1995). The Khmer Rouge also celebrated victory over Vietnam (*Phnom Penh Domestic Service* 1978b), although the Vietnamese had apparently not withdrawn due to having been defeated, but rather because they felt that they needed to develop an allied Cambodian anti–Khmer Rouge force (Dũng 1995). The Khmer Rouge also accused Vietnam of invading Cambodia as early as September 1977, beginning with an incursion along Route 7 into Kratie Province (*Phnom Penh Domestic Service* 1978b). Vietnam responded by dwelling on the "bonds of solidarity and friendship" and "special relationship" between Kampuchea and Vietnam, which some viewed as demonstrating Vietnam's paternalistic attitude toward Cambodia (Pao-Min 1985, 56).

In January 1978, the leadership of Vietnam apparently still hoped for a negotiated settlement with Cambodia. However, on January 25, 1978, four days after the Khmer Rouge ended its most aggressive attacks into southwestern Vietnam to date, Ngo Dien, Director of Vietnam's Ministry of Foreign Affairs Press Bureau, organized a press conference in Ho Chi Minh City to report that the Khmer Rouge had moved most of its army up to the border and had conducted large-scale attacks deep inside Vietnam. Mr. Dien stated that, "Cambodian armed forces not only murdered Vietnamese citizens; they also killed a number of Cambodians living along the border. They disemboweled these people, ripped out their livers, and they filmed and photographed the corpses to try to blame Vietnam for these atrocities." Two Khmer Rouge prisoners of war who Ngo Dien brought to the press conference reportedly "admitted that Pol Pot had done these things" (Huy Đức 2012a, 134).

The following statement, which Pol Pot made on February 1, 1978, to his party's central committee, indicates the view of the Khmer Rouge at the time:

> The war between us and Vietnam will be a protracted war, a "nibbling" war. If we do not strike first, we will not win. . . . All we need to do is to kill a few dozen of them every day, a few thousand every month, a few hundred thousand every year, and in that way we will be able to fight them for ten, fifteen, or twenty years. We must achieve the goal that for every one of our people killed 30 of their people are killed. In that way by sacrificing the lives of two million Cambodian we will be able to kill sixty million Vietnamese. We must take the war into their territory. (Liên 2013)

It is evident that Pol Pot's hatred of the Vietnamese was deep, and that he saw things through a highly essentializing and racialized lens.

Moreover, he too was inspired by Sarin Chhak's 1966 book, *Les Fron-tières du Cambodge.*

Despite the escalation of conflict and the hardline view regarding their fight against the Vietnamese, on February 5, the Vietnam Ministry of Foreign Affairs issued a formal three-point proposal for organizing a conference with the Khmer Rouge to resolve the border conflict. It stipulated that each side withdraw their respective troops five kilometers from the border (Pao-Min 1985). However, the initiative backfired, and the Khmer Rouge became increasingly emboldened (Vu 2014), stating, "The conflict between Cambodia and Vietnam cannot be resolved through negotiations. It must be resolved through military action" (Ấm 2002).

In March 1978, the Central Military Party Committee of Vietnam issued a resolution making it clear that they would support Cambodians taking refuge in Vietnam to build up revolutionary forces. Trần Văn Quang was entrusted with the responsibility of leading this effort (Liên 2013). On April 7, the Vietnamese also issued a lengthy document titled, "On the Indochina Federation Question," in which it was argued that the idea of establishing an Indochina Federation had long been abandoned (Pao-Min 1985). A few days later, Pol Pot accused the Vietnamese of being insincere and of denying Vietnam's goal to establish an Indo-chinese Federation (*Phnom Penh Domestic Service* 1978c). At around the same time, Radio Hanoi started broadcasting in Khmer and openly encouraged the Cambodian people to rise up against the Khmer Rouge (Rathie 2006). The situation became especially tense after the purging of Democratic Kampuchea's east zone and the subsequent "East Zone Revolt" of Khmer Rouge soldiers to Vietnam in May 1978 (Vickery 1984; Vũ 1979).

Recruiting Brao Soldiers from Laos

In early 1978, Bun Mi was sent to Laos to try to convince Cambodian refugees there to join him. Bun Mi traveled to the Lao capital of Vientiane to meet with senior leaders of the Lao People's Democratic Republic (Lao PDR). Since the government of Laos was a close ally of the SRV, it is not surprising that they agreed to the request. Bun Mi, at that point, started working to gain political support from the refugee population in Attapeu Province, southern Laos.[18] However, no refugees from Laos initially volunteered to travel to Vietnam to join the revolutionary forces.

A second delegation to Laos was led by Soy Keo, who initially went by himself to Vientiane to meet Osakanh Thammatheva, himself originally from Voeunsai, to ask for help in looking after the refugees. Then he went to Attapeu to see his old colleagues, including Thang Bai.[19] No actual recruiting was done at this time, but preparations were well underway.

Later, a third delegation, again led by Soy Keo, traveled to southern Laos, this time with the clear goal to recruit soldiers. Soy Keo again met Thang Bai.[20] Yoep Vanson and some Khmers went with him, but no soldiers returned with them, as none of the Brao were ready to join. Many remained skeptical.[21]

In October-November 1978, Kham Phai led the fourth and last delegation to Laos to recruit soldiers. He went with Pa-ao, who came from Kham Phai's village and was a good speaker, and a Vietnamese military advisor named Chang. It took two days and two nights to walk from Gia Poc to Xaysettha District in Attapeu Province. They based themselves in the district center and visited the Brao communities located adjacent to the Xexou River, including Keng Makkheua Village, where a large number of Brao from Cambodia lived, including Veng Khoun. Kham Phai's team traveled by themselves to the villages in the mornings and returned to the district center in the evenings, where they ate most of their meals. They were able to convince about one hundred Brao recruits to return to Gia Poc with them. Kham Phai's team did not, however, visit any non-Brao villages during the trip. The group spent a month in Attapeu so as to allow time for those who volunteered to prepare to go to Gia Poc.[22]

It took much longer to walk back to Gia Poc than it took to come to Laos, as some male recruits—especially those with relatives staying at Gia Poc—decided to take their wives and children with them.[23] The group of 600–700 people was led by Thang Bai and Kham Lai.[24] According to Kham Sai, the group slept eleven nights in the forest during the journey, arriving at Gia Poc on December 5, 1978, just three weeks before the offensive into Cambodia began.[25] One Brao soldier told me, "We had no time to train in Vietnam. We just attacked."[26] The Vietnamese did, however, provide a small amount of training, with Bou Thang and Soy Keo acting as translators.[27] Kham Phai confirmed this, claiming that the group he recruited only had about ten days to train before the Vietnamese offensive began.[28]

Some of the key civilian officials who also made the trip to Vietnam from Laos included Kham Lai (Kreung, Tiem Loeu Village), Thang Bai, and Chan Thon (Kreung, Phak Nam Village). Two key military leaders who came from Laos were Kham Suk (Kreung, Tiem Loeu Village) and Thon Thin (Brao, Phao Village); another less significant soldier was Bun Sou (Tampuon, Kachoan Village), Thang Bai's only son.[29]

On December 26, 1978, a few weeks after the first group of Cambodian refugees from Attapeu had traveled to Gia Poc, a second group traveled to Vietnam. This group included people who could not leave earlier, such as the veteran revolutionaries Nu Beng (ethnic Lao, Voeunsai Village) and Bun Kang (ethnic Lao, Pong Village), as they had been working for the Lao government at the time they were recruited. They had just two days' notice to prepare to move. Two helicopters picked them up in Attapeu and brought them to Pakse, where they boarded a larger Vietnamese plane that took them to Pleiku, the capital of Gialai-Kontum Province.[30]

Those Who Did Not Want to Fight

Although many Brao agreed to join the revolutionary forces, some declined for various reasons. For example, the former military leader Kham Sai resigned from his position, claiming that he had experienced enough fighting.[31] Some claim that Kham Sai was afraid to die in battle.[32] He was not the only one. A Brao woman originally from Cambodia who remained in Laos said that her husband also did not join the revolutionary forces because he was afraid to die.[33] Many others at Gia Poc also expressed fear about attacking the Khmer Rouge from Vietnam.[34] Dop Khamchoeung, who would later become the head of the military in Mondulkiri Province, also initially refused to participate, admittedly due to fear. However, he was later cajoled into changing his mind. He insisted at that time that he would die with the others if necessary.[35] As Khamchoeung put it, "At first I was lazy to attack the Khmer Rouge, but many people encouraged me to join, so I did."[36]

Others, such as Channiang Gle, decided not to join. He had three small children at the time and so chose instead to help look after the women and children who were left behind in Laos when their husbands went to become soldiers.[37] Another Brao man who also returned to Cambodia in 1983 did not join because he was already in the Lao Army when recruiting occurred and therefore was not eligible to join the revolutionary force.[38] A Brao man now living in Laos told me that he did not join the revolutionary forces because he thought he would miss his wife and children too much. He said that he was not afraid to die, as there had been much more harrowing battles before he came to Laos. Instead, he simply did not want to fight anymore.[39] One Brao man— Kro Ban, who until recently was the chief of Taveng Loeu Commune— told me that he opted not to join the new force. He had initially agreed, but at the beginning of the journey to Vietnam, when he spent a night in Xaysettha District Center, he had a dream that his ancestor, Ya Koung, told him that if he went to Cambodia to fight, he would die. This scared him and resulted in him changing his mind and not going further.[40]

What we can see here is a diversity of circumstances. While some Brao and other ethnic minorities were eager to join in the liberation of Cambodia from the Khmer Rouge, others chose not to participate for various reasons.

Group 578

On May 12, 1978, the chief of PAVN's general staff, Lê Trọng Tấn, acting on behalf of Vietnam's Ministry of Defense, signed an order forming Group 578, a unit designed to specifically support Cambodian revolutionary units. Lieutenant Colonel Cung was made the overall group commander (Cung 2011). The first revolutionary unit, called 125 Unit, had only 200 people in it, but it was symbolically important (Liên 2013; Institute of Military History 2010; Hun Sen 2012; Minh Nam 2012). Its headquarters was officially established far to the south of Gia Poc, with Hun Sen in charge. Group 578 developed its headquarters, which consisted of a staff operations agency, a political agency, a rear services agency, and a technical agency (Son 2016; Cung 2011). It was at this time that the Vietnamese military distributed guns to the Cambodian revolutionary soldiers based at Gia Poc.[41]

Once Group 578 was formed, the Northeastern Cambodia Insurrection Committee was integrated into it.[42] This was done by linking the soldiers at Gia Poc with PAVN's 78th Division. According to Bou Thang, it is likely that 578 stood for May (5th month) 1978.[43] Bou Thang was the political leader and Soy Keo was made military leader in the northeast, supported by Group 578, with Kham Phai as Bou Thang's deputy. Kham Chan was the director of the general political department and Heng Khamvan was responsible for the northeast headquarters at Gia Poc (Bou Thang 1993).[44] Three battalions were initially created in preparation for the major offensive against the Democratic Kampuchea, even though there were not nearly enough soldiers to fill them. Kham Chan headed the first, and Bou Thang and Soy Keo led the other two (see Joint Task Force 1994a, 1994b). Bou Thang, however, claims that shortly before the attack, the two battalions were reorganized into five (actually the size of companies), one allocated for each of the provinces of Ratanakiri, Stung Treng, Mondulkiri, Preah Vihear, and Kratie.[45] Kham Chan was made the military head of the Battalion 1, responsible for Mondulkiri, with Heng Khamvan being put in charge of politics. Ma Ranchai (Lun, Taveng Village) was initially made the leader of Battalion 2, with Doeun (Lun, Taveng Village) as his deputy. But Ma Ranchai did not continue on to Preah Vihear as planned, so Doeun later became the military head with Toeua (Brao, Bong Village) in charge of politics.[46] Thao Sim was made the military head of Battalion 3, assigned to Ratanakiri, with Thon Thin in charge of politics. Kham Sanit was the military head of Battalion 4, responsible for Stung Treng; Loeun (Kreung, Khuan Village) was put in charge of politics.[47] The Brao dominated almost all the key positions.

Initially, the hope was that the northeast region would include Kratie Province.[48] However, it was later decided that there were not enough soldiers to populate all five battalions. Therefore, Battalion 5, for Kratie Province, was handed over to Khmer forces to the south.[49] This being the case, Bou Thang did not work with this unit and instead concentrated on the other four provinces.[50] As he put it, "I could not speak Khmer very well at the time, so it was better to let someone else manage that military unit."[51]

Each of the remaining four battalions was made up of three small companies, with each including between just four to ten people. One big gun company was also included in each battalion. In addition, there was an investigation battalion with thirty-one soldiers in it.[52] There was also a military command unit.[53] By July 1978, there were reportedly seventeen operational teams with a total of 600 personnel established with the assistance of Military Region 5 and especially Group 578 (Institute of Military History 2010). However, that number is far from certain. Dop Khamchoeung claims that there were no more than 120 soldiers at Gia Poc.[54] Yoep Vanson estimated the number to be slightly higher, at between 130 and 160.[55] This generally fits with Jampong Jari's claim that the company/battalion he was in—one of the four—had just thirty soldiers in it, which is the size of a platoon.[56] Kham Phai told me that at the end of 1978, there were actually only about two hundred soldiers (almost all Brao), plus another one hundred from Laos.[57] However, one of the Brao leaders at Gia Poc, Ma Ranchai, stated that Battalions 2 and 3, responsible for Preah Vihear and Ratanakiri respectively, each consisted of just three companies with just thirty men each (ninety men per battalion).[58] Muan Hoi claimed that there were about five hundred soldiers based at Gia Poc,[59] while Bou Thang claimed that there were a little more than five hundred.[60] Heng Khamvan initially claimed that there were nine hundred soldiers included in these battalions, although he later adjusted his estimate to six hundred.[61] Kham Sana claimed that there were a total of 282 soldiers at Gia Poc just before the major attack on the Khmer Rouge occurred, which may actually be the closest number to the truth, when including all military personnel.[62] Although the actual number of soldiers from northeastern Cambodia at Gia Poc is uncertain, the previous published claim that UFNSK forces included 1,800 northeasterners, including a few ethnic Lao Cambodian refugees in Vietnam and some Cambodian Brao who had been refugees in Laos (see Joint Task Force 1994a, 1994b), was undoubtedly highly exaggerated.

Officially, the newly formed battalions were referred to as divisions, even though they were more like small companies. The number of UFNSK soldiers was pumped up for political reasons. Bun Mi was the official leader, but in reality Bou Thang and Soy Keo had already taken control. However, they did not participate in the offensive into Cambodia. They stayed in Vietnam to address political and policy issues. The actual leaders of the attacking forces were Kham Chan, Kham Phai, Heng Khamvan, Thao Sim, Dop Khamchoeung, and Kham Sanit.[63]

In late 1978, Vietnamese officials from Sepa District contacted Bui Yung and the other Jarai families who had fled to Tang Village in 1975. They asked if any of the refugees wanted to become soldiers with the UFNSK. Only three volunteered, but later the group was not contacted again, so the three did not join the anti–Khmer Rouge force.[64]

China-Vietnam Tension Escalates

In early 1978, China became increasingly alarmed with Vietnam's carrot-and-stick strategy in relation to Cambodia, and increased its military aid to the Khmer Rouge, including providing, for the first time, tanks and other armored vehicles, as well as long-range guns. Increased numbers of Chinese advisors were also sent to Cambodia to provide training (Pao-Min 1978; Mertha 2014). The actions of China clearly angered Vietnam and caused tensions to escalate, including Vietnam launching a nationwide campaign against ethnic Chinese in Vietnam (Pao-Min 1985; Chanda 1986). Huy Đức (2012) reported that the Vietnamese feared that the 1.2 million ethnic Chinese in Vietnam could become a Trojan horse in a future war with China, one that looked increasingly inevitable. This campaign resulted in 70,000 ethnic Chinese fleeing from Vietnam to China in April and May alone (Pao-Min 1985; Huy Đức 2012a).

On May 12, 1978, China cancelled twenty-one factory aid projects to Vietnam (Pao-Min 1985), and in June China shut down all three Vietnamese consulates in China, and also cancelled all aid to Vietnam. China also announced that all of its technicians would be withdrawn from Vietnam by July 3 (Pao-Min 1985). On June 17, Hanoi, which up to then had not openly criticized China, accused Beijing of having "ceaselessly given all-round support to the Kampuchean authorities in launching their border war of aggression against the Vietnamese people . . . and in carrying out an anti-Vietnamese policy aimed at . . . sabotaging the tradition of solidarity and friendship between Vietnam and Kampuchea" (quoted in Pao-Min 1985, 63). On June 30, Vietnam also unilaterally suspended Sino-Vietnamese talks regarding territorial disputes, and on July 11, China announced the closure of its land border with Vietnam (Pao-Min 1985).

In late June and July, Hanoi further stepped up verbal attacks, blaming China for promoting genocide in Cambodia and aggression against the Vietnamese to destroy the Kampuchean race and pave the way for China's conquest of other parts of Asia. China, in response, accused Vietnam of wanting to annex Cambodia. Indeed, not only were tensions between Vietnam and the Khmer Rouge escalating, but so were tensions between China and Vietnam. These tensions were exacerbated by Vietnam moving closer to the Soviet Union. Armed skirmishes along the Vietnam-China border started in late August 1978 (Pao-Min 1985).

Preparing for War

On June 16, 1978, Vietnam's Politburo issued Resolution 20, which formed a new national-level Cambodian operations section (called Section B-68 for short), which was created specifically to support the Cambodian revolution, and had its headquarters in Ho Chi Minh City. The first chief of Section B-68 was Major General Nguyễn Xuân Hoàng, the deputy director of Vietnam's Military Science Institute (Anh 2015). He had considerable experience assisting Cambodian revolutionaries and had previously headed the Party Central Committee's Section CP48. Later, Major General Hoàng Thế Thiện took over as chief of Section B-68 (Dũng 1995).

When Section B-68 was first formed, Comrade Lê Đức Thọ, a member of the Politburo and the chief of the Central Committee's Organization Department,[65] was put in charge of broadly overseeing the "special operation" to prepare for the offensive against the Khmer Rouge (Huy Đức 2012b). According to Lê Đức Anh, "Lê Đức Thọ was the designer [of the plan] from the very beginning. He was the person who made the decisions on big questions such as building up forces, methods of implementation, outlining general combat plans, directing troop movements, and issuing orders to generals" (Huy Đức 2012a, 377). Indicative of this, on July 15, Lê Đức Thọ signed a Party Secretariat Directive stating that, "Our people have an obligation to assist them [the Cambodians who fled to Vietnam], to protect them, to organize their lives while they are here in our country, and to help them to continue their revolution against the Cambodian reactionary clique" (Yen 2005, 351). Linked to the above directive, on July 19, 1978, Vietnam's Central Military Party Committee issued Decision Order No. 68/QD-QUTW, which authorized the formation of a Forward Command Element within the Ministry of Defense. This unit was given the following responsibilities: to provide unified command over all combat operations of the different military regions, army corps, and military services in the south for the purpose of fighting to defend Vietnam's sovereignty along its southwestern border (Anh 2015). Cung found Lê Đức Thọ to be a very strict and serious cadre and later wrote that he was proud to have worked with him (Cung 2011).

In July 1978, Cung received a cable from Lê Đức Thọ, informing him of the formation of B-68. During the same month, Lê Đức Thọ asked Cung and Khang Sarin to invite the Standing Committee of the Northeastern Cambodian Insurrection Committee to come to B-68's headquarters in Ho Chi Minh City to hold important talks (Son 2016). Thus, Bou Thang, Bun Mi, and Soy Keo traveled to Ho Chi Minh City via Pleiku and Nha Trang, where they met with other important resistance leaders originally from Cambodia, including Pen Sovan, Heng Samrin,

Chea Sim, Hun Sen, and Ros Samay. Both Lê Đức Anh and Lê Đức Thọ
played leading roles in the meetings, along with Major General Lê
Ngọc Hiền, deputy chief of the PAVN general staff; Major General
Nguyễn Xuân Hoàng, the leader of B-68; and the commanders of
PAVN's Military Regions 5, 7, and 9. The meeting was seen as historic
(Bou Thang 1993; Son 2016), as it was clear at this point that the Viet-
namese were committed to removing the Khmer Rouge from power
(Bou Thang 1993).

Before the meeting, Major General Nguyễn Xuân Hoàng told Cung
that he intended to allow the Cambodian leaders to speak freely and
make their own recommendations regarding what they needed in terms
Vietnamese assistance. However, Cung was somewhat concerned that
the northeastern leaders might not be able to articulate their needs and
desires.

After all the delegates introduced each other, the representatives
of each group, including Hun Sen, Chea Sim, and Heng Samrin made
presentations. The last group to speak was from the northeast. It had
previously been agreed that Bou Thang would present on behalf of the
group, since he could speak Vietnamese fluently. He proposed the
following:

1. Bring together the Cambodian dissident forces who had fled to
   Vietnam, the forces rising up inside Cambodia, and the individuals
   who had been previously living in Vietnam to form a united force
   that would be called the Anti-Pol Pot–Ieng Sary Alliance;
2. Resurrect the Cambodian Party;
3. Move forward to topple of the genocidal regime and form a military,
   establish a radio broadcasting station, and establish a new Cambodian
   State (government, regime). First of all, help the northeastern Cambodia
   dissident forces that need assistance to become the base and the rear
   guard of the Cambodian revolution.

After listening to Bou Thang, Lê Đức Thọ looked at him and then at
Cung. He was impressed and praised Bou Thang, saying that what he
proposed made a lot of sense. Suddenly, however, Bun Mi—who the
Vietnamese described as a direct and sincere person—stood up. He
said, "I request that Uncle Sau [Lê Đức Thọ's Communist Party name]
allow me to speak!" Lê Đức Thọ smiled and said happily, "Certainly.
I invite you to speak your mind." Bun Mi responded surprisingly

honestly, with Bou Thang translating for him: "Uncle Sau has praised what we said, but in reality we had help from Brother Cung here!" Everyone laughed out loud, except for Cung, who sat silently. Lê Đức Thọ said quickly, "Well, that's enough. The groups should now go back home to continue discussions and reach agreement with one another, after which we will implement your decisions" (Son 2016).

Later in 1978, the Vietnamese stepped up their actions at least partially due to continued Khmer Rouge raids and massacres of Vietnamese people living on the Vietnam side of the international border (Guan 2013). In addition, the ethnic Vietnamese population living in Cambodia had been subjected to abuse and many fled to Vietnam. According to the PRK Foreign Ministry (1985), by August 1978, 268,000 ethnic Vietnamese refugees from Cambodia had arrived in Vietnam, although it is unclear from when they started counting.

Although Vietnam's overall response to Khmer Rouge border aggression was appropriately characterized as "moderate" by Evans and Rowley (1984), there was indeed a limit to their patience, as Khmer Rouge border attacks from northeastern Cambodia increased to many each day in June 1978 (Hồng 2004). Thus, on June 23, Vietnam's Military Region 5 sent the 31st Regiment and the 95th Infantry Regiment to attack Khmer Rouge forces in the southeastern part of Ratanakiri Province. They reportedly easily defeated the Khmer Rouge forces situated along the border and rapidly gained control of an approximately twenty kilometers long and ten to fifteen kilometers deep piece of territory inside Cambodia, which they would later use to launch their full-scale attack against the Khmer Rouge. However, the Khmer Rouge's 801st Division initiated a series of small operations designed to disrupt PAVN's 31st Regiment, which had been designated as the frontline unit responsible for defending the Cambodian territory previously taken. During the rainy season of 1978, the 31st Regiment experienced significant hardships due to difficulties transporting supplies along extremely poor quality muddy roads and continued Khmer Rouge ambushes. As conditions deteriorated, the 31st Regiment was replaced by the 95th Regiment, along with the 93rd and 94th Regiments, thus allowing the 31st Regiment to rest and regroup (Hồng 2004).

In 1978, *Izvestiya* (Moscow) (1978) reported that localized rebellion against the Khmer Rouge was occurring in sixteen out of Cambodia's nineteen provinces, including in the northeast. This claim was false and was designed to set the stage for the Vietnamese ousting of the Khmer

Rouge without making it look like it was actually them who was behind it.

In November 1978, it was reported that a large number of leaflets had been distributed in eastern and northeastern Cambodia to encourage Cambodians to join the revolution against the Khmer Rouge (*Hanoi VNA* 1978). However, *Hanoi VNA* (1978) did not mention how the leaflets had been distributed; only that they had been found in various parts of Cambodia. One leaflet cited was signed by Bun Mi and Soy Keo. Interestingly, only their previous positions with the Khmer Rouge were mentioned. It was not stated that they had been in Vietnam since 1975. Even though it seems likely that these leaflets were never widely distributed, the content of their text is worth reproducing in full:

> Fellow countrymen and soldiers of various nationalities [ethnicities] in the provinces of Ratanakiri, Mondulkiri, Stung Treng and Kratie and compatriots throughout the country. We are Bun Mi, former deputy party secretary of the third region of Ratanakiri Province in the northeastern zone, and Soy Keo, commander of Battalion 703 in the northeastern zone. Unable to suffer the daily killings and misery, and the national discrimination and contempt practiced by the Pol Pot–Ieng Sary clique traitors against our people of different nationalities, and in the face of their reckless and stupid acts of provoking an unjust war of aggression against the fraternal Vietnamese people at the instigation and with the help of the Chinese authorities, we and many other officers and soldiers have left the ranks of this traitorous clique, organized our forces and built fighting bases against them in the northeastern zone.
>
> Our forces continue to grow and are pressing attacks to join together with the insurgent forces in other localities throughout the country to smash the administration of the Pol Pot–Ieng Sary clique, to save the people and the nation, to regain independence, freedom and genuine democracy, to build Kampuchea into a new, progressive, and genuinely revolutionary country and to bring about happiness and a plentiful life to our people of all nationalities throughout the country. This is also aimed at putting an end to the war against Vietnam so that our people may live in peace and restore our solidarity with the Vietnamese people.

> We ardently call on our people of all nationalities in the north-eastern zone and the rest of the country to rapidly join their forces and smash all dark schemes of the Chinese authorities. (*Hanoi VNA* 1978)

Bou Thang claims that he was not aware of any informants or allies that his group or the Vietnamese had in Cambodia in late 1978. He suspected that the leaflets had simply been dropped in Cambodia by Vietnamese planes. He admitted that, "The Vietnamese just made up the story that people were rebelling against the Khmer Rouge in the northeast for political reasons and to prepare for their attack on Pol Pot."[66]

In the latter part of 1978, both Vietnam and Cambodia built up their military forces on the Vietnam-Cambodia border. In September-October, PAVN apparently increased its troop allocation along the border from 60,000–80,000 to well over 100,000 (Pao-Min 1985), and in late 1978, nineteen of the Khmer Rouge's twenty-three regular army divisions were deployed to the Cambodia-Vietnam border to launch attacks into Vietnam (Hòa and Tường 2008). A military build-up was occurring on both sides of the border.

In November 1978, Lieutenant Colonel Cung was confronted with a dilemma. Vietnam's Military Region 5's 307th Division was planning to launch a counterattack against the Khmer Rouge. Thứ, the deputy commander of Military Region 5 and the plan leader, said to Cung, "We are launching a counterattack across the border but no one here knows the routes or knows the language so that our forces can carry out civilian proselyting work. You have five operations units, so why don't you loan them to us for a while" (Son 2016). Cung did not know what to do. On the one hand, the military units at Gia Poc were considered strategic forces, and if General Văn Tiến Dũng found out he had loaned them out, Cung would surely be disciplined. On the other hand, if he did not loan the forces out, the combat power of the 307th Division would be reduced. Moreover, Cung and his forces were based in Military Region 5, which had given him a great deal of assistance, so he did not want to disappoint them (Son 2016). Cung had a plan. He talked with Bou Thang and proposed that rather than providing the five units as requested, they would instead cobble together five so-called "fake" units made up of inexperienced people to support the 307th Division, while allowing the actual five units to continue with their training undistracted (Son 2016).

The plan proceeded, but to everyone's surprise, the newly formed units actually performed well when the attack occurred. In fact, the deputy commander of Military Region 5 wrote a report to the Ministry of Defense, in which he praised the units for their outstanding contributions. However, when General Văn Tiến Dũng heard of what had happened, he sent Lieutenant General Hoàng Thế Thiện to interrogate Cung about why he had offered these units to support the 307th Division. Cung feared he was going to lose his position, but when he briefed Thiện on what actually happened—including how the five fake units had been formed—the lieutenant general slapped his hand on the table, laughed out loud, and proclaimed, "Excellent! You are really good!" (Son 2016). Interestingly, however, the *Voice of the Cambodian People* (1978), along with the Soviet news agency, TASS (1978), reported that only Cambodian anti–Khmer Rouge forces had launched the attacks into Cambodia at the end of November, without mentioning any involvement of the Vietnamese in the offensive, thus greatly distorting reality.

Establishing the UFNSK

As part of preparations for taking control of Cambodia, Boua Chuong and Kham Len had already been, since September-October 1978, secretly designated as the chairman of Ratanakiri's provincial People's Committee and secretary of the Ratanakiri's Party Committee, respectively. Similar decisions had been made for other provinces in Cambodia. Future military positions in the provinces were also allocated well before the offensive, of course with Vietnamese assistance. That way there would be no confusion or time wasted once the offensive had succeeded. Early on there were no ethnic Khmer people involved in preparing at Gia Poc for the attack again the Khmer Rouge other than Cung's translator Khang Sarin.

On October 23, Bou Thang, Bun Mi, and Soy Keo were called to travel to another important meeting in Ho Chi Minh City, this time about officially forming the UFNSK. Other key members of the Cambodian resistance attended, including Pen Sovan, Heng Samrin, Chea Sim, Hun Sen, Chea Sot, Ros Samay, and Keo Chanda (Bou Thang 1993; Son 2016). At the meeting, Bou Thang and Bun Mi were elected to UFNSK's Central Committee (Son 2016). By late 1978, UFNSK reportedly included a total of 107 people who had previously held senior positions in the Cambodian military (Liên 2013).

From November 26 to 29, the first Congress of the Central Committee of the UFNSK was held at Group 977's Thu Duc Public Security School in Ho Chi Minh City. One hundred and eight delegates attended, including forty-two Khmer Hanoi who had stayed in Vietnam to work there; thirty-five members from the Eastern Military Region; sixteen who had fled to Vietnam in June 1977; eleven from the northeast; and four notables. The congress elected a fifteen-member Central Committee (Liên 2013; Institute of Military History 2010). The leadership of the UFNSK was further designated on November 30 (Bou Thang 1993, 2011; Gottesman 2002). When the first fourteen-member cabinet for the UFNSK was established, under the leadership of Heng Samrin, there was just one representative from the northeast: Bun Mi (Bou Thang 1993), even though he continued to suffer from mental health problems. Not surprisingly, the Vietnamese elevated many of the few remaining Khmer Hanoi to senior positions (Huy Đức 2012a).

The UFNSK was not publically announced until a week later, on December 2, 1978, at a ceremony organized at a clearing in a rubber plantation in a secure liberated zone in Cheung Khlou Commune, Snoul District, Kratie Province, in Cambodia.[67] According to some accounts, thousands were in attendance (Slocomb 2003), including several hundred Cambodian refugees trucked into Cambodia for the occasion (Gottesman 2002). Early on, it was reported that the nucleus of the Cambodian resistance to the Khmer Rouge had organized in the Snoul area, on Cambodian soil, after which time the resistance requested support from the Vietnamese (Vickery 1984). However, it is now acknowledged by everyone I have spoken with that the resistance was actually organized among refugees who had fled to Vietnam, but that for political reasons the Vietnamese wanted to give the impression that resistance had emerged inside Cambodia. In any case, many local villagers attended the initial public ceremony announcing UFNSK.[68] Kham Suk, an ethnic Kreung soldier with UFNSK, claims that one hundred soldiers from Gia Poc attended, even though he was not one of them.[69] The red flag with a yellow, five-towered Angkor Wat symbol on it, the one used by the Khmer Issarak during the First Indochina War against the French, was flown during the event (Slocomb 2003).

Heng Khamvan told me that he led, with Kham Chan, a group of over three hundred people from Gia Poc to go to Snoul on November 25, and that his group arrived at Snoul via Pleiku on November 28, three days before Bou Thang and other UFNSK leaders arrived on December

2.[70] According to him, the Khmer Rouge had retreated from the area, and Vietnam's big guns had been moved in. Nevertheless, the road to the site in Snoul was heavily guarded by PAVN soldiers.[71]

According to Bou Thang, senior members of UFNSK traveled from Ho Chi Minh City at 6 am on December 1, and after traveling twenty-four hours via Pleiku and Dak Keu, they arrived at the Vietnam-Cambodia border and entered forty kilometers into Cambodia to near Snoul (Gottesman 2002), during which time the purpose of the UFNSK was formally announced by its leader, Heng Samrin (Slocomb 2003, Pribbenow 2006; Heng 2018), and witnessed by Lê Đức Thọ (Chanda 1986). The group then rapidly returned to Vietnam, arriving there on the afternoon of the same day.[72] Chanda (1986), however, claims that the site was just two miles inside Cambodia, east of Snoul, and Dop Khamchoeung reported that the location was about ten kilometers inside Cambodia.[73] Wherever the exact location might have been, there was not actually any substantive discussion about the UFNSK during the event in Snoul. Only a formal address was made, one that had been prepared earlier in Vietnam's Dong Nai Province.[74] The Vietnamese and their new partners, the UFNSK, were, in any case, preparing the political landscape for ousting the Khmer Rouge. The PRK government's Ministry of Foreign Affairs (1985) put it this way in a White Paper they prepared, years later: "In late November 1978 a national congress of revolutionary patriotic forces convened in one of these districts and formed the United Front for the National Salvation of Kampuchea (UFNSK). On 2nd December, the UFNSK Central Committee adopted an 11-paragraph political program and called on the people to mount a nationwide uprising against the hateful Pol Pot regime. At the same time, it applied to Vietnam for help."

During the December 2 ceremony, Slocomb (2003, 45) reported that Heng Samrin announced the establishment of "a people's democratic regime, to develop the Angkor traditions, to make Kampuchea into a truly peaceful, independent, democratic, neutral, and non-aligned country advancing socialism, thus contributing actively to the common struggle for peace and stability in Southeast Asia." Key to his speech was the eleven-point program, which was expected to be implemented following the overthrow of Democratic Kampuchea (Slocomb 2003; Heng 2018), and which was apparently written by Vietnamese advisors (Huy Đức 2012a). These eleven points were to:

1. Consolidate national unity to overthrow the Khmer Rouge.
2. Establish the UFNSK and all its associated organizations to politically organize to overthrow the Khmer Rouge.
3. Develop and strengthen the UFNSK revolutionary military to bring the Khmer Rouge down from power.
4. Uphold free and democratic rights that respect the value of human life. That includeds allowing people to return to their homes and live normal lives, and to be able to travel freely within the country.
5. Identify and develop a new economic path to rehabilitate the country.
6. Abolish forced marriages.
7. Eliminate the culture promoted by the Khmer Rouge and replace it with a culture that would really fit with the people's lives. These changes include eradicating illiteracy and generally supporting Khmer language education throughout the country.
8. Encourage people to join the new UFNSK military forces to fight against the Khmer Rouge.
9. Develop new and friendly relations with other foreign nations.
10. Solve disputes with neighboring countries using peaceful means, including stopping hostilities along the Vietnam-Cambodia border.
11. Promote solidarity with other revolutionary and developed countries, including promoting peace, independence, sovereignty and social development, and opposing imperialism and new or old colonialism.

Generally speaking, the UFNSK claimed "they would make Cambodia into an independent and democratic state, one 'progressing towards socialism'" (Vickery 1984, 216). They also claimed to have the support of "millions" of Cambodians (Pao-Min 1985).

Heng Khamvan reported that a total of thirteen battalions of soldiers assembled in Snoul, although these battalions were undoubtedly greatly under strength. He said that once the leaders arrived, the statement was read, everyone had lunch, and then they departed back to Vietnam in the afternoon.[75] Dop Khamchoeung claims that he only slept one night in Snoul before returning to Vietnam, even though both Vietnamese and Cambodians asked him to stay longer. He was worried about being attacked so he ignored their pleas and returned early.[76]

After leaving Snoul and returning to Vietnam, Heng Khamvan traveled to Ho Chi Minh City with Kham Chan and some Vietnamese officers, where they stayed in the Binh Nhe Guest House. After participating in meetings to establish the leadership of the UFNSK, Khamvan returned with Kham Chan to Gia Poc, arriving there on December 15, 1978.[77]

The Attack

On December 6 and 7, 1978, the SRV's Politburo and the Central Military Party Committee of Vietnam met and made the final decision to launch a general offensive to annihilate the Khmer Rouge and bring the border war to an end (Institute of Military History 2010). Vietnam probably felt that China was too weak or would be unwilling to militarily intervene in a major way. Indeed, China's leader, Deng Xiaoping had already openly stated that while China intended to continue supporting the Khmer Rouge, they did not plan to send Chinese troops to Cambodia (Pao-Min 1985).

There was a short lull before the storm, but on December 20 to 21, the Khmer Rouge launched a number of fierce attacks into Vietnam's Tay Ninh Province, some involving the massacre of large numbers of women and children. According to Son (2016), at that time a total of ten Khmer Rouge Divisions were mobilized to attack the Vietnamese along the border. This being the case, Vietnam's military leaders decided to launch their own attack one week ahead of schedule, beginning on December 22, under the command of Lê Đức Anh (Gottesman 2002; Pribbenow 2006; Hồng 2004).

On December 20, prior to the attack, Soy Keo, Bou Thang, and Bun Mi traveled to Gia Poc to prepare the troops to invade Cambodia. The three met their troops on December 21, and then returned to Pleiku the following day, the day the attack began. They immediately flew to Ho Chi Minh City for crucial meetings with other leaders, including Veng Khoun, Thang Ngon, Jandrun (Brao, Kapong Commune), Seang Kalpeuhop, Boua Chuong, Lao Nyai, and Kham Len, who had been in Ho Chi Minh City since after the event at Snoul.[78] Soy Keo left Ho Chi Minh City on January 6, 1979, and arrived in Phnom Penh the next day.[79] Bou Thang and the other members of the Central Committee traveled directly to Phnom Penh but did not get there until mid-January.[80]

The senior Brao military leaders actually involved in the attack were Kham Chan, responsible for policy and the deputy chief of the rebel army, and Kham Phai, the deputy responsible for military affairs. Thao Sim was chief of staff. However, Kham Phai acknowledged that, "The

Vietnamese led the attack. The Cambodians did not lead themselves."[81] He claimed that he was personally guarded by thirty Vietnamese soldiers, including a radio man. They also had a vehicle.[82]

When the actual penetration of Cambodia began, the Vietnamese 5th and 578th Divisions became especially important. The UFNSK's Battalion 2, destined for Preah Vihear, followed Vietnamese forces from the 5th Division into Cambodia via Route 19 (now Route 78), which crosses through Ratanakiri's present-day O Yadao District. Traveling by vehicle, the military moved farther west. The Khmer Rouge initially put up stiff resistance against PAVN's blitzkrieg attack, although they were quickly overwhelmed and forced to gradually retreat. They planted landmines as they moved back, and also unsuccessfully tried to flank the incoming PAVN forces from both sides. Two Khmer Rouge soldiers hiding in trees used B-40 (RPG-2) and B-41 (RPG-7) anti-tank weapons to destroy two PAVN tanks before they were shot dead. However, the Vietnamese forces continued to move forward (Hồng 2004), with Vietnamese snipers playing an important role in protecting them.[83]

According to one Brao informant, ten Vietnamese soldiers were assigned to protect each Brao soldier. The Vietnamese believed that they could afford to lose lives, but there were much fewer Brao, and they were told that they would be needed once the Khmer Rouge had been driven from power.[84] Vũ (1979) also reported that during the offensive into Cambodia, special efforts were made to avoid putting UFNSK units into places where there was fierce fighting, to prevent the Cambodians from suffering casualties.

By December 25, PAVN forces were able to punch a hole between the Khmer Rouge's defending 801st and 920th Divisions, and before long the advancing forces had liberated Bokeo City along Route 19. The Khmer Rouge's 920th Division pulled back, and soon after, PAVN's 31st Regiment overran the Khmer Rouge's 801st Division's headquarters at Voeunsai. By the end of December, the Khmer Rouge's 801st and 920th Divisions had sustained some losses, and most of Ratanakiri was under PAVN control. However, Khmer Rouge losses were not as great as PAVN hoped for, as the Khmer Rouge decided to adopt a strategy of "strategic withdrawal," which resulted in only a relatively small number of Khmer Rouge soldiers being killed during attacks (Hồng 2004).

UFNSK's Battalion 2, which had avoided fierce fighting by coming in behind PAVN troops, reached Stung Treng after it was taken by PAVN forces on January 1 (Pribbenow 2006), and by January 4, the northeast had been largely liberated (Bou Thang 1993). Once in Stung Treng, Battalion 2 continued on to Preah Vihear under Kham Phai's command.[85] Veng Khoun would arrive sometime later to become the chairman of the Preah Vihear Provincial People's Revolutionary Committee and later secretary of the provincial People's Committee.[86]

Meanwhile, on December 29, Battalions 3 and 4 entered Cambodia by vehicle via Route 19. Kham Chan and Kham Sanit traveled with those two battalions.[87] Those assigned to work in Ratanakiri Province arrived at Voeunsai on December 30, and the unit assigned to Stung Treng arrived soon after. As Dop Khamchoeung explained, "It only took us two days to reach Stung Treng from the Vietnam-Cambodia border."[88]

Meanwhile, UFNSK's Battalion 1 had left Gia Poc to prepare to enter Mondulkiri on December 18, just three days after Heng Khamvan had returned from engaging in political meetings related to the UFNSK in Ho Chi Minh City.[89] He was initially supposed to come into Stung Treng, but because he could speak Vietnamese better than many other military leaders, it was decided at the last minute that he should enter into Mondulkiri instead. He claimed that these sorts of last minute changes occurred regularly.[90] Heng Khamvan led the group as one of the division leaders. Yat Bleo was the head of political affairs for the battalion, while Kham Sana (Kreung, Phak Nam Village) was responsible for military strategy. Kavet La-In (Kreung, Khuan Village) and Kham Suk were other soldiers in the group. Kham Loeua also traveled with Khamvan's battalion and was responsible for logistical supplies.[91] He would later be appointed as head of the Education Department of Mondulkiri Province.[92]

This group did not have it as easy as the other three battalions and did not travel into Cambodia by vehicle. Instead, they were only transported by vehicle to near the border and then they had to cross the Srepok River and enter Cambodia at Dak Dam by foot. From there, they had to continue by foot because there were no roads on the Cambodian side of the border.[93] However, Vietnamese forces went in front so the Cambodians were protected. They were commanded by Colonel "Châu Khải Định" (pseudonym), the military commander of Daklak Province, and a special emissary from Military Region 5. PAVN's 250th Infantry Regiment (minus 2nd Battalion), 142nd Regiment (minus 5th Battalion), 407th Sapper Battalion (minus one company) and independent 83rd Infantry Battalion were involved in the attack.[94] Some Vietnamese paratroopers were parachuted into part of Mondulkiri.[95]

Five hundred and sixty Vietnamese soldiers[96] reportedly traveled by foot with 120 UFNSK soldiers.[97] The Cambodians reportedly only had fifty guns between them. The group walked thirteen days until January 2, 1979, when they reached Kaoh Nheaek, in Mondulkiri Province. It had been emptied of people by the time they arrived.[98] Even a couple days later, they did not know where the Khmer Rouge had retreated to.[99] Although UFNSK forces did not suffer any casualties on their way to Kaoh Nheaek, as ten Vietnamese soldiers were assigned to protect each Cambodian soldier traveling with them, many Vietnamese soldiers stepped on mines and were killed or lost limbs on the way. When they first entered Cambodia from Vietnam, they had to pass over a four-kilometer-wide mine field. Other Vietnamese soldiers were frequently attacked as they traveled in guerrilla-like small groups under the command of the Khmer Rouge's 920th Division. Many Khmer Rouge soldiers also died during this fighting.[100]

According to a former Vietnamese soldier in Regiment 250th, on January 3, after they had entered an empty Kaoh Nheaek, they saw an old man waving his arms back and forth above his head in the distance. All Vietnamese units moved into their fighting positions, fearful that it could be a trap. The Vietnamese sent a Cambodian specialist [advisor] out to talk with him. The specialist learned that the civilians were hiding in the treeline of the forest, and he sent the old man back to call them to come back into the town. Soon the civilians had returned. However, the Vietnamese soldier wrote, "For some reason I don't understand, few of the residents of the town were able to speak Khmer. They all spoke Lao."[101] Indeed, the people of Kaoh Nheaek primarily spoke Lao.

According to Heng Khamvan, the first thing that needed to be done in Mondulkiri after the Khmer Rouge had retreated, the civilians had returned, and the security situation had become stable, was to begin releasing information to the general population about the eleven point plan that had been announced in Snoul on December 2.[102]

The Khmer Rouge tried to claim (*Phnom Penh Domestic Service* 1978a), including via the Chinese media (NCNA 1978), that they had inflicted a heavy blow to the invading Vietnamese forces, including killing or wounding 600 along Route 19 in O Yadao, and another 400 along Route 7 north of Snoul, in Kratie Province, causing the Vietnamese to retreat in disarray. It would, however, soon become obvious that nothing of the sort had actually occurred, although there were certainly some Vietnamese casualties during the initial attack. Not surprisingly, they also condemned the "Vietnamese aggression" in a letter sent to the United Nations Security Council on December 31, 1978 (*Xinhua* 1979a).

By January 7, the Vietnamese had full control of Phnom Penh (Chanda 1986; Pribbenow 2006), and by January 17, all the provincial and district towns in Cambodia were under Vietnamese/UFNSK control (Liên 2013). Chanda (1986) reported that some Vietnamese units entered Cambodia from Laos, and the Khmer Rouge also reported this to be the case (VODK 1979c, 1979d). However, my interviews, as well as the work done by Merle Pribbenow (2006), suggest that this was not the case. Once PAVN had control of Phnom Penh and most of the rest of Cambodia, Lê Đức Anh became the commander of the Ministry of Defense Forward Headquarters in Cambodia (Institute of Military History 2010).

Mopping Up Operations and Bringing the People Back from the Forest

After taking control of all the main towns and cities, the Vietnamese continued to hunt for Khmer Rouge forces in mopping up operations. They reportedly had informants in the Khmer Rouge's 920th Division. Vietnamese pursued Khmer Rouge forces after withdrawing from Lumphat town, and after crawling up a hill all night, the Vietnamese were finally able to attack the Khmer Rouge early the next morning. After thirty minutes of heavy fighting, however, the main Khmer Rouge force retreated, leaving thirty-five child soldiers to defend the position with eighteen medium-sized machine guns. But the morale of the remaining Khmer Rouge soldiers was low, and the position was soon taken, with three Vietnamese soldiers killed and five wounded.[103]

Then on January 27, 1979, PAVN's 812th Regiment/309th Division attacked the Khmer Rouge's stronghold at Prey Khieou, which was thirty kilometers from Kaoh Nheaek. Despite having a hard time finding water on the way, and having to filter muddy and bad smelling water through their scarves to get anything to drink, the Vietnamese eventually made it to their target. The attack occurred on the first day of the Vietnamese New Year, *Tet*, and at 6:00 am in the morning all the heavy weapons in each PAVN battalion simultaneously opened fire. As one former Vietnamese soldier involved in the attack put it, the attack occurred "to celebrate the arrival of the Year of the Goat." Fierce fighting continued for four days. The conditions were difficult, and Vietnamese food rations were insufficient, causing considerable hunger during the fighting. One soldier reported that he was so hungry that he was willing to eat uncooked rice. Finally, the fighting ended when return fire stopped coming from enemy positions. The Khmer Rouge had retreated, but they left a large amount of weapons and munitions. Vietnamese forces then continued to the Chbar area where they intended to attack FULRO's 91st Regiment. However, by the time they reached there at the end of February, the FULRO forces had retreated, although the Vietnamese were able to recover a large quantity of elephant tusks, which the Vietnamese military loaded onto two trucks and took away.[104] Similar operations were happening in various parts of northeastern Cambodia. The Voice of Democratic Kampuchea (VODK) (1979b) tried to claim that the Khmer Rouge was making military gains, such as reporting in early February that sixteen T-54 Vietnamese tanks had been wiped out near Banlung, Ratanakiri, with all those in the tanks perishing, but such reports were simply not credible.

As the Vietnamese pushed forward, the Khmer Rouge had little choice but to retreat toward the border with Thailand. Some also fled into Laos. The Khmer Rouge leaders wanted to take as many civilians with them as possible, and told the people that the Vietnamese would kill everyone who remained, so most were fearful and either voluntarily fled or were forced to flee with the Khmer Rouge (Vickery 1984). The reality was that the Vietnamese were not doing anything like that. They had a political agenda, and they did not want to scare people away from coming out of the forest and giving up. However, at least initially, the people did not know that. One ethnic Lao man who was in Talao Commune (presently in Andong Meas District) when the Vietnamese entered Cambodia, explained that he was told by the Khmer Rouge leaders of his cooperative that if they were caught, the Vietnamese would kill them. The local Khmer Rouge leaders also told the villagers that if the Vietnamese caught them, they would rape their wives and tie them up to watch.[105]

In another case, when the Vietnamese arrived, an ethnic Lao man from Voeunsai District initially fled to the forests with the Khmer Rouge. He spent twenty days hiding in the forest close to Kamen Village, which is itself near the Vietnam border. He finally, however, gave up to the Vietnamese. What prompted him to do so was that his wife had recently given birth to a baby, and they were suffering from a lack of food. Although the Khmer Rouge also told him that the Vietnamese would kill him if he gave up, he finally decided that he would die of starvation if he did not surrender. Therefore, he walked out of the forest to give up to the Vietnamese with 150 other villagers from Voeunsai. The villagers were relieved when they realized that the Vietnamese had no intention of killing them.[106]

Another man in Ratanakiri Province told me that when the Vietnamese entered Cambodia, he fled to the forest with many others. They initially lived off of wild tubers, but after six months there was little to eat, so he decided to try to steal some cultivated cassava from someone's swidden field. However, he was caught and once he realized that he was not going to be killed as the Khmer Rouge claimed, he freely gave himself up. Once the informant and others had surrendered, they were given some land to cultivate, and during the first year after the Khmer Rouge had left the area, his group began cultivating lowland wet rice. Because they did not have any draft animals or other machinery, they did the very laborious work of tilling the fields using hand spades. Many local level Vietnamese soldiers stayed with them to provide security.[107]

Ho Hong, who is ethnic Khmer but married to an ethnic Lao woman, explained that in 1979 he fled with the Khmer Rouge to the end of the Khampha and Trabok streams, near the border with Laos, in what is now northern Taveng District. However, when the Khmer Rouge leaders of the 801st Division decided to travel to the Thai border in 1981, he decided not to go with them, as they said that no children could make the trip, in case they made noise on the way. In addition, the Khmer Rouge planned to swim across the Mekong River in Khong District, Champasak Province, southern Laos, and children would not be able to cross the river. He was unwilling to abandon his small child, as the Khmer Rouge leaders urged him to do.[108] Later in 1981, after most of the Khmer Rouge soldiers had moved to the Thai border, Ho Hong determined that his wife's relatives were living in Siempang District, in Stung Treng Province, so he brought his family there to give up in 1982.[109]

The Aftermath

The Cambodians, including the Brao, played a relatively insignificant role in the offensive that forced the Khmer Rouge from power. No Brao I have met refutes this. However, Bou Thang stressed, when interviewed in early 2017, that there was not a single ethnic Khmer soldier, not even one, involved in the "liberation" of northeastern Cambodia. Khang Sarin was the only Khmer involved in supporting the soldiers from the northeast, but he was just a translator at the time (Son 2016) and did not participate in the fighting. Bou Thang exclaimed, "Some Khmers claim that ethnic Khmers fought to liberate the northeast, but that is not true."[110] His comments were significant, as it indicates how many minorities view this important history.

In the end, only a small number of Brao soldiers were reportedly killed in the attack. According to one source, only one was killed, and that was because a Khmer Rouge unit that was already believed to have been disabled was able to launch a surprise attack against vehicles and troops following the first wave of attacks into Cambodia.[111] Another source claimed that three UFNSK soldiers were killed once they entered the northeast; one from being shot by a Khmer Rouge sniper and two others from stepping on landmines.[112] In addition, Phuong, one of the Vietnamese provincial committee members from Galai-Kontum Province, was ambushed and killed by remnants of the Khmer Rouge on the Bokham–Bokeo Road, as he was traveling from Vietnam to a victory celebration in Ratanakiri. Eleven people were killed in the ambush, with only three surviving.[113]

Deth (2014) reported that the UFNSK contributed 20,000 troops, and Rathie (2006) claimed that there were 20,000 to 30,000 UFNSK troops in total. It seems likely, however, that the actual number was greatly inflated for propaganda purposes. The Vietnamese wanted to gain political legitimacy for the offensive by emphasizing the role of Cambodians. On the other hand, there were apparently at least 150,000 Vietnamese troops involved in the attack (Pribbenow 2006; Gottesman 2002), which is 50,000 more than Ea Meng-Try (1981), Rathie (2006), and Pao-Min (1985) reported. This is probably more than twice as many soldiers as the Khmer Rouge had to defend against the attack.[114]

China was shocked by the rapid success of PAVN in at least initially defeating the Khmer Rouge, but they were not about to allow Vietnam to simply get away with taking down their most important ally in the region and making them look weak. Therefore, on February 16 to 17, 1979, China launched its own surprise one-month punitive invasion into Vietnam (Pao-Min 1985). The Chinese wanted to teach Vietnam "an appropriate limited lesson" (Kamm 1998, 156), and "destroy the myth that Vietnam is the third largest power and therefore could do anything it wants" (Pao-Min 1985, 88). According to Pribbenow (2006), 600,000 Chinese soldiers crossed into Vietnam. But they faced stiff resistance from PAVN, and ultimately both sides suffered heavy losses before the Chinese withdrew a month later (Chanda 1986; Pribbenow 2006). More importantly for this book, the Chinese invasion into Vietnam does not appear to have significantly altered Vietnam's objectives and work in Cambodia.

After the Vietnamese arrived in Phnom Penh, there were two opinions within the Vietnamese leadership as to how to proceed. Some felt that the Vietnamese should only spend a relatively short period of time in Cambodia, and then hand power over to their Cambodian allies before returning to Vietnam. Ngo Dien confirmed this, reporting that when he first arrived in Phnom Penh in 1979, Lê Đức Thọ told him, "We will strive to do our best for a while, perhaps three to six months, and then turn the country over to our [Cambodian] allies" (Huy Đức 2012a, 370). However, another group felt that withdrawing from Cambodia prematurely would only allow the Khmer Rouge to return to power, because the Khmer Rouge had been defeated but not crushed. Lê Đức Anh led that camp. As history has now shown, Lê Đức Anh's view would ultimately prevail (Anh 2015).

Conclusion

A series of events between 1975 and 1978 led to the Vietnamese attack on Cambodia in late 1978, beginning with vicious Khmer Rouge attacks across the border into Vietnam. Indeed, these attacks started almost immediately after Phnom Penh fell to the Khmer Rouge in April 1975. Inspired by Sarin Chhak's ideas from *Les Frontières du Cambodge* (1966) about Cambodia's "lost territories," the Khmer Rouge leaders were focused on killing the Vietnamese little-by-little, with the intention of eventually wiping them out and gaining control of the territory that now encompasses southern Vietnam or Kampuchea Kraom. Initially, the Khmer Rouge leadership was largely cordial with the Vietnamese, claiming that the border attacks were simply mistakes made by local military leaders stationed along the border, but over time it became increasingly clear that the border attacks were not simply a series of misunderstandings, but actually a plan to wage a slow but brutal border war against Pol Pot's most hated enemy, the Vietnamese.

While the border situation was becoming increasingly tense, the geopolitical circumstances in the region were also intensifying, with relations between the People's Republic of China and the SRV rapidly deteriorating for various reasons. The global rift between China and the Soviet Union had widened, with the two communist superpowers becoming increasingly hostile toward each other. With the Vietnamese aligning itself with the Soviet Union and the Khmer Rouge siding with the Chinese, the border conflict between Vietnam and Cambodia increasingly felt like a proxy for the broader geopolitical circumstances that were dividing the communist world, even if tensions were related to much more than that and had much deeper roots. The leaders of the People's Republic of China became especially enraged when the Vietnamese started mistreating the ethnic Chinese population in southern Vietnam, while Vietnam was unhappy when China increased the amount of military aid it was providing to the Khmer Rouge.

As conflict along the border escalated, the Vietnamese became increasingly inpatient, even though they were weary of war and wanted to avoid full tilt conflict with the Khmer Rouge because the American war had only ended a few years earlier, and Vietnam had only recently been reunited and was weary of conflict. Finally, in 1977, after enduring over two years of borderland massacres of Vietnamese communities inside Vietnam at the hands of the Khmer Rouge, the Vietnamese began to realize that resolving the conflict with the Khmer Rouge peacefully was not likely to be possible. At that point they started to seriously consider how to overthrow the Khmer Rouge. However, there were not many dissidents in Cambodia for them to support, and so in mid-1977, they began politically organizing and militarily training the northeastern Cambodians based at Gia Poc, with the idea that they could play a role in eventually bringing down the Khmer Rouge. However, the Vietnamese still had some hope that full-scale war could be averted, but finally, in 1978, the situation escalated even further, and a military build-up on both sides of the border intensified. The training and arming of the northeasterners also rapidly picked up pace, as did political organizing, including the establishment of the UFNSK in late 1978, bringing the ethnic minority refugees from the northeast together with ethnic Khmer refugees to the south. Efforts were also made to recruit Brao Cambodians in southern Laos to join the UFNSK.

Finally, the campaign began on December 22, 1978. Vietnam's PAVN was the main force involved in the offensive against the Khmer Rouge. While the UFNSK were also involved in the attack, they played a very minor role, and furthermore, the Vietnamese went to considerable efforts to prevent the Cambodians from suffering casualties, as they would be needed once the Khmer Rouge was ousted from power. It appears that the strength of the UFNSK was greatly exaggerated, as the Vietnamese wanted to reduce international criticism against themselves by making it look like the Cambodians had risen up against the Khmer Rouge themselves, including groups allegedly based in Cambodia. In any case, once the attack began, the Khmer Rouge found themselves greatly outgunned and outnumbered, and despite putting up strong resistance, they were no match for the battle-hardened and better equipped Vietnamese, and the Khmer Rouge were soon defeated and forced to scatter and retreat, before eventually regrouping along the Thai border. However, the Khmer Rouge were not totally devastated. Instead, they were intent on biding their time to be able to fight another day.

We now turn to Part 2 of this book, considering how the northeastern Cambodian provinces of Ratanakiri, Stung Treng, Mondulkiri, and Preah Vihear were reorganized and governed following the defeat of the Khmer Rouge in early 1979, and particularly how so many seemingly underqualified Brao and other former northeastern Cambodian refugees from Vietnam and Laos were catapulted to important positions of power in the new PRK government and military. Indeed, the ethnic minorities from northeastern Cambodia who had fled to Vietnam and Laos in the mid-1970s had one crucial quality that helped them rise to power: because they had spent a number of years as anti-Khmer Rouge refugees in Vietnam and Laos, and they had a history of being pro-Vietnamese communists, so they could be trusted in ways that the Cambodians who stayed in Cambodia during the late 1970s could not. For those who returned to Cambodia from Vietnam and Laos, it was the beginning of their golden age, a time when they had more power in government than any ethnic minorities in Cambodia ever had before.

Bou Thang and Vietnamese advisor, Thanh, at Gia Poc, 1977 (Bou Thang)

Bou Thang at Gia Poc calling for northeasterners to join the resistance against the Khmer Rouge, 1977 (Bou Thang)

Mainly Brao young men doing military training at Division 578, Gia Poc, 1977 (Bou Thang)

Bun Mi and Thanh Van at Danang hospital in Vietnam, 1978 (Bou Thang)

Eighteen people from northeastern Cambodia at first party meeting on October 10, 1978 (Bou Thang)

Thanh Van, Soy Keo, Lang from Taveng, Bun Mi, and a Vietnamese, Bou Thang, in Pleiku before Snoul event, 1978 (Bou Thang)

Bou Thang visiting Pong Village, Voeunsai, Ratanakiri, October 1979 (Bou Thang)

Phnom Penh PRK leaders Heng Samrin, Chea Sim, Bou Thang, Kham Chan, Pen Sovan, Chan Si, and Mat Ly (next to Bou Thang) in Phnom Penh, 1981 (Bou Thang)

Soy Keo hugging Vietnamese in Gialai-Kontum Province, 1982–83 (Soy Keo)

Reko (ethnic Lao from Stung Treng), Kham Toeung, Glawng, Veng Khoun, Ya Yang, Khmer, Ya Ee, and Jadawng (daughter of Veng Khoun) in Stung Treng, 1984 (Kham Toeung)

Kalang, Kham Sai, Ma Ranchai, Kham Len, Kham Kheoun, and Boua Chuong, Khmer soldiers sitting, on study trip to Gialai-Kontum Province, Vietnam (Kham Len)

Bou Thang, Soviet Union military leaders, and translator on a walk, Moscow, 1985 (Bou Thang)

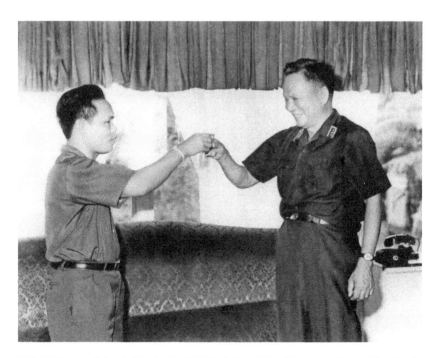

Chief Vietnam advisor in Cambodia, Lê Đức Anh, and Bou Thang meeting in Hanoi, 1985 (Bou Thang)

Kham Len standing next to Gialai-Kontum Province General-Secretary and Attapeu Governor, Pheo Saiyavong (Kham Len)

Bou Thang, Osakanh Thammatheva (Minister in Laos, originally from Ratanakiri Province), and Nguyễn Quyết (Vietnamese), Vientiane, 1988 (Bou Thang)

Division 315 Pen Sovan visits in Ratanakiri, with Boua Chuong wearing white shirt behind, 1981 (Kham Len)

PRAK Soldiers in O Chum District, Ratanakiri Province, receiving clothes (Kham Len)

Bou Thang, Ky (Brao), and unidentified Vietnamese teacher at Gia Poc, 1978 (Bou Thang)

Eating food at Khamphan Thivong's house in Stung Treng (with Thang Bai), 1980 (Khamphan Thivong)

Bou Thang, Tea Banh, and Phạm Văn Đồng (*from left to right*), Hanoi, Vietnam, 1987 (Bou Thang)

Kham Khoeun toasting Gialai-Kontum Province counterpart during trip to Vietnam (Kham Len)

Bou Thang visiting Brao people in Taveng District, Ratanakiri Province, 1983 (Bou Thang; an altered version of this photo appears on the cover of this book)

PART 2

Organizing Post–Khmer Rouge
Northeastern Cambodia
and the Rise of the Brao

Having explained the role of the Brao and other northeastern minorities in the organization of the UFNSK and the ouster of the Khmer Rouge from power, we now turn to considering how the Vietnamese and their Brao and other ethnic minority allies from northeastern Cambodia initially went about governing the PRK government in early 1979, particularly in the northeastern part of the country. Indeed, the new government faced many challenges. On the one hand, they desperately needed qualified people to help run the government, but on the other, they were wary of hiring people who might be Khmer Rouge spies and infiltrators. Therefore, large numbers of Brao and other ethnic minorities who had previously been refugees in Vietnam and Laos but had little formal education were elevated to senior positions in the central government, and especially in the northeastern provinces of Ratanakiri, Stung Treng, Mondulkiri, and Preah Vihear. They were valued not because they were highly skilled, but because they could be trusted by the Vietnamese since they had already proven their opposition to the Khmer Rouge.

Some of the important challenges that affected the new government included preventing people from taking revenge against Khmer Rouge leaders held responsible for the deaths of family members and other atrocities. The PRK policy was deemed politically crucial, as the government wanted to convince the remaining Khmer Rouge in the forests to surrender. However, they realized that few would come in if they believed that revenge would be taken against them. Indeed, one of the biggest challenges facing the new government was how to convince those still hiding in the forests to give themselves up.

The demise of the key Brao political leader, Bun Mi, was significant. Bun Mi's condition had been in decline for some years already, as Bun Mi had become increasing mentally unstable when in Vietnam, and when he was staying in Phnom Penh during the early days of the PRK. Thus, the leadership of the northeast transitioned from Bun Mi to Bou Thang, who became the paramount ethnic minority from Cambodia.

Another important issue addressed in this chapter relates to misinformation spread about famine in northeastern Cambodia soon after the Khmer Rouge was ousted from power. Indeed, northeastern Cambodia did not face nearly as severe food security problems as some outsiders reported in 1979 and the early 1980s.

Taking Control

On January 5 to 7, 1979, at the same time as Vietnamese PAVN troops were fighting their way toward and taking control of Phnom Penh, the third Communist Party of Kampuchea Congress was being convened in Ho Chi Minh City (Liên 2013). Slocomb (2003) reported that Phnom Penh was taken so quickly that developments in Cambodia interrupted the congress. Indeed, some people departed from it early to quickly travel to Phnom Penh, including Soy Keo, who departed on January 6.[1] During the congress, sixty-two original members of the previous Cambodia communist parties were recognized as key figures within the new organization, the existence of which was kept secret until it came out as the Revolutionary People's Party in May 1981.[2] Crucially, eighteen of the sixty-two were ethnic minorities from northeastern Cambodia.[3] Prior to the congress, the Vietnamese consulted with Bou Thang, Soy Keo, and Bun Mi, who identified the eighteen. The Vietnamese apparently did not decide who would be admitted into the party. According to Bou Thang, "It was a joint decision."[4] Both Bou Thang[5] and Slocomb (2003) reported that the sixty-two represented the over 200 party members at the time.[6] Bun Mi had always been the key northeastern leader of the UFNSK, but Bou Thang became the northeast representative in the central committee, as by that time Bun Mi was clearly mentally unstable and his condition could no longer be hidden (see, also, later in the chapter).[7] Seven people were initially appointed to the party's central committee: Pen Sovan, Chea Sim, Heng Samrin, Hun Sen, Bou Thang, Chan Kary, and Van Son.[8]

On January 8, the eight-member People's Revolutionary Council of Kampuchea was elected to form the publicly proclaimed provisional government, including Heng Samrin as president; Pen Sovan as vice-president in charge of national defense; Chea Sim as interior minister; Hun Sen as minister of foreign affairs; Keo Chanda as minister of information, press, and culture; Mok Sakun as minister of economy and living conditions; Nu Beng as minister of health and social affairs; and Chan Ven as minister of education (Slocomb 2003; Fawthrop and Jarvis 2004).

Once PAVN—rhetorically on behalf of the UFNSK—had gained control over most of Cambodia, including the capital city of Phnom Penh, on January 10, 1979, UFNSK became an adjunct to the secret Communist Party and the public PRK government. However, as Loschman (2006–2007, 98) has accurately pointed out, "The People's Republic of Kampuchea found itself largely dependent on Vietnam from the very hour of its birth." Indeed, it would be accurate to even go as far as to say that the PRK depended on the Vietnamese from when it was still in the womb.

The People's Republic of Kampuchea

By February 1979, the central committee of the party included Pen Sovan as secretary; Heng Samrin as chairman of the People's Revolutionary Council of Kampuchea and president of the front; Chea Sim as vice-president of the front and minister of interior; Van Son as secretary of the Phnom Penh Party Committee; Bou Thang as chairman of the propaganda and education commission; Hun Sen as minister of foreign affairs and member of the front; and Chan Kary as chair of the monitoring committee (Slocomb 2003).

On September 29 to 30, 1979, the front central committee was expanded to thirty-five members, with the top three positions still held by former east zone Khmer Rouge: Heng Samrin, Chea Sim, and Mat Ly (Vickery 1984). Bun Mi was still a member of this central committee (Carney 1986). The rather ad hoc People's Revolutionary Council of Kampuchea was, however, replaced in June 1981, by a seven-person state council led by Heng Samrin, and a seventeen-member council of ministers headed up by Pen Sovan (Vickery 1984; Heng 2018). Bun Mi was not included in the latter line-up, but Bou Thang was.

Fawthrop and Jarvis (2004) reported that three groups came together to form the new government: 1) the former members of the Communist Party of Kampuchea who had gone to Vietnam after the Geneva Accords of 1954—the Khmer Hanoi, 2) those without previous communist or revolutionary experience, and 3) Khmer Rouge dissidents who had defected in 1977 and 1978. However, Fawthrop and Jarvis, like many other observers, failed to recognize that a key group of leaders in the new government were ethnic minority Khmer Rouge dissidents from the northeast.

The Vietnamese and their Cambodian allies battled the armed forces of the government of Democratic Kampuchea, a loose coalition made up of the Khmer Rouge's National Army of Democratic Kampuchea (NADK),[9] which was established in late 1979 with Pol Pot as its chairman;[10] the Sihanouk-supported National Army of Sihanouk; and Son Sann's Khmer People's National Liberation Front (KPNLF). The government of Democratic Kampuchea fiercely opposed Vietnam and the Vietnam-backed government in Phnom Penh (Conboy 2013; Bekaert 1997; Gottesman 2002; Chanda 1986). In northeastern Cambodia, however, the National Army of Sihanouk and KPNLF were virtually absent. Only the NADK, or the Khmer Rouge, which were sometimes referred to as "bandits" by the PRK government, posed any real threat. However, the security situation varied considerably from place to place and from time to time.

On May 1, 1981, a 117-member National Assembly was "elected,"[11] for the first time in the PRK period, from 148 candidates nationally (Vickery 1984). There were three people elected in Ratanakiri: Nu Beng (ethnic Lao), Kham Len (Lun), and Ms. Lak On (Khmer), while Bui Yung (Jarai) was a candidate but was not elected. Bou Thang (Tampuon/ Lao), Veng Khoun (Brao), and Sok Somaing (Khmer) were elected for Preah Vihear. There were only two members elected for the smaller Mondulkiri: Thang Ngon (Brao) and Chan Yeun (Bunong). In Stung Treng, Thang Bai (Tampuon) and Bun Koeung (ethnic Lao) were elected. Soy Keo was also elected as a representative of Kratie Province (*Phnom Penh Domestic Service* 1981a, 1981b).

Although only ten of the 117 seats in the National Assembly were designated for the four northeastern provinces, the People's Revolutionary Party of Kampuchea's (PRPK) influence in the northeast was nonetheless stronger than in most other regions. To make this point, Bou Thang told me that some provinces had just one party member in 1981,[12] and party influence was especially lower at the local levels in various parts of the country (Vickery 1984). Prior to the public Fourth National Party Congress, which was held from May 26 to 29, 1981, with Vietnamese support (Dũng 1995), the secretaries of the provincial party committees of Preah Vihear, Mondulkiri, Stung Treng, and Ratanakiri—Veng Khoun, Thang Ngon, Kham Len, and Thang Bai respectively—all expressed their strong support. Veng Khoun was reported as stating, "The Pol Pot-Ieng Sary-Khieu Samphan clique's party called itself Marxist-Leninist to fool the people but, under Beijing's inspiration, it applied a policy of genocide and destruction in all domains" (*Phnom Penh SPK* 1981a). Thang Bai was also reported as stating that, "the minorities of Stung Treng have obtained successes in all domains" (*Phnom Penh SPK* 1981a).

Not surprisingly, the PRK government mainly chose people they trusted to fill positions in the new administration, especially from the ranks of those who had been refugees in Vietnam and Laos during the latter part of the Khmer Rouge period. As Gottesman (2002, 55) wrote, "The Vietnamese tended to prefer Cambodians who had been refugees in Vietnam or who spoke Vietnamese." The Vietnamese, like the Khmer Rouge before them, also tended to be more sympathetic to rural dwellers as compared to city people (Gottesman 2002). This favored the ethnic minorities from the northeast. As one Brao leader who fled to Vietnam in 1973 put it, "The government got Brao to take high positions in the government after 1979 because they [the Vietnamese] didn't trust people who had worked with the Khmer Rouge."[13]

According to Dam Chanty (ethnic Lao/Tampuon, Talao Village), the future head of the Department of Women's Affairs in Ratanakiri Province,[14] after the establishment of the PRK government, it was officially prohibited to distinguish between those who had been in Vietnam and Laos during the Khmer Rouge period and those who had remained in Cambodia.[15] Nonetheless, there is no doubt that the Vietnamese did favor those they knew well and had worked with, and as a result, many ethnic minorities from the northeast gained important positions in the new government, including the Brao who came to dominate the PRK government in the northeast. Much needed to be done to build up the PRPK, but in the meantime, with so few members, almost all party members were expected to take on significant roles in the new government, even those who were not particularly competent (Kamm 1998). In fact, only four or five people in the original group of party members were apparently not selected to fill senior positions in the new PRK government.[16]

The Vietnamese generally preferred to appoint educated Khmers to the central government, provided that they were believed to not be sympathetic to the Khmer Rouge (Vickery 1984). Some minorities from the northeast did, however, gain important central-level positions. According to Bou Thang, his specific responsibilities during the PRK period included developing the northeast part of the country, convincing the remaining Khmer Rouge to surrender, and generally improving the efficiency of the government.[17] Bou Thang was clearly the most important representative of the northeast. Not surprisingly, he became well-known for controlling the appointments of local leaders in the northeast (Gottesman 2002).

Bou Thang developed his own ideas about how to economically develop the northeast. He admitted to me, in 2017, that he had to overcome various obstacles. For example, some people suspected that he was actually ethnically Vietnamese, even though that is not the case.[18] This was probably because he is light skinned and speaks Khmer with an accent. In fact, according to him, he only started learning to speak Khmer when he was about twenty years old.[19]

Other key figures from the northeast who gained positions in the post–Khmer Rouge central government included the former Khmer Hanoi Nu Beng,[20] who was appointed as minister of health and social welfare in 1979. In the military, Di Phin (ethnic Lao, Siempang District) would rise up to become deputy minister of defense in charge of military administration. Other northeasterners in the military included Bun Kang and Cheng Thone (Kreung, Khuan Village), who became deputies under Di Phin. Kham Chan became deputy minister of defense responsible for politics. He worked directly under Bou Thang. Heng Khamvan was made the head of the military's Statistics Department. He was also put in charge of village-level volunteer forces. Nuan Pak (Kreung, O Chum District) became a central-level colonel in the army.[21] He was also the head of the Ratanakiri military in around 1987, and he became the deputy chief of the northeastern military region betweem around 1988 and 1989.[22] Bou Thang is, however, rather critical of Nuan Pak, claiming that he did not work regularly and was too interested in making money.

He attributed these circumstances to the fact that he had a greedy ethnic Khmer wife,[23] indicating how important an ethnic lens was. Other people who were given positions in the central military included Khem Thatda (ethnic Lao, Pong Village), who was also a deputy under Di Phin, responsible for looking after weapons. Puay Nuchan (ethnic Lao, Kalan Village) was given a position in the military looking after armaments, but he only held it for a couple of years before returning to his village in Ratanakiri Province.[24] Bou Thang's brother, Bou Lam, also held a logistics position in the army for a number of years in Phnom Penh before returning to Ratanakiri.[25] He is presently the member of parliament for Ratanakiri Province. Bou Thang emphasized that most of the minorities from the northeast who worked for the central government were in the military. As he put it, "The minorities controlled the military back then."[26] Indeed, Michael Victory (2010) has noted that up to 1985, the PRK military was dominated by northeasterners and men who had previously worked extensively with the Vietnamese. According to Bou Thang, at the time, the Khmer people in the PRK did not like the fact that ethnic minorities dominated the military, but the Vietnamese protected them. He noted that once the Vietnamese were gone, most northeasterners lost their positions,[27] an important point that I will return to later.

Although the Vietnamese had considerable power, they often worked with and through Cambodian leaders. These collaborations resulted in the Vietnamese sometimes appearing to have less power than they actually had. Indeed, that was the impression they hoped the Cambodian public would gain.

Who Are Our Friends?

Generally speaking, one of the biggest challenges the new PRK government faced was identifying qualified people to work as government officials. The government had a tricky balancing act to negotiate, as it did not want to hire people who had worked with the Khmer Rouge or who might be Khmer Rouge spies or operatives, but they desperately needed people to help govern the country. In addition, many of the most competent Khmer Rouge had fled when the Vietnamese arrived, and most of the competent people from the former regime had died during Khmer Rouge rule.

In early 1979, the Vietnamese recontacted the Jarai Cambodian refugees at Tang Village. They asked for volunteers to join a group that would work on a six-month mission in Cambodia. Two people agreed to join, Bui Yung and another Jarai named Thai, Bui Yung's nephew. The mission was to support the Vietnamese occupation force by going to villages to identify and arrest those who had killed people during the Khmer Rouge period. Those who had not committed crimes and wanted to work for the new government were, at the same time, targeted to be recruited to join the government, with the idea that if they worked well they could eventually join the party.[28]

From February 15 to 26, a training course was organized in Pleiku, the provincial capital of Gialai-Kontum, in preparation for the mission. It was explained that the new PRK government had low capacity and could not be sure who their enemies and friends were. Therefore, they needed volunteers from Vietnam to help. All sixty-six of the trainees were ethnic Jarai from Vietnam, except for Bui Yung and his nephew, who were Jarai refugees from Cambodia. After the training, all the trainees were given guns: hand guns for the leaders and AK-47s for the others. However, twenty-three of the trainees became afraid soon after and fled rather than go to Cambodia, leaving only the forty-three remaining trainees to continue. They made it to Voeunsai on March 23, and from there they were sent to Jarai villages in Bokeo District, Ratanakiri Province. They basically did their work according to plan, but virtually all the trainees were simply villagers, and so had themselves limited capacity to carry out their duties. In the end, Bui Yung did not continue on with the group. Because he spoke all the local languages of Ratanakiri, as well as Khmer, he was asked to do the same sort of work for six months in other parts of Ratanakiri Province. By September he had traveled to all four of Ratanakiri's districts: Lumphat, Voeunsai, Bokeo, and O Chum. After the work was completed, most of the Jarai from Vietnam returned home, but Bui Yung was asked to stay in Cambodia. He agreed and was made the head of Ratanakiri's Agriculture Department. He was also appointed to the province's newly formed elders committee. Bui Yung was one of the few literate people who the Vietnamese trusted at the time, so he was desperately needed. He would hold those positions for six months, and then on April 12, 1980, he was made head of the province's Commerce Department.[29]

Rebuilding the Northeast

In the northeast of Cambodia, the problem of reconstruction was, at least in some ways, even more problematic than at the central level, as there were few buildings in working condition that the government could immediately occupy. Moreover, there were very few educated people or former officials to drawn from. Therefore, virtually all of the key positions were allocated to those who had fled from Cambodia to Vietnam and Laos in 1973 and 1975, even though few spoke much Khmer, and even fewer had received an even basic formal education. For example, Kham Toeung became vice-chairman of the Stung Treng provincial People's Committee, even though he sometimes required a translator because he was much more fluent in Brao and Lao than Khmer. An ethnic Lao man originally from Khinak, southern Laos, helped translate for him from Khmer to Lao.[30] There were also efforts to convince loyal refugees to return from Laos and Vietnam to work for the new government. For example, in 1980, a small group of Cambodian refugees from Attapeu, in Laos, were recruited to return. They traveled by airplane from Pakse to Ho Chi Minh City. Bunhom Many (ethnic Lao, Pong Village), the future deputy governor of Ratanakiri Province, was among the group.[31]

Prior to entering Cambodia, considerable planning had already occurred in Vietnam, although some of it was rather rushed. In particular, the top leadership in the northeast had already been determined. Indicative of the major positions given to those who had fled from the Khmer Rouge in the northeast, ethnic Brao people were made chairmen and vice-chairmen of provincial People's Committees (governors and vice-governors) and secretaries of all the northeastern provincial Party Committees, including Ratanakiri, Stung Treng, Mondulkiri, and Preah Vihear (US Library of Congress 2006). They were also allocated most other senior military and civilian positions in the northeast.

Considering the low levels of formal education of many government officials in the northeast, including those in senior positions, it was necessary to immediately promote education so as to gradually build up human resources. Solving this problem was not, however, easy. There were no educational facilities in northeastern Cambodia at the time, so many northeasterners were sent, at least for short periods, to study in Vietnam (see chapter 7). However, some potential government officials did not agree to travel far from home to study. For example, one ethnic Lao man from Voeunsai was offered the chance to go to study in Hanoi to become a district chief. He decided not to take up the offer, apparently because he was illiterate and did not want to reveal his weakness.[32]

Ethnic Minorities in Ratanakiri Province

In 1979, Voeunsai became the first capital of Ratanakiri Province during the PRK period (see Figure 2 for post-1979 northeastern Cambodia). Initially, the province had just four administrative units: the chairman of the People's Committee office, the military office, the police office, and the PRPK office.[33] Boua Chuong became the chairman of the provincial People's Committee, and Kham Len became secretary of Ratanakiri's Party Committee. Thao Sim, Thon Thin, and Thao Sin (Brao, Haleum Village) were made the first military leaders in Ratanakiri,[34] and Bun Pan (ethnic Lao, Voeunsai Village), a man who apparently was easily angered, became the police chief of the province. Kreng Siengnoi did not initially have an official position in the government in Voeunsai, as shortly after the new government was established, one person from each province was sent to study in Phnom Penh, and Siengnoi was designated to represent Ratanakiri.[35] Crucially, all the people initially appointed to senior positions in Ratanakiri were ethnic minorities who had fled to Vietnam and Laos in 1973 and 1975.

A key task was building up the PRPK, since it was initially quite weak. In February 1979, thirty people from Ratanakiri were sent to Voeunsai for three months to study about "the nation" and the "morals of the party." Some had come from Vietnam and Laos, while others had spent time in Cambodia during the Khmer Rouge period. Each of those involved in the training were required to drink "sacred water" and take an oath to sacrifice themselves to the country. A bullet and a knife were soaked in the water. This ceremony was apparently specific to northeastern Cambodia,[36] and resembled what had been done in the 1960s during the early years of the revolution.[37] Moreover, this sort of water drinking ceremony occurred during the time of Siamese and Lao control, and then later during the French colonial period (Baird 2008). Those who passed the six-month trial period, and then took the oath of loyalty, were granted full party membership. However, only eight of the thirty were appointed to the PRPK Committee: Thao Jip was initially made the party head for Voeunsai District, although he soon left the position.[38]

Later in 1979, the Ratanakiri provincial committee was expanded, with Boua Chuong and Kham Len remaining chairman of the province's People's Committee and secretary of the province's Party Committee respectively. Their deputies were Kreng Siengnoi, who was made PRPK deputy secretary of the province's Party Committee in charge of organization, Bui Yung, who was responsible for commerce, and Seang Kalpeuhop (Kreung, Phak Nam Village), who was put in charge of managing the rubber plantations in the province. Thao Sim was made head of the provincial military, with Thon Thin responsible for politics in the military. Ma Ranchai was put in charge of elders. Bun Pan continued as chief of police, but the stress seriously wore on him and he started to see ghosts everywhere and he wanted to indiscriminately arrest people. Finally, he shot and killed his wife, with whom he was apparently not having any conflict, before turning the gun on himself and ending his life.[39] In any case, ethnic minorities held all the key positions.

In 1980, the first *Khana Munty Khet* or provincial office's committee of Ratanakiri Province was established with seven members: Boua Chuong, chairman of the provincial People's Committee; Kham Len, secretary of the province's Party Committee; Kreng Siengnoi, personal administration; Thao Sim, head of the provincial military; Thon Thin, responsible for politics within the provincial military; Kham Khoeun; and Ma Ranchai.[40] All those in the People's Committee for the province were supposed to be literate, but in reality, Kreng Siengnoi was not. He was older and a veteran revolutionary, so he was not required to study basic literacy.[41] Some others who were marginally literate were allowed to work.

While the government of the province initially only had four offices, in 1980 the number was expanded considerably. Apart from the chairman of the provincial People's Committee office, the military office, the police office, and the PRPK office, which existed in 1979, Yoep Vanson, the former medic at Gia Poc, became the head of the provincial Health Department,[42] Ms. Lak On, one of the few Khmers to hold a senior position in the northeast at the time, became the head of the Education Department. Bui Yung was made the head of the Commerce Department. Samone (Khmer, moved to Ratanakiri in Sihanouk period, married to ethnic Lao) became head of the Information Dissemination Department, Tha Thoeng (Khmer) became head of the Department of Agriculture, Jampong Jari (Kreung, Phak Nam Village) became head of the bank,

even though there was no Cambodian currency yet.[43] Kham Toeung
(Pheng Phol) (Kachok, Kachut Village) was appointed as head of the
Transportation Department, while Sak (Brao, Haleum Village) became
head of the Construction Department. Feuay Bunma (ethnic Lao, Voeunsai Village) took the position of head of the Department of Youth Affairs.
Tan Sisuphon (ethnic Lao, Hat Po Village) also became the first head of
the military police (*Sanitsok*) in the province.[44] Notably, no justice positions existed in the government at the time, as the PRK government did
not begin to develop a legal system until after they adopted a constitution on June 17, 1981 (Sorpong 1981).

According to Kham Sai, the Vietnamese decided who would be
appointed to each senior position in the provinces,[45] but Bou Thang
and Yoep Vanson claim that Cambodians chose their own people, albeit in consultation with Vietnamese advisors.[46] In any case, most of
those appointed had little relevant experience related to the positions
they became responsible for, and so they had to learn as they went.
Yoep Vanson reported learning on the job when he was chief of the
Health Department.[47] Efforts were also made to integrate some talented
people who had lived in Cambodia under Democratic Kampuchea before 1979 to join the government and the party.

In 1981, Thao Sim was replaced as head of the Ratanakiri provincial military by Mong Then,[48] because Thao Sim was suspected of being
involved in the murder of Thang Bai's son, Bun Sou, who was shot
and killed one evening in late 1980 as he rode a bicycle near the newly
established provincial capital of Banlung (see later in this chapter for
more details). Even though definitive evidence was not available, Thao
Sim was implicated but never actually punished for the death. Although
Kham Khoeun, Boua Keo (ethnic Lao, Voeunsai Village), and Dam
Chanty believe that Bun Sou was probably shot and killed by one of the
many Khmer Rouge resisters in the Banlung area, or possibly by mistake by Vietnamese soldiers patrolling the area,[49] others, including Bou
Thang, continue to suspect otherwise. According to Bou Thang, it was
widely believed by people in Banlung that Thao Sim was responsible
for Bun Sou's death, although Bou Thang admitted that there was no
specific evidence implicating Thao Sim. Bou Thang said, "Some people
believe that Bun Sou was killed by the Khmer Rouge, but I do not."[50]
Bou Thang said that Thao Sim might have killed Bun Sou over a conflict
related to money, since Bun Sou managed the finances for the military

unit that Thao Sim commanded. Others have speculated that Thao Sim might have been worried that Bun Sou was going to be promoted to replace him, but Bou Thang said that no such plan was in the works. Ultimately, Thao Sim resigned from his position due to the incident.[51]

Ethnic Minorities in Stung Treng Province

Ratanakiri was not the only province dominated by ethnic minorities who had fled from the Sesan River basin in Ratanakiri Province between 1973 and 1975. In Stung Treng Province, Thang Bai became secretary of the party committee, a position he held until succumbing to illness in 1984 (*Phnom Penh SPK* 1984b). Some believe that he died due to a curse, as his stomach became bloated before he passed away. Indeed, a water buffalo was sacrificed on his behalf in Kachoan Village, in Ratanakiri Province, before he died, and he also visited Lao and Khmer spirit doctors as well, but to no avail.[52] In the end, he died in Phnom Penh while receiving treatment. His body was flown back for a large funeral in Kachoan Village.[53] Bun Koeung (ethnic Lao) was appointed chairman of Stung Treng's provincial People's Committee (*Phnom Penh Domestic Service* 1980b). Kham Toeung (Brao) became the vice-chairman of Stung Treng's Party Committee. Khamphan Thivong (ethnic Lao, Voeunsai Village) was appointed to be the first vice-chairman of the province's People's Committee, after spending a year as vice-chairman of Kampong Thom's provincial People's Committee. Other ethnic minorities from Ratanakiri Province also took up senior positions in Stung Treng.

Ethnic Minorities in Mondulkiri Province

Many ethnic minorities, and especially Brao people from the Sesan River basin in Ratanakiri Province, were assigned to work in Mondulkiri Province after 1979. Moi Choem was made chairman of the provincial People's Committee, while Thang Ngon became secretary of the Mondulkiri provincial Party Committee. Dop Khamchoeung was an early member of the leadership committee of Mondulkiri. He replaced Heng Khamvan as the military leader of Mondulkiri Province soon after the Khmer Rouge had been ousted from power. Yui Khamteu (Kavet, Siempang District) was initially his deputy, but he died soon after taking up the position. Yat Bleo replaced Yui Khamteu.[54] They were all Brao or from Brao subgroups.

Moi Choem remained chairman of Mondulkiri's provincial People's Committee until 1983, when efforts began to bring more ethnic Bunong people into the government leadership, since the majority of the province's population were Bunong. A Bunong named Buay Keuk replaced him. Moi Choem then became vice-chairman of the provincial People's Committee, with responsibility for elders' affairs.[55] He finally retired and returned to Ratanakiri in 1988, the same year as Thang Ngon. The government wanted Thang Ngon and Moi Choem to stay in the province upon retirement, but both quickly returned to their home province of Ratanakiri, with Moi Choem choosing to settle in Banlung,[56] and Thang Ngon moving back to his original village of Trabok. "If he [Moi Choem] had stayed in Mondulkiri, it would have been too far for him to visit his village," explained his widow, Tom Mut. She also expressed regret that after Moi Choem passed away, she only received 3,000 riel per month in lieu of his pension. She was facing hardship when I interviewed her in 2009, as she only had one child of her own, and she is mentally ill. She did, however, have two other adopted children.[57] Thang Ngon took all the wood that he was given by the government to build his retirement house, and convinced the government to move it for him by truck all the way to his home village of Trabok in Taveng District, Ratanakiri Province, where his house was built.[58]

I asked the wife of Moi Choem how the Brao got along with the Bunong. She responded, "I never heard that the Bunong complained about the Brao staying there. They respected us. They cried when we returned here [to Ratanakiri Province]. It was not difficult in Mondulkiri." Neither Moi Choem nor his wife spoke any Bunong, but they apparently got along well with the locals. They used Khmer language to communicate.

Kavet La-In (Kreung, Khuan Village) was another ethnic minority from Ratanakiri who held senior positions in Mondulkiri Province during the PRK period. In 1979, after arriving at Kaoh Nheaek with the Vietnamese and serving as a soldier there for two months, he was appointed chief of Kaoh Nheaek District. In 1981, however, he was transferred to become the chief of Ou Reang District. He stayed there for three years, but he did not like being there, as the ethnic Bunong people in the area were generally afraid of him, but more importantly, he missed his home and his parents in Ratanakiri. He also found it difficult to be district chief, as he only spoke a little Bunong. When he went to villages, large numbers of Vietnamese and Cambodian soldiers had to go with him for security reasons. The district center was attacked twice when he lived there, resulting in the deaths of some Bunong civilians. Therefore, in around 1984, he abruptly quit his position and returned to his village in Ratanakiri Province to become a farmer again. He did, however, complement his Vietnamese advisor at Ou Reang, Hung, and told me that he was sorry that he let him down when he returned to Ratanakiri.[59] There was one other Brao person with Kavet La-In at Ou Reang, a man named Lia, a Brao from Trabok Village in Taveng. He became a military leader in the district and married a Bunong woman. He settled there and did not return to Ratanakiri.[60]

Ethnic Minorities in Preah Vihear Province

In Preah Vihear Province, the Brao former committee member at Taveng Loeu Commune, Veng Khoun was made secretary of Preah Vihear's provincial Party Committee and also chairman of the province's People's Committee. Initially, the veteran ethnic Lao revolutionary Bun Chan (ethnic Lao) was supposed to take up the position of chairman of the People's Committee, but he decided that he did not want to go there, so Veng Khoun took on both positions.[61] Kham Lai became vice-chairman of the provincial People's Committee responsible for elders, while Kham Phuy, from Kachoan Village, was made an elder advisor, working with Kham Lai.[62] However, Kham Phuy only stayed in that position for two years before moving back to Ratanakiri Province.[63]

Other members of the leadership in Preah Vihear included Kham Phai, a Lun who became head of the provincial military; Doeun, his deputy; Mong Then became chief of staff of the military, responsible for politics; and Kham Dy (Brao, Bong Village), the son of the early revolutionary, Yoep, became police chief.[64] Although Kham Phai was the military leader of Preah Vihear, he admitted that he could only speak "half of Khmer language" when he was first based there in 1979. However, he at least knew enough to communicate with ethnic Khmers and did not require a translator. He also spoke some Vietnamese, but the Vietnamese military advisors he worked with had translators.[65]

Beginning in 1979, Doeun became the deputy head of the military in Preah Vihear. In 1984, Doeun was transferred to Stung Treng, but he only spent a short time there before being forced into retirement due to having a nerve ailment and, probably more importantly, due to his heavy alcohol consumption.[66] In 1989, the government built a house for Kham Len in Taveng Village, Taveng District. However, Kham Len, who was the son-in-law of Doeun, gave it to Doeun, since he did not have a good house to live in and was not eligible for a military pension.[67]

In addition, Kham Suk, who had been involved in the Mondulkiri attack from Vietnam in late 1978, became deputy chief of staff of the military in Preah Vihear Province in 1982. His father was Kham Lai, the vice-chairman of the provincial People's Committee. Kham Suk held that position until 1985, when Military Region 1 was established in Stung Treng and he was transferred there to head up the office of strategic planning, a position he held until November 1988, when he became the head of the provincial military in Stung Treng Province.[68]

After Thang Bai died in Stung Treng in 1984, Veng Khoun moved to Stung Treng to replace him. At around the same time, most of the other Brao in Preah Vihear Province also moved to either Stung Treng or back to Ratanakiri Province. Kham Dy, for example, who had taken Veng Khoun's daughter as his minor wife, moved back to Ratanakiri to become deputy police chief, working under Kham Kheoun. Kham Dy later became chief of police for the province.[69] A few Brao stayed on temporarily in Preah Vihear but not many. According to Bou Thang, it was appropriate that the Brao depart, as by then the province had enough competent and trustworthy local people to fill all the civilian and military positions, so the Brao were no longer needed.[70] Apparently only one Brao man decided to permanently settle in Preah Vihear: Toet (Brao, Paroe Touich Village), as he married an ethnic Khmer woman from there. When Kham Phai was still in the province, Toet was one of the many Brao assigned to guard him. As Kham Phai put it, "I wanted Brao guards because I could trust them more than Khmers." However, Kham Phai generally found it easy to live in the province when he was there.[71]

Returning Home to Cambodia

Once the Vietnamese military had gained control over the country in early 1979, they started directing people who had lived under the Khmer Rouge, including those relocated to southern and central parts of Cambodia, to return to their original villages in the northeast. By the end of 1979, most Kreung and Brao Tanap were in the general areas where they lived before the war. A man from Wang Kraom Village commented, "After 1979 people were allowed to go where they wanted. People did not have to stay in the lowlands and do wet rice agriculture as previously required" (Baird 2008, 248).

While there was not much pressure put on people to change their livelihoods or spatially organize in particular ways for "development" purposes during the PRK period, security concerns did dramatically affect spatial organization nonetheless, dictating that people needed to be located adjacent to roads or in other places where they could be easily monitored. These strategic hamlets near roads were specifically designed to ensure that they could be protected from Khmer Rouge attacks (Baird 2008), and during periods of insecurity, villagers were often required to stay within them (VODK 1982). *Phnom Penh Domestic Service* (1980d), the government media, explained it this way: "Our brothers and sisters of all nationalities in Ratanakiri Province are fully pleased with, support and defend the revolutionary power and new regime. They go voluntarily into the forest to fell trees for the building of strategic hamlets (Cambodian: *Phum Yutthasas*)."

Although the vast majority of the Brao from Taveng District fled to Vietnam and Laos in 1973 and especially 1975, a few were away fighting with the Khmer Rouge during this period and did not have a chance to escape. One of those was the Brao military leader, Bun Chan. He stayed with the Khmer Rouge throughout the 1975 to 1979 period. However, he was arrested in Preah Vihear Province along with most of his military unit on February 2, 1978 (Baird 2008), as part of the many internal purges orchestrated by the Khmer Rouge between 1976 and 1978 (Short 2004).

Bun Chan was probably only a few days away from being executed (his deputy had already been killed) when the Vietnamese entered Phnom Penh and rescued him.[72] According to Kham Toeung, only Bun Chan and two others out of over one hundred survived.[73] Bun Chan was eventually sent by the Vietnamese to Stung Treng, after Dop Khamchoeung vouched for him with the Vietnamese.[74]

Revenge in 1979

In 1979, after the fall of the Democratic Kampuchea regime, many villagers took revenge and killed local Khmer Rouge leaders responsible for the deaths of family members (Vachon 2017). However, the Vietnamese and the PRK government planned to convince Khmer Rouge who were still hiding in the forest to surrender, but that plan strongly depended on making sure that the Khmer Rouge understood that they would not be punished if they gave themselves up. Indeed, in Snoul in December 1978, the UFNSK's manifesto stated that the government would "welcome and facilitate traitorous government's armed forces, cadres and staffers who defect and join forces with the people" and "provide leniency to the loyalists who understood and remedied their past mistakes faithfully." They also made it clear that they intended to reeducate captured Khmer Rouge soldiers (Vachon 2017).

Nonetheless, and as I have previously reported, some revenge killings still occurred. The northeast was not an exception. For example, villagers from Kachoan Village killed the Khmer Rouge leaders who fled to the forest with them on the arrival of the Vietnamese military in late 1978. As one ethnic Lao man put it, "They killed Khmer Rouge leaders who had killed their relatives earlier."[75]

In one of the most famous cases of revenge, ethnic Lao villagers mob-killed the former ethnic Lao Khmer Rouge leader named Thang Sing (also known as Comrade Kham and Thang Si), after he gave himself up to the Vietnamese. Apparently the Vietnamese chief of Voeunsai District—remembered by locals as being named Chao—made the crucial decision to bring Thang Sing before villagers so that villagers could confirm if Sing had killed any of their relatives. He apparently admitted to ordering the deaths of one hundred people. The villagers confirmed that he was responsible for forty deaths in Pong Village and another ten in Fang Village, but Chao apparently did not count on being unable to control the relatives of the people who Thang Sing had ordered killed. Chao lost control, and the villagers attacked and beat Thang Sing to death in mob fashion. Chao apparently realized that he had committed a serious breach of protocol by not stopping Thang Sing from being killed, and that his actions could set back efforts to convince other Khmer Rouge leaders to surrender.[76] Indeed, Thang Sing's death apparently resulted in some Khmer Rouge who had been planning to give up to change their mind.[77] Chao apparently feared that he would be arrested or seriously disciplined by his superiors, and he shot himself in the head a week after Thang Sing was killed.[78]

Bou Thang, however, blames Boua Chuong, the chairman for Ratanakiri's People's Committee, for allowing the villagers to kill Thang Sing. Bou Thang told me that he warned Chuong not to allow revenge killings, but that he did not listen, and therefore indicated his short sightedness. "Chuong committed a sin, and that led him to die early," commented Bou Thang in 2017, still visibly upset with what happened almost forty years earlier.[79] Chuong apparently wanted revenge, as Thang Sing apparently tried to kill him before he escaped to Vietnam in 1975. Chuong was also angry that Thang Sing had order Khmer Rouge soldiers to shoot at him when he was trying to escape in 1975.[80] Bui Yung also criticized Boua Chuong, claiming that because he had been a soldier, Chuong sometimes used violence to solve problems. Bui Yung said that the main reason that Chuong ended up as chairman of Ratana-kiri's People's Committee was because he had gained favor with the communists before becoming a Khmer Hanoi in 1954, by leading part of a French military company he commanded to switch sides and join the Viet Minh.[81] In any case, it is clear that the Vietnamese recognized that the biggest battle they faced was the one to win over the loyalties of local people, and they knew that revenge killings constituted a heavy political blow to their efforts (see also chapter 5). Indeed, even in later years, there were strict orders not to kill Khmer Rouge soldiers who surrendered or were captured. The Vietnamese generally spearheaded military operations against the Khmer Rouge, but it was the job of their Cambodian colleagues to deliver "reeducation"[82] lectures to those apprehended. Villagers were then typically sent back to their villages,[83] although they were only granted clemency and allowed to return home after having spent time in prison (*Phnom Penh Domestic Service* 1983b).

The policy to not take revenge was not always easy to follow. For example, in 1981, about fifty percent of the villagers in Kaleng Village, in Bokeo District, Ratanakiri Province were still cooperating with the Khmer Rouge. During a meeting involving those Khmer Rouge, the Vietnamese attacked and injured one person. About twenty villagers loyal to the Khmer Rouge carried the man out and brought him to the Bokeo District hospital for treatment. They were, however, mistaken for villagers loyal to the PRK, and so were not bothered. But when they met two Vietnamese on the way back, they decided to attack the unsus-pecting soldiers. They killed one but the second had a grenade, which he was able to ignite, causing the death of four of the Khmer Rouge–aligned villagers.[84]

This became an important story and led to an important meeting being organized in the district capital of Bokeo. Sev Luo, the district chief,[85] expressed extreme anger at Kaleng Village for allowing this to happen and suggested that all the people from Kaleng should be killed for the crime. Most people in attendance loudly clapped when he proposed taking revenge. However, the headman of Kaleng, an older man who was loyal to the PRK, silently cried. Bui Yung spoke out, stating that if revenge was taken, it would hurt the reputation of the Vietnamese. He also said that taking revenge would not end the problem, as it would result in the government having more enemies. It would be like lighting a wasp nest on fire, as some would escape and take revenge. Instead, he proposed relocating the villagers to other villages temporarily, and once the area was again peaceful, the people could return to the village. In the end, his recommendation was accepted, but it could have easily gone the other way.[86]

The Demise of Bun Mi

In 1975, Bun Mi was the most important leader of the ethnic minorities in northeastern Cambodia, and especially the Brao who fled to Vietnam and Laos. On the Khmer side, Heng Samrin was the top leader from the eastern zone of Cambodia. Chea Sim was apparently slated to be deputy of Bun Mi, with Hun Sen expected to have an even lower position.[87] This being the case, it is not surprising that Bun Mi represented the northeast resistance to the Khmer Rouge at the first planning meeting for the Northeast Cambodian Insurrection Committee in 1977.[88] However, as previously mentioned, Bou Thang eventually became the key member of the leadership of the UFNSK from the northeast after Bun Mi became increasingly mentally unstable, making him unable to continue in a leadership role.[89] Thus, Bun Mi did not meaningfully participate in the planning work done with the Vietnamese directly leading up to the attack on the Khmer Rouge, even though he had been one of the main contacts with the Vietnamese at Gia Poc earlier, along with Bou Thang, Soy Keo, and Kham Len. His condition had deteriorated by that time.[90]

Bou Thang claimed that when they took Bun Mi to meet with Heng Samrin in 1978, he could hardly talk. Moreover, he was exhibiting other unusual behavior. For example, he insisted on sleeping on the floor during that trip. Bou Thang felt that Bun Mi was already seventy to eighty percent debilitated by then. Although in 1978, Bou Thang was actually in charge of the northeastern wing of the party, Bun Mi was still officially the leader.[91] Other leaders from the northeast hoped that Bun Mi's health would eventually improve, so he still officially held a position within the party central committee.[92] In 1979, in an attempt to cure him, a water buffalo was sacrificed at Gia Poc according to Brao animist tradition, but nothing changed.[93]

In 1979, after Phnom Penh fell, Bun Mi was too mentally unstable to take on any real responsibilities in the party or the new government.[94] He was, instead, moved to a house in Phnom Penh near the former residence of Norodom Sihanouk.[95] But Bun Mi's condition continued to deteriorate, and he started indiscriminately and inappropriately grabbing women on the streets of Phnom Penh. He was also increasingly exhibiting other abnormal behavior.[96] At that point, the northeastern leaders started thinking seriously about how to treat Bun Mi's illness. They considered sending him to the Soviet Union, but everyone involved in the discussion was afraid of flying,[97] and he would have had to have been accompanied on the plane, so that plan was rejected. It was finally decided to send Bun Mi overland for treatment in Laos. A Brao man named Jem Yen was assigned to accompany him, together with Khamteu and a few other Brao. In 1979, they traveled together to Xaysettha District, Attapeu Province. Another water buffalo was sacrificed for Bun Mi in Keng Makkheua Village, but his condition did not improve,[98] and after about a month in Laos he was escorted back to Phnom Penh.[99]

By 1980, Bun Mi could still converse, but his condition continued to worsen. After about two years in the capital city without doing any actual work, his behavior became so embarrassing for the PRK government[100] that in 1981, it was decided that Bun Mi could no longer stay there. He was sent to Stung Treng and then Ratanakiri Province, and from there Yoep Vanson, who was by then the head of the hospital in Ratanakiri Province, personally accompanied him to Gia Poc in Vietnam.[101] Bun Mi wanted another water buffalo to be sacrificed for him to try to remedy his illness. The sacrifice at Gia Poc went as planned, but once again proved ineffective.[102] Vietnamese doctors also examined him, but they could not cure him either. Bun Mi could apparently start conversations normally, but after a short period, his condition would deteriorate and he would start speaking incomprehensibly.[103] Finally, in 1983, it was decided that it would be best for Bun Mi to be admitted to a state institution in Dong Thap, Vietnam. The political career of one of the most important revolutionaries in northeastern Cambodia was over. Indeed, Bun Mi and Thang Bai may have been the most important revolutionaries of their generation,[104] so many were dismayed when they learned of Bun Mi's decline.[105] Thang Bai had joined the revolution before Bun Mi, so he was considered more senior, but Bun Mi had been the most influential Brao revolutionary,[106] which was crucial because in the 1960s, the Brao made up the majority of the revolutionaries.

The Cause of Bun Mi's Illness

According to Bou Thang, after Voeunsai was attacked by Vietnamese communists in 1950, Bun Mi joined the revolution and went to Attapeu with Thong Dam (later governor of Attapeu before retiring in Vientiane), Osakanh Thammatheva (later military general and finally Lao PDR politburo member and minister), and Nu Beng (PRK minister of health and social affairs), where he worked with Thongphoun Sipraseuth, a key communist political figure in Laos. At that time Bou Thang was still a novice at the Pong Village Buddhist temple, which was adjacent to the Sesan River in Voeunsai District.[107] However, Bun Mi did not become a Khmer Hanoi like other early revolutionaries, opting instead to remain in northeastern Cambodia.

Bou Thang, Kham Phai, Jyao Dawl, and others believe that Bun Mi's mental illness resulted from a wound he suffered during a battle against FARK forces in 1968.[108] Bun Mi and six other soldiers had gone to Hat Po Village, adjacent to the Sesan River in Voeunsai District, to secretly meet an official there. However, when they were in the village, they were unexpectedly surrounded by FARK soldiers. The only weapons that Bun Mi and his fellow soldiers had were traditional Brao crossbows. Bun Mi was shot with a gun while trying to escape and was badly injured. Jyao Dawl, a Brao soldier from Bang Koet Village, had to carry Bun Mi away. Bun Mi's shoulder bone was showing, and a Vietnamese doctor put a piece of metal into his shoulder to repair the bone.[109] Bou Thang believes that Bun Mi was affected by tetanus caused by the operation. The metal was not taken out when it should have been, and the wound began to fester and smell bad; liquid oozed out. Bun Mi did not realize how serious the problem was, and he was also fearful that if he went to Vietnam to get the wound treated, he might be accused of collaborating with the Vietnamese. But the problem persisted, and his shoulder was still hurting in 1980.[110]

Yoep Vanson also believes that it is possible that Bun Mi's condition was somehow genetic, as Bun Mi's younger brother, Bun Ren, also reportedly developed a similar condition, and eventually became mentally ill as well.[111] However, Kham Phai thinks that Bun Ren's condition was not nearly as severe as Bun Mi's, and that the two were probably unrelated.[112] In addition, Kham Toeung told me that Bun Mi was mentally ill because he thought too much, not because he was really ill. Eung Saneuk, a Brao leader in Trabok Village, had a similar opinion.[113] But Kham Phai put it the clearest. Although he too believes that Bun Mi's injury was part of the reason for his mental collapse, he suspects there was another factor that contributed to his mental instability. As Kham Phai put it, "Bun Mi was elevated to too high a position, and that put too much pressure on him."[114] In any case, the direct cause of Bun Mi's decline remains uncertain.

Bou Thang and Soy Keo went to visit Bun Mi in Vietnam in 1985, but the Vietnamese doctor in charge of looking after him told them that Bun Mi's nerves were bad. Shockingly, for Bou Thang, even though Bun Mi was physically in seemingly good condition, by that time he could not even recognize his former close colleagues. He was being treated like a senior citizen who could no longer look after himself.[115] According to Kreng Siengnoi, Bun Mi came back to visit Ratanakiri once in the late 1990s, but was still mentally unstable.[116] Bun Mi was still alive and living in Vietnam in 2007,[117] but he is believed to have died in Vietnam a few years ago.

After the demise of Bun Mi, Bou Thang played an even more crucial role in the northeastern faction of the PRK government. He essentially determined who was appointed to the senior positions in the northeastern provinces. He became the power broker for the northeast. According to Bou Thang, the initial key objectives of the new PRK government were to: 1) maintain security, 2) strengthen the military, 3) not allow the Khmer Rouge to return to power, 4) make connections with supportive foreigners, and 5) not allow the United States to gain any influence in Cambodia.[118] Indeed, building up the military was seen as particularly important and urgent (Bou Thang 1993).

Famine in Northeastern Cambodia

In 1979, various media outlets outside of Cambodia reported that famine had gripped parts of Cambodia, as the agricultural cycle had been greatly disrupted due to the fighting and the breaking up of the Khmer Rouge agricultural communes. In some cases, rice had

been left unharvested due to the confusion and fighting, and also sometimes because people left agricultural communes to return to where
they originally came from, without being able to carry substantial rice
stocks with them (Kamm 1998; Ea Meng-Try 1981). This was also the
case in northeastern Cambodia. Ea Meng-Try (1981) pessimistically
speculated that only about ten percent of the total 1979 rice crop was
actually harvested, and claimed that famine was severe in 1979, as the
160,000 tons of food aid provided by international organizations during
the last five months of 1979 was apparently stock-piled in Phnom Penh
and not distributed to the people. This situation reportedly left only
food aid distributed by PAVN and the new PRK government, which
had insufficient stocks to feed the whole country. Still, Ea Meng-Try
(1981) acknowledged that there was variation depending on the part of
the country.

It appears that the situation in northeastern Cambodia was less
severe than it might have been in some other parts of the country. Bou
Thang told me that while there was hunger in parts of Cambodia, this
was not the case in the northeast. "There were no beggars in the northeast like in other parts of the country," he commented.[119] Indeed, I did
not hear of any significant food shortages in 1979, although that may
have been because most of the people I spoke with worked closely with
the Vietnamese, so were probably given priority for receiving food
supplies. I did hear of rice from Khmer Rouge rice banks being distributed to people who gave up to the Vietnamese in 1979,[120] but these supplies were not enough to subsist on for an extended period. In addition,
in early 1980, Ratanakiri Province received rice, vegetable seeds, and
agricultural tools from Nghia Binh Province in Vietnam, while Daklak
Province in Vietnam provided one hundred tons of food to Mondulkiri Province, and Quang Nam–Da Nang Province in Vietnam provided
food and other necessary goods to Stung Treng Province (*Phnom Penh
SPK* 1980). This was certainly not enough to feed everyone, but it helped.
Ultimately, it appears that many people in the northeast simply relied
on forest foods to survive, as they had done historically during times of
food shortages. For example, many dug wild tubers and cassava to subsist on that year. They also utilized their knowledge of nature to forage
for other foods and to hunt and fish to survive. In that the Khmer Rouge
did not allow much fishing during the time they were in power, there
were plenty of fish in the Sesan and other rivers and streams in northeastern Cambodia in 1979.[121]

It appears, however, that initially a serious potential blunder occurred, one that was eventually corrected. According to Bui Yung, in 1979, Boua Chuong in Ratanakiri, the People's Committee of Stung Treng, and maybe other provincial governments too, ordered that bicycles and domestic animals be confiscated from villagers who had taken them from cooperatives as the Khmer Rouge fled. They were ordered to bring them back to the provincial capitals to establish new "cooperatives." In reality, it appears that the confiscated domestic animals served more as spoils for the revolutionary winners than the basis for new cooperatives. In Ratanakiri, for example, whenever there was an important provincial meeting, a pig or water buffalo would be killed for food. Bui Yung was particularly concerned about this practice, and told the Vietnamese advisors that taking domestic animals from villagers would leave them with nothing and cause serious problems in relation to food security. He used Ho Chi Minh's own words to make his point, which apparently impressed the Vietnamese. Finally, the advisors supported his view and told Boua Chuong to stop ordering the confiscation of domestic livestock from villagers. By that time, however, most of the animals had already been confiscated in Voeunsai District and part of O Chum District, and those animals were not returned, but at least the practice ended from that point onward. Thang Bai, who was doing the same thing in Stung Treng Province, also ordered an end to confiscations in response to Ratanakiri stopping.[122]

During the following years, many farmers were unable to produce sufficient rice to fully feed themselves, but unlike during the Khmer Rouge period, they had many more options to make up for the shortfall: hunting, fishing, and foraging in particular (Gottesman 2002), something that suited the ethnic minorities of the northeast particularly well. In addition, private commerce and market activities were not discouraged, especially after the security situation further improved in 1981. The PRK government and their Vietnamese advisors believed, however, that these market activities needed to be closely guided and inspected (Gottesman 2002).

Conclusion

With much assistance from the Vietnamese, the PRK government was politically organized in 1979. The ethnic minorities, and especially the Brao, who had been refugees in Vietnam in Laos, were allocated most of the important government and military positions in the four northeastern provinces of Ratanakiri, Stung Treng, Mondulkiri, and Preah Vihear. They also took some key positions in the central government, particularly in the military. Many Brao were put in senior positions despite the fact that most spoke little Khmer and were illiterate or just marginally literate. In fact, few had received any formal education. Thus, under regular circumstances they never would have risen to such powerful positions in government. But they did because they had the right political credentials, and crucially, they had proven themselves to be loyal to the Vietnamese Communists who had led the advance on the Khmer Rouge. No wonder so many Brao and other ethnic minorities from northeastern Cambodia, especially those who had fled to Vietnam and Laos in the mid-1970s, felt like the PRK period was a kind of golden age for them, even if civil war continued and times were tough for everyone.

Having explained how the PRK government was initially organized, particularly in the northeast, we now turn to the general political and livelihood circumstances in northeastern Cambodia during the PRK period, from 1979 to 1989, particularly how the government gradually developed and changed over time, with the Brao and other ethnic minorities continuing to play important roles up until the end of the 1980s, when the Vietnamese withdrew their troops from the country, after having spent a decade fighting resistance groups, particularly the Khmer Rouge.

The Development
of Northeastern Cambodia,
1979 to 1989

Compared to Democratic Kampuchea, the PRK government was much more moderate in its approach to
socialism. It reopened schools and markets, introduced relatively moderate policies related to collective agriculture, reestablished a Buddhist sangha, and generally allowed for the return to normal family life
throughout the country. The government had, however, a difficult time
mobilizing the population based on the idea of "Khmerness," due to
the PRK's close ties with Vietnam. Instead, it had to rely on the threat
of the return of the Khmer Rouge as its main tool for mobilizing the
public. The PRK government also had a difficult time organizing itself
in a centralized way, due to various infrastructure and human resource
limitations (Hughes 2009). In some ways both these points bode well
for the minorities of the northeast, who were not particularly enthusiastic about Khmerness because they are not ethnic Khmers, and because
the lack of effective central control in effect granted considerable flexi-
bility and autonomy to the minorities of the northeast to govern and live
in ways that made sense to them.

Development of the four northeastern-most provinces was not easy
during the 1980s, and many suffered during this period. But, as illus-
trated using examples from Ratanakiri Province, the region gradually
changed and developed, and people's lives slowly improved and became less precarious during the 1980s. The Brao and other ethnic minorities, especially former refugees from Vietnam and Laos, played particularly important roles in rebuilding the northeast and the country more

generally, and thus deserve some attention, even though little has been written about them until now.

Provincial Capitals

On February 17, 1979, the province of Ratanakiri was officially reestablished. In 1959, when Ratanakiri Province was first declared, the provincial capital was moved from Voeunsai, which is adjacent to the Sesan River, to Lumphat, on the banks of the Srepok River in the southern part of the province (*La Depeche* 1959; Meyer 1979). However, in 1979 the provincial capital was moved back to Voeunsai. Taveng was officially established in 1986, along with An-dong Meas, Koun Mom, and O Yadao Districts. Banlung District was created a year later, in 1987. Bui Yung claims that he justified establish-ing these new districts as a way to counter the remaining Khmer Rouge in the province, but in reality he wanted the districts established to in-crease Cambodia administrative control over the border areas so as to prevent Vietnam from taking more land from Cambodia.[1] Bou Thang agreed with the plan, both to help protect the border and also because Voeunsai and Bokeo Districts were too large to easily govern.[2]

In 1979, when the capital of Ratanakiri was still Voeunsai, there was debate about where the capital should be permanently located. Boua Chuong led a group that favored keeping Voeunsai as the provincial capital, while Ms. Lak On[3] and some others preferred the old provincial capital, Lumphat.[4] Somebody suggested, however, that Banlung would be an appropriate location for the new capital. There are, however, con-flicting reports regarding whose idea it actually was. Some claim that the Vietnamese suggested Banlung as the new capital,[5] and that other Cambodians agreed, including Bou Thang, due to its central location in the province, half way between the Sesan River to the north (Voeunsai) and the Srepok River to the south (Lumphat). The Vietnamese may have also thought that hydropower dams would be built on the Sesan River in the future and so did not want the provincial capital there, in case of future flooding.[6] Banlung was also situated in a central location for traveling to Vietnam or Stung Treng, and another advantage was that the city would not be under any risk of natural flooding, as would have been the case if it had been located near the Sesan or Srepok Rivers. Bou Thang claims, however, that he made the decision, although he says that he did so after consulting with the Vietnamese.[7] Possibly prior to that, Bui Yung claims that he offered the suggestion to the chief Vietnamese advisor at the time, Lok, arguing that it was the most central location. He claims that Boua Chuong asked how boats could travel to the provincial capital if there was no nearby river, and also suggested that there would be a shortage of fish in Banlung.[8] He also argued that there was insufficient drinking water and wood available.[9] Finally, according to Bui Yung, the Vietnamese ignored these concerns and made the final decision to establish the capital at Banlung.[10]

The main problem was, as previously mentioned, that there is no river located near Banlung, only Beung Kansan Wetland and Yak Loam Lake.[11] As feared, there was initially insufficient drinking water in Banlung, which caused many to hesitate to move there.[12] Bou Thang also confided that he was afraid that gold or another precious metal might be found on the site of Banlung in the future, and that he would be blamed for locating the provincial capital there. He apparently continued to worry about this until about 1985.[13]

In any case, the Vietnamese prepared a plan in Binh Dinh Province in Vietnam for constructing the new capital,[14] and in late 1979 or early 1980, Banlung began to be built, although progress was initially slow. The first few buildings were built in what was previously a small ethnic Tampuon village. Sak (Brao, Haleum Village) was put in charge of this early construction work and over ten other people worked with him, including Feuay Chan (ethnic Lao, Pakke Village) and Tong Lieu (ethnic Thai from Thailand). Only ethnic minorities, including both highlanders and ethnic Lao, played significant roles in constructing the new capital. They obtained building wood from nearby forests and received salaries for their work. The first provincial government offices built in Banlung were all made of wood, as cement was not available at the time.[15] The Vietnamese government specifically assisted in constructing houses in Banlung for Boua Chuong, Kham Len, Kreng Siengnoi, and Lak On.[16] By April 1980, it was decided that enough had been constructed to warrant moving the provincial capital to Banlung. The move occurred less than a month after the Cambodian currency was reintroduced to the country,[17] following a five-year hiatus during the Khmer Rouge period (Slocomb 2003; Chanda 1986). However, in the 1980s, trading for commodities using gold became common in Cambodia.

In 1979, the first people to move to Banlung were the Vietnamese and Cambodian soldiers. Kham Sana, the deputy head of the sector military training school, was one of the first to settle there.[18] The soldiers established camps in two places in Banlung, but these camps were near each other. Two days later some officials started arriving. Then ten to twenty days after that, Boua Chuong and Kham Len followed. Later in 1980, a fifty-bed provincial hospital was built (BBC 1980). According to Bou Thang, by 1981 the move was completed.[19]

Life in the new capital was not initially easy, as there were insufficient accommodations for officials, resulting in most having to construct their own houses, but with only minimal resources to do so. Initially three or four families often occupied single, shanty-like long houses. Early on officials also often ate together, as there were few places where one could purchase food. There were no shops yet.

It was initially not safe to travel outside of Banlung, as the threat of the Khmer Rouge remained significant. There were, in addition, dangers related to landmines planted by the Khmer Rouge on the outskirts of Banlung. According to an ethnic Thai Communist who worked in Banlung during the early period, "In 1979, when the Vietnamese first took over Ratanakiri, there were a lot of anti-personnel and anti-truck landmines along the road. It was very dangerous."[20] Indeed, since the Vietnamese engaged in most of the direct military confrontations with the Khmer Rouge, the main threat to Cambodian soldiers allied with the Vietnamese were landmines. Indeed, many lost legs and feet or were killed due to stepping on mines.[21] However, over time the threat gradually subsided. Vietnamese soldiers were often required to provide protection for people traveling outside Banlung, especially in the early 1980s. One early resident recalled, "Between 1980 and about 1988 the Khmer Rouge would come to the outskirts of Banlung and stay for five or six, or sometimes ten nights. They came in groups of between three and six people, to collect information. When they were shot at they would run away."[22] Another woman who moved to Banlung in 1980 told me, "Sometimes the Khmer Rouge were just outside of Banlung. Therefore, we didn't travel outside of town much [unless it was necessary]."[23] One female government official said, "In 1980 Banlung was still surrounded by forest. It was scary at night."[24] Although Tan (n.d.) reported that by mid-August 1980, Khmer Rouge forces in northeastern Cambodia had been severely weakened, the reality was that the Khmer Rouge were still relatively strong, but in the early 1980s, instances of Khmer Rouge intrusions gradually declined, and by some reports, the Khmer Rouge was only really a serious threat to Banlung until around 1981.[25] Moreover, the Vietnamese reportedly bore the brunt of the risk, especially in the early years. According to one Brao man who served in the military from 1979 until 1994, "There were lots of Khmer Rouge in the area at first, but none of us [Brao] died. Only the Vietnamese died because they went to fight. We just stayed in the camp." He commented later, "The Vietnamese soldiers were good to us. They protected us."[26]

Indicative of improved security in the Banlung area, by 1983, Phuy Bunyok was carrying goods to sell in the villages surrounding Banlung, including tobacco, cosmetics, and also cooked noodles and sauce. She also sold to Vietnamese soldiers stationed in the villages. She told me that she would walk from Banlung to the villages, and that there were no Khmer Rouge in the area at the time so it was safe.[27]

After 1985, when more wells began being dug and drilled in Banlung, greater numbers of people moved to the capital. Banlung also gradually developed to be a site of commerce, albeit quite limited at first (Baird 2008).

The provincial market at Banlung was built in 1988 (Baird 2008), not long after the central government announced the introduction of major market reforms, which started being implemented around 1987 (Slocomb 2003; Loschman 2006–2007). One of the early inhabitants of Banlung, who initially moved there to do construction in 1980, stated that, "People began to come to Banlung when they had money to spend." This was especially evident between 1990 and 1992, when Banlung grew significantly.[28] According to Bou Thang (1993), the numbers of cows, buffaloes, and pigs being raised in the province also rapidly increased between 1986 and 1988, probably due to improved security and increased opportunities for marketing livestock.

In 1979, there was also some controversy related to establishing the capital of Mondulkiri Province. Initially, the capital was located at Kaoh Nheaek, in the northern part of the province. For some, it was ideal, as the Khmer Rouge had built up the area. It had ample lowland rice paddy land, and the Khmer Rouge had built an irrigation dam to supply the fields with water. Thang Ngon and Moi Choem apparently both wanted to situate the provincial capital there, but the Vietnamese made it clear that they wanted to return the capital to its original location, Sen Monorom. Dop Khamchoeung was the most outspoken in objecting to the Sen Monorom plan. Some Vietnamese became angry with Khamchoeung for questioning them. Two years later, the move occurred, with everyone having no choice but to abide by the decision and make the best of it. The one advantage of Sen Monorom, Khamchoeung later admitted, was that there were a number of large Lon Nol–era houses there where government officials could stay.[29] However, a disadvantage of Sen Monorom was that there were very few trees nearby, which meant that there was little protection from the strong winds that are common there.[30]

Moving Back Home from Vietnam and Laos

Although the return of people in Cambodia to their villages after the fall of the Khmer Rouge in early 1979 has already been touched on in parts of the previous two chapters, there is also the matter of the ethnic minorities, and particularly the Brao, who gradually returned to Cambodia from Laos and Vietnam in the early 1980s. Some Brao refugees in Laos joined the UFNSK at Gia Poc and participated—albeit from the rearguard—in the attack on the Khmer Rouge from Vietnam at the end of 1978, but most remained in Attapeu Province. There is also the matter of the return of other ethnic minorities, particularly the Kavet, who stayed with the Khmer Rouge in the forests longer than most others.

Some of the inhabitants of Gia Poc in Vietnam began returning to Cambodia in late 1979. Four Vietnamese trucks transported most of the people originally from Kachoan Village to Cambodia via O Yadao District in Ratanakiri.[31] The returnees initially stayed almost a month near the Vietnamese Military Division Camp 35 near present-day Banlung. However, near the end of 1979, the people of Kachoan and a small number of people from Fang Village decided to move near the district center of Voeunsai on the south side of the Sesan River. The people from Fang Village were particularly anxious to return home, as they wanted to cultivate lowland wet rice paddy during the coming rainy season. Eventually the people from Kachoan and Fang were allowed to return to their original villages.[32]

In late 1979, efforts also began—albeit not major ones—to repatriate the remaining civilian refugees from Laos. The first delegation, which included Jem Yen,[33] Kham Khoeun, and Yoep Vanson, traveled to southern Laos to assess the situation and encourage the population to return to northeastern Cambodia. Those who volunteered to come back were given clothing as an incentive, but many were still concerned about the security situation in Ratanakiri and chose to stay in Laos.[34]

The second attempt to entice refugees from Laos and Vietnam to return was launched in 1980, when a second delegation traveled to both Laos and Vietnam to identify members of the refugee population who were at least marginally qualified to work in the PRK government. Some refugees returned to Cambodia as a result, but most were still afraid to move.[35]

However, in early 1981, as a result of the 1980 trip to Gia Poc, most of the remaining Brao villagers in Vietnam did agree to move back to Cambodia (Baird 2008), although it would take longer to convince those in Laos to return.

In the early 1980s, the United Nations became aware of the Cambodian refugee situation in Laos. Robert Cooper, a Brit who was working for the UNHCR in Laos, was sent to Attapeu to learn more. It was not easy to get to Attapeu at the time, and he was not able to arrange to do so until late 1980, when he traveled by biplane from Vientiane, Laos' capital city. Over the next three years, he spent a total of three months in Attapeu working largely with the Brao refugee population. He provided some vegetable seeds at the end of 1980, and also some rice, although he told me in 2012 that the food security situation of the refugees at the time was not particularly precarious. He remembers there being 10,400 refugees in Attapeu, but he thought that there might have been 11,429 when most were repatriated to Cambodia in 1983.[36]

In 1982, trucks came from Cambodia to take some Brao back from Attapeu Province. Veng Khoun was said to have ordered the trucks to get the people in Attapeu, but most were still not confident to return.[37]

In 1983, yet another delegation traveled to Laos with the goal of returning civilian refugees to Cambodia.[38] By that time the security situation in the northeast of Cambodia had improved somewhat, and so more refugees agreed to return during this trip, although some never did return, and still live in Laos to this day. The leaders of the delegation were Bou Thang, Kham Chan, Nu Beng, Bou Lam, Kham Len, and Dop Khamchoeung. Large trucks took people from Laos to Cambodia, with a convoy of trucks traveling from Attapeu to Pakse, in Champasak Province, and then from Pakse south to Khinak, and then to the border between Laos and Cambodia's Stung Treng Province. The trucks continued on to Stung Treng town and then to Banlung.[39] None of the heavily potholed roads along the route were paved at the time, so it was a long and arduous journey.

Those who returned to Cambodia mainly gave the rice paddy farmland that they had developed in Laos to relatives or to their host villages. Land did not have a clear value, and in any case, the refugees were grateful to their host communities for the tremendous support that they had provided during a difficult time. As in other communities, the host villagers from Saisy did a *"sou khouan"* soul-calling traditional Lao ceremony for the refugees to wish them a safe trip back to Cambodia. There were tears in the eyes of those who left and those who stayed.[40] One Brao man said, "The returning refugees mainly just gave their paddy fields to relatives. We helped them, they helped us."[41] It must be remembered, however, that most of the Brao had mainly been doing swidden cultivation because that was the type of agriculture that they were most familiar with.

Those Who Stayed in Laos and Vietnam

A number of Brao Cambodians chose to stay in Laos permanently and not return to Cambodia. In April 2017, I met some of these people in Keng Makkheua Village, where over two hundred Brao families from Cambodia had stayed between 1975 and the early 1980s, and where five Brao families who originated in Cambodia still live.[42] One seventy-year-old Brao man originally from Phao Village in Taveng District decided not to leave Laos in the early 1980s because he married a Brao Lao woman, and she did not want to go to Cambodia with him.[43] A fifty-four-year-old woman who fled to Laos with others as a teenager in 1975, was an orphan, and did not know where her relatives lived in Cambodia. She also married a Brao man from Laos. In 1983, she saw the trucks come to pickup other Brao families, but she decided to stay in Laos.[44] Another woman in her seventies claimed that her whole family decided not to return to Cambodia because her husband's younger brother had been killed by the Khmer Rouge in 1974, and so he was fearful that he too might be killed if he returned. In fact, ten people in her family fled to Laos in 1974, before the main group arrived in 1975. The woman said that her family was not overly pressured to return to Cambodia in 1983.[45] Another older Brao woman told me that she did not return because the Khmer Rouge had killed both her father and husband when she was still in Cambodia, and so she dared not return.[46] A sixty-year-old Brao man told me that he did not return because his mother preferred to stay in Laos, and he did not want to leave her alone.

However, his younger brother joined the UFNSK in 1978 and returned to Cambodia after initially going to Gia Poc.[47] Some Brao people living in other villages, and also some Kavet and Brao who had come up to Attapeu in the late 1960s and early 1970s to work at the CIA-supported base at Kong My, chose to remain in Laos (see Baird 2010d).

There was apparently just one Brao person in Gia Poc who chose to stay in Vietnam. Jarang (Kreung, Tiem Loeu Village), called Phoeung in Vietnamese, decided to stay in Vietnam because he married an ethnic Jarai woman there. Although Gia Poc Commune, and the twelve villages that once encompassed it, were all abandoned and ceased to exist, he settled in one of the nearby Jarai villages.[48]

Back in Cambodia

Once back near Banlung, the returning refugees could not immediately return to their original villages north of the Sesan River due to Khmer Rouge security concerns. Therefore, they settled adjacent to Drao stream near Yak Loam Lake, not far from Banlung, the new provincial capital of Ratanakiri. They stayed there for various amounts of time, between one year and three years and five months, before relocating to the south side of the Sesan River in soon-to-be established Taveng District.[49] The security situation north of the Sesan River still did not make it possible for them to move back to where most originally came from, as Khmer Rouge units populated by mainly Kavet and Kreung were still operating near the Lao border.[50] In that the Brao from Taveng were strongly anti–Khmer Rouge and very pro-Vietnamese, the Khmer Rouge dared not make contact with the Brao Amba villages near the Sesan River. Instead, they only contacted some ethnic Tampuon, Jarai, Kavet, and Kreung villages in other areas because some of those people were more sympathetic to the Khmer Rouge.[51]

Many of the Brao who returned to Taveng were still afraid of the Khmer Rouge north of the Sesan River. However, as the number of people returning increased, everyone started feeling more confident and secure, and this resulted in more people relocating. Indicative of the fact that the security situation had improved, there were only two Vietnamese soldiers and no Vietnamese advisors stationed in Taveng District when it was first established in 1986. When the security situation north of the Sesan River in Taveng improved significantly, which was not until the mid-1990s, the Brao Amba resumed agriculture production north of the Sesan River.

One Brao former official who came to work in Banlung after returning from Laos in 1983 explained that by the time he arrived, the security situation near Banlung was good, but before then many Khmer Rouge were still staying in the forests near Banlung. There were still Khmer Rouge elsewhere in the province, but he never saw any. He believed that they were mainly operating near the road from Banlung to Stung Treng, in Koun Moum and Sesan Districts.[52] Indeed, in July 1985, the NADK reported ambushing a Vietnamese Jeep at Trapaeng Kraham, on the road between Stung Treng and Ratanakiri, reportedly killing a Vietnamese regiment commander and four other Vietnamese (VODK 1985b).

One Cambodian Brao man named Jyao Dawl, who had not become an UFNSK soldier in 1978, decided in the early 1980s to return to Stung Treng to work for Rao Nuong as a policeman. There were over twenty Brao policemen in Stung Treng at the time, and their main job was to protect the provincial leadership, including Thang Bai, Kham Toeung, and later Veng Khoun. The leaders apparently wanted their closest guards to be Brao, as they trusted them more than others.[53] The same was true in Mondulkiri, where the secretary of the Party Committee, Thang Ngon, convinced his son-in-law, Khameng (Brao, Bang Koet Village), to join the army so that he could help guard him. Khameng became one of the four most trusted guards of Thang Ngon, going everywhere he went.[54] Loi (Kreung, Chuay Village) was the head of the *"kang karpear munty pak"* (Party Office Defense Unit). Khameng, however, hated being a soldier and resigned a year later and returned to stay at Drao stream in Ratanakiri Province.[55] After eight years, Jyao Dawl also resigned from his job as a policeman in Stung Treng because he was illiterate and the police started putting more emphasis on literacy. Essentially, he was embarrassed by his inability to read or write.[56]

When Dop Khamchoeung, the former military leader of Mondulkiri, moved back to Ratanakiri in the mid-1980s, he initially lived with some other Brao near Drao stream, where they stayed for three years. Two Brao elders, Joebong (Lun, Paroe Thom Village), and Hoertoong (Lun, Paroe Touich Village), were also living at Drao stream after returning from Vietnam and wanted to wait for permission from the ministry before returning to live near the Sesan River. The Brao did not want to stay in the territory of the Tampuon and so were restless. Therefore,

Khamchoeung proved himself to be, once again, quite daring, and traveled to Phnom Penh via Vietnam to ask for official permission to move. He went on the recommendation of Kham Len, the party secretary in Ratanakiri. Once in Phnom Penh, Khamchoeung met Chea Sim, Heng Samrin, and Hun Sen. In the end, they granted the Brao permission to move back to the Sesan River.[57]

Another Brao man who had been living in Laos and doing agriculture with his uncle returned from Attapeu Province in 1983. He managed to get a job with the provincial government in Banlung, working for the Department of Logistics. He worked for the government with ten others selling salt, tobacco, clothes, and other basic items. There was no market at the time, so one could only make purchases at government shops. There were also branches of these shops in each district center. He did not speak any Khmer, but according to him, only Lao and Brao were spoken by people who worked with him, and all the customers used languages other than Khmer. Therefore it was not a problem. Kong Bat was the head of his group, but Oen (ethnic Lao) succeeded him in 1986. However, Oen was not replaced after he passed away a couple of years later, as by that time the private market at Banlung was being developed, thus making the state shops redundant.[58]

The Kavet Return from the Forest

The situation was particularly difficult for the Kavet subgroup of the Brao, many of whom supported the Khmer Rouge in the 1980s. In both Voeunsai and Siempang Districts some of the most notorious Khmer Rouge leaders were Kavet, and when the Vietnamese entered Cambodia in late 1978, most Kavet fled to the forests. A large number ended up in the mountains in the general vicinity of the Ratanakiri–Stung Treng border with Laos' Attapeu and Champasak Provinces. They suffered greatly during the 1980s. Faced with frequent Vietnamese attacks, the Kavet were always on the run and were unable to produce sufficient food to feed themselves. Many died as a result of military conflict, but even more perished as a result of illnesses at least partially attributed to malnutrition. However, the Khmer Rouge leaders told the Kavet that the Vietnamese would kill them if they gave up, and so many initially dared not surrender. However, between 1981 and 1985, the Kavet civilians either gave up little by little or were captured by the Vietnamese, with the largest group of 700 civilians coming down in 1985. Those who surrendered or were captured were relieved when the Vietnamese did not punish them. Some Kavet Khmer Rouge soldiers remained in the forests (Baird et al. 1996), and a small number did not give up until the surrender of the Khmer Rouge in 1998 and 1999 (see chapter 6).

Organizing the Villages

Ironically, the PRK government, or the Heng Samrin government, as it was often referred to, continued to promote the idea of linear rather than circular villages, just as the Sangkum and Khmer Rouge governments had done in the 1960s and 1970s. However, PRK government officials were much more lenient in their implementation of measures that had the potential to upset the location population. Therefore, the only laws that were typically enforced during this period, at least in remote parts of the northeast, related to security. It was only during the UNTAC period in 1993 that a set of clear laws started being developed in the country.[59]

The PRK government was also careful not to implement unpopular resettlement schemes. When villages were located for security reasons, the highlanders were often encouraged to make long linear settlements, which continued to be a symbol of modernization and were also easier for the government to monitor and defend. For example, in 1982 and 1983, people from the Kreung village of Kalai were told to settle in a linear village along both sides of the road between Banlung and Voeunsai (Baird 2008). Bou Thang explained that he was one of the main advocates of these linear villages next to roads, but that those living away from roads were still allowed to establish circular villages. He had studied in Vietnam for many years and believed that he knew more about modernizing than others in the northeast.[60]

Transportation after 1979

In 1979, the "door to Ratanakiri" had been opened, but the irony was that there were no roads to get there.[61] Indeed, there were not any roads in the province that could be traversed year-round. Neither were there any paved roads in all of northeastern Cambodia. What few roads had existed prior to the FANK's withdrawal from the northeast in 1970 had deteriorated during the Khmer Rouge period, which spanned almost nine years in the northeast, as compared to less than three years and nine months in Phnom Penh. Road travel was difficult, but in any case there were few vehicles in the northeast outside of Soviet-built military vehicles. Most people either walked or traveled by river using paddleboats. Still the transportation situation gradually improved in the 1980s; for example, the old disabled French colonial bridge across the Srepok River was rehabilitated early on, with work being completed in 1980 (Bou Thang 1993). In 1986, when Taveng District was established, only an old Vietnamese road could reach there, and it could only be passed by military vehicles during the dry season. However, in 1992, construction of a better road began, and that road became usable in 1993.[62]

In the 1980s, the main route to Phnom Penh overland was via Vietnam, as the road from Phnom Penh to the northeast was very difficult to pass. Luon Vandy, who worked in Stung Treng, explained that it generally took four days to travel overland from Stung Treng to Phnom Penh. Travelers would sleep the first night in Pleiku, the second night in Nha Trang, and the third night in Ho Chi Minh City.[63] Apart from being in poor physical condition, the stretch of the road from Banlung to Stung Treng was insecure, and the stretch from Stung Treng to Kratie was even more insecure. Indicative of the circumstances, in 1983, the driver of Boua Chuong, the chairman of Ratanakiri's People's Committee, was killed along the road from Stung Treng, not far from Banlung. The car he was driving was ambushed by Khmer Rouge soldiers under the ethnic Tampuon Khmer Rouge leader, Kham Veang (see Chapter 6).[64] In November 1987, the VODK (1987) also reported that the NADK had ambushed a truck traveling the road, killing three "Vietnamese–Heng Samrin enemy soldiers," wounding two others, and seizing an AK-47 gun, a rucksack, Cambodian and Vietnamese banknotes, and a "Marxist-Leninist book."

The transportation situation in Mondulkiri Province was even worse because in the 1980s there were virtually no roads in the province. According to Thang Ngon, the Brao secretary of the provincial Party Committee there, he only left the provincial capital once in the 1980s, and he traveled on the back of an elephant. He had ten soldiers assigned to protect him, while the Vietnamese advisor that traveled with him had fifteen soldiers protecting him. According to Thang Ngon, vehicle travel did not make sense at that time.[65] However, later the roads gradually improved, especially from Kratie to Sen Monorom.

Dop Khamchoeung, the Brao military chief of Mondulkiri in the early 1980s, traveled to the countryside more often, although with Vietnamese

soldiers guarding the routes that he traveled. Many Vietnamese soldiers were apparently shot by Khmer Rouge during trips outside of
the provincial capital. The security situation in the province was particularly difficult during the first few years of the 1980s, but it gradually
improved.[66]

Some long distance government travel to and from the northeast
during the 1980s was done by airplane.[67] There were initially no commercial flights to northeastern Cambodia. There were, however, government and military flights to Banlung, and there was one flight to
Voeunsai in the early 1980s.[68] Bou Thang reported that in the 1980s, he
mainly traveled to the northeast by Soviet airplanes or helicopters.
Sometimes he also flew to Banlung. Even along the road from the airport he was occasionally shot at by the Khmer Rouge, but he claimed
that he was not afraid of the danger associated with traveling.[69] By the
late 1980s, however, the Cambodia national airline, Air Kampuchea,
was flying internally. Kamm (1998) reported that all the planes and
pilots were Soviets, but in fact, many pilots were Cambodians, since by
1987, 150 aviators and specialists had received training in the Soviet
Union, and fifty others were still receiving training (*Phnom Penh Domestic Service* 1987).

During the 1980s, due to security concerns, it was the law for everyone to obtain written permission to travel outside of one's village. This
rule remained in place until after the Paris Peace Treaty and the arrival
of UNTAC in 1992.[70] However, Vickery (1984) reported that many
people in Cambodia were willing to travel without permits in 1980, and
that in any case, most village committees freely gave out permits to
those wanting to travel from village to village. Vickery (2010) acknowledged, however, that more travel restrictions existed in border areas.
Moreover, it was not true that "complete freedom of movement" was
tolerated, as Vickery (2010, 167) reported. Instead, the circumstances
varied according to place and time. In the early 1980s, in Ratanakiri,
the Khmer Rouge frequently ambushed Vietnamese and government
troops traveling along roads. It was a dangerous and difficult time to
travel in the northeast; so long distance trips were rare. According to
one ethnic Lao person from Voeunsai District, "During the Vietnamese
period, we typically did not travel far. We only went to our agricultural fields."[71] Between 1991 and 1993, security improved considerably,
and at that time the requirements for travel documents were largely
eliminated.[72]

Developing Ratanakiri Province (1979–1989)

As previously mentioned, in 1979, the PRK government had a hard time finding qualified people to work for the government, and this was especially the case in northeastern Cambodia. In Pone, an ethnic Lao woman originally from Voeunsai, and the niece of Nu Beng, the PRK government's first minister of health and social affairs, was one of those who initially agreed to take up a government position in the new capital of Banlung because there were no positions open in Voeunsai, where she would have preferred to have been based. Despite having no previous government experience, she was immediately made the chairperson of the provincial Department of Women's Affairs (*Prathean Naree Khet*). After agreeing to relocate to Banlung, she was encouraged along with many other new government recruits, including Kham Khoeun and Dam Chanty, to study for three months at a school for Cambodians in Thu Duc, a suburb of Ho Chi Minh City. However, she felt a need to be home to look after her parents and found it too difficult to complete her studies. Therefore she resigned from her position and returned to Ratanakiri.[73]

In 1980, Lak On replaced In Pone as chairperson of women's affairs. She actually held two positions, as she also led the Department of Education. In August 1982, Dam Chanty became her deputy in women's affairs,[74] just after returning from studying one and a half years in Ho Chi Minh City. Lak On continued as head of the Department of Education, and she also joined the provincial PRPK Committee. In 1988, however, Dam Chanty took over the position of president of women's affairs,[75] with Jop Moer (Kachok) as her deputy.[76] Bou Thang told me, in 2013, that he believed that Dam Chanty was the most capable woman in Ratanakiri Province.[77]

In Phnom Penh, monetary salaries were introduced in April 1980, which coincided with the return of Cambodian currency use. Before then salaries were paid in rice and other food provided by the Vietnamese (Vickery 1984) or in Vietnamese currency (Vickery 1989). Salaries all over the country, including in the northeast, were—in any case—meager and not enough to live off of. However, wages came with other basic supplies that were not monetarized. For example, Dam Chanty received sixteen kilograms of rice per month, as well as sweetened condensed milk and salt.[78] Her salary was 90-riel per month in 1979, although there was no money to actually pay her until she returned from studying in

Vietnam in 1982. When she was finally paid, she received a full bag of small Cambodian bills, including a large number of Kak notes, with 10-Kak being equal to 1-riel (at present, the exchange rate is about 4,000-riel/US$). At the time the largest bill available was 5-riel, but she did not even get one of those.[79]

Another junior ethnic Brao who was working in Banlung for the government in the mid-1980s told me that while he worked for the government, his wife did swidden agriculture nearby to feed the family because his salary was insufficient. Apart from getting a small salary of 3,000-riel per month (the rate rose considerably higher after 1980, due to hyperinflation), he received about twenty kilograms of rice per month for each of his family members and five meters of cloth per year for each child (adults did not receive a cloth allowance).[80] He also received blankets and mosquito nets from the state. Soldiers apparently received more supplies than civilian officials.[81]

Jampong Jari, after spending a few months in Bokeo District, was appointed head of the Ratanakiri provincial bank, and in May 1979, he went to Phnom Penh for three months to receive technical training related to banking because he only had two years of basic education and no knowledge of banking prior to being appointed. He was appointed to the position because human resources were so limited at the time.[82] As Bou Thang recollected, "Looking for good government officials was like looking for gold, except that gold was easier to find."[83] One person from each province was sent to receive banking training, which was led by a Vietnamese advisor who spoke Khmer. Apart from limitations regarding human resources, the most pressing initial challenge for Jampong Jari after he returned to Banlung was security associated with the bank. Initially, a small wooden building was constructed in Banlung to serve as the bank, but it was not secure enough to effectively safeguard money. In any case, there was still no Cambodian currency to look after. Initially, the government provided US$20 a week to store in the bank. Although this may seem like a rather trivial amount, US$20 was considered to be a substantial sum at the time. Considerable effort was put into building a more secure bank made of concrete. There was, however, no cement available in Ratanakiri, so it had to be sourced from Kratie. But since there were still a large number of Khmer Rouge along the road to Kratie, a substantial number of Vietnamese soldiers were needed to escort the cement safely back to Banlung. The sand required was taken from the Sesan River near Kachoan Village in Voeunsai

District. The security situation along the road to Kachoan was tenuous at best. As Jampong Jari put it, "The bank was the first concrete building constructed in Banlung, but it was very difficult to source the materials to build it." Finally, however, the concrete bank was built, and the fifteen employees were able to feel more confident to be able to secure money.[84]

Banking during the early PRK period was certainly different from the high-tech and large volume banking of today. Personal and commercial accounts were unheard of, and the main purpose of the bank was to facilitate the payment of monthly government wages. When the Cambodian currency was reintroduced, money was sent to Banlung by plane, and then it was kept in the bank for safekeeping.[85]

Heng Bunthan (ethnic Lao, Voeunsai Village), the younger brother of Heng Khamvan, started working for the Organization Department in Banlung in the early 1980s, and was assigned the job of gaining central-level permission to pay government employee salaries. This is how it worked. A list of names of government employees to be paid and the budget needed to pay them would be prepared in Banlung. It was then Heng Bunthan's job to carry the list by hand to Phnom Penh via Vietnam. It was not safe to travel via Cambodia, due to Khmer Rouge security concerns. Indeed, until the late 1980s, virtually all the travel from Ratanakiri Province to Phnom Penh went through Vietnam.[86]

Once Heng Bunthan arrived in Phnom Penh, he would deliver the list to the Ministry of Planning and the Ministry of Finance to approve the budget. It would typically take between one and two weeks to receive these approvals. Then Bunthan would return to Banlung and give Jampong Jari the approved plan. Jampong Jari would then release the funds to pay the government salaries, which would be delivered to government offices for distribution to individual employees. The military and police prepared their own salary plans and followed the same process. Salaries were sometimes late being paid, but typically not more than a month. In any case, government officials depended much more on food rations than their salaries, and those were typically delivered on time.[87] According to Muan Poi, he initially received forty kilograms of milled rice, some monosodium glutamate (MSG), five packs of cigarettes, and two bars of soap each month. In addition, each year he received enough cloth to make two sets of clothing (two shirts and two pairs of pants). After currency was reintroduced into the system, government employees had to buy cloth to make clothing.[88]

One of the main jobs of the Organization Department was checking on the histories of potential new employees before they were hired, including scrutinizing political histories and considering their abilities. Sometimes trips had to be made to check on the backgrounds of potential new employees, including traveling through Vietnam to reach southern Cambodia.[89] Because it was difficult to find people to work for the government, people with low qualifications were often hired. For example, it was not initially necessary for government officials to be literate, provided that they were loyal to the PRK government.[90] Indeed, much more care was taken not to hire people who were allegedly sympathetic or working undercover with the Khmer Rouge.[91] Indicating the importance of loyalty above skill, the *Phnom Penh Domestic Service* (1980a) reported, in specific reference to Ratanakiri, that, "We have flushed out many two-faced officials among us."

The department also investigated reports about inappropriate behavior by government employees, but they did not have a mandate to investigate Vietnamese soldiers or advisors. The Vietnamese did that themselves. The department also compiled the personnel documents of candidates for becoming party members after other party members had nominated them. The documents would then be sent to the provincial party office for consideration.[92]

Constructing a Formal Education System in Ratanakiri Province after 1979

As with most other PRK governmental departments after 1979, and particularly in northeastern Cambodia, the formal education system in Ratanakiri Province was virtually nonexistent. Therefore, it had to be built from scratch. Chan Khamkhoeua, who would later become the head of Ratanakiri's Education Department, became one of the first school teachers in Ratanakiri Province in 1979. She was initially an elementary teacher in Lumphat District. In early 1979, the new government began searching for people in the villages who had even a basic education and were willing to become teachers. Because Chan Khamkhoeua was not a leader in the Khmer Rouge, she was eligible to join the ranks of the first group of new teachers chosen. Before starting teaching, however, she was sent with other recruits for one month of teacher training in Voeunsai, which at the time was still the provincial capital. One person was chosen from each village or commune in the province to receive this basic teacher training. According to Chan Khamkhoeua, "Basically anyone who was literate had the chance to become a teacher. If a person had studied grade one, that person could teach grade one, and then the next year the teacher could potentially teach grade two even though he or she had never studied grade two before."[93] During this period, the PRK government motto was something like, "Those who know a lot teach those who know a little. Those who know a little teach those who know nothing."[94] This certainly applied to northeastern Cambodia. Heng Bunthan was another early teacher. He spent the Khmer Rouge period in Cambodia, but because he was literate in Khmer, he was made head teacher in Voeunsai in March 1979.[95]

On October 6, 1979, after Chan Khamkheua finished her initial training at Voeunsai, she started teaching elementary school at Lumphat. However, before she began teaching there were not any schools in the province, so all the new schools in the villages, including the one she taught at, were very basic bamboo structures built by the villagers using materials from the forest. Each of the communes had a Vietnamese advisor stationed there, at least early on. These advisors helped mobilize local people to construct the buildings. It was not until 1992 that better schools made out of sawed lumber and concrete began being constructed.[96]

At the end of her first year of teaching, Chan Khamkheua received an additional three months of teacher training, from June to October 1980. Then, after completing her second year of teaching, she was sent to Banlung for a third round of teacher training. This time she specifically studied how to teach grade one and two students in the same class, and grades three, four, and five in the same class. In 1981, she was chosen to go to Phnom Penh for more advanced teacher training. She stayed there until 1983, and then returned to Ratanakiri Province, where she was appointed as the principle of the elementary school in the provincial capital of Banlung.[97]

In 1980, there were reportedly just twelve schools, seventeen teachers, and six hundred students in Ratanakiri Province (*Phnom Penh Domestic Service* 1980c), but the education system expanded quickly, and late in the same year there were reportedly thirty-nine schools, 140 classrooms, 150 teachers, and 3,500 students in the province (BBC 1980). Still, the Ratanakiri Education Department was not officially established until 1983.

In 1983, for the first time, Ratanakiri Province sent thirty people who had grade three education (most were seven to eighteen years old) to study for a year in Phnom Penh. Called the 3+1 program, those who returned from this training taught grade three. In 1984, there were students in Ratanakiri who had studied grade four, and forty of them were accepted for teacher training in Banlung. This program was similar to the previous one, except that all the training took place in Banlung and was one year more advanced than was the case the previous year. It was known as the 4+1 program. Although teaching qualifications gradually improved, from 1979 to 1984, it was still only possible to study as high as grade four in Ratanakiri Province.[98]

In 1985, forty people who had completed grade five were sent to study for a year at the newly established teacher's college in Stung Treng, as part of the 5+1 program. From 1985 onward, it was possible to study as high as grade five in Ratanakiri. In 1986, thirty students were sent to Stung Treng to study for the time in a three-year teacher training regime known as the 5+3 program. They also organized 4+1 and 5+1 teacher training programs in Banlung for those who had been teachers before 1970 but needed some updated instruction. Most of those who enrolled in these programs graduated and returned to Ratanakiri to teach.[99]

Although the number of teachers in Ratanakiri Province gradually increased throughout the 1980s, school enrollment remained low, especially among the ethnic minorities. Chan Khamkhoeua claimed that less than 40 percent of the ethnic minorities went to school in the 1980s, and that many of those only studied at certain times of the year.[100] This was due to both sporadic teaching, and also because children often traveled to remote areas with their parents to farm during the rainy season, thus making it difficult for them to study. Many parents also did not want their children to commute to school, fearing that they might be abducted or attacked by the remaining bands of Khmer Rouge in the province. According to Chan Khamkhoeua, it was mainly only possible for children living in the provincial capital or district centers, and some communes, to attend school, as few villages had schools in them. Security concerns also made it difficult for government officials from Banlung to provide support in some of the villages. For example, officials were wary about traveling on the road between Banlung and Voeunsai for fear of encountering Khmer Rouge along the way.[101] Indicative of the education problems, the *Phnom Penh Domestic Service* (1984b) reported that in 1984, Ratanakiri was the only province in the country where it had not yet been possible to establish a high school.

During the 1980s, some opposed to the PRK government and their Vietnamese allies accused the Vietnamese of trying to impose Vietnamese language education in Cambodia (see Vickery 1984), but in Ratanakiri and Stung Treng there is no evidence to support such claims. Indeed, only people who wanted to study Vietnamese did so, but many chose to, so that they could talk with the Vietnamese advisors working with the government.[102] French and English languages were discouraged during the PRK period, but that mattered little in the northeast, as very few people were interested in these languages or had much knowledge of them.[103] The focus was developing basic Khmer-language teachers. More important, the indigenous languages of the minorities were not discouraged by the PRK government (Gottesman 2002), much to the relief of those in the northeast, where Khmer was not well-known. Generally speaking, minority languages were respected, and each ethnic group was given the right to write, speak, and teach in its own language (US Library of Congress 2006), even though in reality none of the minority languages were being taught at the time.[104] Indeed, a system for writing Brao did not begin to develop until the 1990s.

Developing Infrastructure in Ratanakiri Province

In 1979, there was virtually no physical infrastructure in northeastern Cambodia. In fact, there was little even before the Khmer Rouge came to power, and even less by the PRK period. There were a few buildings here and there, but not many, and what existed was generally in poor condition. No urban water supply or sewage systems existed, and nobody in the northeast had access to electricity. Therefore, considering that the main priority of the PRK government and the Vietnamese was to maintain security and prevent the Khmer Rouge from returning to power, there was little effort made to develop infrastructure in the northeast during the 1980s apart from constructing a small number of government buildings, including those built in the provincial capitals, such as Banlung. Even then, most building were made of wood. The Vietnamese military did, however, build some strategic military infrastructure. For example, in April 1979, it completed a 200-meter long bridge across the Srepok River in Sesan District, Stung Treng Province (*Phnom Penh Domestic Service* 1979a).

One substantial infrastructure project that was initiated in the northeast during the PRK period was the O Chum hydropower project in Ratanakiri Province. In 1985, Vietnamese "specialists" agreed to build one or more moderate-sized hydroelectric dams in Ratanakiri Province, primarily to provide electricity for the provincial capital. They identified the O Chum stream, in O Chum District, as having potential for the development of two medium-sized hydropower dams. The lower dam was built first. It flooded a relatively small area belonging to the two Kreung villages of Trawng Jong and Jou (Svay). In 1987 or 1988, not long after he had returned from working in Kampong Som Province to become vice-chairman of Ratanakiri's People's Committee, Bunhom Many was invited to visit France to learn about hydropower dams. In 1990, following his return, construction on the upper dam began (*Phnom Penh Domestic Service* 1990), which resulted in flooding of a much larger area, including fifty to sixty hectares of lowland paddy land. The flooding caused significant hardship for the ethnic Kreung people from Trawng Jong and O Chum Villages, the owners of the land. Although the dams, with a combined electricity generating capacity of 1 MW of power, were able to provide moderate electric supply to a small town like Banlung, their development was problematic, as no compensation was offered for any of the land that the locals lost. Initially, the Vietnamese dam builders and their Cambodian counterparts promised that those impacted would receive free electricity, but after the project was completed the villagers found themselves paying the same rate as everyone else (Baird 2008). With support of Vietnam's Water Conservancy Construction Enterprise No. 1, the O Chum hydroelectric power plant was finally completed in late 1991, at a reported cost to the Cambodian government of between US$3.5 and 4 million. The expense was partially borne by the government of Cambodia, with the government of Vietnam being responsible for design, construction, and the provision of equipment and machinery (BBC 1991; *Phnom Penh SPK* 1991; *Hanoi Domestic Service* 1991).

Pro Ethnic Minority Policies

In the introduction of this book, I mentioned a comment made by Kham Sai, in which he stated that one of the reasons for Pen Sovan being arrested was because he was not as pro ethnic minority as the Vietnamese. It is certainly true that one of the things that ethnic minorities in Ratanakiri Province and other parts of northeastern Cambodia often say is that the PRK government and their Vietnamese allies were strongly pro ethnic minority. Indeed, one of the main reasons that many Brao see the 1979 to 1989 period as a sort of golden age is because of their understanding that the PRK period was a time in which ethnic minorities were given priority by the government. Minorities tend to point to a few key issues to demonstrate this. First, almost all the leaders in northeastern Cambodia at the time were themselves ethnic minorities. Many still speak about this today and bemoan the fact that the local governments in northeastern Cambodia are now mainly dominated by ethnic Khmers, something that was not the case at the time the Vietnamese were in Cambodia (see, also, Chapter 8). Second, the Brao often mention that during the PRK period anyone could go to school for free and receive medical treatment at the hospital for free. In contrast to today, those without money (especially the ethnic minorities) presently have a hard time studying because teachers demand small under-the-table daily student fees. Teachers also frequently require that students pay for "extracurricular classes" that are necessary to pass important tests. Teachers also often demand that students pay them fees to graduate, especially from high school in Banlung. Fees can sometimes reach US$1,000 per student or higher, making it very hard for poorer students, and particularly ethnic minorities, to make it through the system. The same goes for medical services.

Illustrative of this, Baird and Hammer (2013) learned through their research on health care in Ratanakiri that many ethnic minorities in the province do not believe that present-day medical services are better than those available in the 1970s and 1980s. That is mainly because the service (not necessarily the treatment) that they received back then was generally better. Crucially, patients were treated with more dignity. Now doctors and nurses often treat patients without money with disdain, something that was rarely the case during the PRK period. Overall, many ethnic minorities point to the fact that they never had to pay fees to go to school or access health care services during the PRK period, but now they do. The former head of the Department of Women's Affairs in Ratanakiri Province, Jop Moer, who is herself ethnic Kachok, told me, "The Vietnamese didn't look down on people [the ethnic minorities] like the Khmers do. The ethnic minorities had a strong role during the Vietnamese period."[105]

Indicative of the pro minority policy of the PRK government, in

1984 a resolution was released at the PRK's National Cadres Conference entitled "Policy toward National Minorities," which made it clear that minorities (with the exception of the Chinese) in Cambodia were considered an integral part of the Cambodian nation, and were therefore especially acknowledged. As Bou Thang put it, "The PRK supported minorities, but we were wary of the Chinese. We did not utilize them in government."[106]

In addition, during the 1980s, the PRK government established a "Nationalities Committee" (*Khana Kamaka Chun Cheat*), but it was apparently dissolved in 1993, which was disappointing to Bou Thang.[107] According to him, in the early 1990s, he proposed to members of the FUNCINPEC Party that were in the national constitution drafting committee that more needed to be done to recognize ethnic minorities in Cambodia's new constitution. According to Bou Thang, he told them, "Every forest has many kinds of trees." However, Loy Sim Chheang, FUNCINPEC's first vice president of the National Assembly, reportedly responded by saying that Cambodia did not need any minorities, which was a Sangkum Reast Niyum period position.[108] Not surprisingly, this shocked Bou Thang.[109]

The district chiefs in Ratanakiri Province in 1987 were Sev Luo (Jarai, O Yadao), Len Noeung (Tampuon, Bokeo), Raman Pun (Jarai, Andong Meas), Ha Nen (Tampuon, Kachoan), Heng Bunthan (ethnic Lao, Voeunsai), Bien Thavoen (Kreung, O Chum), and Sieng Plung (Brao, Taveng). Koun Moum and Banlung districts had not been established yet.[110] Crucially, all these leaders were ethnic minorities.

Ethnic minorities also dominated other senior government positions in northeastern Cambodia during the latter part of the PRK period. For example, the following ethnic minorities held leadership positions in departments in the province: Dam Chanty (ethnic Lao/Tampuon, women's), Yoep Vanson (Brao, health), Feuay Bunma (ethnic Lao, youth), Kham Dy (Brao, police), Muan Poi (Brao, organization), Thon Thin (Brao, military), Kham Toeung (Pheng Phol, second name) (Kachok, transportation), Bui Yung (Jarai, trade and construction), Kham San (Kreung, agriculture), Euang Sari (ethnic Lao, information), and Lat Vansao (ethnic Lao, propaganda). Kreng Siengnoi (Brao) was the head of the provincial PRPK, with Yoep Vanson (Brao) as his deputy.[111] The provincial PRPK Committee had twenty-one members at the time.[112] The only ethnic Khmer leader in the province apart from Lak On was Yeul Sari, who headed the Education Department.[113]

While the policies of the PRK government were certainly more sensitive to minorities than previous governments, and were also generally more sensitive to minorities than Khmer-dominated governments since the 1990s, government policies were still aimed at transforming the highlanders into modern Khmers. The Stalinist view related to the evolution of humankind was politically dominant. Ideas related to legal pluralism and the empowerment of "Indigenous peoples" were not yet known.

Life of the General Population in Ratanakiri after 1979

Despite a lot of propaganda, including many outrageous accusations leveled against the PRK government and its Vietnamese supporters during the 1979 to 1989 period (see Ea Meng-Try 1981; Shawcross 1984, for examples), the PRK government was quite moderate, especially compared to the Democratic Kampuchea government that preceded it (Vickery 1984, 2010). This was particularly the case because the country was entangled in civil war throughout the 1980s. Indeed, the civil war was one of the main reasons that the PRK government and its Vietnamese allies were especially careful not to upset the local population. They feared—and rightfully so—that being too harsh could have serious political and ultimately security implications, specifically if locals supported the Khmer Rouge. For example, the PRK government decided to not collect taxes from the peasantry, opting instead to just collect some small market stall fees from those involved in trading (Vickery 1984). The PRK government also issued guns to highlanders in Ratanakiri to defend themselves against the Khmer Rouge, and was quite moderate in restricting their use, an act that might have seemed necessary for security reasons at the time, but later was blamed for considerable declines in wildlife populations, since many of these weapons ended up being used for hunting (Zweers and Sok 2002).

The government reintroduced Buddhism in 1979, as Buddhism was fully embraced by the PRK leadership, although they chose to drop the traditional schools of ordination, the *Mahanikay* and *Thommayuth* (Loschman 2006-2007) just as its neighbor, the Lao People's Democratic Republic (Lao PDR) had done. In fact, Loschman (2006-2007) conducted research in the mid-1980s—albeit in other parts of Cambodia and not in the northeast—regarding the reestablishment of the Buddhist sangha in Cambodia. Loschman reported that the idea was to "develop a monastic order which, as an active pillar of support to the new rulers, would use the opportunities and means at its disposal to help carry out the programme of reconstruction of Cambodia in which social progress would become a reality" (p. 101). Essentially, rather than simply wanting monks to return to traditional Buddhist thought and practice, they encouraged them to adopt "reason and rationality," to be a productive force in reconstructing the nation. This policy included promoting the idea of social equality between monks and laypeople (Loschman 2006–2007, 104). While the revival and promotion of Buddhism was not nearly as important for most of the ethnic minorities in the northeast as compared to other parts of the country, as most northeasterners were not Buddhists, the change was significant for two groups in the northeast: the Lao, who largely profess to respect Buddhism, and also ethnic Khmers living in the province. While there were no Buddhist Brao at the time, some Tampuon, especially those from Kachoan Village where Bou Thang and Thang Bai came from (remember that Bou Thang was once a Buddhist novice), also greatly promoted the PRK's reintroduction of Buddhism.[114]

Another important change was that people were no longer prevented from organizing and participating in animist rituals and were generally allowed to follow their traditional spiritual practices, including sacrificing chickens, pigs, and water buffaloes, and practicing various rituals associated with swidden agriculture (Mallow 2002; Ruohomaki 2003). This change was particularly important for the Brao, but also for various other minority groups in northeastern Cambodia, including the Lao. It is not that such practices were necessarily encouraged, as the government still followed a Marxist-Leninist ideology that generally saw animist rituals as primitive and superstitious, but as previously mentioned, the PRK government and their Vietnamese allies were particularly attentive about keeping the people from joining the Khmer Rouge, so they did not discourage more traditional ways of life, even if the leadership might have privately disapproved of some rituals. The relaxation on religious freedoms pleased most highlanders, and some animist practices became reinvigorated. Others, however, never did, and in some cases, animist rituals were abandoned or reduced in importance and frequency during the 1980s (Mallow 2002).

In northeastern Cambodia, as in other parts of the country, "solidarity teams" (*kraom samakhi* in Khmer) or mutual aid teams were established, but only with considerable care (Slocomb 2003), and they were not created for rice cultivation. The argument used to justify not establishing collective agriculture at the time was that the people did not have enough surplus rice to support such a system. Also, after experiencing Khmer Rouge rule, the people were generally not interested in full-scale communal farming or anything else that resembled the system that Democratic Kampuchea had forced on them. Therefore, the people were generally happy that they were allowed to grow rice independently. In 1979 Hun Sen stated, for example, that "collective exploitation is our policy, but without the methods of Pol Pot. . . . We will not force farmers into participating, and those who are capable of farming individually may do so" (Gottesman 2002, 91). Some communal agriculture was, however, established for rubber cultivation in Ratanakiri Province,[115] as rubber was considered a key export for the PRK government (Slocomb 2003).

After 1979, each village was encouraged to cultivate a single small solidarity or communal swidden field as a community to serve as a safety net for community members who encountered unexpected hardships. These were called "solidarity swiddens" (*chamkar samakhi* in Khmer). According to Yoep Vanson, many people in Ratanakiri Province, correctly or incorrectly, believed that the idea of *chamkar samakhi* emerged from Kreung traditional practices. Essentially, the idea was to create one collective swidden field for each village, so as to support people in need.[116] They were specifically encouraged to participate in collectivization, or the creation of solidarity groups. According to Bou Thang, this system was especially important early on, as there were many elderly and disabled people and orphans who could not fend for themselves and therefore required support from other community members (Bou Thang 1993). The PRK government also encouraged the establishment of solidarity groups consisting of ten to fifteen families that would essentially exchange agricultural labor with each other. This practice is in line with Brao traditions of labor exchange, which I frequently observed in rural Taveng District in the early 2000s, long after the government stopped promoting such exchanges (Bou Thang 1993).

In 1982, commune or subdistrict elections were organized for the first time. In Talao Commune, in what is now Andong Meas District, but which was in Bokeo District at the time, the elections were conducted in a very basic way. The officials allocated one tin can for each candidate. Then each voter was given a single kernel of corn to vote with. Each voter put the kernel of corn into whatever can was being used to represent the candidate that the voter preferred.[117] This indicates the way things were in the early years of the PRK. There were no official voting boxes or ballots for elections, just tin cans and kernels of corn.

The civil war continued on for many years, and the government established the Disabled Peoples Department in the 1980s, with branches in all provinces to support disabled war victims, which was indicative of the toll the war took (especially with regard to injuries caused by landmines).[118]

Border Demarcation with Vietnam

In 1984, Dop Khamchoeung traveled to Galai-Kontum Province to negotiate with the Vietnamese regarding the border between Mondulkiri Province and adjacent parts of Vietnam. It must have been somewhat awkward because the Vietnamese still maintained considerable power in Cambodia, and the memory of the arrest of Pen Sovan remained fresh in the minds of many. Khamchoeung went to the border twice during the year, and it took him five or six days to travel from Sen Monorom to the border and back each trip. Yet according to Khamchoeung, the Vietnamese were fair regarding the border and did not unduly use their influence to gain additional territory from Cambodia.[119]

Bui Yung, however, had a very different experience in relation to border demarcation with the Vietnamese. In April 1986, when he was vice-chairman of Ratanakiri's People's Committee, two senior Vietnamese military advisors, Quang and Hat, reportedly asked him to "sign away land on the border to Vietnam." Initially, when they approached him, he asked them why he was expected to sign, and not Boua Chuong, the chairman of the province's People's Committee. They responded that Boua Chuong was old and would soon retire, and Bui Yung would replace him, so it was appropriate for Bui Yung to sign. Bui Yung then asked why the chairs of the People's Committees in other provinces were not being asked to sign, but he did not receive a clear response.[120]

Bui Yung, who was also the head of the provincial Planning Department,[121] asked others in the department to review the maps that the Vietnamese wanted him to approve, including Yat Sokhan (ethnic

Lao, Lumphat), Khen Phosy (ethnic Lao, Lumphat), Ho Hong (Khmer), and Chanma Savat (ethnic Lao, Lumphat). However, the documents and maps were all in Vietnamese, which presented a serious problem for those who were supposed to review them but did not read Vietnamese.[122] In any case, after examining the maps, Bui Yung asked the others whether they thought he should sign or not. None were brave enough to provide a clear recommendation one way or the other. Instead, they said that it depended on him. He believed that the Vietnamese were proposing to take a large piece of land north of the Sesan River from the headwaters of the Lalay stream, in Stung Treng Province, to the Dragon's Tail triborder area between Cambodia, Laos, and Vietnam. He felt that the proposal was inappropriate and so did not sign, and ultimately walked out of the room on the Vietnamese advisors, apparently leaving them "red-faced." They tried to call him back, but he kept going.[123]

Bui Yung claimed that he never told Kham Len, the secretary of Ratanakiri's provincial Party Committee or Bou Thang about the incident, as he feared they would not believe him and side with the Vietnamese.[124] However, when I asked Bou Thang many years later what his impression was of Bui Yung's story, he responded that he thought that it might be accurate, as his own experiences indicated to him that the Vietnamese were gradually taking land in the northeast of Cambodia. He commented that the Vietnamese expanded their control over land like *"man keo"* (the Lao language work for a type of tuber). Bou Thang also claimed that he had argued with a Vietnamese advisor once, in the 1980s, after he claimed that part of O Yadao District was the property of Vietnam. Bou Thang believes that once the Vietnamese failed to convince him to go along with this idea, they may have moved on to Bui Yung to try to convince him to sign.[125]

In a related matter, Bou Thang said that in 1981 and 1982 he worked with Bui Yung as an advisor to develop a special market sector in the area that now encompasses O Yadao, Andong Meas, Lumphat, and Bokeo Districts, partially to try to prevent the Vietnamese from taking territory along the border. Part of the plan was also to move some disabled and retired Khmer soldiers into the area to protect the border. However, some people misunderstood that he was trying to make some sort of autonomous area for himself. Lak On was apparently especially opposed to the idea, as was Hun Sen, and the Vietnamese lobbied strongly against the plan, claiming that Bou Thang was trying to separate from the country. The Vietnamese asked the PRK government to stop the plan, and Hun Sen apparently specifically told Bou Thang to abandon the initiative, which he did. According to Bou Thang, the Vietnamese were angry with him.[126]

Bui Yung claims that after he refused to sign away Cambodian territory as the Vietnamese requested, the Vietnamese advisors in Ratanakiri proceeded to orchestrate a secret behind-the-scenes campaign to slander him and make him look bad in the eyes of other leaders. Bui Yung believes that Boua Chuong bought into the plan, and that he subsequently ordered the provincial police to surround his house one day in 1986 or 1987 when ninety people were gathered there playing cards, after Bui Yung's nephew had died of illness. Shots were fired above the house, and the people there were accused of illegal gambling.[127] However, Kham Khoeun claims that Chue Ngong of the police, not Boua Chuong, ordered the action to stop people from losing money due to gambling.[128] In any case, in 1987 Bui Yung was demoted and transferred to the Education Department of Ratanakiri Province, where he worked as the deputy of one of the units in the department.[129] Bui Yung was, however, also given the position of deputy head of development for the province. However, he was no longer invited to party meetings and was generally shunned. He finally left government service in 1995, resentful of how he had been treated.[130]

Conclusion

Northeastern Cambodia, like other parts of the country, was in shambles when the PRK government was established in 1979, as the Khmer Rouge left behind very little infrastructure or human resources. Indeed, in 1979 there was almost nothing to build on in the northeastern provinces of Cambodia—including Ratanakiri Province. The situation, however, made it possible to start anew. For example, in the 1980s, the capital of Ratanakiri Province, Banlung, was developed on the site of a small Tampuon village. In addition, basic infrastructure and the education system were gradually built up from being almost nonexistent during the Khmer Rouge period. Crucially, the pro ethnic minority policies that the PRK government adopted help explain why so many Brao and other ethnic minorities in the northeast saw the PRK government as being on their side, even if other ethnic minorities sided with the Khmer Rouge. Significantly, most of the senior government positions in northeastern Cambodia were held by ethnic minorities, which made the Brao and others feel more politically represented than ever before. We finally considered some of the tensions that emerged with the Vietnamese regarding border issues, especially in Ratanakiri Province. It was nothing like what occurred between the Khmer Rouge and the Vietnamese in the late 1970s. However, subtler but important tensions did emerge, ones that have not been well documented.

We now turn to considering the security situation, and particularly the military conflict that occurred in northeastern Cambodia between the Vietnamese and People's Revolutionary Army of Kampuchea (PRAK) on one side, and the Khmer Rouge on the other. In the chapter, we can see how political divisions often trumped ethnic connections, although ethnicity certainly remained a crucial factor.

6

The Security and Military Circumstances in Northeastern Cambodia, 1979 to 1989

The People's Army of Vietnam (PAVN) provided the vast majority of the fighting force that drove the Khmer Rouge from power. They were also, however, crucial for maintaining security in Cambodia for years to follow. Most of the Vietnamese stayed near the Cambodia-Thailand border where much of the fighting occurred, but there were also a considerable number based in northeastern Cambodia and other parts of the country. Although the number of Vietnamese troops in Cambodia gradually declined after 1985, a substantial number remained in the country until 1989, and even a smaller number for a short period afterward.[1] Cambodia faced a conundrum. On one hand, the heavy Vietnamese presence in the country made it possible for the opposition to claim that Vietnamese colonialism was occurring (Gottesman 2002), whether it was or not. On the other hand, the Vietnamese were militarily essential for keeping the Khmer Rouge from returning to power, as the NADK, the army of Democratic Kampuchea, remained largely intact as a fighting force since in early 1979 they withdrew from the cities and moved to the forests to establish bases, especially near the border with Thailand.

The military conflict in northeastern Cambodia between the PAVN and their Cambodian allies in the PRAK and the NADK had a tremendous impact on life in northeastern Cambodia throughout the PRK period, even if the security situation varied from place to place and gradually improved as PRAK was built up with Vietnamese support. But northeasterners were not only affected by security issues, many ethnic minorities from the northeast were recruited into PRAK and were sent to support security initiatives such as the program known as K5, which was an extremely controversial plan launched near the Thai border in the 1980s. Many northeastern ethnic minorities also learned Khmer and even Lao languages when they were soldiers.

Vietnamese Operations in Northeastern Cambodia

By early 1979, PAVN had secured control over most of Cambodia, including the northeast. However, the security situation remained precarious, although throughout 1979 Hanoi denied that armed resistance was occurring in Cambodia. Instead, they claimed that there were just operations to mop up "hordes of bandits" (Pao-Min 1985, 134). In fact, there were still significant Khmer Rouge units operating in many parts of the country, including in the northeast. Although PAVN initially mainly worked alone because there were few Cambodian forces to collaborate with, over time, as the PRAK strengthened, the Vietnamese gradually coordinated operations more closely with them.

In early 1979, PAVN's 309th Division was the main Vietnamese force operating in northeastern Cambodia east of the Mekong River. However, on March 15, 1979, Military Region 5 Headquarters ordered the 315th Division to replace it, with the task of continuing to hunt down the Khmer Rouge's 801st Division, to support supply transportation along Route 19 (the road from the Vietnamese border through Ratanakiri to Stung Treng), and to help the PRK government "mobilize the masses, restore production, build political organizations and local governments, attack hunger and disease, and stabilize the lives of the people" (Institute of Military History 2010).

Based in Banlung, and led by division commander Trương Đức Chữ and political commissar Trương Trung Thắng, the 315th Division did not, however, have it easy, as they were required to conduct combat operations over a wide and sparsely populated area with rugged terrain (Institute of Military History 2010). There were apparently 3,000 soldiers in the 315th Division, which was the only Vietnamese unit based in Ratanakiri.[2] The 315th Division supported PRAK's 179th (named after January 1979) Battalion, the PRK government's military force in Ratanakiri Province. The 179th Battalion was much smaller and less capable than Vietnam's 315th Division, but it gradually strengthened during the 1980s. The 315th Division also worked closely with the 280th Engineer

Regiment and assault youth forces of the Vietnam Volunteer Army (VVA) assigned to mobilize on Route 19 to protect traffic along the main road corridor from the Vietnam-Cambodia border to Stung Treng (Institute of Military History 2010). They faced frequent attacks from NADK forces, especially in 1979 and the early 1980s.

In late March 1979, a plan for the deployment of Vietnam's 315th Division was approved at the zone headquarters in Stung Treng. The 142nd Infantry Regiment was based in Lumphat District, Ratanakiri Province, and a part of the regiment was sent to southern Bokeo District in Ratanakiri Province and eastern Stung Treng Province. Their area of operations was south of Route 19 to the border between Mondulkiri and Kratie Provinces. One of its tasks was to protect the area near the Srepok ferry crossing to Kaoh Nheaek District, in Mondulkiri Province, and also Route 141 and its intersection with Route 19 (Institute of Military History 2010). The 143rd Infantry Regiment was based in Voeunsai District, Ratanakiri Province and Siempang District, Stung Treng Province, north of the Sesan River. Their main task was to attack NADK forces in the headwaters of the Lalay stream and in other parts of the district (Institute of Military History 2010), which was mainly populated by ethnic Kavet people. The 733rd Infantry Regiment would be responsible for the Banlung area, O Chum to the north, and the eastern part of Voeunsai District up to the triborder "Dragon's Tail" area, where the borders of Laos, Cambodia, and Vietnam meet (Institute of Military History 2010). The 729th Artillery Regiment was deployed east of Banlung and the western part of Bokeo District in Ratanakiri Province. It concentrated on turning its soldiers into artillerymen and on defending its area of operations and Route 19 (Institute of Military History 2010).

The 315th Division conducted sweep operations against pockets of NADK forces, and from March 20 to April 14, 1979, the division's units reportedly fought sixteen battles, killed and captured hundreds of enemy troops, and confiscated a quantity of weapons and ammunition (Institute of Military History 2010). AFP (1979) also reported, based on information received from Khmer Rouge soldiers, that 4,000 Khmer Rouge troops in northern Ratanakiri and Stung Treng Provinces had been "dispersed" by the Vietnamese in March 1979. Some apparently fled into Laos and were captured by Pathet Lao communist soldiers, while others traveled to the northwest. Some Khmer Rouge continued to fight, but they were suffering from a lack of anti-tank weapons, thus leading some soldiers and officials to defect. There were, however,

Vietnamese casualties as well, including one serious case reported from Ratanakiri when a Vietnamese military truck ran over a mine, reportedly killing everyone on board (*Xinhua* 1979b).

In 1979, before the provincial capital was moved to Banlung, the Khmer Rouge spread rumors that it would attack the Cambodian provincial office at Voeunsai. Correctly guessing that the Khmer Rouge was trying to lure Vietnamese troops to defend Voeunsai, the 315th Division's leadership sent only a small force and instead mobilized most of their troops to hunt down NADK units in the Lalay stream area and near the border with Attapeu Province, southern Laos. During this operation, the Vietnamese were reportedly able to "liberate" 3,000 civilians, including Boua Chuong's oldest son and grandson (Institute of Military History 2010).

Vietnam's 315th Division was reportedly able to move many people in northeastern Bokeo District back to set up new villages along Route 19. NADK forces came to try to burn down the houses of people who moved to the road, to chase the inhabitants back out into the forest, but the 733rd Regiment quickly attacked and was able to successfully defend the people (Institute of Military History 2010). However, VODK (1979c) reported a very different situation, claiming that a company of Vietnamese soldiers came to Kang Le Village, in northern Bokeo District, and burned all 250 houses down, a large amount of food stuffs, and then—quite unbelievably—publically executed forty people, including older people, pregnant women, and children. Furthermore, the Vietnamese were accused of disemboweling some victims, burying others alive, and using chemical weapons.

During the Cambodian New Year celebrations on April 14 and 15, 1979, units of the 315th Division provided the security that allowed the people to celebrate and have fun. According to the Vietnamese, "Cambodians were so moved that they tied strings around the wrists of our soldiers and poured water on them as part of their prayers for our Vietnamese volunteer troops. Those noble and selfless actions helped to cement the bonds of trust between Vietnamese volunteer army troops and Vietnamese military specialists and the Cambodian revolutionary army and the Cambodian people" (Institute of Military History 2010).

During the rainy season of 1979, the 315th Division reportedly took advantage of the high water level of the Sesan River and used its 733rd Regiment to commandeer civilian boats in Voeunsai and use them to move up the river to Taveng and then deep up the Khampha and

Trabok streams to coordinate with Gialai-Kontum provincial armed forces units in conducting an attack deep into the base of NADK's 801st Division, which was located along the Cambodia-Laos border. During this operation, Vietnamese forces reportedly destroyed many enemy logistical support facilities (Institute of Military History 2010).

To further strengthen the Cambodians at the grassroots level, in August 1979, Vietnam's Military Region 5 formed four additional local battalions and fifteen district companies to assist the Ratanakiri, Mondulkiri, Stung Treng, and Preah Vihear Provinces (Institute of Military History 2010). Kratie was being supported by Vietnam's Military Region 7.[3] At the same time, the Vietnamese sent personnel to help the PRAK form unified military headquarters in each of the four northeastern provinces, as well as a PRAK cadre training school near Banlung (Institute of Military History 2010).

During the 1979 to 1980 dry season, NADK reestablished the 801st Division command center, after being driven from the Lao-Cambodia border, in the three borders area between Cambodia, Thailand, and Laos (Institute of Military History 2010), near the Tonle Repou (Xelamphao) River, which borders with Mounlapamok District, Champasak Province, Laos, and Yeun District, Ubon Ratchathani Province, Thailand.[4] They concentrated their forces to attack areas west of the Mekong River in Preah Vihear and western Stung Treng Provinces.

NADK's 920th Division, on the other hand, operated east and west of the Mekong River in a number of districts in Mondulkiri, Kratie, and Kampong Thom Provinces. NADK's 612th and 616th Divisions established a rear supply base in the area of Hill 547 and dispersed their forces along the Thai-Cambodian border in western Preah Vihear Province and eastern Siem Reap Province (Institute of Military History 2010).

The Khmer Rouge had two main goals in the northeast: west of the Mekong, they intended to intensify guerrilla operations, including conducting heavy weapons/artillery attacks and small ambushes. They also planned to use various types of landmines to expand attacks on road and water traffic. Those NADK forces located west of the Mekong also actively recruited supporters with the intent of expanding their military strength. They were successful in capturing a number of Vietnamese-manned border outposts to so as gain control of more territory and populated areas (Institute of Military History 2010). Although it is hard to verify either Khmer Rouge or Vietnamese reports, in January and February 1980, the NADK reported that 2,089 Vietnamese troops had been either wounded or killed in the northeast, of which 1,325 were killed by punji stakes, punji pitfalls, and booby traps (VODK 1980).

On May 18, 1981, Vietnam's Central Military Party Committee issued Resolution No. 36/QUTW, officially forming the VVA in Phnom Penh, designated as Command Headquarters 719. Directly subordinate to Vietnam's Ministry of Defense, the resolution specified that the headquarters was directly responsible for commanding the VVA (actually made up of PAVN forces) and the Vietnamese military specialist group assisting its Cambodian allies. Then on June 29, 1981, Vietnam's chief of state signed an order appointing Lê Đức Anh as deputy minister of defense with the concurrent position of commander of the VVA in Cambodia (Anh 2015). Less than a year later, on June 8, 1982, the Vietnam Politburo issued Decision Order No. 132, forming the specialist group in the Cambodia leadership section, which replaced the section responsible for Cambodian operations. A total of seven members were appointed to the section, but Lê Đức Anh remained the head (Anh 2015).

In northeastern Cambodia's four provinces, VVA units massed their transportation equipment, primarily trucks, to transport a total of 290,536 people in two separate waves back to their old villages so that they could resume their daily routines. Local area VVA battalions reportedly worked closely with these returnees, helping the PRK government form 386 self-administering committees and saving 114,644 people from hunger. VVA soldiers helped them resettle and provided food, tools, seeds, and breeding livestock to make it easier for the people to expand agricultural production. Children in some areas were also able to go to school for the first time in many years. There were also reports of some villagers providing Vietnamese forces with crucial information about NADK troop movements (Institute of Military History 2010).

On the other side, the Khmer Rouge's goal was to gain control of the majority of Battambang, Siem Reap, and Preah Vihear provinces along with western Stung Treng by 1982, to use this area as a springboard for expanding operations further inside Cambodia. They hoped to expand guerrilla activities throughout the country and gain control of 60 percent of the villages and 50 to 60 percent of the population. From that foundation, the Khmer Rouge expected to be able to raise the strength of its military to 60,000 soldiers. They also hoped to seize and disrupt Cambodian markets to sabotage economic recovery and make the economy continue to decline (Anh 1986, 71, cited in Institute of Military History 2010), which they believed would help them raise further support among the population.

In the late 1970s and early 1980s, the Khmer Rouge accused the Vietnamese of using chemical weapons against them on many occasions, including in Ratanakiri in November 1978 (*Hanoi Domestic Service* 1978) and August 1983 (VODK 1983b), but there is not any credible evidence to support such claims. Not surprisingly, the Vietnamese government directly rejected the allegations, calling them "a fabrication that can deceive no one" (*Hanoi Domestic Service* 1978).

Building up the People's Revolutionary Army of Kampuchea (PRAK)

Although the VVA were quite active in the early 1980s, it was not deemed sustainable for the Vietnamese to shoulder so much of the fighting in the long term. It was therefore seen as particularly important to build up the PRAK so that it would be able to eventually takeover security operations. Indeed, over time the PRAK's strength did gradually increase, including in the northeast. The VOPK radio reported that the people of Ratanakiri Province were encouraged to call their relatives out of hiding to join their families and send their children to the revolutionary army as a sign of their lofty national conscience. At important ceremonies, combatants going into battle were blessed. During operations in dangerous areas, ethnic minorities were also encouraged to guide military units (*Phnom Penh Domestic Service* 1980d). However, one of the concerns was that admitting people into the PRAK too easily could allow the enemy to infiltrate the military, which might result in tragic circumstances. Therefore, recruitment needed to happen quickly, but also cautiously. There needed to be a balance.

One of the strategies adopted by PRAK was to implement a five-year military service draft for men. The PRK government opted for this long draft period to reduce turnover and quickly build up its military strength (Gottesman 2002). According to Bou Thang, the focus needed to be put on two groups of people to develop the military. First, efforts were made to draft and otherwise recruit appropriate civilians into the military. Second, efforts were made to increase the capacity of the Cambodians who were admitted into the military. The government tried to do both, but not always in a particularly efficient manner. Early on, the goal was to recruit at least thirty good PRAK regular soldiers for each district in the country.[5] However, conditions in the military were generally harsh. Salaries were low, food was poor, and almost all the equipment provided came from outside of the country and was not always high quality. Even the PRAK's uniforms had to be imported from Vietnam, as there were not yet any garment factories in Cambodia.[6]

Another problem was that Cambodian soldiers—especially ethnic Khmers but also others—often did not like receiving orders from Vietnamese officers. Therefore, morale was frequently poor, and as a result of a combination of factors, desertion rates were high, especially on the Cambodia-Thailand border. Therefore, even though *Phnom Penh Domestic Services* (1979b) reported, in a celebratory manor, that "thousands" of men and women had joined the PRAK during the first six months of the PRK period, the reality was that retention of military personnel was an ongoing challenge. The situation did, however, gradually improve, although not as quickly as hoped. These circumstances resulted in the Vietnamese continuing to engage in most of the serious fighting,[7] although the Khmer Rouge claimed that large numbers of Vietnamese troops in northeastern Cambodia were also deserting (VODK 1983a). Indeed, a small number of Vietnamese soldiers did desert, apparently mainly because they missed their homes and families in Vietnam.[8] Bou Thang claimed that he did not know VVA desertion rates, as the Vietnamese handled their own military affairs.[9]

Beginning in 1979, Ki (Brao, Tangaich Village) was appointed as head of the sector military training center in Banlung, with Kham Sana as his deputy. They were responsible for training soldiers from the five northeastern provinces of Ratanakiri, Stung Treng, Mondulkiri, Preah Vihear, and Kratie. Yung, one of UFNSK's military trainers at Gia Poc, became one of the four Vietnamese military advisors at the school, which offered six-month programs. These included military and political training and also general literacy education for soldiers. There were one hundred students enrolled in each course, including about twenty people from each of the five provinces (including Kratie) that the school was responsible for.[10] Interestingly, many illiterate ethnic minority soldiers in northeastern Cambodia became marginally literate during the time they were in the army.

Prior to 1980, the military region headquarters (*Phum Pheak*) for the northeast, based in Stung Treng, was almost fully staffed by Vietnamese. However, in 1980, a transition to Cambodian leadership began, although it would take some time to complete.[11] Indeed, the headquarters for Military Region 1 was not led by Cambodians until 1985 (*Phnom Penh SPK* 1989), when Kham Chan was transferred from Phnom Penh to take up the command, after previously being the head of military security or *Sanitsok Yothea* in the Mministry of Defense. Kham Phai was transferred from Preah Vihear at that time and became Kham Chan's deputy.[12]

In 1985, the Sector military training school in Banlung was moved to Stung Treng and became the training school for Military Region 1. Its leaders, Ki and Kham Sana, moved to Stung Treng from Banlung to run the school. However, the old military school in Banlung remained open, but from that point onward it was only responsible for training new recruits from Ratanakiri Province.[13]

Dam Jyun became the head of the school in Banlung after Ki and Kham Sana departed for Stung Treng. Three Vietnamese advisors were assigned to work with him, Hong, Yieu, and Kak. An ethnic Lao Cambodian, Leng, translated for them.[14] In 1986, the school organized two three-month military training courses for new recruits. The first had 180 students, while 120 were enrolled in the second. In 1987, another two trainings were organized, one for 200 students and another for 80.[15] In 1988, a single training was organized for 90 students, but in 1989 there were no trainings organized, as the Vietnamese advisors had returned home.[16] This happened despite the fact that late in the 1980s was a crucial period for building up the Cambodian military (*Phnom Penh Domestic Service* 1989b) because the Vietnamese were preparing to withdraw from Cambodia.

According to Dop Khamchoeung, there were between fifty and seventy Brao soldiers working in Mondulkiri Province during the early PRK period, and that about ten of those had been killed by the time he left the province in the mid-1980s. While there were very few other PRAK soldiers during the first few years after the Vietnamese gained control over Cambodia, by 1983 and 1984, the PRAK's 180th Battalion was operating in Mondulkiri Province. A PRAK battalion was also established in Stung Treng Province, where the PRAK was gradually being built up. Previously, there had only been a much smaller number of PRAK soldiers there, and they mainly guarded the provincial capital and the roads near the capital.

Sometimes Khmer Rouge spies were able to infiltrate the military. In one case, three ethnic Khmer men joined the military in Mondulkiri Province. Later, they prepared a plan to kill Dop Khamchoeung one night. They prepared 7,800 bullets for the attack. However, their secret was discovered the night before the attack, and all three operatives were arrested and imprisoned. They were kept in miserable conditions, with chains and cement blocks attached to their legs. After two years, two had died. The last one was able to use a knife to stab a Vietnamese guard and escape to Kratie with his gun. He was eventually apprehended and extrajudicially killed in captivity.[17]

Dop Khamchoeung received a salary of just 700-riel per month prior to 1982, while regular soldiers received 350-riel/month. However, over time Khamchoeung's salary increased to 1,500-riel per month, which was enough to buy three water buffaloes. Regular soldiers received 800-riel per month, which was sufficient to buy one adult water buffalo and one baby. Inflation was high though, so people did not hold onto much cash.[18]

It was dangerous being a soldier in Mondulkiri. In one 1986 incident in Kaev Seima District, a military convey was ambushed by the NADK, resulting in forty-five government soldiers being killed, including thirty-six in a single vehicle. Six of the dead were Brao. Only one person in the convoy survived. The group had been on the way to register villagers and to provide political training. There were more NADK forces in Mondulkiri compared to Ratanakiri and Stung Treng, but there were even more NADK in Preah Vihear Province.[19]

Dop Khamchoeung's son, Glee, joined the military in Mondulkiri in 1984. Rather than being assigned to a dangerous front line position, he worked as a guard for the Brao provincial leadership, who preferred to have Brao body guards, as previously mentioned. However, in 1987 he returned to Taveng with his father. Apparently the main reason why Dop Khamchoeung decided to leave the military was because Glee was considering marrying an ethnic Khmer woman. He disapproved, and so wanted to get him back to where he could find him a Brao wife. Once back in Ratanakiri, Glee worked three more years as a soldier before also leaving the military and moving back to his village.[20]

Apart from the Brao who worked as soldiers guarding the provincial capitals and the Brao leadership, there were not a lot of rank-and-file Brao soldiers in the military, as most Brao had been assigned to higher military and government positions or preferred to not work for the military or government at all. The Vietnamese were apparently afraid that their Brao PRAK allies would be killed by the Khmer Rouge, so the Vietnamese generally did not put them in dangerous front line positions.[21]

Seven or eight Brao soldiers ended up settling in Mondulkiri permanently. Bin was one. He was initially the chief of staff of the military in Mondulkiri. He later married an ethnic Bunong woman and settled in Kaev Seima District. Other Brao, such as one named Le (Phayang Village) settled in the province, as did Bong Loit, who looked after guests in Ou Reang District for many years and ended up settling there.[22]

The Khmer Rouge in Northeastern Cambodia after 1979

Despite generally experiencing defeat during the early period of Vietnamese advancement into Ratanakiri and Stung Treng Province, the Khmer Rouge were able to regroup and fight back in many parts of the country (Slocomb 2001), including in the northeast. When the Vietnamese entered the northeast in late 1978, the main Khmer Rouge military units there were, as mentioned earlier, the 801st and 920th Divisions. Between early 1982 and 1992, the 920th Division mainly operated in Mondulkiri and Kratie Provinces, as well as western Stung Treng Province and a little in Ratanakiri Province. The 801st Division operated mainly in Ratanakiri Province and eastern Stung Treng Province.[23]

Although the Khmer Rouge's military units were somewhat diminished in 1979, significant forces remained active after the arrival of Vietnamese troops. They did, however, change their strategy by separating into small groups to launch guerilla-type attacks against their enemies.[24] Ironically, the NADK used similar tactics to fight the Vietnamese as the South Vietnamese Communists had used to fight the Americans during the Second Indochina War. The NADK's bases also moved to the Dangrek Mountain Range, near the border between Preah Vihear Province and Thailand's Ubon Ratchathani Province. In the 1980s, apart from the 801st and 920th Divisions, there were also other NADK units operating in the northeast from Zones 105 and 107.[25] The chairmen or secretaries of these military units were responsible for politics, while the deputy secretaries dealt purely with military matters, and standing committee members were responsible for logistics and other auxiliary functions. Between 1979 and 1981, the NADK was divided into northern and southern sectors, but in early 1982, an eastern sector (1001) was added with Son Sen as chairman and Chantha (Thot) (Tampuon, Patang Village) responsible for the northeast.[26] Eastern Sector 1001 was based in

Ubon Ratchathani Province, in northeastern Thailand, near the border with Preah Vihear.[27] In the early 1980s, the 801st Division, led by So Saroeun,[28] was the main military unit operating in Stung Treng and Ratanakiri Provinces, while the 920th Division, led by another Khmer named Nhem San, operated farther south. In March 1982, the 801st Division was apparently composed of only 700 troops, but it was still considered to be one of the nine most active NADK Divisions in terms of attacking Vietnamese forces.[29]

In 1984 and1985, the Vietnamese, with limited assistance from the PRAK, were successful in defeating NADK (the 801st and 920th Divisions) and the National Army of Sihanouk, and also allied FULRO (central headquarters and Zone 105) and the Lao right-wing resistance, as all were based in the triborder area between Preah Vihear Province, Ubon Ratchathani Province in Thailand, and Champasak Province in Laos (Tan n.d.). At that time resistance forces lost control of much of the territory that they had previously controlled along the border with Thailand (PRK Foreign Ministry 1985).

Later in the 1980s, the Khmer Rouge's 801st Division was disbanded and together with some troops taken from the 920th Division, five new divisions were created, including the 105th, 607th, 709th, 802nd, and the 809th. In some parts of the northeast, the NADK was able to strengthen as Vietnamese military units withdrew. In 1991, the 709th Division was operating in Stung Treng and Ratanakiri Provinces, and also in western Preah Vihear Province, on both sides of the Mekong River; the 607th Division was active in southern Preah Vihear Province; and the 105th Division was based in Mondulkiri Province. The 612th Division was another NADK military unit that was located in the northeast in the early 1990s. They operated in the northern and eastern parts of Preah Vihear Province. Although a full NADK Division was supposed to be composed of about 3,000 soldiers, the average strength in 1991 was apparently only 1,080 soldiers, although the strength of different divisions varied greatly. For example, the 920th Division reportedly had 2,328 soldiers, while the 105th Division had 589, and the 612th Division had just 386. Moreover, many of these troops were stationed in rear bases. For example, the 105th Division had only 94 of its 589 soldiers stationed in Mondulkiri Province.[30] The NADK units in northeastern Cambodia were all supplied from the Dangrek Mountain Range along the Thai-Cambodia border (Institute of Military History 2010). Indeed,

I heard stories in the 2000s from Kavet Khmer Rouge leaders about long treks they took from north of the Sesan River to Preah Vihear to transport arms and other supplies.

Overall, NADK's strength is believed to have begun to increase in 1983 after initially decreasing. However, after the Vietnamese offensives of 1984 and 1985, their strength again declined. Afterwards, it gradually increased again. In 1985, Vietnamese troops began gradually withdrawing from Cambodia (*Hanoi VNA* 1985), although the PRK government claimed at the time that 1985 marked the fourth yearly withdrawal of VVA troops from Cambodia (*Phnom Penh SPK* 1985b). In any case, after 1985, the NADK was able to gain control of more rural areas, which was crucial for recruiting more soldiers.[31]

Although the NADK were generally weaker than the better equipped Vietnamese, they had the advantage of knowing the terrain, speaking the languages of the locals, and making use of guerilla tactics, which allowed them to achieve some significant military victories.

Di Thin

Di Thin was the secretary of the Office 102 Party Committee in Ratanakiri Province prior to the arrival of the Vietnamese in late 1978, when he apparently fled the province. Later, he is believed to have become one of the leaders of the Prey Khieou Sector of northeastern Cambodia. However, in the 1980s, Di Thin probably moved around quite a bit.[32] He was, for example, sometimes based at the Cambodia-Thailand border,[33] and he also spent time near the Lao border in the Jai Yook Mountains in the northern part of Siempang District in Stung Treng Province.[34] In 1992, Di Thin was reported to be the commander of NADK's 709th Division.[35]

Soy Keo commented that in the early 1990s, Prey Khieou became less important for NADK, and that most of the NADK forces in Stung Treng Province were based in the Jai Yook Mountains because the mountainous geography there was easily defendable. According to Soy Keo, "The Vietnamese could not attack the Khmer Rouge positions there. The Cambodians could not either. We tried in 1984, but it was too difficult. Some soldiers stepped on landmines. Seventeen of our soldiers were killed, including my own nephew. We carried him back to Samakhi Commune [near Stung Treng], but he died there. The terrain in the area was simply too steep."[36] There were apparently no Vietnamese involved in that campaign.

Somewhat ironically, in the early 1970s, Di Thin was a close colleague of Bou Thang and Soy Keo. As Soy Keo explained, "In the 1980s I fought against my old close friend [Di Thin]."[37] Somewhat surprisingly, however, Soy Keo claimed to not have any ill feelings toward Di Thin. "He was a good friend, and we were from the same ethnic group [Tampuon]," he commented.[38] As has been previously mentioned, ethnicity did not always fit with political affiliations. Ethnicity was important, but sometimes politics was more important. During the time that Di Thin was the sector secretary in Ratanakiri Province before the Vietnamese occupation of Cambodia, he apparently committed many atrocities. In fact, before he died in 2007, he had been one of those targeted for possible charges related to the international criminal court's Khmer Rouge tribunal.[39]

The Khmer Rouge in Ratanakiri Province

Initially, in 1979 and the early 1980s, there were four main Khmer Rouge strongholds in Ratanakiri Province, where the NADK's 801st Division initially operated. The first was north of the Sesan River in present-day Kok Lak Commune, Voeunsai District; the second was in present-day Koun Mom District, in the southwestern part of the province;[40] the third was in the Goor Mountains northeast of Banlung, and the fourth was in the "3 *Srok*" area in the southwest part of Ratanakiri. The leader of the Khmer Rouge in the mountains north of the Sesan River near the border with Laos was reportedly Vi Prar (Kavet, Ndrak Village).[41] Between 1979 and 1981, he stayed near the Lao border at the end of the Trabok and Kampha streams in what is now northern Taveng District, Ratanakiri Province. He led one of the regiments of the 801st Division.[42] Another important Kavet leader was Nan.[43] Other more minor Kavet Khmer Rouge leaders included Bun Som and Bun Ma. According to the VODK (1979a), in January 1979, soon after the Vietnamese entered Cambodia, Kavet in the Kok Lak area of Voeunsai District, north of the Sesan River, were able to inflict significant casualties on Vietnamese forces, particularly through using punji stick pitfalls and other indigenous traps, just as they had done against Sihanouk's soldiers in the 1960s (see Chapter 1). Later, the Kavet led Khmer

Rouge forces to attack villages on the north side of the Sesan River, such as Eetoop and Lameuay Villages. Later, however, life became more difficult, and in the mid-1980s, Bun Ma and Bun Som surrendered, along with most of the rest of the Kavet initially in the forest with them. According to Bun Ma, he did not plan to surrender, but after his wife was captured by the Vietnamese, he became lonely and decided to give up so he could be with her.[44]

Chantha (Thot) is believed to have been the leader of the Khmer Rouge in the "3 *Srok*" area.[45] Kreng Siengnoi reported that Chantha was head of the NADK forces in Ratanakiri, with Kham Veang (Tampuon, Sai Yo Village, Sida Commune) as his deputy.[46] At some point Chantha apparently moved to the Khmer Rouge stronghold of Anlong Veng, near the Thai border, in present-day Oddar Meanchey Province, but he returned to the 3 *Srok* area in 1988, where he is believed to have died in battle.[47] Chantha was another Khmer Rouge leader who worked closely with Bou Thang and Soy Keo in the early 1970s.[48]

Kham Veang had a reputation for killing many people during the 1975 and 1978 period.[49] His forces in Ratanakiri were apparently diminished in 1979, so he operated in the "3 *Srok*" area with small groups of five to ten soldiers, or maybe thirty soldiers at most.[50] The NADK was active in the area in 1984, and on March 19, VODK (1984a) reported that they had "totally liberated" three communes (Patang, Labang, and Chhip) and five villages in Lumphat District, causing a number of casualties to Vietnamese forces. Then, on July 15, the VODK (1984b) claimed that NADK forces had destroyed a "Vietnamese commune Office" in La-ak Commune, in Voeunsai District, killing a number of "Vietnamese enemy soldiers," destroying a rice barn with 500 bushels of rice in it, and confiscating some weapons and other material. They claimed to have liberated five villages in the area. The NADK also claimed to have overrun the district capital of Lumphat in February 1985 (VODK 1985a). Although Supha Subin claimed that the Khmer Rouge had essentially disappeared from present-day Andong Meas District of Ratanakiri Province by 1985,[51] the VODK (1985c) reported that the NADK was able to "liberate" the district capital of Bokeo in July 1985, and that they ambushed a Vietnamese regiment in Bokeo District in October 1985 (VODK 1985d). Another informant reported that Kham Veang had many soldiers in the early days, but that between 1985 and 1987, the Vietnamese devastated NADK forces in Ratanakiri.[52] There were also some minor Khmer Rouge leaders operating in the 1980s. For example,

Kanan (Kavet, Rok Village) and Thit Bunloeu (ethnic Lao, Voeunhoi Village) operated in Voeunsai District after 1979. They were often based at the end of the Lalay stream near the border with Laos. They frequently engaged in fire fights with soldiers based in villages near the Sesan River. Voeunhoi Village, located on the north side of the Sesan River, was particularly disputed. They only gave up in the early 1990s after the Vietnamese had left the country.[53]

Some lower level NADK soldiers surrendered when their forces in Ratanakiri were decimated, but crucially, no senior NADK leaders are believed to have given up until well into the 1990s.[54] Bou Thang pointed out that the four main NADK leaders in Ratanakiri Province in the 1980s were Di Thin, Chantha, Kham Veang, and Chan, and that they were all ethnic Tampuon.[55] Other key NADK leaders believed to be under their command were also mainly Tampuon, including Khum An (Tampuon, Sida Commune) and Than (possibly also known as Kouich Thoeun)[56] (Tampuon, Sida Commune).[57] Than was the head of the Khmer Rouge in O Chum, Andong Meas, and Bokeo Districts in Ratanakiri. He apparently died in 1988. By the late 1980s, there were apparently only small groups of five to ten NADK soldiers operating in remote parts of the province,[58] including north of the Sesan River near the border with Stung Treng Province and with Laos in the headwaters of the Lalay stream,[59] as well as in the 3 *Srok* area.

Some informants claim that after leaving Ratanakiri in the mid-1980s, Kham Veang stayed in the Prey Khieou Mountain area.[60] Stephen Heder recorded him as still operating in Mondulkiri Province in 1992.[61] Dam Kalang reported that Kham Veang was killed on the order of the Khmer Rouge leader Chan, after Kham Veang slept with Chan's wife when Chan was away receiving political training.[62] Kham Veang's nephew, Kham Voen, substantiated this story, reporting that Kham Veang died in 1993, during the UNTAC period. He was apparently shot when bathing in a wetland area in the 3 *Srok* area, not far from where he was born.[63]

The Khmer Rouge in Mondulkiri Province

In Mondulkiri Province, the NADK were much more of a threat than they ever were in Ratanakiri Province, and security concerns were considered serious throughout the 1980s. One informant claimed that the NADK forces entered the provincial capital a few times,[64] which demonstrated that no parts of the province were considered totally safe from NADK attacks. However, Thang Ngon, the Brao secretary of Mondulkiri's provincial Party Committee in the early 1980s, reported that only Khmer Rouge spies were able to infiltrate Sen Monorom, and that the provincial capital was never seriously threatened.[65] Phoet Phoeua commented that Khmer Rouge agents frequently entered Sen Monorom to contact relatives and collect information. "There were a lot of Khmer Rouge in Mondulkiri. I rarely left the provincial capital when I was there," he stated.[66] Dop Khamchoeung suspected, however, that there were more spies in Kaoh Nheaek District, where the NADK was particularly strong.[67] One key NADK leader in Mondulkiri Province during the 1980s was Ham, who was ethnic Lao from Kaoh Nheaek District. However, the Brao I interviewed did not know the names of most Khmer Rouge leaders in the area.[68] There were also significant NADK forces in Keav Seima District.[69] One division of Vietnamese soldiers were based in the province throughout the 1980s due to the strength of the NADK there.[70] The difficult security situation greatly limited the movements of senior provincial government officials, most of whom hardly left the provincial capital.

During the 1980s, some former FULRO soldiers from Vietnam were based in Mondulkiri Province. They cooperated closely with the Khmer Rouge.[71] According to Tan (n.d.), in early 1981, the 2nd Division's 38th Infantry Regiment conducted sweep operations against FULRO forces in eastern and southeastern Ratanakiri Province and in Mondulkiri Province. Dop Khamchoeung heard that there were FULRO in the province, but he never encountered any. He also heard that there were some FUNCINPEC-aligned National Army of Sihanouk soldiers in the province, but that they eventually changed allegiance and joined the NADK.[72]

The Khmer Rouge in Stung Treng Province

In Stung Treng Province, there were a number of pockets of NADK. As previously mentioned, the Prey Khieou Mountains was an important base area for NADK after 1979. In addition, there were NADK on Kalapouk Mountain to the north of the Sesan River in Sesan District, near the border with Kalapouk and Khsach Thmei (Saisamy in Lao) Villages in Sesan District.[73] For at least part of the 1980s, Vi Prar was the leader of NADK there,[74] but Pong from Phluk Village was the best-known Khmer Rouge leader in the Kalapouk area.[75] As previously mentioned, the Jai Yook Mountains in northern Siempang District was also a key NADK stronghold, especially in the later 1980s.

Villagers living in areas where the Khmer Rouge were active rarely left their villages for fear of encountering the Khmer Rouge, but still, they sometimes met them nonetheless. For example, in the early 1980s, a government official from Khamphun Village, Sesan District, was out preparing his lowland rice fields when four NADK soldiers approached him. They had apparently come to spy on the village. He knew them, as they originally came from a nearby village. They told him not to report that they had been in the area, and even commented that if he did report them, they knew where his house was. This attempt at intimidation scared him, and he decided not to tell anyone what had happened.[76]

In another case, in 1986, the village headman of Phluk Village, in Sesan District, was out fishing on the Sesan River with a friend. It was 10 am when they were surprised by a group of eight heavily armed NADK soldiers. They told the two villagers not to be afraid and asked for help from them to cross from the south side of the river to the north. The villagers felt that they had no choice but to oblige. Soon another thirty-six Khmer Rouge soldiers arrived. Because the villagers only had one small boat, it took a number of hours to take them all across the river. While they waited for others, some Khmer Rouge happily bathed in the river. Before everyone had crossed, a long-tail motorboat traveling from Stung Treng to Srekor Village arrived by chance, and the Khmer Rouge forced the owner to hand over the goods that he had bought in the provincial capital and had planned to sell in the village. Interestingly, however, the Khmer Rouge paid for everything they took. But not selling to them was not an option. As they departed into the forest, the leader of the group told the villagers to report to the Vietnamese that they had crossed the Sesan River. He also said that Khmer should not fight Khmer. He also warned the villagers that if they came into the Kalapouk forest where they stayed, they should not venture farther than five meters from the foot path, as there were landmines planted a little away from the path.[77]

Indicative of the difficult security situation in Stung Treng Province in the 1980s, in 1984 about thirty PRAK soldiers based themselves in Phluk Village to carry out anti–Khmer Rouge operations north of the Sesan River. They stayed at the village's Buddhist temple, but one day when the soldiers were away on an operation, a group of Khmer Rouge attacked the temple, apparently in retribution against the villagers for allowing PRAK soldiers to stay there. There were no soldiers there at the time, but two women and two children were killed in the attack, and the village's sacred temple building was burned to the ground. The villagers in Phluk fled to some islands in the middle of the Sesan River. Later, when the PRAK soldiers returned, they tried to follow the Khmer Rouge soldiers who had by that time left the area. They recruited a villager to lead the way, but he stepped on a landmine and lost a leg. Following the attack, more PRAK troops came to stay in the village.[78]

Khmer Rouge reconnaissance elements were reported to occasionally enter Stung Treng town at night. Therefore, the VVA and PRAK had to be mindful of the safety of their high-level officials. Indicative of this, the Brao vice-chairman of the provincial People's Committee, Kham Toeung, had ten soldiers to protect him and his house, and when he went to villages, he usually traveled with a group of fifty soldiers.[79]

The Khmer Rouge in Preah Vihear Province

There was a strong NADK presence in Preah Vihear Province throughout the 1980s, as it borders with Thailand, which provided the NADK with access to important logistical support. Although Kham Phai claimed that he did not know the names of the Khmer Rouge military leaders in Preah Vihear,[80] in the early 1980s, Men Keov, who was a senior NADK officer, operated along the border between Stung Treng and Preah Vihear Provinces, west of the Mekong River. Men Keov could apparently speak Khmer, Lao, Thai, and English.[81] He also reportedly operated near Charap Village in Sesan District, Stung Treng Province, which is located east of the Mekong River.[82] In the early 1980s, Men Keov reportedly commanded the 84th Regiment of the 801st Division.[83] For part of the 1980s, he was believed to be among the most senior NADK military commanders in northeastern Cambodia.

However, after he surrendered and was integrated into the Cambodia military in 1993 and 1994, he apparently helped convince other Khmer Rouge to defect. Kong (Kreung, Tiem Loeu Village) may have taken over after Men Keov surrendered. According to Kham Toeung, however, Khieu Moeun (Khmer, Satung, Kampong Thom Province), not Kong, replaced Men Keov as NADK zone head.[84] Khieu Moeun was apparently based in Siempang District at some point.[85] Doeun remembers Khieu Moeun as being the leader of the NADK in Preah Vihear Province when he was based there in the 1980s.[86] Stephen Heder reported that Khieu Moeun was the 802nd Division's political commander up until 1988.[87] He then became the military commander of the 802nd Division, which was based in Choam Khsan District in Preah Vihear Province,[88] near the border with Laos. Later Khieu Moeun either surrendered or was shot and killed during an internal Khmer Rouge dispute.[89]

Although there were a lot of Khmer Rouge in Preah Vihear when Kham Phai was based there, he reported being able to travel to villages in the province, but generally with a large number of soldiers supporting him, otherwise it was dangerous. Kham Phai claimed that the provincial capital of Preah Vihear, Tbaeng Meanchey, was never attacked by the Khmer Rouge during the time he was there. However, after he left, the Khmer Rouge were apparently able to take control of most of Choam Khsan District. In addition, San Khum Thmei District was among the most insecure parts of the province, and it was only possible to travel there for short periods of time. The PRK district chief there, a Khmer, was assassinated by the Khmer Rouge during the time Kham Phai was based in the province.[90]

Security against the Khmer Rouge

According to one of the early volunteer soldiers for the PRK government in Voeunsai District, during the early part of the PRK period, there were usually seven Vietnamese soldiers assigned to maintain security in each village. They typically teamed up with ten Cambodian volunteer soldiers. Patrols were organized each night, with these groups rotating. Typically, three of the seven Vietnamese would go on patrol each night, together with five Cambodians.[91]

Political propaganda was crucial for the PRK government's efforts to defeat the Khmer Rouge, and Lat Vansao, who was head of the Information Dissemination Department in Ratanakiri Province, was put in charge of distributing political propaganda to the villages. He was apparently given the job because he was trusted, but also because he was in Cambodia during the main Khmer Rouge period between 1975 and 1979, so he could speak about what happened then from personal experience. He had seventy employees working with him at the time, as the work was considered particularly important for improving security.

According to him, the main point that his group needed to counter was that Vietnam was trying to takeover Cambodia. Lat Vansao heard that the Khmer Rouge would frequently refer to him as *"khluan Khmer, kabal Yuon"* (body of Khmer, head of a Vietnamese). The main points that his side made were that (1) the Khmer Rouge had killed a lot of people, (2) they had moved people from their villages during the Khmer Rouge period, (3) they had made everything communal, and (4) there was no freedom under the Khmer Rouge. He also argued that it was not true that the Vietnamese did bad things to the Cambodians.[92] Because the Khmer Rouge were heavily supported by the Chinese, and were Maoist, those who supported the PRK government often referred to them as *"khluan Khmer, kabal Chen"* (body of a Khmer, head of Chinese),[93] or *"kabal Pol Pot"* (Pol Pot head).[94] These narratives reflect the regional geopolitics of the conflict in Cambodia (see Pao-Min 1985; Chanda 1986).

Lat Vansao and one or two other officials under his command traveled from Banlung with Vietnamese soldiers, but once they reached the districts, they would take about five Cambodian soldiers to the villages, not the Vietnamese soldiers, as according to him, it would not have looked good politically to have taken Vietnamese soldiers to the villages. The Vietnamese would only be called down to the villages if security problems became serious. Still, Lat Vansao carried three guns when he left to work outside of the provincial capital. When he went to highland villages he lectured in Khmer, and his speeches were translated into local languages. However, he spoke Lao when he went to ethnic Lao villages.[95]

Yoep Sat, a Brao man from Bong Village, took up a government position like so many others who had spent time in Laos and Vietnam during the Khmer Rouge period. According to him, many ethnic minorities like him were assigned to go to the villages to try to convince the villagers not to support the Khmer Rouge. Unlike Lat Vansao, he claimed that the Vietnamese went with the minorities to the villages to provide security, but that the Brao were the ones who talked with the villagers. He explained that his group especially went to villages in Voeunsai, Lumphat, and Bokeo because there were more NADK forces there than elsewhere. He claimed that the Brao mainly went to Brao villages, while the Tampuon went to Tampuon villages, and so on. If they met people in the villages with relatives who were still with the NADK, they would encourage them to tell their relatives that if they gave up there would be no punishment against them. On the contrary, if they continued to fight, they would be shot and killed.[96]

Although some people were still afraid of the Vietnamese, the PRK government had no choice but to rely heavily on the VVA for support, as the PRAK was still weak and was also prone, especially in the early years, to desertion (Vickery 1989). As Lat Vansao put it, "The Vietnamese helped a lot. If anyone says otherwise, they are bad."[97] Bou Thang explained that many Cambodian recruits initially lost confidence in the PRAK due to Khmer Rouge propaganda that accused the Vietnamese of trying to colonize Cambodia. However, once the situation stabilized in 1980 and 1981, the desertion rates declined significantly.[98] Still, Lat Vansao claimed that the security situation was good enough for him to be able to go to all districts in Ratanakiri Province to do his work.[99]

Initially the Vietnamese set up a big camp along the road to Vietnam, but later they spread themselves out at posts located every two to three kilometers along the road. Each post had more than ten Vietnamese soldiers stationed at it. These Vietnamese apparently planted vegetables near each post to help supplement their food supply.[100] In insecure parts of Cambodia, Ea Meng-Try (1981) reported that for security reasons, villagers were sometimes discouraged or prohibited from planting crops far from communities. Security concerns affected various parts of the northeast.

The Department of Women's Affairs also played a role in disseminating information designed to help improve the security situation, although their focus was on the role of women. According to Jop Moer, who was deputy of the department in Ratanakiri Province, her main job was going to villages to encourage women to help resist the Khmer Rouge and to support their husbands when they were away serving in the military. She generally traveled separately from her boss, Dam Chanty, who also moved from village to village doing the same sort of work. Jop Moer explained that they also encouraged villagers to grow rice and raise domestic animals to improve their lives, rather than relying on the government like during the Khmer Rouge period. "They had to help themselves," she explained. "It wasn't that fun," she stated, "At that time there were no vehicles to travel to the villages." She mainly walked by foot, starting from Banlung and first going to the district centers. She picked up women working for women's affairs there and they went together to meet women working at the communes and then the villages.

Unlike people in higher positions, she generally did not have any military support, either Vietnamese or Cambodian, unless she was on a special mission that required security. However, she commented that women were given more attention during the PRK period than at present, as the Department of Women's Affairs was located in the provincial party office, which had considerable power at the time.[101] When the Vietnamese advisors in the districts went to the villages with people from the provincial Department of Women's Affairs, three or four Vietnamese soldiers would often travel with them. This pattern was especially evident in the early period when there were very few PRAK soldiers. However, by 1983 and 1984, security had improved, and at that point provincial members of the Department of Women's Affairs generally went to the villages without security.[102]

Despite the security provided by the Vietnamese, it was still dangerous to travel. In one case in the 1980s, the vehicle that Lat Vansao was traveling in was shot at by NADK forces, flattening its wheels. Nobody was injured, but it could have been much worse if the Vietnamese traveling with him had not shot back.[103]

In 1985, Vietnam's 2nd Division was carrying out combat missions, but it also organized sixteen operational units that were assigned responsibility for maintaining security in the four districts in Ratanakiri Province (Lumphat, Banlung, Bokeo, and Voeunsai) as well as a number of villages in the neighboring provinces of Mondulkiri and Stung Treng. They received guidance from Vietnamese Specialist Group 5501, and the operational units held well-attended study seminars on the policies and programs of the PRK government. In addition, 2nd Division units provided supplementary training to twelve village cadres and a total of 850 guerrillas, and they recruited and trained 125 village guerrillas and 214 hamlet guerrillas, so as to ensure that each hamlet had one guerrilla squad (five to seven personnel) and each village had one guerrilla platoon (with fifteen to twenty personnel) that were strong enough to maintain security at the local level. The division also helped form hundreds of solidarity production organizations (with each production cell consisting of between seven and twenty families) and more than 100 security cells (with each cell consisting of two to three people) at the village level (Tan n.d.).

Through all these efforts, the security situation throughout Ratanakiri Province gradually improved, especially after 1987.[104] In early 1987, most of the troops in the 2nd Division moved to Preah Vihear Province and southern Laos (Tan n.d.). The strength of the PRAK had increased by then, and the threat from the NADK had also been significantly reduced. As a result, the number of VVA troops based in the province apparently declined to less than one hundred, who remained there to protect the provincial Vietnamese advisors.[105]

In 1988, the Vietnamese prepared to withdraw their forces from Cambodia, following an agreement reached during a joint conference of the Vietnamese Communist Party Politburo and the Politburo of the PRPK organized in August 1985. As a final task, the military region commander ordered the 2nd Division to launch a wave of sweep operations in coordination with allied Cambodian units to clear the provinces of Stung Treng and Mondulkiri in preparation for turning full responsibility for security in these provinces over to the PRAK (Tan n.d.). To carry out this order, the 2nd Division sent its 1st Infantry Regiment to conduct operations along the Mekong River in Stung Treng Province. After this work was done, in April 1988, the 2nd Division reportedly withdrew all of its personnel back to Vietnam, ending its ten years of fighting in Cambodia (Tan n.d.).

The Brao Military Contribution

The Brao frequently speak about the important military contributions that they made during the post-1979 PRK period, but while many Brao did spend years in the army, it appears that their military contributions were generally much more modest than some have implied.

Battalion 2 was one primarily ethnic Brao unit based in Preah Vihear during the 1980s. There were between forty and sixty Brao soldiers attached to it, and Kham Phai was the leader. Some ethnic Khmer soldiers were also part of the unit. They had one big gun, which was given to them by the Vietnamese.[106] The Brao in Preah Vihear worked closely with Vietnam's 307th Division. Although one Brao man reported to me that, "A lot of people died in Preah Vihear, at least 20 a day, mainly from being shot," in fact, very few if any were Brao. Although some Brao did engage in major battles, most were rarely put in front line combat situations, and in Preah Vihear Province, they apparently rarely left their base in the provincial capital. Like during the main 1978 attack against the Khmer Rouge, the Vietnamese tended to be sent to the front lines first, with the Brao following at a relatively safe distance. As far as

I have heard in interviews, it does not appear that any died from being shot in battle,[107] but a few did die due to stepping on landmines.[108] Indeed, landmines were the main danger for the Brao in Preah Vihear. Also, one Brao accidentally shot another Brao when hunting one night. The victim was mistaken for a barking deer because he was wearing a black coat.[109]

Even as the threat of NADK in northeastern Cambodia gradually subsided during the 1980s, PRAK still had to take security threats seriously. One of their strategies was to send soldiers to rural villages to prevent the Khmer Rouge from sending reconnaissance elements into the villages. However, those I spoke with reported that these soldiers were never able to identify any spies.[110]

K5

The K5 or "*phaenkar bram*" in Khmer was one of the most well-known and ambitious military plans developed during the PRK period. As Slocomb (2001) pointed out, K5 was specifically focused on defending the Cambodia border with Thailand. The "national defense plan" that was apparently most closely linked to K5 was drafted in March 1983, following important discussions held at the PAVN's general staff's forward headquarters at Tan Son Nhat Airbase, near Ho Chi Minh City. Those who attended the meeting included military region cadres, army corps cadres, front cadres, and the commanders of forces operating on the battlefield in Cambodia (Hồng 2004).

K5 was, however, not launched until March 1984, and it was not officially abandoned until the end of the 1980s. Vietnamese forces in Cambodia and the PRK's Ministry of Defense jointly directed K5. According to Slocomb (2001), the barrier that was the lynchpin of the plan was supposed to be 700 kilometers long, two kilometers wide, and include about 500 meters of cleared terrain, a fence, a mine field, another fence, and then more cleared area. However, Bou Thang explained it somewhat differently. He claims that K5 was intended to establish strong border defenses at five specific locations near the border with Thailand to support front line troops. Those five locations were (1) Choam Khsan District, Preah Vihear Province, (2) the O Smach area in Samraong District, in present-day Oddar Meanchey Province, (3) Poipet Commune in Ou Chrov District, present-day Banteay Meanchey Province, (4) Pailin Province, previously part of Battambang Province, and (5) Koh Kong

Province. According to Bou Thang, the "K" in K5 referred to *phaenkar* or plan and the "5" referred to the five key focus locations. It was apparently recognized that not all the border could be sealed, so the idea was to develop strong defenses and infrastructure at five key locations, including improved roads and accommodations for front line soldiers. It was hoped that this would improve defenses and also troop spirits. However, according to Bou Thang there were not enough materials or equipment to fully implement the plan. He still believes that K5 was partially successful.[111]

According to General Mai Xuân Tân, the chief of specialist of the VVA's military specialist unit, Group 478,

> The building of K5 had a very clear and practical significance. First, it was a border defense project, so the armed forces units of our [Cambodian] allies felt more secure, and only then did they dare to take over the defense of the border on their own, which meant that our volunteer army forces were free to perform the role of a strategic mobile [reserve] force. Second, at that time if we had told our [Cambodian] allies to step forward to fight big battles or a major campaign, a big revolutionary effort, they were not yet capable of performing such a task. However, telling them to organize the civilian population to cut down trees, dig trenches, and plant sharpened bamboo stakes to build a road to use to patrol and protect the border, that was something that they could do and that they were gradually able to do it well. (Huy Đức 2012a, 372)

Villagers in Preah Vihear, Stung Treng, and Ratanakiri Provinces were sent to work on K5 in Preah Vihear Province for a few years beginning in 1984. Mondulkiri apparently did not send anyone to help, as the province was considered to be too far from the Thai border. Other parts of the border were the responsibility of people from other provinces outside of the northeast. Those recruited generally had to work a couple of months before returning home. They did not receive any salary for this work, but they were supplied with food rations when working.[112] Bou Thang claimed that many soldiers from Ratanakiri Province participated in K5. "Everyone had to go to dig holes. Soldiers rotated every two or three months," he commented. He reported that every military region in Cambodia had to send some PRAK soldiers to work on the project.[113] In 1985, Kham Phai visited K5. He noted that a small number of Brao were working on it. Most recruits were, however, ethnic Khmers.[114]

Huy Đức (2012a, 372) claimed that K5 made Cambodians easy "live targets," victims of ambushes, and that generally "K5 was a place of fear and horror for the Cambodians." There were apparently between 146,000 and 381,000 laborers recruited to work on K5 between 1984 and mid-1987 (Gottesman 2002), after which time the program was scaled back heavily, although not officially ended. Boliek (2007) claims that over one million people were forced to work on K5 over the years. Chan Si, the PRK government prime minister who died in late 1984, apparently opposed K5 (Deth 2014).

As senior military leaders in the PRAK, Bou Thang and Soy Keo both became military generals who played key roles in the highly controversial K5 program (Boliek 2017). Bou Thang was the minister of defense and party politburo member when K5 was launched, and Soy Keo was vice-minister, party central committee member, and general chief of staff of the PRAK.[115] However, Bou Thang was dropped as minister of defense in October 1985 (the Fifth Party Congress), and not surprisingly, at that time, his close friend Soy Keo was also removed from being a Party Central Committee member and the general chief of staff (Slocomb 2001). According to Bou Thang, it was deemed more politically correct to put a Khmer in charge of the Ministry of Defense at that time, since the Vietnamese were preparing to withdraw from Cambodia.[116] However, it seems likely that Bou Thang's power declined as the Vietnamese reduced their role in Cambodia because he was apparently one of Vietnam's favorites.[117] Indicative of the circumstances, Bou Thang claimed that Soy Keo was dropped because while he could work well with Vietnamese because he spoke Vietnamese, he was not skilled enough to lead by himself. Soy Keo was also apparently deemed to not be a very good motivational speaker, which was key at the time because PRAK recruiting was emphasized.[118]

Most scholars recognize K5 as having come at a very high cost, both for the military and for civilians who were either forced or who "volunteered" to work on the project. Large numbers were infected with malaria or became victims of landmines planted as part of the program, or by those wanting to thwart it (Conboy 2013; Bekaert 1997; Slocomb 2003; Gottesman 2002).

In 2009, Soy Keo claimed that K5 had been "a success,"[119] although he pointed out that while he was appointed to seemingly powerful military positions throughout the 1980s, including ones related to K5, in reality he never really had the power to make independent decisions. He reported that the Vietnamese military advisors had much more power.[120] Most of those opposed to the PRK government in the 1980s believed this to be the case, although it must be emphasized that many decisions were made based on joint discussions. In this case, however, Soy Keo seemed to want to distance himself from the generally unpopular initiative.

In 2017, however, Bou Thang strongly defended K5, claiming that although many have criticized the plan and claimed that a large number of people died when involved with K5 due to malaria, in reality things were not nearly so bad. He suggested, rather oddly, that some people contracted malaria, but then returned home, had sex, and died. He said that K5 should not be blamed for that![121]

Deth Sok Udom, an expert on the PRK period, agrees that it is likely that much fewer people died due to K5 than is sometimes alleged by critics. "Maybe 50,000 died, instead of the 500,000 that some critics claim," he roughly estimated.[122] Perhaps 25,000 people died from malaria alone, and a large number also became victims of landmines (Deth 2014). In any case, it is certainly not true, as Sam Rainsy (as quoted in Boliek 2007) has alleged, that K5 was concocted by Vietnamese specifically to kill Khmers. Nevertheless, most do not consider K5 to have been particularly successful. This success is at least partially because the plan was implemented without sufficient demining or adequate equipment.[123] The unpopularity of forced labor to implement K5 may also have benefited Khmer Rouge recruiting.[124]

Bou Thang continues to take responsibility for K5.[125] In particular, he told me that K5 was his idea, not the idea of the Vietnamese, a claim that is rather surprising considering all the criticism that K5 has received. Indeed, K5 has generally been considered a plan developed by the Vietnamese (Deth 2014), with Lê Đức Anh being especially associated with the initiative (Huy Đức 2012a). Nevertheless, Bou Thang claims that he came up with the idea for K5 when he was touring border areas in Eastern Europe in May 1983 (*Phnom Penh Domestic Service* 1983a), a couple of months after the national defense plan apparently linked to K5 was drafted in Vietnam. In any case, Bou Thang claims that he thought, when viewing the border with Western Europe, that Cambodia could make a similar sort of fence to keep enemies from infiltrating government defenses.[126] Indeed, Boliek (2017) claims that K5 was sometimes thought to have been a Cambodian version of the "Berlin Wall," but according to Bou Thang, it was not so much the Berlin Wall that inspired him as the border defenses in forested areas in Bulgaria and Hungary because they resembled the situation in Cambodia to a greater extent.[127] According to Bou Thang, when he returned to Cambodia, he proposed the idea to the Vietnamese, and later after some discussion, a plan for developing K5 emerged.[128]

Kham Phai commented, when I asked him if K5 had been successful in closing off the border to the Khmer Rouge, that the border was very long so it was not possible to fully do so through K5.[129] Indeed, even after K5 was developed, the Khmer Rouge were able to move across the border and establish bases deep inside Cambodia (Huy Đức 2012a). However, Slocomb (2001) has pointed out that the huge success of the 1984 to 1985 dry season offensive along the Cambodia-Thailand border was probably largely due to improved roads facilitated by the K5 plan. Hồng (2004, 204), the former deputy commander of PAVN's Military Region 5, provided the following assessment of K5:

> [A] number of people have expressed the opinion that the building of the K5 defense line cost too much and was not very effective, and there is some basis for this position. In reality, there are no perfect solutions. The general opinion is that the decision to build the K5 defense line that was made by us and our [Cambodian] allies was a correct and necessary decision. Although it had many limitations and weaknesses, it was a measure aimed at building a people's war posture to fundamentally improve the ability of the Cambodian revolutionary government and its armed forces to govern the country, and it also allowed Vietnamese volunteer army units and Vietnamese specialists to bring our historic mission to an end on our own initiative.

Epilogue: The Decline of the Khmer Rouge in the 1990s

It is beyond the scope of this book to seriously consider the security situation in northeastern Cambodia after the departure of the Vietnamese from the country in 1989. Beginning in the 1990s, however, despite Khmer Rouge hopes that they could overwhelm the PRAK after the departure of the Vietnamese, the Cambodian military was generally able to hold their own, although the NADK did gain control of some rural areas after 1989, especially near the Cambodia-Thailand border, including Pailin and Anlong Veng. But they were unable to turn the tables throughout much of the northeast, and after the mid-1990s, many NADK leaders in the northeast gradually defected. Vi Prar and Di Thin, two key Khmer Rouge leaders in Ratanakiri and Siempang, for example, finally gave up and were integrated into the Cambodian army in 1998.[130] Vi Prar's last position with the Khmer Rouge had been commander of the 800th Division and deputy chief of staff for Military Region 1. He was integrated into the Cambodian armed forces during a ceremony held in Stung Treng on August 25, 1998 (BBC 1998). However, he died in Stung Treng Town of a stomach illness just two years later, in around 2000.[131]

Soy Keo spoke of Di Thin's surrender, claiming, "I told him to give up, and said that we would give him his old position in the Khmer Rouge if he came over to our side."[132] Di Thin apparently admitted that he had made mistakes when he gave up.[133] In 2007, however, Di Thin was killed when a car ran into his motorcycle near Stung Treng City. Although there were rumors that he had been intentionally run down by relatives of some people who Di Thin ordered killed when he was a Khmer Rouge leader, Heng Khamvan dismissed such speculation, pointing to the fact that the family of the person who hit his motorcycle gave Di Thin's family 6,000,000-riel (US$15,000) in compensation, something that almost certainly would not have happened if the driver had intended to kill Di Thin. Heng Khamvan claimed that Di Thin was run over partially because his motorcycle did not have a strong headlight and so could not be seen easily in the dark.[134]

Conclusion

Security and military matters had an important impact on the lives of people living in the four northeastern provinces between 1979 and 1989, including soldiers, officials, and regular villagers. While the Vietnamese initially achieved important victories, the Khmer Rouge proved much more resilient than originally expected. While they were quite easily defeated in late 1978 and early 1979, they were not wiped out, and soon they were able to reorganize along the Cambodia-Thailand border and begin causing serious security problems for the VVA and the PRAK, including in northeastern Cambodia. The PRK government needed to strengthen militarily because they were initially very weak, but recruiting soldiers into the PRAK proved difficult and desertion rates were high. Over time, however, the security situation gradually improved, and the PRAK slowly gained strength. Still, the fighting was far from over, and in the second half of the 1980s, many ethnic minorities from the northeast were sent to work on the notorious and controversial K5 plan near the border with Thailand, a plan that most believe was created by the Vietnamese, but which Bou Thang claims was actually his idea. He asserts that he was inspired by what he saw when he visited the borders of Eastern Europe in 1983. Although the extent to which Bou Thang actually played in devising the K5 plan remains unclear, it can certainly be said that security issues were paramount throughout the PRK period, including in northeastern Cambodia.

We now turn to examining the experiences the Brao and other northeasterners had during the PRK period in relation to people and places from outside of Cambodia. The first part examines relations between Brao and other ethnic minorities from the northeast and Vietnamese soldiers and particularly the civilian and military specialists/advisors who worked with those in senior positions in the PRK government. The second part considers the experiences that the Brao and other northeasterners had traveling in Vietnam, Laos, and Eastern Europe, as those who traveled abroad were often deeply affected by their short-term experiences outside of Cambodia.

Experiences with People
from Vietnam, Laos, and
Eastern Europe, 1979 to 1989

Virtually all the people who play an important role in this story were born in rural and relatively remote parts of northeastern Cambodia, mainly in the Sesan River basin in the northern part of Ratanakiri Province. They had virtually no opportunities to travel long distances when they were young; nor did large numbers of outsiders travel to where they lived. There was considerable ethnic diversity nearby, but their geographical knowledge was not expansive, even for within Cambodia. However, their involvement in communist movements beginning in the early 1950s, 1960s, and early 1970s put them in contact with many more "outsiders." They met ethnic Khmer leaders from Democratic Kampuchea, including Pol Pot, Ieng Sary, Son Sen, Ya (Ney Sarann), Ny Kan, and others. They also interacted with the Vietnamese beginning in the 1950s and in the 1960s and early 1970s.

However, once they fled to Vietnam and Laos in the mid-1970s, and after the establishment of the PRK government in early 1979, northeastern leaders came into contact with Vietnamese soldiers and advisors, and also people from other countries who were part of the same global political alliances, such as Laos, the Soviet Union, and various other Eastern European countries. The PRK period is typically characterized as an era of political isolation for Cambodia due to opposition and embargoes organized and supported by China, the United States, and ASEAN, as well as most noncommunist European countries. However, for the ethnic minorities of northeastern Cambodia—especially those appointed to leadership positions—this period offered some opportunities for new interactions beyond what they had previously experienced.

The interactions that ethnic minorities from northeastern Cambodia had with people from outside of the country, including the roles and behavior of Vietnamese soldiers and advisors in northeastern Cambodia, is an important topic. Apart from working with Vietnamese in Cambodia, in the 1980s, the ethnic minority leaders from the northeast also had important interactions with foreigners outside of Cambodia. Few northeasterners traveled to Eastern Europe for long periods (although many ethnic Khmers from other parts of the country did) but some took short trips to Eastern Europe, including the Soviet Union, East Germany, Czechoslovakia, Poland, Hungary, and Bulgaria. They also traveled frequently to Vietnam and, to a lesser extent, Laos. These trips were important for ethnic minority leaders because most northeasterners had little experience traveling before the 1980s.

The Behavior of Vietnamese in Cambodia

The behavior of so-called volunteer Vietnamese soldiers assigned to work in northeastern Cambodia during the PRK period is worth considering, especially because in sheer numbers there were many times more Vietnamese soldiers based in Cambodia compared to advisors, although the number of both soldiers and advisors declined over the 1980s. As previously discussed, when Vietnam made the final decision in 1978 to remove the Khmer Rouge from power in Cambodia, they were well aware that many ethnic Khmers viewed Vietnam as their historical enemy or at least with considerable suspicion. This understanding certainly affected the relations that emerged between Cambodians and Vietnamese after 1979. The Vietnamese understood that if they were to have any hope of winning over the hearts and minds of most Cambodians, they needed to be disciplined in their behavior when in Cambodia. Huy Đức (2012b) reported that when he was training to be a volunteer advisor in Cambodia at Military Specialist School 481, his instructors prepared their students mentally for "a long-term assignment helping our allies."

Vu (2014), in a similar vein, explains that Vietnamese soldiers and advisors were carefully taught about what became known, in Vietnamese, as the "three prohibitions and five nos," before they were allowed to go to Cambodia. Essentially, the Vietnamese were taught to demonstrate absolute respect for Cambodian property and persons, so as not to provide their enemies with any reasons to criticize them and ultimately turn the population of Cambodia against them. Moreover, the Vietnamese required their soldiers and advisors in Cambodia be entirely self-sufficient, allowing them only to "breath [Cambodian] air and drink their water" (Vu 2014, 16). Essentially, the Vietnamese were not supposed to rely on Cambodia for food, clothing, medicine, or anything else. This background is crucial when considering the behavior of Vietnamese soldiers and advisors in Cambodia.

Vietnamese soldiers were obviously crucial to maintaining security after 1979, as previously demonstrated. They often worked closely with ethnic minorities from the northeast, and some developed close relationships with them. For example, at the time Dop Khamchoeung arrived in Mondulkiri in 1979 and became the head of the provincial army there, the Vietnamese still dominated the military. Therefore, he stayed with them. He did not have a translator, and the Vietnamese soldiers could only speak Vietnamese, so his Vietnamese language skills quickly improved. He got to know many Vietnamese soldiers quite well.[1]

Another Brao soldier from Ratanakiri told me, "It was not difficult when the Vietnamese were here. They didn't do bad things. The South Vietnamese were stealers, but the soldiers that came here were from Hanoi, so they were fine." He also said, "If the Vietnamese sent people to go cut wood, the Vietnamese would go ahead to protect the wood collectors."[2] Although those from Hanoi, whether soldiers or advisors, were considered more hardline and rigid than those from the south, they were also believed to be more disciplined (Gottesman 2002), which many in northeastern Cambodia appear to have appreciated. However, while Vietnamese advisors frequently received special training before coming to Cambodia, rank and file soldiers received much more rudimentary instruction. Therefore, they were much less politically astute. Moreover, the soldiers tended to be young draftees, and they were typically sent directly from Vietnam to take up positions in the villages to provide security.[3] But even before leaving Vietnam, they were certainly told to behave or be punished.

When asked about the behavior of the Vietnamese soldiers who stayed in Cambodia during the 1980s, Dam Chanty told me that the Vietnamese soldiers did many good deeds, such as giving rice to poor people to show solidarity. She also claimed that she only rarely heard of Vietnamese soldiers misbehaving. She then commented, "And when they did occasionally do bad things, the culprits would be quickly arrested and handed over to their leaders to be punished."[4] Bou Thang commented that most of the Vietnamese soldiers were young and immature, and therefore they sometimes behaved inappropriately. "Some chased girls and stole things," he commented. "They stole coconuts and other agricultural products, mainly because they were hungry."[5] Similarly, an ethnic Lao man from Voeunsai District who spent the Khmer Rouge period in Cambodia, not in Vietnam or Laos, stated that, "The Vietnamese were generally good, but some soldiers stole bananas and sugar cane from our fields. They probably did not have enough to eat."[6] Dop Khamchoeung reported that there were occasionally fights between Vietnamese and Cambodian soldiers, but that these "squabbles were relatively minor and did not occur often."[7]

There was a small company of fifty Vietnamese soldiers stationed at Voeunsai in 1979.[8] An ethnic Lao man who lived nearby told me a story that seems to be a good indicator of the reality of the time. In 1982, he became quite unhappy with the thievery of what he cultivated by Vietnamese soldiers, so he took his gun (he was a village volunteer soldier at the time) and bravely went to the Vietnamese military camp located near the capital of Voeunsai District Center, in Fang Village, where he asked to meet the camp commander. He was granted a meeting, and subsequently explained that thievery was occurring and that if it continued relations with villagers would undoubtedly suffer. The Vietnamese camp leader took his complaint seriously, and shortly afterward assigned Vietnamese military police to strictly work to prevent further stealing. The man who brought the issue to the camp leader's attention felt that his complaints had a good result, and that even though the Vietnamese were not always well behaved, at least their leaders made a serious effort to reduce the amount of bad behavior when there were complaints.[9]

One woman in Banlung explained that there were some cases in the early 1980s, albeit exceptional cases, when Vietnamese soldiers based near Banlung raped Cambodian women. "Even though there were not a lot of instances, many women dared not walk alone at night," she explained. However, in other cases Vietnamese soldiers married local women and later took them back with them to Vietnam or ended up staying in Cambodia as civilians after the war ended.[10] Not surprisingly, circumstances varied from case to case.

Dop Khamchoeung explained that, "Some of the Vietnamese soldiers drank too much, and there were instances when they raped local
women. But if caught, they would be punished and sent back to Vietnam. The Marxist-Leninist policies of the Vietnamese were good. It was
just that some individuals did not always follow them. I knew the rules
of the Vietnamese, and they were strict."[11] This seems to sum up the
overall situation when it came to the behavior of Vietnamese soldiers in
northeastern Cambodia, including how the Vietnamese leaders were
determined to limit bad behavior as much as possible.

According to one Cambodian source, the Vietnamese often behaved
well with the Cambodians, as some were apparently afraid that if they
treated Cambodians poorly, they might turn on them, kill them, and
then claim that the Khmer Rouge had actually killed the Vietnamese in
battle. Who would know the truth? Some believed that this kept the
Vietnamese soldiers in-line.[12] However, as already mentioned, the Vietnamese were also under orders to maintain good relations with their
Cambodian colleagues, so it was clearly more complicated than simply
fearing the Cambodians.

Sometimes, however, conflict arose between the Cambodian volunteers and the VVA soldiers. In one case, in 1981, an ethnic Lao man from
Voeunsai District was grieving over the death of his one-year-old son,
who died due to illness. A Vietnamese soldier approached him and
told him that he was required to go on guard duty that evening. In that
his son had died just hours earlier, the ethnic Lao man felt that such a
request was insensitive and inappropriate, and he became enraged and
took his rifle and shot the Vietnamese soldier in the leg. The Lao man
was not punished for his transgression, but he was no longer allowed
to be a village soldier, and his gun was taken away. Reflecting on this
incident many years later, the man who shot the Vietnamese in the leg
said, "Some Vietnamese were good and some were not."[13]

The Vietnamese Advisors in Vietnam

Vietnamese advisors began working with the ethnic minorities of the northeast in 1977 when UFNSK was first being established at Gia Poc, as previously mentioned in Chapter 3. Lieutenant
Colonel Trần Tiến Cung was the key PAVN advisor to the UFNSK beginning in 1977 (Son 2016). When at Gia Poc, Bou Thang also worked
closely with an advisor named Thanh, who Cung assigned to help

strengthen the UFNSK. Thanh and Bou Thang developed a close relationship, as Bou Thang already spoke Vietnamese at the time.[14] This was, however, only the beginning. Bou Thang explained that, "Every place I worked there was one Vietnamese advisor." He emphasized that there were various types and levels of Vietnamese advisors, from the high political level to much lower levels.[15] He clearly wanted me to see the advisors as a diverse set of actors, which seems appropriate. Yoep Vanson reported that when he was a medic with the military command at Gia Poc, there were four Vietnamese advisors, two men and two women.[16] There were also other Vietnamese advisors at Gia Poc, including one named Quang, who provided general support.[17] Each had their own personalities, strengths, and faults.

Interestingly, however, when Vietnam formed the organizational structure to begin helping Cambodia in 1977 and 1978, Lê Đức Thọ did not use southern Vietnamese cadres, even though they already knew some of the players and had helped the Cambodian Party for many years. Instead, almost all of the cadres who were initially chosen to be in charge of the advisors to the Cambodians were from northern Vietnam (Dũng 1995).

The Vietnamese Advisors in Cambodia

Some advisors from the Soviet Union and other Eastern Bloc countries came to work in Cambodia, along with a few from other sympatric nations, including volunteers who did not come to Cambodia with their governments' support. However, for security reasons, most non-Vietnamese foreigners were based in the capital city of Phnom Penh or in nearby areas (Gottesman 2002), and none are known to have been based in remote parts of the country, including the northeast. Indicative of the circumstances, during the UNTAC period of the early 1990s, Henry Kamm (1998) was told by the vice-chairman of Stung Treng's People's Committee that during the 1980s no Soviet or other Eastern European "experts" had reached his province. Bou Thang, however, was based in Phnom Penh and had two Soviet advisors when he was minister of defense, with each changing their position every three years. They too mainly stayed in the capital city. Bou Thang only had Soviet and Vietnamese advisors, but always regarded the Vietnamese as being his most important advisors.[18] I too have not heard of any Soviet or Eastern Bloc advisors based in northeastern Cambodia during the 1979 to 1989 period. Therefore, when we talk about foreign advisors during the PRK period in northeastern Cambodia, we are really only talking about the Vietnamese.

Vietnamese advisors or specialists worked with all PRK government departments, from the military and the police to the ministries, departments, People's Committee offices, and different provincial departments and district and commune offices. They especially supported the development of the fledging PRPK. In many cases, they also developed close relationships with the Brao and other ethnic minorities they worked with. By April 1979, a network of Vietnamese advisors or specialists assigned to assist the Cambodian revolution was in place, from the central level down to the villages (Anh 2015).

On May 15, 1979, apparently at the request of the Central Committee of the PRPK, the secretariat of the SRV's Party Central Committee issued Directive No. 75/CT-TW, which was designed to set the conditions for large numbers of Vietnamese advisors—or specialists as they were also known—to serve in Cambodia's provinces, districts, and communes (Nhan 2005). These advisors were drawn from various places, including PAVN military units, as well as from civilian positions in the government. The plan was to send these specialists to work on specific jobs for defined periods of time (Institute of Military History 2010). Section B-68 was the main Vietnamese specialist group in Cambodia.

Also on May 15, 1979, Party Secretariat Directive No. 39-QD-TW was issued, stating:

> Because of the requirements of our international mission to assist the Kampuchean revolution, the [Vietnam] Party has sent and will continue to send rather large numbers of cadre and Party members to assist our friends' Party Central Committee, Government, branches, and province and district Party affairs committees. Many of those sent are or will be high-ranking cadre from central, national-level sections and branches and from the provinces. Our Friends' revolutionary duty is growing swiftly on a nation-wide scale and the size of our specialist [advisory] forces is steadily growing, so we must quickly strengthen and perfect the Party's organization within the specialist apparatus to improve the capabilities and increase the fighting strength of Party chapters to

ensure that all responsibilities entrusted by the Party Central
Committee to the Party chapter involved in operations assisting
our friends are carried out properly. (Nhan 2005, 145)

Apart from the main civilian advisory unit, B-68, unit A-40 was
established as an economic and agriculture production specialist group
to help Cambodians to quickly rebuild and stabilize living conditions
and social activities. Nguyễn Cồn, member of the Party Central Committee and chief of the Central Committee's economy and plans section,
was appointed as head of this specialist group. Hồ Viết Thắng, vice-
chairman of the state planning commission, was made deputy specialist
group chief and the group's general, overall standing committee member. Nguyễn Tuân, deputy minister of the Ministry of Electricity and
Coal, was put in charge of the industrial section of the group (Anh 2015).
A-50 was responsible for the municipality of Phnom Penh (Carney
1986). Vietnam's Party Central Committee also established a security
specialist group (codenamed K-79), which was led by Trần Viễn Chi,
deputy minister of interior. The specific goal of K-79 was to help Cambodian allies build their security forces (Anh 2015).

Finally, there was a powerful Vietnamese military specialist unit
named Group 478, led by Lê Đức Anh (Huy Đức 2012a), which was
directly subordinate to the Central Military Party Committee. Group
478 was mandated to oversee all aspects (political, ideological, and organizational) of the formation of party chapters in Cambodia, although
provincial-level specialist groups were under the overall administrative control and direction of Section B-68 (Nhan 2005). According to
Bou Thang, there were basically two varieties of Vietnamese advisors
in Cambodia: military and civilian, although the military advisors generally had more power.[19]

In that the focus of this book is particularly on northeastern Cambodia, it is especially notable that province-level specialist groups and
district-level specialist cells were mandated to form unified party chapters directly subordinate to the secretariat of the Party Central Committee, and that these were called "Specialists Assisting the K Friends
Party Chapters." A-40 and Section B-68 each set up their own party
chapters made up of subordinate party chapters in the different compo-
nents of these two agencies. Party chapters were formed in each province, made up of provincial specialist group party chapters and district
specialist cell party chapters. These chapters could both introduce and

expel members (Nhan 2005). This structure was critically important for the organization of Vietnamese advisors working in Cambodia.

Another important part of Vietnam's plan to assist Cambodia related to the creation of "sister provinces" for supporting Cambodia. Party Secretariat Directive No. 75 CT/CW approved a plan to assign Vietnamese provinces the responsibility of assisting particular Cambodian provinces (Nhan 2005, 152). The Vietnamese provinces would not, however, send operation units to their Cambodian sister provinces to "mobilize the masses and form revolutionary governments and mass organizations." That duty was assigned to specific military units operating in the Cambodian province that the Ministry of Defense forward headquarters and the military region headquarters entrusted with the mission of "mobilizing the masses and building local government." Those units could form operations units and they would be required to assign political and civilian cadres to carry out assigned responsibilities. They were also required to coordinate closely with provincial-level specialist groups (Institute of Military History 2010).

Ea Meng-Try (1981, 222) wrote, rather cynically, that, "The colonization efforts [of Vietnam] began with a pairing of Kampuchean provinces with Vietnamese provinces," but it seems that the efforts of many Vietnamese were quite sincerely intended to assist Cambodia. Indicative of this, Bou Thang commented that these special province-to-province relationships played a role in encouraging some Vietnamese advisors to come to work in Cambodia from these linked provinces. For example, often Cambodians struck up close friendships with Vietnamese they met through these linkages, and these friendships sometimes later became important when trying to convince Vietnamese specialists to come to be advisors in Cambodia.[20]

Considering the importance of establishing a strong group of specialists to work in Cambodia, on December 30, 1979, Party Secretariat Decision No. 60-QD/TW was issued. This decision mandated the establishment of "Special Political School K," which was directly subordinate to the Secretariat of the Vietnam Party Central Committee. The school was mandated "to develop a program of theoretical and political research for senior cadre of our K [Kampuchean] friends" (Nhan 2005, 517). It was located in the Tay Tuu part of Hanoi (Nhan 2005).

The Vietnamese Ambassador to Cambodia, Ngo Dien, is considered by some to have been the principal architect of Vietnam's policy toward Cambodia from the beginning until its end (Kamm 1998). However, during the early years of the PRK, Lê Đức Thọ was the most important Vietnamese figure in relation to Cambodia. He was the member of the Politburo who most closely oversaw Section B-68. Moreover, on August 24, 1979, acting as the representative of the Politburo of the Vietnamese Communist Party, Lê Duẩn signed Decision Order No. 19, forming the Section Responsible for K [Kampuchean] Operations. Lê Đức Thọ was appointed as head of the unit, with Lê Đức Anh as his first deputy (Nhan 2005; Anh 2015).

According to Gottesman (2002, 144), Lê Đức Thọ is most remembered "for his condescending lectures to the Cambodian leadership." Indeed, Gottesman (2002) viewed Tho as the embodiment of "Vietnamese arrogance," although it is hard to know to what extent these comments reflect the views of his key informants. This view extends to Pen Sovan, who may have wanted to tarnish the name of the Vietnamese leader due to his role in Pen Sovan's imprisonment years earlier. Bou Thang dared not state if Lê Đức Thọ was arrogant. Instead, he commented that Lê Đức Thọ was a leader of Vietnam, and therefore it should not have been considered unusual for him to have a strong personality.

As far as Bou Thang is concerned, "Lê Đức Thọ had a lot of ability." To back up his point, he mentioned the successful negotiations with Henry Kissinger that Tho led in the early 1970s; the negotiations that eventually led to an end of US involvement in the war in Vietnam.[21] Ngo Dien admitted, however, that Vietnamese condescension [toward the Cambodians] was unavoidable, as the Vietnamese prepared most of the PRK's important documents, and did most of the work organizing government affairs (Huy Đức 2012a). In any case, in February 1980, Lê Đức Thọ returned to Vietnam from Cambodia, and the Politburo appointed Lê Đức Anh as his replacement (Anh 2015). However, Lê Đức Thọ continued to be the member of the Politburo responsible for overseeing the situation in Cambodia well into the 1980s (Carney 1986).

In early 1980, the Vietnamese decided to disband their district-level specialist groups (Anh 2015), although there were still Vietnamese advisors working in districts and even in the communes. By the end of 1980, the Vietnamese apparently had a total of twenty-two central specialist groups and twenty-two province and city specialist groups (Anh 2015).

Gottesman (2002, 143) described the Vietnamese advisors in Cambodia as essentially "wield[ing] tight control over the [PRK] regime." He pointed out, for example, that "[d]eference to the advisors was a matter of official policy," with the PRK government encouraging its officials to work closely and ask the opinions of Vietnamese advisors regarding virtually all important matters. This policy is likely to have been in place, at least early on, but despite having considerable influence over the matters that they presided over, the advisors did not all act dictatorially. Many were modest people who received very little compensation for their efforts, and often lived in quite humble conditions. This included advisors based in Phnom Penh (Gottesman 2002), and especially ones stationed in much more remote parts of the country, including the northeast.

Were the Vietnamese advisors qualified to do the work that they have been assigned to do? Speaking about Vietnamese advisors in Cambodia generally, Huy Đức (2012a, 394) wrote that, "Except for a small number of Vietnamese cadres who were truly capable and talented, the majority of the specialists were simply people who were enthusiastic and eager to mechanically apply the experiences and the work methods of Vietnam's bureaucratic subsidy system to Cambodia." This seems a bit unfair. Although enthusiasm and motivation were certainly important factors, it does seem that many of the advisors were also fairly skillful, even if the standards in the northeast were not very high.

Henry Kamm (1998, 188–189) also discussed the role of the Vietnamese advisors in Cambodia, although in an overly simplistic way. He wrote: "Vietnamese officials were advising the government of poorly educated Cambodians that Hanoi had installed in every ministry." Kamm (1998, 189) also stated, however, that "In the provinces, Vietnamese officials were less tactful or sensitive to Cambodian's self-esteem than in the capital." This may have been the case in some parts of the country, but the evidence that I have been able to collect in Stung Treng and Ratanakiri Provinces tends to contradict, or at least greatly complicates and nuances, our understanding of the nature of the relationships that emerged between the Vietnamese advisors and Cambodians, at least the ethnic minorities from the northeast. My many interviews with Brao and other highlanders who worked closely with Vietnamese advisors during the 1979 to 1989 period, as well as some ethnic Lao Cambodians, tends to indicate that the advisors in the northeast behaved quite well, although with some exceptions, as might be expected.

In 1982, Vietnamese advisors were apparently expected to stay in Cambodia three or four more years, but five years later most were still in their original positions (Gottesman 2002). My interviews similarly indicate that many of the advisors in the northeast worked for many years in their original positions, and some stayed from the beginning right up until the advisors were finally withdrawn from the country. However, many also worked for much shorter periods, and in fact, Slocomb (2003) reported that the number of Vietnamese advisors had already declined by 1980, although this was not reported by my informants in the northeast. In any case, according to Gottesman (2002), by March 1988, most advisors had returned home to Vietnam. This information generally fits with what I heard from informants in northeastern Cambodia. I was told that most Vietnamese advisors left before the last Vietnamese soldiers departed, although a small group of military advisors were apparently the last to leave. They reportedly departed a few months after the soldiers did.[22] This makes sense, due to concerns that the PRAK would not be able to stand up to NADK forces once the VVA had left the country.

It is difficult to estimate exactly how many Vietnamese advisors worked in Cambodia during the 1980s, including in the northeast. Nationwide, however, Dũng (1995) estimated that there were probably over 10,095 Vietnamese civilian advisors over the decade. One thing that is certain is that the vast majority were males. There were, indeed, very few female advisors from Vietnam, and even fewer female Vietnamese soldiers.[23] Indicative of the situation, even the advisors for the Department of Women's Affairs in Ratanakiri Province were always men, although it must be acknowledged that these advisors also worked with other departments at the same time as they were responsible for supporting the Department of Women's Affairs.[24] There were, however, a small number of Vietnamese female advisors, but the vast majority were nurses. Overall, apparently only 2 to 3 percent of the advisors in the northeast were women.[25]

When the capital of Ratanakiri Province was initially based in Voeunsai, near the Sesan River, Teuk was the first main Vietnamese advisor to the province. Nin advised about organizing human resources, while Treu provided economic advice. Most Northeasterners I interviewed could only remember the given names of the advisors they worked with, but nonetheless, most remembered their names twenty or more years after they last left.[26]

Later, however, each province, including Ratanakiri, was allocated one Vietnamese advisor for every provincial department or group of two or three departments. There was also one Vietnamese advisor assigned for each district and commune. Advisors were not assigned to work in specific villages.[27]

Lok, a Vietnamese from Binh Dinh Province, became the chief Vietnamese advisor in Ratanakiri. He generally monitored the work of all the departments in the province. He was said to have been dedicated and to have performed well. Lat Vansao worked with Lok in 1979, along with Lok's Vietnamese translator, and he had a good opinion of him.[28] As one senior Brao official put it, referring to Lok, "He was like a governor," as he was recognized as being the leader of the other advisors. Lok apparently retained his position from 1979 until March 1980, when he was replaced by Yen, followed by another advisor, and finally Kwen became the province's chief advisor in 1986.[29]

Teuk, who was also from Binh Dinh Province, was another important Vietnamese specialist in Ratanakiri, as he was specifically responsible for advising the PRPK, and therefore was considered one of the province's key advisors. He also took up his position in Ratanakiri in 1979. After spending a few years in the province, he returned to Vietnam for a period, before coming back to Ratanakiri and continuing in the same position until around 1987.[30]

There were advisors for almost every major enterprise in the province, although sometimes a single advisor was assigned to work with two or three units. For example, there was one advisor assigned to the propaganda branch of the PRPK, and he also worked with the Department of Women's Affairs and the Department of Youth Affairs. It appears that many Vietnamese advisors were chosen through party lines. Still, most government units had an advisor. Indicative of this, one Brao official pointed out—with apparent surprise—that there was not a Vietnamese advisor assigned to the provincial sawmill.[31] In that there was only a single Vietnamese advisor attached to the Department of Women's Affairs, Department of Youth Affairs, and the propaganda branch of the PRPK, the advisor came to the Department of Women's Affairs about once a week, depending on how much work there was to do. According to Jop Moer, he taught people in all three departments how to 1) encourage villagers not to join the Khmer Rouge, 2) teach women how to help husbands who were soldiers, and 3) encourage other villagers to help military families. Jop Moer explained that after receiving this training, she spent most of her time doing this in the villages, albeit unaccompanied by the advisor.[32]

At the fifty-bed hospital in Ratanakiri Province there was only one Vietnamese advisor. The first of those was named Lien, but advisors to the hospital typically changed every year. In some offices, however, advisors stayed longer, often two or three years.[33] In reflecting on the Vietnamese advisors who worked with him over the years, Yoep Vanson, the head of the hospital in the 1980s, said that they all did a good job. However, he also commented that some Cambodians made trouble by bringing up "ancient conflicts" with the Vietnamese that went back to the precolonial era. He said that these people, although few in number, brought up these conflicts to try to discredit the Vietnamese. Most, however, appreciated the Vietnamese, he explained.[34]

In Mondulkiri, Thang Ngon, the Secretary of the province's PRPK Committee, reported that he had two Vietnamese advisors. One, whose name was Dak, came from Hanoi and worked with him for three years. Another, named Keng, was from Daklak Province. He stayed in Mondulkiri until the Vietnamese withdrew from Cambodia. Each advisor had his own translator. Thang Ngon also reported that in the 1980s all the government departments in Mondulkiri had Vietnamese advisors attached to them.[35]

The Vietnamese were organized separately from their Cambodian colleagues. For example, they participated in Vietnamese-only party meetings, ones that were only open to Vietnamese advisors. Essentially, they maintained their own party cells. The PRPK rules in Cambodia were exactly the same as they were for the party in Vietnam. However, Vietnamese advisors were allowed to join the PRPK's meetings as well, but without having voting rights. Lok, the key Vietnamese advisor to Ratanakiri Province, often attended provincial PRPK Committee meetings.[36] The PRPK rules were also exactly the same as they were in Laos, where Vietnamese advisors also observed party meetings.[37]

After a six-month probationary period, new PRPK members were given full party rights. However, Slocomb (2003) reported that party rights were initially given out slowly, for fear that enemies might be admitted into the PRPK. Thus, by late September 1980, only three new PRPK members had been approved throughout the country (Slocomb 2003). However, not long after, the number of new party members began increasing. For example, Dam Chanty became a full member on December 17, 1980,[38] even though she had lived with the Khmer Rouge throughout the 1970s.

The Vietnamese advisors did not receive their salaries through regular provincial budgets in Cambodia, like Cambodian government officials, but were instead paid directly from Vietnam by the Vietnamese. Therefore, nobody in Cambodia knew what their salaries were. The Vietnamese also secured their own food, supplies, and so on.[39]

Sai Sopheap knows more about Vietnamese advisors in northeastern Cambodia than most, as his job was to teach them the Khmer language. He taught about one hundred Vietnamese for about a year. The advisors studied at three levels. Only Cambodians (although he is ethnic Lao) taught Khmer to the Vietnamese. His students included one of the key Vietnamese military advisors, Quang.[40] Sai Sopheap was under the impression that all the Vietnamese advisors were officially soldiers, and that there were no civilian advisors. My research, however, indicates that many advisors did hold civilian government positions before coming to Cambodia as specialists. But most also had at least some military training as well. As Sai Sopheap put it, "They had to get people who could fight, in case they were attacked." However, those who worked as civilian advisors wore regular clothes, not military uniforms.[41] When Vietnamese advisors first came to Cambodia, they typically studied for a year. They apparently all had to take a special course before coming to Cambodia, although it was not clear to some Cambodian observers, such as Sai Sopheap, what the course curriculum included.[42]

Sai Sopheap claimed that the advisors in the communes changed every year, but that this was not the case at the provincial level, where they tended to hold their positions longer.[43] Another informant from Andong Meas District, Ratanakiri Province had a similar story, reporting that commune advisors changed every six months to a year, while advisors at the district and provincial levels tended to hold their positions much longer.[44]

Most of the Vietnamese advisors were at a disadvantage because they did not have much knowledge of local languages. If they did study a language, it was only Khmer, and even then they were rarely able to speak much. In any case, people in the northeast rarely used Khmer. Some advisors found Lao easier to learn, especially those who had spent time in Laos. Furthermore, most of the Cambodians working at the local government level in northeast Cambodia did not speak Vietnamese well either, but those who had spent time as refugees in Vietnam generally spoke Vietnamese better. Moreover, some of the older Khmer Hanoi who had spent many years studying in Vietnam spoke Vietnamese quite well. However, even though Boua Chuong studied the Vietnamese language for many years when he was in Hanoi, he was already older than other Khmer Hanoi who went to Vietnam, and so was never able to master the language, even though that was all he studied in Vietnam.[45] Still, he knew enough Vietnamese to at least maintain good relations between Ratanakiri Province, which he governed, and the Vietnamese.

When Vietnamese advisors went to villages, they generally had to use translators.[46] Some translators were Vietnamese, but some were Cambodians belonging to various ethnic groups. One informant, who was a policeman during the PRK period, reported that most Vietnamese advisors who worked in Andong Meas District spoke some Khmer and Lao. However, they were generally not able to speak either language fluently. Therefore, they often used translators, but the translators were usually Cambodian ethnic minorities who lived in the area, and they were not fluent enough in Vietnamese to translate all details effectively. Moreover, none had ever received any formal training regarding translation. Instead, they often summarized the results of discussions or meetings to the Vietnamese advisors, which only provided them with partial information.[47]

In some cases, Cambodian officials translated themselves. For example, Dam Chanty, from the Department of Women's Affairs, sometimes translated for Vietnamese advisors in Ratanakiri, as she had studied in Vietnam and is quite fluent in Vietnamese.[48] In early 1980, for example, Chanty remembers going with Vietnamese soldiers to Phi Village near the border with Vietnam to translate for Vietnamese soldiers. On the way back, the Vietnamese were checking the road ahead of them when one Vietnamese soldier was killed by a landmine planted on the road they were traveling on. Later, during the same year, she went to translate for Vietnamese soldiers who were dispatched to deal with the Khmer Rouge in Malik Village. A Jarai woman named Liem was also sent to translate with her. They slept in the forest with 200–300 Vietnamese soldiers. The translators were protected by the Vietnamese soldiers. Dam Chanty remembers one inhabitant of the village, who was actually her relative, being arrested and jailed in Banlung for a couple of months for having contact with the NADK. In still another case, she traveled to near the Vietnamese border with Lak On.

They were supposed to ride in a Toyota truck, but luckily they decided to ride in a Vietnamese vehicle, as the Toyota was shot at during the trip and two Vietnamese soldiers in it were killed.[49]

The overall picture that emerges is that there was considerable variation when it came to advisors, including how long they stayed and where they came from. Moreover, the translator situation also varied widely from place to place.

Vietnamese Military Advisors

Probably the most important Vietnamese advisors in Cambodia were, not surprisingly, those who worked in Group 478, the unit led by Lê Đức Anh and set up to provide military advice. Military advisors played important roles in various fields, from advising on political and battlefield strategies and recruiting drives for new soldiers to providing various kinds of specialized military training.

Soy Keo reported that Lê Trọng Tấn, the Vietnamese two-star general who had previously signed, as PAVN's general chief of staff, the order to form Group 578 in May 1978, was his personal military advisor when he was general chief of staff of the PRAK. The ethnic Kinh man was apparently a revolutionary soldier from southern Vietnam and was originally from Saigon.[50] Each province had a number of Vietnamese advisors assigned to work specifically with the PRAK.

Beginning in 1979, Quang, who was based in Stung Treng, was the head Vietnamese military advisor of the northeast. He had previously stayed in Laos for over ten years supporting the war effort there, and so he could speak Lao. Later he was based in Pleiku in Vietnam, where he worked with Military Region 5.[51] Soy Keo commented that after 1979, Quang was the one who investigated Cambodians who were believed to have violated regulations.[52] His deputy was another Vietnamese military advisor named Ti, who could also speak Lao.[53] Hat was another Vietnamese military advisor of the northeast zone, but he spent a considerable amount of time in Ratanakiri Province and could not speak Lao.[54] The Brao man, To Bioe, frequently assisted with translating for Quang because Bioe was based in Stung Treng and spoke Khmer and Lao, whereas Quang only spoke Vietnamese and Lao.[55] Bioe also worked closely with Theng, another Vietnamese military advisor based in Stung Treng. Although Theng spoke no Khmer, Bioe felt that he was well disciplined and that his policies were good.[56]

Relations with Vietnamese Advisors—A Generally Much More Positive Perspective

As is evident from the previous discussion, I heard many stories about the behavior—good and bad—of Vietnamese advisors from the people interviewed, and they generally had a good impression of those they worked closely with. For example, Chenh, an ethnic Kinh man from Nha Trang Province and the Vietnamese advisor to the secretary of Stung Treng's provincial PRPK Committee from 1979 to 1988 was well liked by the people he worked with, as was Jo, an ethnic Kinh translator.[57] In Preah Vihear Province there was a Vietnamese military advisor from Danang who worked with the Brao soldiers in the 1980s, and was quite popular with the soldiers.[58]

The Brao generally appreciated that the Vietnamese advisors were careful not to criticize them.[59] Kreng Siengnoi claimed that it was easy to work with the Vietnamese, and that they hardly ever complained to the Cambodians. He stated, "There was consensus (*akhapheap*) when the Cambodians [in Ratanakiri Province] worked with the Vietnamese. We would make requests and they would work with us to achieve the goals. If Cambodians could do something by themselves, the Vietnamese did not get involved. If their help was needed, they were happy to assist us. They helped a lot to build up our capacity."[60] Thang Ngon had similarly positive things to say about the Vietnamese. He commented about one of his advisors, stating that, "Dak's policies were high level. I liked him."[61] Joeun Wel, an ethnic Jarai man who now lives in Talao Village in Andong Meas District, but originally came from Phi Village in O Yadao District, reported that the Vietnamese advisors who came to Ratanakiri "were quite disciplined." He continued, "They didn't cause any problems. They didn't want to fall into the Khmer Rouge's trap."[62] Luon Vandy, an ethnic Lao man in Stung Treng, also expressed his support for the Vietnamese advisors and soldiers, stating, "They helped fight the Khmer Rouge. I didn't hear of them doing any bad things. They stayed [in Cambodia] the right amount of time."[63]

Two Brao former government officials provided some telling comments that relate to the difference between how the Brao and the Khmer frequently viewed Vietnamese advisors. One said, "There wasn't much conflict with the Vietnamese. But most of the time we followed them, although sometimes the Vietnamese agreed with Cambodian ideas, provided that they were well founded." He continued, "In Stung Treng,

Mondulkiri and Ratanakiri there were no problems between the Vietnamese and the Brao, as they had similar histories of being with the Indochina Party before." They claimed, however, that in Preah Vihear Province the situation was more complicated, as most of the people there are ethnic Khmers. The other said, "In other parts of Cambodia it was different. The Vietnamese and the Khmer could not work together well. There was bad history from before. But for us, nobody was bored with the Vietnamese advisors."[64] Similarly, Ma Ranchai, who is ethnic Lun, stated, "It was easy to work with the Vietnamese. They taught us." Because Ma Ranchai was illiterate when he began working for the government, he was particularly grateful when the Vietnamese wrote documents for him. He felt that the Vietnamese encouraged him to learn things, but did not force him to study anything. He, therefore, felt sorry when the Vietnamese advisors left Ratanakiri. "If they didn't help, I wouldn't have been sorry to have seen them go," he offered.[65]

Some people were, however, more skeptical about the motives of the Vietnamese advisors. One ethnic Lao man from Voeunsai District said, for example, "The Vietnamese were good in some ways, but not in all ways. They did not come to Cambodia just to help the Cambodians. They came to help themselves."[66] Bui Yung made similar comments. As he put it, "The Vietnamese said that they came to Cambodia to put the fire out, because if they did not it would have crossed into Vietnam. In reality, they did not come into Cambodia to help the Cambodians. They came to help themselves."[67] Indeed, there may be much truth to this view.

In one case, a Vietnamese commune advisor in Bo Kham Commune (now in Andong Meas District), named Tat, raped a local woman when she was cooking rice for government officials in the commune. The woman was apparently unmarried and single, and was forced to have sex from behind while she was cooking rice. She later reported the incident to the authorities, and when he was confronted with the allegations, the advisor admitted his guilt. He knew the gravity of the mistake he had made, but initially tried to convince the commune officials not to report his offense to the district government in Bokeo, where the Vietnamese advisors there would certainly learn of what happened. The local police said that they had no choice but to report what had happened. In response, Tat wrote a letter in Vietnamese, apparently explaining what had happened, and asked the policeman to deliver the letter to the Bokeo District government. However, before the letter

251

could be delivered, Tat returned and asked for the letter back. It was returned to him and was never sent. The next day Tat went to Bokeo District. Later in the same day, the policeman also traveled to Bokeo District center and reported the incident to officials there. The officials were still not aware of what had happened, even though Tat had met them earlier in the day. It is unclear what happened after that, but Tat was never seen again. Because this happened near the end of the Vietnamese occupation period, in 1988, Tat was not replaced.[68] Although it appears that this sort of incident was quite rare, it is quite likely that there were more incidents than were revealed to me in interviews.

There is also one more category of Vietnamese behavior that deserves mention. This was behavior perceived as being against the interests of Cambodians. One such example became evident after the PRPK's 5th Party Congress in October 1985, when it was decided that economic reform was necessary, and that the provinces would need to be more self-sufficient (*Phnom Penh Domestic Service* 1985). Bui Yung claims that a Vietnamese advisor asked him how Ratanakiri could become more self-sufficient. He responded that the province had three main resources: 1) forests, 2) minerals, and 3) rubber plantations. Bui Yung felt that the best options were to develop mining and logging, as the government was already managing the rubber plantations. The province did not, however, have enough technical ability or equipment to develop logging or mining. Therefore, Bui Yung suggested that Ratanakiri partner with its two sister Vietnamese provinces, Gialai-Kontum and Nghia Binh, to do this (*Phnom Penh Domestic Service* 1983c). He proposed that Gialai-Kontum provide technical assistance and gasoline, and that Nghia Binh provide technical assistance and equipment. The Vietnamese advisor liked the idea.

Indeed, promoting cooperation between Gialai-Kontum, Nghia Binh, and Ratanakiri Provinces in relation to logging had already been discussed when Vietnam's Politburo member, Võ Văn Kiệt, visited Ratanakiri in July 1983 (*Phnom Penh Domestic Service* 1983c). Moreover, Nghia Binh developed a plan to log in Ratanakiri during the same year (*Hanoi VNA* 1983). However, Bui Yung was disappointed with what actually happened. According to him, all the trees cut down that had a girth wider than sixty centimeters were taken to Vietnam by the Vietnamese, and Cambodia was only allowed to retain the smaller trees. He felt that the Vietnamese had taken advantage of the Cambodians, and that they had gained most of the benefits and had not actually helped the Cambodians.[69]

Having reviewed the relations between Vietnamese advisors and soldiers and minorities in northeastern Cambodia and the behavior and consequences of inappropriate behavior by Vietnamese soldiers and advisors, we now turn to the second part of the chapter, which considers the experiences of ethnic minority leaders who traveled outside of Cambodia.

Traveling in Vietnam, Laos, and Eastern Europe (1979–1989)

Prior to the establishment of the PRK, few of the ethnic minorities from the northeast had ever traveled far from where they were born, except possibly to southern Laos or Vietnam. However, those who gained senior positions in 1979 often had opportunities to travel, mainly to Vietnam and Laos, but also as far as Eastern Europe.

Trips to Vietnam

Not surprisingly, one way in which the Vietnamese hoped to generate loyalty among Cambodians was through offering them opportunities to travel to Vietnam to develop relationships with Vietnamese leaders there. Indeed, people in leadership positions in the northeast frequently traveled to Vietnam for various reasons, including to join training courses, participate in study trips, and attend political meetings and events. High-level officials also frequently went to Vietnam for medical treatment.

As previously mentioned in the first part of this chapter, one of the ways in which the Vietnamese tried to strengthen ties between Vietnam and the PRK government and engage the provincial governments in Vietnam with the development of Cambodia after 1979 was through the "sistering" of Cambodian border provinces and neighboring provinces in Vietnam. One potentially positive aspect of these sister province arrangements was that they provided opportunities for ethnic minorities from northeastern Cambodia to travel to—and receive support from—neighboring provinces in Vietnam. Indeed, delegations of ethnic minority leaders from northeastern Cambodia frequently traveled to Vietnam to participate in study trips that allowed them to meet and develop relationships with their counterparts. They were also expected to learn more about Vietnam. Certainly it was hoped by the Vietnamese that some of what they learned in Vietnam would be emulated in Cambodia. These study trips were significant events in the lives of many of ethnic minorities, and everyone I spoke with who participated in these trips reflected positively on their experiences, some even stating that the trips represented some of the most memorable times in their careers.

Education opportunities in Vietnam were also crucial. As mentioned in previous chapters, in 1979 most people from the northeast had very low levels of formal education, and literacy rates were extremely low (Bou Thang 1993). Therefore, most of those who occupied senior positions in the northeast participated in three-month, short-term Khmer literacy and political training trips. In 1979 and 1980, many completed these three-month training sessions in Ho Chi Minh City, including leaders from the northeast, such as Boua Chuong, Lak On, Kham Khoeun, Yoep Vanson, Kham Chan, Kavet La-In, and Dam Chanty, just to name a few.[70]

Many also participated in longer training programs, from six months to up to two years, especially younger people with leadership potential. For example, Luon Vandy studied economics and policy in Ho Chi Minh City in 1981 to 1982,[71] and between March and September 1983, Bui Yung went to study public policy in Hanoi for six months, after which time he became vice-chairman of Ratanakiri's provincial People's Committee.[72] Sai Sopheap studied architecture mapping in Vietnam in 1984,[73] and in 1985, Lat Vansao went to study politics in Ho Chi Minh City for six months.[74] During the same year, Kham Khoeun did a six-month special police training course at the police school in Ho Chi Minh City.[75] Others, such as Yoep Vanson and Dam Chanty, participated in Khmer literacy, politics, and government administration courses that took one and a half years to complete. For example, after completing the three months of initial training, future chairman of Ratanakiri's provincial People's Committee Kham Khoeun studied basic literacy skills for one and a half years in Ho Chi Minh City.[76] The same is true for the future chairperson of the Department of Women's Affairs, Dam Chanty.[77] Khmer teachers were brought from Phnom Penh to teach Khmer language, while Vietnamese provided training about politics and government administration, using translators to convey their messages. In 1979, one group of thirty-eight people from Ratanakiri Province went to study in Vietnam. There were six hundred people there from all over Cambodia, and they were encouraged to compare the old and the new situations in Cambodia. Comparisons with Laos and Vietnam were also frequently drawn. The instructors explained that if the Cambodians did a good job governing the country, many countries would support them, including France and the United States. The teachers also explained to the Cambodians that their country would develop in the future, provided that there was no war. But if war persisted, foreign countries would not help them to "develop." However, some, such as Yoep Vanson, did not know what "development" was yet, so he asked and was told that it was related to progress and modernization.[78]

Special training opportunities were organized for the military and the police. For example, in 1984, Kham Sana was one of three hundred people from all over the country who went to study technical military matters in Ho Chi Minh City for a six-month period. He enjoyed studying in Vietnam, as he did not need to be wary of Khmer Rouge military attacks when he was there, as was the case in Cambodia. He could just study and enjoy himself without fear. Strict discipline was enforced at the military school where all the students boarded, but on weekends students were permitted to relax a bit. Relaxing included being allowed to drink alcohol. Drinking on regular days of instruction was, however, prohibited, and those who violated the rule were punished.[79]

There were also shorter touring study trips to Vietnam designed simply to expose Cambodians to circumstances in Vietnam, with the goal of improving relations between Cambodia and Vietnam. For example, Boua Chuong, Kham Len, Ma Ranchai, and Yoep Vanson went on one study trip early on to Pleiku. Notably, during the group study trip, the son of the former prime minister of Vietnam, Phạm Văn Đồng, gave each person from Ratanakiri a photo album full of photos of the trip so that everyone would remember it. The idea was to capture the memories and cement relationships between Cambodia and Vietnam.[80] I heard stories about these trips from many of the senior northeastern minorities who worked for the PRK government. They often spoke of the lasting and fond impressions they had from these trips. Clearly, the Vietnamese were trying to cultivate these memories of friendship. Because there were many trips organized during the PRK period, sometimes government departments would rotate different officials to participate so that as many people as possible could have chances to visit Vietnam.[81]

Bou Thang also officially visited Vietnam four times between 1979 and 1989 specifically for political reasons. First he went as the head of the Propaganda Department.[82] His second trip was a result of an invitation to visit the Ministry of Defense in Vietnam in December 1982, as the leader of a high-level military delegation from Cambodia (Institute of Military History 2010). He also visited Hanoi in December 1984 to attend fortieth anniversary celebrations for PAVN (*Phnom Penh SPK* 1984a), and in August 1989, he visited the Vietnamese province of Lang Son for a week (*Phnom Penh Domestic Service* 1989a).

Trips to Laos

Some ethnic minorities from northeastern Cambodia traveled to the Lao People's Democratic Republic (Lao PDR) during the PRK period, but travel to Laos was generally much less frequent than to Vietnam.[83] Still, a treaty of "peace, friendship and cooperation" was signed between the PRK and the Lao PDR on March 22, 1979 (*Phnom Penh Domestic Service* 1984a). Moreover, the Lao PDR apparently offered to send troops to Cambodia to support them, if requested (VODK 1984c); although an official request was never apparently made. Moreover, sister relationships were developed between Ratanakiri Province and Attapeu Province, and between Stung Treng Province and Champasak Province. Even though the Lao provinces had much less resources to offer,[84] the sistering program resulted in some aid being provided to Cambodia from the sister provinces in Laos. For example, Champasak and Attapeu provided Cambodia with limited support in building infrastructure, such as the O Kandea Bridge on Route 13 in Stung Treng. They also gifted some coffee, plywood, and fuel to Cambodia in the late 1980s, along with various other products (*Phnom Penh SPK* 1990).

Sister province relations also resulted in a number of delegations being sent from Stung Treng and Ratanakiri to neighboring provinces in Laos. For example, Thang Bai led a delegation to Champasak Province in September 1982, to strength "friendship and cooperation between the two provinces" (*Phnom Penh SPK* 1982). Yoep Vanson also traveled frequently to Attapeu Province to attend events, such as a celebration for the anniversary of the Lao People's Army.[85] Indicative of these trips, in December 1989, Lak On led a delegation from Ratanakiri to its sister province of Attapeu to participate in celebrations related to the fourteenth anniversary of the founding of the Lao PDR (*Vientiane KPL* 1989).

The Lao PDR government did not, however, offer much educational or other study trip opportunities for traveling to Laos, and the PRK government did not have funds to support such travel either. Moreover, because Laos was quite poor and undeveloped itself, it was not considered particularly useful for Cambodians to travel there specifically to study. Also, Laos had few institutions for educating its own people, and so was not in a position to offer Cambodians opportunities to study there.[86] Still, in the late 1980s, six Cambodians were provided with educational scholarships to study pepper planting, mineralogy, and veterinary medicine in Laos (*Phnom Penh SPK* 1990).

In addition, many senior minority civilian and military leaders from northeastern Cambodia visited Laos in the 1980s for political reasons. The relationship between Cambodians from the northeast and people from Laos were particularly good because most of the ethnic minorities from the northeast spoke Lao well, making communication relatively easy. Bou Thang told me that when he went to Laos he would typically start off by speaking Khmer for five minutes, and then would switch to Lao for the remainder of his speech. If ethnic Khmers were traveling with him and could not speak Lao, he would sometimes tease that they were stupid for not being able to speak Lao.[87]

Furthermore, some of the ethnic Lao leaders in the Lao PDR government, such as Osakanh Thammatheva, were born and raised in northeastern Cambodia, before later traveling to Laos during revolutionary times and becoming Lao citizens. In addition, General Somsak Saisongkham, the deputy minister of defense in Laos for part of the 1980s, came from Champasak Province and was ethnic Brao, which helped facilitate relations between him and some of the ethnic minorities from the northeast, such as Kham Chan, Kham Phai, Soy Keo, and Bou Thang, all of whom spoke Brao.

Bou Thang went to Laos three times during the 1980s. The first was in March and April 1980. He met Prime Minister Kaysone Phomvihane in Vientiane and then flew to Luang Phrabang in northern Laos and then to Pakse in southern Laos. Phou Kim Moeur, an ethnic Lao man from Voeunsai working for Lao National radio, served as his translator, even though Bou Thang spoke Lao with native fluency. Bou Thang visited Laos the second time for eight days in January 1983, together with Kham Chan, Thao Kong (the military commander in Stung Treng), and others (*Vientiane Domestic Service* 1983). The group visited Lak Sao, Bolikhamxay Province with Osakanh Thammatheva, and Xieng

257

Khouang Province, and Vieng Xay and Sam Neua Districts in Houa-phanh Province, as well as Champasak and Attapeu Provinces. Bou Thang went to Laos the third time in 1985, with PRPK General Secretary Heng Samrin.[88]

Trips to Eastern Europe

Probably the most exciting and memorable trips for a number of the highest-ranking northeasterners, including Bou Thang, Soy Keo, Kham Chan, Thang Ngon, Kham Toeung, Kham Phai, Veng Khoun, Kreng Siengnoi, Boua Chuong, and others, were to Eastern Europe. Indeed, many Cambodians traveled to Soviet Bloc countries for various "training courses" during the 1980s (Kamm 1998). Some of these trips were designed to simply expose Cambodians to their Eastern European allies and to help foster good relations between Cambodia and other socialist countries. Ohers seemed more focused on actual training. I was struck by the importance many of those who went on these trips put on them.

Bou Thang, for example, went to the Soviet Union two or three times in the 1980s.[89] He visited the Soviet Union and also Bulgaria, Hungary, Czechoslovakia, and East Germany between May 3 and 26, 1983, when he was minister of defense (*Phnom Penh Domestic Service* 1983a). He claims to have come up with the idea for the K5 program when he was in Eastern Europe (see Chapter 6). In May 1985, Bou Thang also went to Moscow to attend the fortieth anniversary celebrations of the Soviet people's victory over Nazi fascism (*Phnom Penh SPK* 1985a).

Thang Ngon, the former secretary of Mondulkiri's provincial Party Committee, went on a study trip to East Germany. He was fascinated with Europe,[90] and he spoke of the trip frequently when I was spending a significant amount of time with him in the early 2000s. In 1983, Boua Chuong, Lak On, Ma Ranchai, Kham Sai, and Kuan went on a study trip to the Soviet Union. Once they arrived in Moscow, they were split up into different groups based on their specialties. Ma Ranchai was in the group with Kham Sai and Kuan. They spent a month there. They saw many things that might seem mundane to many but were brand new to them. For example, European food amazed them, even if they did not particularly like it.[91]

Between late 1983 and early 1984, Feuay Bunma went to East Germany for three months of training at a university. He was the only one of the ten Cambodians on the trip to travel from Ratanakiri. They had a translator who could speak Khmer—he had lived in Cambodia, but moved to Germany in 1975. One of the fascinating things about the trip was that the group traveled there in the winter, and so they saw snow for the first time in their lives. They had never imagined what snow was before coming to Europe.[92] In 1983, Kham Khoeun and Noon (ethnic Lao, Voeunsai Village), both of whom headed the Information Dissemination Departments—Kham Khoeun in Ratanakiri and Noon in Mondulkiri—studied for a month in the Soviet Union.[93] In 1984, Kreng Siengnoi went on a study trip to India and then to the Soviet Union, and he also passed through Canada for one day. The trip fascinated him.[94] In 1984, Kham Toeung went on a three-month study trip in Czechoslovakia,[95] and in 1985, Lat Vansao traveled to the Soviet Union after studying in Vietnam for fifteen days.[96] However, after serious economic reforms associated with perestroika began in the Soviet Union in 1985, the number of Cambodians, including northeasterners, who traveled to Europe dramatically declined.

In around 1986 and 1987, Kham Phai was sent to Moscow for three months of special military training. He traveled there together with eleven other Cambodians who were in leadership positions in other military zones in the country. He was, however, the only person from the northeast. Two Khmer-Russian translators also traveled with the group from Phnom Penh. The group received serious training five days a week and boarded at the military school where they studied. Because there was a lot to learn, Kham Phai did not get a chance to do any traveling outside of Moscow.[97] At this time, the Vietnamese government was already preparing to withdraw from the country, so this trip must have been designed to increase the competence of Cambodian military leaders in preparation for the departure of the Vietnamese. I asked Kham Phai if he enjoyed the food in Moscow. He said that all the Cambodians bought rice and made their own food. "We didn't want to eat bread," he commented. Kham Phai claimed, however, that he enjoyed his time in the Soviet Union. I asked him what the most difficult thing about the trip was. He said that the language barrier was the major problem. There were translators, he said, but they could not translate everything.[98]

In what was probably one of the last training trips from Cambodia to the Soviet Union, in 1989, Luon Vandy and ten other people from other parts of Cambodia outside of the northeast traveled to Moscow for six months of political training. At first he found the food difficult to eat, but later he became used to it. He commented that he enjoyed watching snow plows pushing the snow aside. He enjoyed traveling to Moscow, but he noticed that the political situation was already in turmoil at the time he was there.[99]

A large number of Cambodians went to the Soviet Union and other Eastern European countries for education opportunities during the 1980s. Reportedly between 7,000 and 8,000 traveled just to the Soviet Union, after an education scholarship program between Cambodia and the Soviet Union began in 1982 (Masis 2010; Ellen 2013). It appears, however, that ethnic minorities from northeastern Cambodia were not sent to Europe for longer study opportunities. Bou Thang explained that this was because the education levels of those from the northeast were particularly low, even by Cambodian standards, and so they were not deemed eligible. As Bou Thang put it, "People in the northeast did not have the capability to conduct upper level education. They only went to Europe for shorter trips to gain some exposure."[100]

Conclusion

Between 1979 and 1989, the relationships between the Brao and the other northeasterners and Vietnamese advisors—and Vietnamese soldiers to a lesser extent—were significant and generally positive. Relations between the Vietnamese and ethnic minorities in the northeast differed considerably from the experiences in some ethnic Khmer parts of the country, where the Vietnamese were viewed more as invaders than liberators, especially as the 1980s progressed and people became increasingly concerned that the Vietnamese would never withdraw from Cambodia. Occasionally Vietnamese soldiers and, to a lesser extent, advisors did inappropriate things or committed crimes, but when they were reported, their leaders generally punished the offenders.

In addition, those from the northeast had generally positive experiences when they traveled to Vietnam for short- and long-term studies and for other purposes. They also had good experiences when they went to Laos, although they did not go there to study. They were particularly fascinated with the experiences they had when they traveled to Eastern Europe, although they mainly traveled there for short trips because they were not deemed educated enough to study in Europe for longer periods like people from other parts of the country. Still, they saw many new things, such as snow, and tried many new foods, even if they didn't take a liking to them. But for most, it was such a huge change from what they had known in northeastern Cambodia, that memories of those trips remained highlights of the PRK period.

The next chapter serves as a kind of epilogue, one in which the views and the circumstances of Brao and other ethnic minorities from northeastern Cambodia regarding the PRK period are reflected on. It is clear that the Brao and other ethnic minorities from the northeast have lost a lot of ground in terms of representation in government since the 1980s, and that they have also been badly affected by logging concessions, large hydropower dam development, large-scale mining, economic land concessions for plantation development, and the migration to the northeast of large numbers of Khmers from other parts of the country. The important implications of these changes in the loss of political representation and also land and natural resources for the ethnic minorities in northeastern Cambodia are reflected on, including the many ironies associated with what has been happening since the 1990s, and especially since the 2000s.

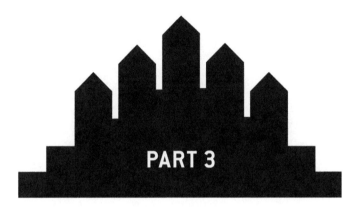

PART 3

Transitions in Northeastern Cambodia in the Late 1980s and Early 1990s

The Vietnamese withdrawal from Cambodia in 1989 led the way for all four warring parties to sign the Paris Peace Treaty in 1991. Soon after, UNTAC was established to help maintain security and create the conditions amenable for multiparty democratic elections in 1993. Essentially, by the early 1990s, it seemed certain that the country would not be returning to the days of "soft socialism" that existed during the 1980s.

So how do the Brao and other northeasterners evaluate the PRK period, and how do they compare it with the present-day circumstances? Life was certainly not easy during the 1980s, due to the trade embargo on Cambodia by most Western and allied countries, and because of the continuing security threat posed by the Khmer Rouge. However, by far the majority of the ethnic minorities interviewed for this study are positive about the PRK government and the Vietnamese who stayed in the country for over a decade. While many ethnic Khmers view the 1980s as a rather dark period, this is not generally the case for most Brao and other ethnic minorities from northeastern Cambodia, who tend to see the PRK period as one that favored ethnic minorities and provided them with opportunities to become leaders in government and the military in ways that can hardly be imagined at present.

Global Changes and Changes in Cambodia

By the mid-1980s, long before the UNTAC-sponsored elections were organized on May 28, 1993, most of the Brao and other ethnic minorities from Ratanakiri Province who had worked as senior government officials and as military and police leaders in northeastern Cambodia had already left the government and returned to Ratanakiri. They were replaced by local people and by ethnic Khmers with higher educational qualifications and better political and economic connections. However, the Brao continued to hold some senior positions in the military and police forces in the northeast, particularly in Ratanakiri and Stung Treng Provinces. For example, Kham Chan, Kham Phai, Heng Khamvan, and Kham Suk continued as the leaders of the northeastern Military Region 1 well into the 2000s, and as of 2018, Kham Suk, a Kreung, is still the head of the military of Ratanakiri Province.

In the mid-1980s, when the Soviet Union decided that it could no longer provide the financial and political support to Vietnam that it had earlier, the Vietnamese were forced to adapt to the changing global political environment and seriously consider Vietnam's ability to sustain its position in Cambodia. This was also a time when Vietnam was facing particular economic problems at home and wanted to open up to the outside world (Co 2003). However, to gain international support for economic policy reforms associated with Đổi Mới, it was necessary for the "Cambodia problem" to be resolved. In particular, the West demanded that Vietnamese forces be withdrawn from Cambodia (Kamm 1998; Co 2003). Thus, global shifts necessitated serious political changes regarding the governance of Cambodia.

Taking a step back, in August 1985, after discussions with the PRPK Politburo, representatives of the Vietnam's Politburo first agreed on a time frame for the PRAK to take over responsibility for its own security. It was also agreed that it was time for the VVA to prepare to return to Vietnam. Then on November 5, 1986, Vietnam's chief of state signed Decision Order No. 1318/NQ/TW. This order relieved Lê Đức Anh of his positions as commander of the VVA and chief of the leadership section of the Vietnamese specialist group in Cambodia. Đoàn Khuê, a member of the Party Central Committee and deputy commander of the VVA in Cambodia, replaced Lê Đức Anh in all his positions in Cambodia. This change in leadership was followed, in 1987, with moves for the PRAK to take full responsibility for security and military matters in the country, even though there were still Vietnamese troops in Cambodia (Anh 2015).

In 1987, Heng Khamvan was made deputy head of the Ministry of Defense's committee for negotiating with the Khmer Rouge and the

CDGK more generally, and particular efforts were initiated to try to end the armed conflict. Since October 1985, Koy Buntha had replaced Bou Thang as minister of defense, but Heng Khamvan continued as deputy chief of the negotiating committee until 1990.[1]

At the end of 1987, the PRK government appointed Bou Thang as political head of the military, with Tea Banh becoming the minister of defense. As a member of the Politburo, and as the head of politics in the military beginning again in 1987, Bou Thang was reinvigorated and remained powerful.

In July 1988, the first face-to-face talks between all four warring parties took place in Bogor, Jakarta, Indonesia (Gunn and Lee 1991), and in the same year, the Vietnamese military began quietly stepping up their withdrawal from Cambodia. At that point many were anticipating that the Vietnamese would soon completely withdraw from Cambodia, and so it was crucial to ensure that Cambodia's soldiers were in good spirits and were prepared to defend the country. Moreover, the government was more open than ever to negotiating peace. The PRK government saw that changes in the Soviet Union brought on by Mikhail Gorbachev's perestroika (restructuring) and glasnost (openness) at the time were occurring and realized that they had to prepare for the future—they had to prepare to be independent and strong.[2]

In February 1989, there were more talks in Indonesia, leading to considerable optimism regarding the prospects for peace (Gunn and Lee 1991). Two months later, in April 1989, the final obstacle for peace was seemingly removed when Vietnam announced that it would unilaterally withdraw all its troops from Cambodia by July and August 1989 (Kamm 1998; Jennar 1998). The withdrawal was, however, officially completed by September 1989. A decade of battling with the NADK and its sometimes oddly matched government of Democratic Kampuchea allies had finally come to an end (Gunn and Lee 1991; Tomoda 1997).[3]

On April 30, 1989, just months before the last Vietnamese soldiers were scheduled to depart, Cambodia's National Assembly ratified a new constitution, and the country's name was changed to the State of Cambodia (Sorpong 2000). Sorpong Peou (2000, 63) referred to the State of Cambodia as a "socialist dictatorship," whereas he felt that the PRK government had ruled a toletarian state. According to Bou Thang, the name of the country was changed to promote a new image and mark the beginning of a new era, one not associated closely with the

Vietnamese. The hope was that the new name would make it easier for the government to convince its enemies to negotiate an end to the civil war.[4] The actual political implications of the name change were, however, minimal, as the PRPK remained in control of the political system (Ovesen and Trankell 2004) and most people knew it. In 1990, the name of the PRPK was also changed to the more neutral sounding Cambodian People's Party (CPP), and over time momentum for peace built. Thailand, for example, adopted its new "battlefields to marketplace" policy, with the intent of ending Cold War–era conflict in mainland Southeast Asia (Gunn and Lee 1991).

There were further talks in Indonesia in February 1990, and in mid-1990, the United States announced that it would no longer support the Khmer Rouge in holding the Cambodian seat at the United Nations (Gunn and Lee 1991). A strong diplomatic push involving a number of countries and world leaders gained strength, and finally, on May 1, 1991, following the creation of draft settlement agreements the previous November, a ceasefire was agreed to by all warring parties.

The Arrival of UNTAC and the 1993 Elections

On October 23, 1991, the final peace agreement was signed in Paris by the four parties, the five permanent members of the Security Council of the United Nations, and the governments of Vietnam, Laos, Japan, India, Australia, Canada, and Yugoslavia (representing the Non-Aligned Movement). The document was called, "An Agreement on a Comprehensive Political Settlement of the Cambodian Conflict" (Kamm 1998; Jennar 1998). Speeches by Norodom Sihanouk, Perez de Cuellar from the United Nations, the French President Francois Mitterrand, and others were made at the signing ceremony in Paris (Kamm 1998). Following the signing, UNTAC was constituted in February 1992, and on March 15, 1992, it commenced operations in Cambodia.

The government administration of Taveng District, Ratanakiri Province—the homeland of the Brao of northeastern Cambodia who have been the focus of this book—was one of the most hostile to UNTAC in 1992. In fact, some claim that Taveng was the only non–Khmer Rouge controlled district in the country to resist the arrival of UNTAC. Led by district chief, Khieou Bunchia (Brao, Phnom Kok Brao) and his deputy, Ap Khamdeu (Brao, Labat Village), the government initially decided to not allow UNTAC to establish a presence in the district. This move was supported by many of the former Brao leaders from the 1970s and 1980s, including Veng Khoun, Thang Ngon, Dop Khamchoeung, Kham Toeung, Doeun, and Hai He, the commune chief of Taveng Kraom, and Kro Ban, the commune chief of Taveng Loeu. They were concerned that the arrival of UNTAC would erase the hard-fought successes that had been achieved since collaborating with the Vietnamese to remove the Khmer Rouge from power in 1979. They were particularly afraid that UNTAC would allow the ideology of the Khmer Rouge to return through permitting other political parties to operate in the district. They were intensely supportive of the Cambodian People's Party (CPP) and were fearful of any changes that might provide the Khmer Rouge with a chance to return to power. Some also believed that UNTAC was bringing Americans back to Taveng, and many Brao hated the Americans due to the United States bombing that occurred in northeastern Cambodia in the early 1970s.[5] After initially refusing access to UNTAC, however, Kham Len made a trip to the district and convinced the reluctant leadership there that they had to allow UNTAC to come in. They eventually did, but the district administration of Taveng never fully cooperated with UNTAC.[6]

The results of the UNTAC sponsored May 1993 elections, which the Khmer Rouge boycotted, were a shock to many ethnic minorities in the northeast, as the CPP easily received the majority of the votes in the four northeastern provinces. However, FUNCINPEC, led by Norodom Ranariddh, Norodom Sihanouk's son, received 45.5 percent of the popular vote nationwide, compared to just over 38 percent for the ruling CPP.[7] The CPP led by Hun Sen, Heng Samrin, and Chea Sim, the former PRPK leadership in the 1980s, was shocked and initially charged that there had been election fraud. However, UNTAC rejected the complaint.

One week later, on June 10, Hun Sen announced that eight unspecified eastern provinces had decided to secede from Cambodia under the leadership of then-deputy Prime Minister Norodom Chakrapong and Interior Minister Sin Song.[8] Not surprisingly, the provinces were believed to have included Ratanakiri, Stung Treng, Mondulkiri, Preah Vihear, and others, but Bou Thang told me that even he was never certain what provinces had joined the movement.[9] Moreover, Hun Sen did not indicate his own specific support for the secession threat, but the move was clearly designed to put pressure on UNTAC and FUNCINPEC. Moreover, supporters of the rebels attacked the offices of their political opponents in the provinces and also ordered UNTAC officials to leave the provinces they controlled. Norodom Ranariddh feared a resumption of civil war in the country and finally agreed to a political compromise. Thus, on June 14, Norodom Ranariddh and Hun Sen were appointed as co-prime ministers (prime minister #1 and #2, respectively), with each having equal levels of executive powers, at least in theory. This agreement resulted in Chakrapong and Sin Song dropping their secessionist threat (Ker 1993), and an uneasy coalition government between the two rival parties emerged, one that would end in a violent coup de force orchestrated by the CPP over FUNCINPEC in July 1997, thus returning the country to a temporary state of civil war. However, in March 1998, an agreement was reached that allowed Norodom Ranariddh to return to Phnom Penh to contest the 1998 election, which the CPP ultimately won.

In the meantime, the Khmer Rouge continued to oppose the government of Cambodia. In 1996, however, the Khmer Rouge splintered, and Ieng Sary, along with other Khmer Rouge leaders in the Pailin area, and about half of the remaining Khmer Rouge forces (about 4,000 soldiers) decided to defect to the government side. Other so-called hardline Khmer Rouge, based at Anlong Veng to the east, continued to oppose the CPP and the new Royal Government of Cambodia. After the 1997 coup, the hardline Khmer Rouge faction, as they became known, militarily supported FUNCINPEC-aligned forces situated near the border with Thailand in northwestern Cambodia. However, the Khmer Rouge further splintered and disintegrated after FUNCINPEC was allowed to return to Phnom Penh and reengage in politics in early 1998. In April 1998, Pol Pot died, and by the end of the year the remaining Khmer Rouge were preparing to give up the fight. In 1999, most of the remaining leaders either surrendered or were captured, and in December 1999, Ta Mok and the remaining leaders gave up, and the Khmer Rouge effectively ceased to exist.[10] Cambodia's long civil war had finally ended.

It was during this period that large numbers of ethnic minorities from the northeast started resigning from government and military service. For example, in 1996, Jampong Jari decided to leave his position in the CPP's party inspection unit and return to his village to be a farmer again. He felt that the amount of work had increased from the 1980s, and that he was not capable of effectively performing his duties due to having a low level of education. Nobody asked him to resign, but he felt that it was time for him to go. Some tried to convince him to stay on, but in the end he just left his position and returned home without giving any notice.[11] Others felt similarly, and by the end of the 1990s, the number of ethnic minorities in government had dramatically declined.

Of course, there is much to be said about present-day CPP dominance of Cambodian politics, something that others have covered already, and still others will undoubtedly do in the future. I will not endeavor to delve into the topic here, but I will say that while the story told in this book does nuance the 1979 to 1989 era in northeastern Cambodia, it is not intended to fully vindicate the PRK government generally, and it is especially not intended to validate Hun Sen's present-day domination of Cambodia, the CPP's increasingly strong hold on power, or the suppression of the media and civil society more generally.

Reflecting on the Past

So how do the minorities from northeastern Cambodia, and particularly the Brao, view the era when they were empowered like never before and not since? Indeed, one could argue that particularly for the ethnic Brao people—who made up the majority of those who fled from northeastern Cambodia to Vietnam and Laos in the mid-1970s—the 1980s were their golden age. It was the one time in history when they were elevated to high positions in the government and the military. They were treated with dignity, and had their own people in positions of power and influence. Being treated well is undoubtedly important for them. As Baird and Hammer (2013) have emphasized, particularly in reference to the health care system in Ratanakiri Province, Indigenous minorities from the region are sensitive to being treated poorly when they go to the hospital for health care services, something that was actually much less of a problem during the PRK period, especially for poorer people who had little money to pay for health care. This sense has also affected ethnic minority views of the present government more generally. As one ethnic Lao man from Stung Treng reflected, "A lot of Vietnamese died from 1979 to 1989. In Cambodia, the old people from the 1979–1989 period have been forgotten. We need to recognize the contributions of the Vietnamese. They provided a lot and at that time they dared not even steal an eggplant or chili pepper. Some people from the south [of Cambodia] might want to fight Laos over the border, but the local people [in the northeast] are fine the way it is."[12]

According to one Tampuon man, "During the Khmer Rouge period the Tampuon were the leaders, but during the Vietnamese period the Brao gained control, except for the Tampuon from Kachoan."[13] This is certainly not the way most Cambodians think about the Khmer Rouge or PRK periods, times of conflict and civil war. That does not, however, make the stories of the northeasterners, or their views, invalid. But it is true that what has been presented here was never intended to be somehow "representative" of the larger population in Cambodia.

One Brao man stated, comparing present-day circumstances with the PRK period, "People were as poor during the Vietnamese period as now, but at that time it was at least possible for poor people to study and everyone had the chance to work in the government, or to become a soldier or a police officer." He added, "Before there was no stealing like now, but on the positive side, there is no war now, and anyone can travel wherever they want."[14] Of course, this may seem somewhat nostalgic, and undoubtedly statements like this do represent views not held by all, or possibly even most, but it is nonetheless the perspective of some.

These stories are, however, becoming more and more peripheral or marginal in Cambodian history, especially since the late 1980s and 1990s, when the northeasterners mainly returned home to their villages to retire. According to Bou Thang, "The Cambodians have now forgotten the value of the ethnic groups in helping with the revolution. Now the Khmers don't agree to recognize different ethnic groups. They don't want different ethnic representation [in the government]. . . . Now they want to get rid of the minorities, little by little. . . . The minorities are not even mentioned in the constitution. I feel bad about that. When the Vietnamese were here, minorities had a strong role, but the Khmers were not happy." Indicative of the relative importance that ethnic minorities played in the Vietnamese system of governing in Cambodia, the rights of minority peoples' languages and customs was the only right added to the PRK's constitution (Gottesman 2002). Bou Thang also explained, "I was kept in the government due to the Vietnamese, but after the Vietnamese left, I had no power. This was the case for all ethnic minorities."[15]

Bou Thang sees one of the main challenges of today being to reduce prejudice against ethnic minorities. He told me that Cambodia does not want to have any ethnic minorities nowadays, reflecting on comments that he heard Loy Sim Chheang make years earlier, ones previously cited in this book. Bou Thang advocates for keeping the ethnic minority committee in the government, which had existed for much of the PRK period but was shut down in 1993 during the UNTAC period.[16] He also noted on a different occasion that ethnic minorities are often discriminated against in Cambodia. He pointed out that Khmers sometimes say "long ngung douch Phnorng" [ignorant like a highland minority], even if they dare not say it to his face.[17] Bou Thang has remained a strong supporter of the soldiers from the northeast, but commented that, "When the ethnic minorities [from northeastern Cambodia] were needed for fighting, they were wanted, but later they were not wanted."[18]

One particular account of the language politics that emerged is well represented by an encounter between Norodom Sihanouk and Bou Thang in 1992, at an evening event in Phnom Penh. It is worth recounting here. They were sitting at the table with a number of other people, and Norodom Sihanouk started out by speaking to different people at the table in either English or French. Bou Thang does not speak either language and so was a little perturbed. After some time, he started speaking Tampuon with his wife "loudly," as he emphasized to me. This discussion caught Sihanouk's attention, and he asked what language they were speaking; Bou Thang answered that they were talking in Tampuon, a native language of Cambodia, not a foreign language. Bou Thang asked Sihanouk, in Khmer, why he had not spoken Khmer and proceeded to accuse him of speaking English and French to boast. Prior to this exchange, Sihanouk had apparently not spoken one word of Khmer. Bou Thang told me that this story demonstrates that he has had to find ways to keep Khmer people from looking down on him because he is an ethnic minority from the northeast.[19]

One senior Brao official in Ratanakiri Province also provided telling comments: "The Vietnamese policy in Cambodia was good for ethnic minorities. But now there are no ethnic minorities left in high positions in Ratanakiri. There are only a few soldiers left . . . but when they retire there will be no new minorities coming up to replace them." He then went on to say, "Now some say that minorities should not even be allowed to occupy high positions in government. For example, Pen Heng [a Khmer] at the provincial Finance Department said that." The official also commented, "It also seems that they are not allowing any minorities to be the heads of districts either. Now only people with money can work in government." He then said, "In the Vietnamese period, things were easier for minorities. . . . There was only one time when the Brao were high. It was because we were near the border [and could escape from the Khmer Rouge]. Others were farther away and so couldn't flee." Indeed, geography played a crucial role in how circumstances developed.

Another Brao man reflected on how much more accessible education was during the PRK period, compared to the present, pointing out that now only those with sufficient funds have any chance to study to a high level. He particularly commented on how privileged Khmer people with money have been able to gain advantage in Cambodian society today. "It now costs US$2–3,000 [in payoffs] to graduate from high-school, even if you don't do well on the tests, you can still graduate [if you pay]," he stated. Another female minority from the northeast continued, "Khmer people from the south look down on us." She then continued, emotionally,

> Khmer people don't care about minorities. They just care about themselves. . . . I am the last minority working in this office. The Khmer want my position. . . . The policy says to look after minorities, but in reality they don't. The highest level [of government] has a good policy. But there are a lot of problems at the middle level. . . . And the children of our former leaders, who have been brought up in Phnom Penh are just like Khmers. They are not like us. . . . Ethnic minorities need to be allowed to move up the ranks. There needs to be a quota for minorities. . . . When Khmer teachers come from the south, they don't really teach when they should. They can't stay in the villages. They just teach one day a week. During the Vietnamese period they actually got people in the villages to work, but now all the district chiefs are from the south. They just look down on the villagers. Now there are very few ethnic minorities left in the government. It is not like when the Vietnamese were here. During that time the Vietnamese gave minorities a chance, but now the Cambodians are different. The policy during the Vietnamese period was better. When I am gone, there will be no more minorities to follow me.[20]

Indeed, there are not many ethnic minorities in the government in Ratanakiri Province now, except for a few in the police and military. Kham Voeun, who is Tampuon, is one of the few left in the civil service at the provincial level in Ratanakiri. He started working in 1983, and claims that the only reason that he has not been pushed out of the government is because his position in the "News Department" of the province is not profitable and therefore nobody wants it. "In 1980, when Banlung was first established, there were only ethnic minorities in government," Kham Voeun reflected.[21]

Land and Natural Resource Loss in Northeastern Cambodia

Apart from the ethnic minorities of northeastern Cambodia losing representation in government, a crucial issue for many, another serious problem that ethnic minorities in the northeast have been confronted with since the 1990s, and especially since the 2000s, is the loss of land and natural resources. In the 1990s, the main problem was commercial logging concessions granted to Cambodian and foreign logging enterprises, which denuded the forests that many ethnic minorities depended on for their livelihoods (Baird 2003, 2009c, 2010c; Bottomley 2002; Colm 2000). Some efforts were made by nongovernment organizations (NGOs) to support communities to resist commercial logging efforts, set up forest management plans, and gain recognition to manage and protect their community forests in the 1990s and 2000s (Baird 2003, 2009c, 2010c; Bottomley 2002; Colm 2000; Emerson 1997), but despite some small successes, many forested areas ended up being heavily logged (Baird 2010c; Bottomley 2002).

In addition, in the 1990s and 2000s, some ethnic minorities, including many Brao and Kavet people, also partially or fully lost access to many of their lands as a result of the establishment of national parks and wildlife sanctuaries. These protected areas have reinforced central control over their lands and natural resources, and have further left them marginalized (Baird 2009c; Ironside and Baird 2003).

Since the late 1990s, large hydropower dams have also had serious negative impacts on the livelihoods of ethnic minorities living in northeastern Cambodia. In 1996, the Yali Falls Dam, the largest dam in the Mekong River basin up to that point, began being constructed in the Central Highland of Vietnam. During the construction period, the dam caused major changes to the hydrology and water quality of the Sesan River in Ratanakiri and Stung Treng Provinces, including directly and indirectly causing the deaths of a large number of people and domestic animals, which were either washed away by surges of water released from the dam or were negatively affected by poor quality water released downstream from the dam's large reservoir in Vietnam. These changes have also negatively affected riverine biodiversity and riverbank gardening. In the 2000s, after the dam was completed, downstream communities have continued to suffer as a result of changes in hydrology and water quality related to the operation of the dam (Wyatt and Baird 2007; NGO Forum on Cambodia 2005; Hirsch and Wyatt 2004).

Moreover, since the 2000s, a number of other large dams have been built in the Sesan River basin in the Central Highlands of Vietnam, and they have further contributed to various downstream impacts in Cambodia (Wyatt and Baird 2007; NGO Forum on Cambodia 2005). Parts of Mondulkiri, Ratanakiri, and Stung Treng Provinces have also experienced negative impacts as a result of the construction of a number of large dams in the Srepok River basin in the Central Highlands of Vietnam (Swift 2006). In addition, the Sekong River basin in Stung Treng Province has been negatively impacted by the construction of dams on its tributaries in southern Laos (Baird and Shoemaker 2008), although so far no dams have been built on the mainstream Sekong River (Natural History Institute and National University of Laos 2017).

Finally, and most recently, the construction of the Lower Sesan 2 Dam in Sesan District, Stung Treng Province, has resulted in the creation of a large reservoir that has flooded parts of the Sesan and Srepok Rivers and has caused a number of ethnic minority villages in Stung Treng Province to have to resettle away from the rivers (Baird and Barney 2017; Baird 2009a, 2016a). This includes the flooding of the ethnic Lao community of Srekor, where the Khmer Rouge once had their northeast zone headquarters (see Chapter 1). Furthermore, the Lower Sesan 2 Dam is undoubtedly negatively impacting important fish migrations from the Tonlesap Lake in Central Cambodia, and also from as far away as the Mekong delta in Vietnam, and even from southern Laos and northeastern Cambodia (Baird 2009a, 2016a). These impacts are expected to result in the loss of up to 9 percent of wild capture fisheries of the Mekong River basin (Ziv et al. 2012), and this will have devastating effects on the livelihoods of people living in the Mekong River basin and also on the maintenance of important biodiversity values (Baird 2009a). With more dams planned in northeastern Cambodia and also in Laos, both on the tributaries and mainstream Mekong River, the situation could get much worse in the future.

The 2001 Land Law of Cambodia brought hope to some of the ethnic minorities in northeastern Cambodia because for the very first time, the government recognized the existence of "Indigenous peoples" (*chun chiet doeum pheak dich* in Khmer) in Cambodia through this law, a designation that includes the Brao Amba, Brao Tanap, Kreung, Kavet, Lun, Tampuon, Jarai, Kachok, and Bunong peoples (Baird 2011a), but not the ethnic Lao people of northeastern Cambodia, who are so far not legally considered to be Indigenous peoples in Cambodia (Baird 2016b). More specifically, the 2001 Land Law recognized the right of Indigenous peoples to gain communal land titles designed to protect agricultural lands managed through rotational swidden cultivation systems, whereas villages not registered as being Indigenous communities do not have that right (Baird 2011a, 2013a). The 2002 Forestry Law also recognized the existence of Indigenous peoples in Cambodia and specified that they should be given preferential access to non-timber forest products (NTFPs) important for their livelihoods (Baird 2011a).

However, despite the initial hope that these laws brought to many of the ethnic minorities of northeastern Cambodia, excluding the ethnic Lao, the laws have been much less successful in protecting the lands and other natural resources that ethnic minorities in northeastern Cambodia depend on. That is partially because the process for obtaining communal land titles has become much more difficult, time consuming, and expensive than originally expected (Baird 2019), and the issuing of individual land titles has also undermined the communal land titling process (Milne 2013). To make matters worse, the issuing of communal land titles in parts of Ratanakiri Province and especially Mondulkiri Province have helped protect ethnic Bunong swidden agricultural lands from being taken, but have essentially resulted in other forest lands that they are dependent on for their livelihoods having been ceded to nature conservation protected areas established in the 1990s and 2000s (Baird 2013a). While some communities have been successful in applying for community forest permits from the Department of Forestry, these community forestry agreements only provide locals with limited rights, which can be revoked if specific rules are not followed, or after the time periods for the permits run out, thus leaving the people with only tenuous tenure over the forest lands that were once theirs (Baird 2013a).

Probably the worst problem that ethnic minorities are facing in northeastern Cambodia, however, relates to the issuing of economic land concessions to Cambodian and foreign companies since the mid-2000s. These concessions, which can legally be as expansive as 10,000 hectares, but in reality are often even larger, have mainly been granted to companies intent on establishing large-scale rubber plantations (Baird and Barney 2017; Baird 2017; Baird and Fox 2015; Global Witness 2013; Neef et al. 2013; Neth et al. 2013), and like the concession rubber plantations established in Ratanakiri Province in the 1960s (see Chapter 1), they have negatively impacted the livelihoods of large numbers of ethnic minorities, whose newly obtained status as Indigenous peoples has done little to protect them from having their lands and forests taken away. Indeed, in recent years, large parts of the once expansive forests of northeastern Cambodia have been transformed into mono-culture rubber plantations controlled by people who are not ethnic minorities. Furthermore, efforts are underway in parts of northeastern Cambodia to develop mining concessions, which also threaten the lands and livelihoods of large numbers of ethnic minorities from northeastern Cambodia (Keating 2013; Global Witness 2009).

To make matters worse, in recent years, large numbers of ethnic Khmer people have migrated to northeastern Cambodia from other parts of the country (Fox et al. 2018). While it was hard to convince Khmers to move to the northeast in the 1960s (see Chapter 1), since the 1990s and especially since the 2000s, many Khmers have migrated to the northeast without receiving any explicit government encouragement or support to do so. While these migrants initially mainly congregated in the cities and towns where they have come to dominate commerce (see McAndrew 2000 for an early account of this in Banlung), in recent years they have begun gaining access to increasingly valuable rural lands as well. Some, for example, have come to work on the new rubber plantation concessions as laborers, while others are looking for new lands after facing debt and land alienation problems of their own in southern parts of Cambodia (Fox et al. 2018). All this migration from other parts of Cambodia is further contributing to the marginalization of ethnic minorities, which now make up a much lower percentage of the population than they once did (Ironside 2009). These new migrants have contributed to further land alienation (NGO Forum on Cambodia 2004, 2006; Baird 2008). This land grabbing has resulted in many ethnic minorities gaining more of a sense that they are becoming increasingly marginalized in a landscape that once had hardly any Khmers living on it. Indeed, many feel that they have become strangers in their own homeland.

While the losses of lands and other natural resources that ethnic minorities in northeastern Cambodia have increasingly faced since the 1990s and especially since the 2000s are not the main focus of this book, these losses have certainly contributed to the views of many ethnic minorities who see themselves as increasingly losing control over their lands and natural resources. Moreover, these losses have hybridized with past memories to construct new forms of politicized landscapes (see Baird and Le Billon 2012), and this in turn has further contributed to many ethnic minorities feeling nostalgic about the PRK period, as at that time they were not only strongly represented in government, but they also largely controlled the lands and natural resources that they depended on for their livelihoods, even if they also had to contend with security issues associated with the remnants of the Khmer Rouge. These losses have resulted in some resistance from local people (Baird 2017; Keating 2013), but despite limited successes, overall the ethnic minorities continue to figuratively and literally lose ground to outsiders. Nature-society relations are changing.

Conclusion

Following the end of the PRK period, the Brao and other ethnic minorities from northeastern Cambodia largely lost their positions in the government and the military to ethnic Khmers from other parts of the country. Not surprisingly, these losses have frustrated and upset many ethnic minorities. However, many have also experienced more tangible losses of lands and other natural resources. For example, despite being recognized as Indigenous peoples in 2001 (except for the ethnic Lao), which gave some people hope for the future, they have, nevertheless, lost much of their land and natural resources due to commercial logging, large-scale mining, large hydropower dam development, economic land concession plantation development, and migration of ethnic Khmers from other parts of the country, thus further resulting in many feeling disenfranchised and also nostalgic for the PRK period in the 1980s, when they had much more control over their land and natural resources. Indeed, nature-society relations are shifting.

Conclusion

Lessons from the 1980s

So what can a book like this—one that deals with a
small group of mainly Brao, Kreung, Lun, Tam-
puon, Jarai, and Lao ethnic minorities from northeastern Cambodia's
Sesan River basin—tell us about Cambodia in the 1980s, and the PRK
period and Cambodia more generally? In that the particular social, cultural, economic, political, geographical, and historical circumstances of
the northeastern ethnic minorities who have been the focus here are
quite different from the rest of Cambodia, not much. Indeed, the historically and geographically contingent nature of what has been presented
is one of the key points that I have strived to make. Site specific historical, political, cultural, and geographical factors really do matter and
need to be considered carefully in research that takes an ethnic studies
perspective, as I do here. As a human geographer, this message is quite
predictable, but it is worth stating nonetheless.

The story presented, nevertheless, offers some lessons about the
role of the Vietnamese in Cambodia during the PRK period, peripheral
or marginal histories in Cambodia, and northeastern Cambodian regionalism. The book also encourages us to recognize the importance of ethnic differences but not to essentialize those differences, as some authors
do. Finally, I reflect on whether the PRK period should be considered a
golden age, and if so, why? I do this to theorize about how this book can
most usefully contribute to ethnic studies in Southeast Asia and particularly Cambodia. I contend that many Brao and other ethnic minorities
from northeastern Cambodia do indeed consider the PRK period to
have been a kind of golden age, and for good reason.

A More Nuanced View
of the Vietnamese

One of the important lessons from this study is that serious efforts were made to ensure that Vietnamese soldiers and advisors did not behave poorly during the PRK period. It is true that the rank and file VVA soldiers who came to Cambodia were often young and inexperienced, as well as poorly paid and fed, so it should be of little surprise that some did engage in petty thievery and violated other rules. However, when this occurred, impunity rarely followed. Instead, when particular violations occurred and individuals were implicated, swift measures were typically taken to apprehend the offenders and seriously punish them for their indiscretions. In other words, the Vietnamese wanted its troops in Cambodia to behave and took measures to ensure that they did. In particular, they recognized that good behavior was crucial if the Vietnamese were going to have any chance of winning over the local population in Cambodia and convince the resistance to give up fighting. Good behavior was particularly important because many ethnic Khmers were already predisposed to see the worst in the Vietnamese, for ideological reasons linked to historical and ethnic factors, and the Vietnamese knew that.

As for the Vietnamese advisors or specialists, with a few rare exceptions they were much more mature, had relatively high levels of experience and political awareness, and as a result generally behaved. Many Khmers from other parts of the country certainly resented the Vietnamese domination that advisors sometimes imposed, or at least frequently represented. However, most Brao and other ethnic minorities from northern Ratanakiri and other parts of northeastern Cambodia felt that the Vietnamese generally provided useful support. The ethnic minorities, known today as Indigenous peoples (except for the ethnic Lao), had very low levels of formal education and thus generally greatly valued the assistance that the Vietnamese provided. Crucially, the Brao and other ethnic minorities of the northeast are not nearly as inclined to be suspicious of the Vietnamese due to historical and ethnic biases, as compared to the Khmers, because the ethnic minorities from the northeast do not generally have the kind of animosity toward the Vietnamese that many Khmers do. These circumstances made the Brao and other northeastern minorities much more ideologically open to the Vietnamese.

In addition, this book clearly demonstrates that the ways Cambodians viewed the Vietnamese between 1979 and 1989 was contingent on various factors, especially ethnic identities and historical understandings. This is one important way that the book fits well with an ethnic studies perspective. So does this mean that the Vietnamese did not sometimes try to shift benefits toward them? Yes, they did. They sometime did try to gain control over natural resources and even part of Cambodian territory. But it also does not mean that all the Vietnamese had nefarious objectives, something that is often assumed by ethnic Khmers, who sometimes fail to give the Vietnamese the benefit of the doubt.

Peripheral or Marginal Histories

So far much of Cambodian history has been written with its capital, Phnom Penh, as the geographical center. This is not surprising, as Phnom Penh certainly is an important place in the country. While this book does not entirely ignore Phnom Penh, which certainly played a crucial role in what happened in the northeast during the PRK period, the book is firmly centered in northeastern Cambodia, and particularly the Sesan River basin in northern Ratanakiri Province, where most of the people discussed in the book originally come from. We need more studies that look at nationally important periods of history but from the perspectives of minorities.

For me, this book represents a sort of "peripheral" or "marginal" history. It is not that the history is at all "marginal"—from the perspective of being unimportant, either from a local or national perspective—but rather it is centered in what many might describe as a peripheral or marginal part of Cambodia, the northeastern provinces of Ratanakiri, Stung Treng, Mondulkiri, and Preah Vihear. The northeastern part of the country is frequently viewed as remote, backward, and relatively unimportant from the perspective of central governments or regional or international actors, and even scholars. To some degree, my view coincides with how Oscar Salemink (2018, 1) has framed an article written about the Central Highland of Vietnam. In that piece, Salemink points out that while the Central Highlands are typically described as "remote, backward, and primitive," in reality the "region has played a central role in the history of the surrounding states and the wider East and Southeast Asia region." Thus, like me, he intends to resituate a marginalized region so that its role is more clearly recognized and is not simply left in the shadows away from view.

Illustrative of this point, the people from northeastern Cambodia have received little attention from the government despite the fact that they have lost much of their land and natural resources to outsiders, especially ethnic Khmers originally from other parts of the country. It is also marginal in the sense that the people who live there hold views about history and the Vietnamese that rarely conform with those held by people differently situated, whether geographically, socially, culturally, economically, historically, politically, or ethnically. This book demonstrates how a group of ethnic minorities—particularly the Brao—participated in and view a particular period. Crucially, I have sought to demonstrate that while ethnic identities and ethnic group understandings are important, they should not be overly fetishized, as the evidence presented here clearly demonstrates that political views often divide people from the same ethnic groups, and that geography is also important for determining how people end up politically affiliating. Thus, I have tried to identify the appropriate balance between ignoring ethnicity, as some have done, and overly essentializing ethnicity, as others have done. What we need is a balanced position that recognizes that ethnicity really is important in the northeast, but so is individual and small group agency, especially when it comes to politics.

The history and views presented and discussed here have not been well documented, and they deserve much more attention than they have received. The Brao and other northeastern highlanders are not simply marginal nobodies, as some people have described them. They are simply not well-known because few people have attempted to collect or present their stories. For most of those who feature in this book, in early 1979 Cambodia was liberated, it was not invaded, and in the 1980s it was not simply occupied but it was saved from the Khmer Rouge. But there were also ethnic minorities from northeastern Cambodia who saw the Vietnamese as invaders and more generally insincere occupiers. Undoubtedly some were. That is why the civil war went on so long.

Regionalism and Ethnic Minorities in Northeastern Cambodia

Regionalism is crucial to what has been presented in these pages, and this book provides particular lessons about northeastern

Cambodian regionalism, ones that very much link with the concept of peripheral or marginal histories previously discussed. Theoretically, regions are now widely recognized by critical geographers as not simply rigidly bounded spaces defined by states but as socially constructed, through state processes and also by those who live inside and outside of particular spaces defined as regions (Paasi 2011). Furthermore, regions are being increasingly recognized as relational, as being historically contingent, and as being constructed through networks and actor-centered geographic understandings (Jones 2009). Indeed, these geography-centered understandings of regions have been crucial for helping frame the way I have approached this project and the ways in which I have come to analyze my research findings.

In Cambodia, there has generally been less of a focus put on regions, regional differences, and regional imaginaries that produce spaces and identities, especially when compared to most other countries in Southeast Asia, including Thailand, Vietnam, Laos, and Myanmar, just to name a few. This lack of focus on regions is at least partially because over 90 percent of the population of Cambodia are classified as ethnically "Khmer," thus leading many to imagine Cambodia as a single unified geographical national space dominated by ethnic Khmers and cultural Khmerness. However, it also has to do with the lack of scholarly research conducted in Cambodia between the late 1960s and early 1990s, which has resulted in the focus of much scholarly work related to Cambodia being on broad national processes because those were also under-researched in the past.

Furthermore, the ethnic minorities of Cambodia—including those officially designated as Indigenous peoples and also the ethnic Lao—together make up less than 3 percent of the total population of Cambodia, live in relatively remote parts of the country, and speak languages that differ considerably from Khmer. Thus, it should be of little surprise that the voices of ethnic minorities in northeastern Cambodia have generally been muted in accounts of Cambodian history. Moreover, it demonstrates why more efforts need to be made to convey different regional perspectives and identities, including those of people who are linguistically and culturally diverse, something that I have tried to do here. We also need fine-grained historical accounts of other peoples in Cambodia, including particular socio-cultural-linguistic groups, such as the Cham and the Indigenous peoples living in various parts of Cambodia; and we also need more histories of different communes, districts, provinces, and regions in Cambodia, including ones dominated by Khmers. These regional Cambodian stories—whether they come from northeastern Cambodia or other parts of the country—are important, but they have so far received insufficient attention. In particular, few have tried to view parts of Cambodia from an ethnic studies perspective, which has been the focus here, although this is hopefully beginning to change.

The 1980s not only provided the ethnic minorities of northeastern Cambodia with opportunities to gain high-level positions in the PRK government but the political circumstances of this period also provided them with chances to travel to places they had never been and to interact with peoples from many ethnic groups, be it highlanders, Vietnamese, ethnic Lao, or Khmer. For example, one Brao man from Taveng District in Ratanakiri Province told me that he learned to speak the Lao language during the time he was a government soldier. Another ethnic Kreung man from Taveng District who speaks some Lao also claimed that he learned it as a soldier during the PRK period. He also reported that he learned how to read and write Khmer when he was a soldier in the 1980s and early 1990s, at least at a basic level. Crucially, these interactions and learning opportunities, as basic as they may appear, affected the networked understandings and the political and social identities of many of the main characters of this book.

Many Brao, for example, now consider that one of their important "inherent" skills is as soldiers because many held important military positions during the 1980s. Few remember the times long ago when villagers fled to the forest when the French went to Brao villages to recruit soldiers for the French Indochina Army (Baird 2008). The ways that the Brao and other ethnic minorities gained power and influence in the four northeastern Cambodian provinces of Ratanakiri, Stung Treng, Mondulkiri, and Preah Vihear during the PRK period, through particular political networks with Vietnamese Communists and other aligned Cambodian ethnic minorities from the northeast—including powerful leaders such as Bou Thang and Soy Keo, who lived in the capital city of Phnom Penh—has greatly influenced how they have come to understand their own past positions in relation to the state, the region of northeastern Cambodia, and the nation of Cambodia more generally.

Thus, the experiences that the Brao and other ethnic minorities from the Sesan River basin had during the PRK government period in the 1980s have contributed to the construction of historically contingent and relational geographical understandings of northeastern Cambodia as a region, including their own relational places within the broader territoriality of Cambodia as a nation-state. This geographical relationality in Cambodia deserves much more attention than it has so far received. Hopefully, the historical events presented here can help us to better understand this period, the politics associated with it, and the regional geographies that have been produced and reproduced, particularly from the perspective of Brao and other ethnic minorities who fled Cambodia and the Khmer Rouge to Vietnam and Laos in 1973 and 1975, and returned to the country with the Vietnamese military beginning at the end of 1978.

The PRK Period:
A Golden Age?

Finally, I want to address the question of whether the 1980s really represented a golden age in northeastern Cambodia and theorize about its relevance, particularly in a book grounded in ethnic studies and marginal histories in a particular region. Was the PRK government period—between 1979 and 1989—really a golden age? Clearly, this question was always intended to be provocative and to inspire readers to view this important but understudied period in Cambodian history in different ways.

In fact, the PRK period can hardly be considered a golden age for most Cambodians, even for most of the ethnic minorities who have been the focus of this book. By all accounts, times were tough during the PRK period, sometimes very tough. The country was embroiled in a difficult and protracted civil war. Many people died, and there were lots of challenges, hardships, and obstacles to an easy and peaceful life. Nobody can credibly deny this, and I have no intention of doing so either. It must, however, be recognized that for the relatively small group of Cambodians that this book has focused on, the ones who were initially aligned with the Khmer Rouge in the 1960s and early 1970s but later became disillusioned with the Khmer Rouge and fled to Vietnam and Laos in 1973 and 1975, it is not unreasonable to suggest that the PRK period was indeed a sort of golden age; not necessarily with regard to material wealth or human security, but rather because of the amount of political power, ethnic empowerment, and general respect that they received from the state and the Vietnamese. These people were elevated to high positions in the government and military for the first and only time in their histories. They became the chairmen of provincial People's Committees and the secretaries of provincial party committees, as well as provincial military leaders, police chiefs, and department heads. They were also given important positions in the central government, particularly in the military. Even though most were either illiterate or only marginally literate in Khmer (or any other language in most cases) and few spoke Khmer language well, they were trusted by their Vietnamese allies and their PRK government colleagues, and thus gained power and respect in relation to the state like they never had before or have had since the departure of the Vietnamese. No wonder many of these people—especially the ethnic Brao who dominated this group—consider the PRK period to have been a sort of golden age, even if they do not typically use these words to describe it. Crucially, however, many look back fondly on this period, especially when they reflect on the respect they received and the power that they wielded.

While the ethnic minorities of northeastern Cambodia certainly worked under the Vietnamese to a large extent, this did not bother most of them, as the power the Vietnamese granted them was unprecedented in their histories. Even now, it is not unusual to meet older people from the particular group of people this book is focused on and hear them speaking nostalgically about the "Vietnamese period." This is not surprising—although it may be a bit shocking to some ethnic Khmers—as during that period the Brao were represented at all levels of government and politics, but now there are very few Brao or other ethnic minorities working in higher levels of the government or the military, either at the central level or in northeastern Cambodia. There are still a few who maintain positions that are a legacy of the PRK government period, but it is clear that there will be few ethnic minorities to fill their roles as government leaders once they retire in the next few years. In fact, most have already long since retired and have mainly been replaced by ethnic Khmers who often come from other parts of the country and hold very different views of history and of the ethnic minorities of the northeast.

In addition, the ethnic minorities have lost much of their land and natural resources to logging, mining, large hydropower dams, economic land concessions, and migration of lowland Khmers and Cham over the last few decades since the Vietnamese departed from Cambodia, and this has also contributed to the nostalgia many have for the

PRK period. Thus, for most of those ethnic minorities, the golden age is long since over, and the power that they held in the government is rapidly waning and can be expected to decline even further in the coming years, along with their access to land and natural resources. Indeed, nature-society relations are rapidly changing. Part of my hope— and the desire of many of those who I interviewed during the course of this project—is that this book can at least provide a record of the period of history that was so important to a particular group of people from northern Ratanakiri Province, northeastern Cambodia.

I do not claim that the political system adopted by the PRK during the 1980s was laudable; nor do I deny or justify the fact that human rights were frequently violated during the PRK period. I do not claim that life was great or even good for most people in Cambodia during this period; or that great suffering and hardship did not occur for so many during this time. Neither do I intend this book to deny the experiences and views of those much more critical of the Vietnamese or the CPP, or to justify present-day abuses of power in the Cambodian government. But at the same time, at least for the group of people that I have focused on here, the PRK period can certainly be seen as their golden age.

Appendix

Prominent People

Boua Chuong

From Voeunsai Village (although actually born at Kiet Ngong Village in Champasak Province, southern Laos), Voeunsai Commune, Voeunsai District, Ratanakiri Province, Boua Chuong was ethnic Lao. He was a *Garde indigene* soldier for the French, but gained credit with the communists in 1954 when he led part of the French military company he was commanding to switch sides and join the Viet Minh. In 1954, he became one of the Khmer Hanoi, although he returned to northeastern Cambodia in 1970. In 1975, he was one of those who led the large number of people to Vietnam, and he was the first leader for Gia Poc Commune. In 1979, after the Vietnamese took over Cambodia, he was appointed as chairman of the provincial People's Committee (governor) in Ratanakiri Province, a position he held until retiring in 1988. He died in 1993.

Bou Thang

Born in Kachoan Village, Kachoan Commune, Voeunsai District, Ratanakiri Province—adjacent to the Sesan River—Bou Thang is half ethnic Lao and half Tampuon. His father was a wild elephant catcher from Laos and his mother was a farmer from Cambodia. He is among the most influential people featured in this book. He joined the Khmer Issarak against French colonialism on April 14, 1954. During the same year, he walked to North Vietnam and became a communist Khmer Hanoi, where he received advanced military training at Bac

Ninh. In 1970, he walked with Soy Keo and other Khmer Hanoi from North Vietnam to northeastern Cambodia, via the Ho Chi Minh Trail. On his return to Cambodia, Bou Thang became the military leader in the Khmer Rouge's Sector 1 of the northeast zone. Later, he was made deputy head of the Khmer Rouge military in the northeast zone, with Son Sen as his superior. When Ya (Ney Sarann) became secretary of the northeast zone in 1973, Bou Thang became the deputy head of the committee for helping the northeast zone, called *Kho 32*. However, in 1974 Bou Thang began planning to flee to Vietnam, and in 1975 he did exactly that. In 1975, he became the leader of the refugee settlement area at Gia Poc Commune, Sa Thay District, Gialai-Kontum Province. In the following years, Bou Thang gradually replaced Bun Mi as the most important ethnic minority revolutionary from the northeast. He became one of seven members of the Central Committee of the UFNSK when it was formed in 1978, leading the northeast. In 1979, Bou Thang became the chair of the PRPK's central propaganda committee and a member of the Politburo. In 1981, he was elected to the 117-member National Assembly, representing Preah Vihear Province. In 1982 he became the PRK's minister of defense. However, in October 1985 he was removed from that position. But in 1987, he became chairman of the military's general political department. He was also deputy prime minister between 1982 and 1992, and he held a seat in the Politburo until 1992. After the UNTAC sponsored elections in 1993, he became a member of parliament for Ratanakiri Province, and later a senator representing the province. He retired in 2017 and passed away in 2019.

Bui Yung

Born in Yang Commune, O Yadao District, Ratanakiri Province, Bui Yung is ethnic Jarai. He joined the Communist Revolution in 1957 and became a full party member in 1969. In 1970, he was given responsibility for commune-level commerce in District 21. In 1975, he fled to Vietnam. In 1979, he returned to Cambodia to support the new government. He became vice-chairman of Ratanakiri's People's Committee and was also head of the Ratanakiri Province Department of Planning. In 1987, he was appointed head of the Department of Trade and Construction, Ratanakiri Province. He was, however, demoted in 1987, becoming the deputy head of one of the divisions of the

Department of Education in Ratanakiri Province. He later left the government and converted to Islam.

Bun Chan

Born in Phao Village, Taveng Kraom Commune, Taveng District, Ratanakiri Province, Bun Chan is ethnic Brao and the younger brother of Kham Toeung. In 1968, along with Bun Mi, Bun Chan was one of the leaders of the Khmer Rouge unit that attacked Post Lo. He stayed in Cambodia with the Khmer Rouge throughout the 1975 to 1979 period. However, he was arrested in Preah Vihear Province along with most of his military unit on February 2, 1978, as part of the many internal purges orchestrated by the Khmer Rouge between 1976 and 1978. He was transferred to Siem Reap in November 1978. At the end of the year, he was sent with seven hundred others to Phnom Penh. He was accused of being a spy for the Brao who had fled to Laos and Vietnam, although the accusations were apparently false. He was released from prison soon after the Vietnamese took control of Cambodia in 1979. He traveled to Gia Poc Commune in Vietnam, where he spent some time. In 1986, he became deputy district chief of Taveng District. He retired in the late 1990s.

Bun Mi (Brao nickname: Moi)

Born in Savanbao Village, Taveng Loeu Commune, Taveng District, Ratanakiri Province, Bun Mi was a key Brao Amba Khmer Rouge operative in Ratanakiri Province during the 1960s and early 1970s. His ethnic Brao wife was named Kham Phanh. In 1962, when revolutionary party cells from the First Indochina War started being revived, Bun Mi and Moi Choem led the recruiting drive in their areas. In 1962, Bun Mi was also one of the first Brao to re-enter the forest with the Khmer Rouge. In the 1970s, he became the party secretary of 55 *Kaw* District (Taveng) in Sector 3. In 1973, he had a conflict with the Khmer Rouge leadership in the northeast, particularly Ny Kan. Later, negotiations resulted in Ny Kan being transferred and Bun Mi becoming the leader of Sector 3. However, in 1975 Bun Mi led a large number of people to flee to Vietnam. His mental illness worsened during the time he was at Gia Poc Commune, and by late 1978 he was too mentally ill to participate in politics. Bun Mi moved to Phnom Penh in 1979, but his behavior became increasingly outrageous. He was taken to Laos and Vietnam to try to cure his illness. He was finally institutionalized in Dong Nai, Vietnam. He never recovered and eventually died in Vietnam.

Chan Khamkhoeua

Born in Lumphat Town, Ratanakiri Province, in 1957, Chan Khamkhoeua is ethnic Lao. She went to school in Lumphat between 1963 and 1970. Once the Khmer Rouge took over the northeast of Cambodia in 1970, she stayed at a cooperative in Nong Bua Village. In 1979, she became a school teacher, and, in 1984, she was appointed as deputy director of the province's elementary education office within the Education Department. In 1985, she was made director, and in 1987, she became the deputy director of the overall Department of Education. In 2009, she completed a master's degree in education in Phnom Penh, after studying part time for six years. She became the head of the Education Department in Ratanakiri Province in the same year she graduated.

Dam Chanty

Born in Ta Lao Village, Ta Lao Commune, Andong Meas District, Ratanakiri Province, Dam Chanty is ethnically half Lao and half Tampuon. She is also adept in various other languages, including Brao, Kreung, Lun, Kavet, Kachok, Khmer, Vietnamese, and Thai. She was in Cambodia during the main Khmer Rouge period, between 1975 and 1979. However, she quickly rose up during the PRK period. After going to Vietnam to study, in 1982, she became vice-president of Women's Affairs Department in Ratanakiri Province, and in 1988, she was appointed president of Women's Affairs Department, replacing Lak On. She left government service in the 1990s and started working for NGOs. She is presently the director the Highlander Association, an NGO based in Banlung.

Doeun

Born in Taveng Village, Taveng Loeu Commune, Taveng District, Ratanakiri Province, Doeun (he is only known by a single name) is ethnic Lun. He fled to Vietnam with a large number of people in 1975, and in late 1978, Ma Ranchai was initially scheduled to lead the UFNSK battalion responsible for Preah Vihear Province. However, Doeun replaced him. Once in Preah Vihear, Kham Phai was transferred to the province to lead the military there, and Doeun became his deputy. Kham Len was Doeun's son-in-law. In 1984, Doeun was transferred to Stung Treng Province, but due to having a serious alcohol dependency, he was soon forced to retire. He returned to live in Taveng Village.

Dop Khamchoeung (Brao nickname: Jrouk)

Born in Bang Koet Village, Taveng Loeu Commune, Taveng District, Ratanakiri Province, Dop Khamchoeung is Brao Amba. He commanded the Khmer Rouge's northeastern-most border military unit beginning in 1974. However, he decided to flee to Vietnam with many others in 1975. After the Vietnamese gained control of Cambodia in 1979, he became a military leader in Mondulkiri Province. In 1987 he resigned his position and returned to his original village to farm.

Heng Khamvan

Born in Voeunsai Village, Voeunsai Commune, Voeunsai District, Ratanakiri Province, Heng Khamvan was ethnic Lao. His father was the Khmer Hanoi named Heng Sunna, who later became the District Chief of Hatsaifong District, in Vientiane, Laos, before dying in 1986. Heng Khamvan fled to Vietnam in 1975, and he was one of the military leaders of the UFNSK northeastern headquarters at Gia Poc Commune. In late 1978, he was the leader of the UFNSK battalion that invaded Mondulkiri Province. Soon after, he was appointed head of the military's Statistics Department. He was also responsible for the village-level volunteer forces in Cambodia. He was the older brother of Heng Bunthan. In 1987, Heng Khamvan was made deputy head of the Ministry of Defense's committee for peace negotiations. He continued in that position until 1990. In the 1990s, he was transferred to the Military Region 1 in Stung Treng, where he passed away in the 2010s.

Jop Moer

Born in Andong Meas District, Ratanakiri Province, Jop Moer is ethnic Kachok. She started working for the new Education

Department of Ratanakiri on October 15, 1980. She remained in Cambodia during the Khmer Rouge period between 1975 and 1979, and in 1980 she was not literate and spoke little Khmer language. During the first four years of her employment, she cooked food for teachers and people working for the Education Department. In 1983, she studied in Ho Chi Minh City for one year. She learned basic Khmer for three months, and then studied other subjects for eight months. She returned in late 1984, and in May 1985 she started working as deputy director of the Department of Women's Affairs. In 1998, she was promoted to be head of the department. She is now retired.

Kham Chan

Born in Trabok Village, Taveng Loeu Commune, Taveng District, Ratanakiri Province, Kham Chan was ethnic Brao. In 1963, he joined the Khmer Rouge and went to the forest in Ratanakiri, and in 1974 he became deputy head of 55 *Kaw* (Taveng) District, working under Thang Ngon. In 1975 he fled to Vietnam, and in late 1978 he was the on-the-ground leader, with Kham Phai as his deputy, of the anti–Khmer Rouge UFNSK forces that invaded Cambodia along with Vietnamese forces. After the Vietnamese took over Cambodia, Kham Chan took a senior position at the Ministry of Defense in Phnom Penh. In 1985, he became chief of the Stung Treng-based northeast military zone. He rose up to be the highest military leader from the northeast, after Bou Thang and Soy Keo. He retired in the early 2000s and eventually moved back to Trabok Village, where he died.

Kham Khoeun

Born in Pong Village, Pong Commune, Voeunsai District, Ratanakiri Province, Kham Khoeun is ethnic Lao, although he spent much time as a child in the forest with Brao people. In 1979, he became the district governor of Lumphat District, and in 1980 he became one of the seven members of the provincial office's committee in Ratanakiri Province. In 1982, he was appointed chief of the provincial police, head of the Information Dissemination Department, and head of the party's dissemination department, but he gave up those positions a few years later when he became vice-chairman of the provincial People's Committee of Ratanakiri. In 1988, he became chairman of Ratanakiri's People's

Committee (governor). In 1993, he lost his position once a coalition government was established in Cambodia, but in the early 2000s he became governor of Ratanakiri Province again. However, in 2005, due to a logging scandal, he was removed from his position and fled to Laos, where he lived until 2016, when he was pardoned and allowed to return to Cambodia.

Kham Len (Lun nickname: Yoi; Lao nickname: Phalen)

Born in Taveng Village, Taveng Loeu Commune, Taveng District, Ratanakiri Province, Kham Len was ethnically Lun and was the son-in-law of the military leader Doeun. Kham Len joined the Khmer Rouge revolution in the early 1960s and was one of the leaders of the large group of people who fled to Vietnam in 1975. In 1979, Kham Len became secretary of Ratanakiri's Party Committee, and in 1981 he was elected to represent Ratanakiri Province as one of the 117-member National Assembly. In 1989, Kham Len went to work in Phnom Penh for the ministry responsible for ethnic minorities. Kham Len did not return to Ratanakiri until after Boua Chuong died in 1993. He became governor of the province during the same year. However, he passed away in March 1994.

Kham Phai

Born in Paroe Touich Village, Taveng Kraom Commune, Taveng District, Ratanakiri Province, Kham Phai is ethnic Lun. He was one of the military leaders at Gia Poc Commune, after fleeing to Vietnam in 1975. He was the deputy leader of the UFNSK attack forces in northeastern Cambodia, with Kham Chan as his superior. In 1979, Kham Phai became the leader of the UFNSK battalion responsible for Preah Vihear Province. Later, in 1985, General Kham Phai was transferred to Stung Treng, where he became deputy chief of the northeast military zone. He became chief of the northeast military zone when Kham Chan retired. Kham Phai is now retired and lives in Banlung.

Kham Sai

Born in Bang Koet Village, Taveng Loeu Commune, Taveng District, Ratanakiri Province, Kham Sai is Brao Amba. His father was the veteran revolutionary Jareng. In the early 1970s, Kham Sai was the military leader for Sector 3 in the northeast zone. In 1975, he was one of the leaders who fled to Vietnam. However, he refused to become a UFNSK soldier. He returned to Cambodia from Gia Poc Commune in 1980, and in 1981 he was appointed head of the Department of Finance in the PRK government in Ratanakiri Province. He retired in the 2000s.

Kham Suk

Originally from Tiem Loeu Village, Kaoh Pheak Commune, Voeunsai District, Ratanakiri Province, Kham Suk was ethnically Kreung and is the son of Kham Lai, the former vice-chairman of Preah Vihear province's People's Committee responsible for elders. In late 1978, Kham Suk led the UFNSK Battalion 1, which entered Cambodia via Mondulkiri Province. In 1982, he became deputy chief of staff of the military in Preah Vihear Province. He held that position until 1985, when Military Region 1 was established, based in Stung Treng. He was transferred there to head up the office of strategic planning, a position he held until November 1988. He became a general prior to becoming the head of the provincial military in Stung Treng Province. He is presently the military commander of Ratanakiri Province.

Kham Toeung (Brao nickname: Kai)

Born in 1936 in Phao Village, Taveng Kraom Commune, Taveng District, Ratanakiri Province, Kham Toeung is ethnic Brao and fought against the French during the First Indochina War, when he was in Laos, where he initially went to work on coffee plantations on the Bolaven Plateau. After returning to Cambodia, in the early 1960s he was one of the early Brao people to join the Khmer Rouge in the forest. In 1967 he was also among the first group of highlanders to study politics with Pol Pot. By the early 1970s he was one of the leaders of the Khmer Rouge's Taveng Kraom Commune. In 1973, he joined Bun Mi when he initially sought political refuge in southern Laos, but he returned with him when Bun Mi agreed to rejoin the Khmer Rouge. In 1975, however, Kham Toeung was one of the leaders who led a large number of people to Attapeu Province, in southern Laos. In 1979, Kham Toeung was appointed vice-chairman of Stung Treng Province's

People's Committee (deputy governor). He held that position from 1979 to 1984 and was then the head of the provincial elders from 1984 to 1987, before retiring in 1988. After retiring, Kham Toeung initially moved to Banlung, the capital city of Ratanakiri Province. Later he re-settled in the Taveng District Center. He passed away in 2019.

Kreng Siengnoi

Born in Bong (Yorn) Village, Taveng Loeu Commune, Taveng District, Ratanakiri Province, Kreng Siengnoi was ethnic Brao. In 1973, he led the first group of Brao people, from Bong Village, to flee to Vietnam, where his community stayed between then and late 1978. In 1979, he was appointed as head of Ratanakiri Province's Organization Department. However, in 1982 he became head of the PRPK Party Office for Ratanakiri Province, resulting in his deputy, Muan Poi, effectively taking over the management of the Organization Department, even though Kreng Siengnoi remained the official leader. In 1987, he was appointed as head of the Ratanakiri provincial PRPK. He retired in the 1990s and died in Banlung in 2017.

Lak On

Born in Lumphat, Ratanakiri Province, Lak On is ethnic Khmer. She rose to prominence within the political ranks in Ratanakiri Province during the PRK period. In 1980, she became the president of Women's Affairs Department of Ratanakiri Province. She was also made the head of the Education Department. Later, she became a member of the PRPK People's Commi ttee, and in 1981 she was one of three repre-sentatives of Ratanakiri Province in the 117-member National Assembly. In 1988, she became vice-chairman of the provincial People's Committee in Ratanakiri Province. In 1989, Lak On replaced Kham Len as secretary of Ratanakiri's provincial party committee. She is now retired and living in Phnom Penh.

Lat Vansao

Born in Pak Kalan Village, Voeunsai Commune, Voeunsai District, Ratanakiri Province, Lat Vansao was ethnic Lao. He remained in Cambodia during the Khmer Rouge period, between 1975 and 1979. However, he gained the trust of the post–Khmer PRK regime, as he was relatively more educated than others. Therefore, in 1979, he became deputy chair of the Propaganda Department of Ratanakiri Province, and in 1982, he took over the leadership. In 1987, he became one of the twenty-one members of the PRPK Committee in Ratanakiri Province. In the 1990s, he became district chief of Banlung District. He died a few years ago.

Ma Ranchai

Born in Taveng Village, Taveng Loeu Commune, Taveng District, Ratanakiri Province, Ma Ranchai is ethnic Lun. He fled to Vietnam in 1975. During the Third Party Congress, held in Ho Chi Minh City in January 1979, Ma Ranchai was one of the eighteen ethnic minorities from the northeast who were party members. He was initially made the leader of UFNSK's Battalion 2, which was destined to go to Preah Vihear Province, but Doeun, his deputy, ended up replacing him. In 1980, he was made one of the seven members of the Ratanakiri Provincial Office's Committee. He served in that position for a number of years until retiring.

Moi Choem

Born in Pateng Village, Kapong Commune, Voeunsai District, Ratanakiri Province, Moi Choem was ethnic Brao. In 1962, he joined the Khmer Rouge in the forest, along with Bun Mi and Kham Toeung. During the same year, he led, along with Bun Mi, the drive to recruit people to join the Khmer Rouge from those involved in the First Indochina War. However, in 1975, Moi Choem joined the many other Brao who fled to Vietnam and Laos. He led a group of Brao people from Kapong Commune that went directly to Laos. In 1979, once the Vietnamese took over Cambodia, he was appointed chairman of the provincial People's Committee (governor) of Mondulkiri Province. In 1983, Moi Choem became vice-chairman of the provincial People's Committee, with responsibility for elders' affairs. He retired in 1988 and returned to Ratanakiri Province. He stayed in the capital city of Banlung with his wife, Tom Mut, dying in the early 2000s.

Muan Poi

Born in Siangsai Village, Taveng Kraom Commune, Taveng District, Ratanakiri Province, Muan Poi is ethnic Brao. His brother is Muan Hoi, who is in the Cambodian military, based in Stung Treng. Beginning in 1979, Muan Poi was deputy and later head of the Department of Organization in Ratanakiri Province, but in 1982 he essentially took over the everyday management of the department. He was governor of Ratanakiri Province in the 2000s, and in 2018 he became the senator representing Ratanakiri Province, replacing Bou Thang.

Ney Sarann (Revolutionary nickname: Ya)

Ney Sarann, better known by his revolutionary name Ya, was an ethnic Khmer who married a local woman, either ethnic Lao or ethnic Jarai, and was able to speak Lao language. In 1973, he became the secretary of the northeastern zone party committee. In 1977, he was sent to the S21 prison in Phnom Penh, where he was executed after being forced to confess.

Ny Kan

An ethnic Khmer Kraom from Vietnam and the brother of Khmer Rouge leader Son Sen, in the early 1970s Ny Kan became the first political leader of Sector 3 in the northeast zone. In 1973, he had a serious falling out with the Brao leader, Bun Mi. After a series of events, Bun Mi negotiated with the leadership of the northeast zone, resulting in Ny Kan being transferred to a different sector in 1974.

Soy Keo (Seuy Keo)

Originally from Kaoh Pheak Village, Kaoh Pheak Commune, Voeunsai District, Ratanakiri Province, Soy Keo was ethnically half Kreung and half Tampuon, although some mistake him for being ethnic Kachok, since that is the ethnicity of most of the people in the village where he was raised. Soy Keo's official birthdate is June 3, 1943, but he claims he was actually born in 1937. Thus he was seventeen years old when he joined the revolution against the French in 1954. Boua

Choeung recruited him. In 1954, Soy Keo traveled by foot with other Khmer Hanoi to northern Vietnam, where he received medical training at Hai Duong. However, he later transferred into the military school. He studied at Bac Ninh with Bou Thang. In 1970, he walked back to northeastern Cambodia with Bou Thang, and soon after arriving he was appointed as the leader of the Khmer Rouge's first military force in the northeast, Company 703. During the Chenla I campaign, he led Company 703 in intensive fighting to the south in Kampong Cham. Once in Siem Reap, Company 703 was elevated to become Battalion 703. In 1974, Soy Keo began considering defecting from the Khmer Rouge, and in 1975 he fled to Vietnam. In 1978, he became a key leader in the northeastern-wing of the UFNSK, and in 1981 he became one of the 117-member National Assembly, representing Kratie Province. Soy Keo was lieutenant general, vice-minister of defense, Party Central Committee member and general chief of staff of PRAK in the early 1980s. He was, however, removed from being a Party Central Committee member and the general chief of staff in October 1985. In late 1987, however, he was brought back as general chief of staff, although with fewer responsibilities than previously. He held that position until 1990. Soy Keo was appointed as chief of Military Region 1 in northeastern Cambodia in 1993, and in 1998 he became a senator. He lived in Phnom Penh from 1979 until he passed away in 2019.

Thang Bai

Born in Kachoan Village, Kachoan Commune, Voeunsai District, Ratanakiri Province, Thang Bai was a veteran ethnic Tampuon revolutionary. He was also the younger brother of Bou Thang's mother. He joined the revolution even before Bou Thang, who joined in 1954. In 1975, Thang Bai was one of the leaders of the large number of people who fled from the Khmer Rouge to Vietnam. After the Vietnamese entered Cambodia and took over the country in 1979, Thang Bai was elevated to secretary of the provincial party committee in Stung Treng Province. He died of illness while in office in 1984.

Thang Ngon (Brao nickname: Nyawng)

Born in Trabok Village, Taveng Loeu Commune, Taveng District, Ratanakiri Province, Thang Ngon is ethnic Brao. In 1963, he joined the Khmer Rouge revolution and went to stay in the forest. In 1974, he was appointed head of 55 *Kaw* (Taveng) District. However, in 1975 he became one of those who led a large number of people to Vietnam. He was one of the eighteen founding Party members of the sixty-two who attended the Third Party Congress in Ho Chi Minh City in January 1979. He was appointed secretary of Mondulkiri's provincial Party Committee. In 1981, he became one of the 117-member National Assembly, representing Mondulkiri Province. In the late 1980s, he retired and returned to farm in Trabok Village.

Thao Sim

Born in Phak Nam Village, Kaoh Piak Commune, Voeunsai District, Ratanakiri Province, Thao Sim is ethnic Kreung. He was originally named Kreut Sim, but his name was changed to Thao Sim when he fled to Vietnam in 1975. Thao Sim was made the military head of The UFNSK's Battalion 3, assigned to Ratanakiri, and was chief of staff of the on-the-ground attack force leaders in late 1978. He then became the first post-1979 military leader in Ratanakiri Province. However, in 1981 he was removed from his position, following the controversial death of Bun Sou, Thang Bai's only son. Despite being Soy Keo's brother-in-law, Thao Sim did not hold any other positions in the government or army after that time.

Veng Khoun

Born in Bang Koet Village, Taveng Loeu Commune, Taveng District, Ratanakiri Province, Veng Khoun was ethnic Brao Amba and was one of the first five Brao people to go to the forest to join the Khmer Rouge in 1959. Later, in the early 1970s, he became one of the leaders of the Khmer Rouge's Taveng Loeu Commune, and in 1975 he was one of those who led a large number of Brao people to Laos. In 1979, after Cambodia had been taken over by the Vietnamese, he became secretary of Preah Vihear Province's Party Committee and was also simultaneously the chairman of the People's Committee in the province. In 1981, Veng Khoun was elected to the 117-member National Assembly, representing Preah Vihear Province. In 1985, he moved from Tbaeng Meanchey, the capital of Preah Vihear, and became chairman of the People's Committee of Stung Treng Province. He retired in 1988, and he eventually returned to his home village, where he farmed until dying in 2003.

Yoep Vanson

Born in Bong (Yorn) Village, Taveng Loeu Commune, Taveng District, Ratanakiri Province, Yoep Vanson is ethnic Brao. In 1973, Kreng Siengnoi led him and others to flee from Cambodia to Vietnam. Yoep Vanson's father was Yoep, one of the first five people to join the Khmer Rouge in Ratanakiri in 1959. In 1977, Yoep Vanson became a medic for the UFNSK, and in late 1978 he participated in the attack on the Khmer Rouge. In 1980, he became the head of the provincial Health Department in Ratanakiri Province, and in 1987 he was appointed as deputy head of the Ratanakiri provincial PRPK. In the 1990s he became a provincial policeman in Ratanakiri Province, and in the 2000s he worked for different NGOs, including NTFP Project and the Sesan Protection Network. He presently lives in Kalai 2 Village in O Chum District, Ratanakiri Province.

Notes

Introduction

1. Not on December 25, 1978, as often reported (Pribbenow 2006). I have put invasion and liberation in scare quotes because both terms are highly contested and the term used generally depends on what side of the conflict one is on.

2. The members of ASEAN were Thailand, Malaysia, Indonesia, the Philippines, and Singapore.

3. Pol Pot was a revolutionary name. His name at birth was Salot Sar (Short 2004).

4. Ea Meng-Try (1981) also reported that by the end of 1979 there were 200,000 to 300,000 civilian immigrants to Cambodia from Vietnam, but this number seems highly doubtful.

5. Bou Thang, pers. comm., Banlung, 2017.

6. However, an unspecified number of Vietnamese military advisors remained in Cambodia, although in September 1990, Vietnam Foreign Minister Nguyễn Co Thach said that they would be withdrawn as well, although without providing a withdrawal timeline (Associated Press 1990).

7. However, the Khmer Rouge falsely claimed in 1989 that large numbers of Vietnamese families had secretly immigrated to Ratanakiri and Mondulkiri (VODK 1989a, 1989c), and between 1989 and 1992 they also apparently falsely claimed that large numbers of Vietnamese soldiers continued to hide in various parts of the country, including Ratanakiri and Stung Treng Provinces (*Voice of the Khmer* 1989; VODK 1989b, 1991, 1992; BBC 1992).

8. Bou Thang, pers. comm., Banlung, 2012.

9. Prince Norodom Sihanouk was the political leader of Cambodia from the time of independence from France in 1953–54 until he was ousted from power in 1970 (Chandler 1996).

10. Bou Thang, pers. comm., Banlung, 2017.

11. Lê Đức Thọ mainly worked on policy, political theory, and planning and management issues and was an excellent public speaker. He apparently did much of the broad policy work. General Lê Đức Anh was the military and political leader in Cambodia. He did the work on the ground (Bou Thang, pers. comm., Banlung, 2017).

12. Following Pen Sovan's arrest, Chan Si was appointed prime minister in February 1982, a position he held until he passed away on December 27, 1984. Then, in January 1985, thirty-two-year-old Hun Sen became prime minister (Slocomb 2003).

13. Khamphan Thivong, pers. comm., Stung Treng, 2009.

14. Yoep Vanson, pers. comm., Banlung, 2009; Kham Sai, pers. comm., Banlung, 2009.

15. Kham Sai, pers. comm., Banlung, 2009.

16. Dop Khamchoeung, pers. comm., Bang Koet Village, Taveng District, 2017.

17. Kham Sai, pers. comm., Banlung, 2009.

18. The term "ethnic minorities" rather than "Indigenous peoples" is used throughout the book because I am typically referring to highland ethnic minorities, which are presently classified as Indigenous peoples in Cambodia (Baird 2011a), and ethnic Lao people, who are also ethnic minorities but are not considered to be Indigenous peoples in the country (Baird 2016b).

19. Eang Sary was Minister of Foreign Affairs for the Khmer Rouge.

Chapter 1

1. These groups include the Kreung, Lun, Amba, Kavet, and Brao Tanap in northeastern Cambodia, and the Kavet, Lun, Hamong, Jree, and Ka-nying in southern Laos (Baird 2008).

2. Bou Thang, pers. comm., Banlung, 2013.

3. He is believed to have died in Vietnam in 1976 (Vickery 1989).

4. Bou Thang, pers. comm., Phnom Penh, 2012.

5. The Khmer Hanoi were Cambodian regroupees in North Vietnam, including places outside of Hanoi.

6. Kon, whose real name was Ouch Khamkon, was an ethnic Khmer. He married Nang Oudone, the granddaughter of the influential Champasak royal, Chao Thammatheva (or Ya Chao Tham) in Voeunsai (see Baird 2009d, 2010a). Kon's son, Osakanh Thammatheva entered the Pathet Lao Communist Army in southern Laos in 1954 and eventually became a general, a minister, and a member of the Politburo in Laos.

7. Bou Thang, pers. comm., Banlung, 2013.

8. Kham Toeung interview by Ben Kiernan, Phnom Penh, January 15, 1986.

9. Bou Thang, pers. comm., Phnom Penh, 2017.

10. Soy Keo, pers. comm., Banlung, 2017.

11. Malaria was a serious problem in Ratanakiri (Whitaker et al. 1973).

12. On the north side, from west to east, were Paroe Thom, Bong, Pajong, Bang Koet Touich, Jarong Laik, Leang Veng, Trabok, and Kang Dak Villages, and on the west side of the school, from east to west, were Viengchan, Phao

Thom, Tambouan Roeng, Savanbao, Phao Touich, and Bang Koet Thom (Ironside and Baird 2003).

13. Short (2004) is mistaken that the original homes of many highlanders were situated adjacent to the Sesan River before they were moved into the "high mountains" by the Khmer Rouge in the late 1960s for security reasons. In fact, most had been moved from the mountains to near the Sesan River at the end of the 1950s.

14. Also known as Uan.

15. To Bioe, pers. comm., Soin Village, Taveng District, 2017.

16. To Bioe, pers. comm., Soin Village, Taveng District, 2017.

17. Bui Yung, pers. comm., Kate 2 Village, O Yadao District, 2017.

18. This village split in two, Tuh Loeu and Tuh Kraom. Jacqueline Matras worked in the latter (Matras-Troubetzkoy 1983).

19. The *lien* was the form of currency used in Cambodia at the time.

20. Although Yoot was appointed Nai Kong during the French colonial period, he retained his title during the Norodom Sihanouk period, although he was actually commune chief of Taveng during that period (there was only one commune in Taveng at the time). He stayed at Yoot Village, which was on the north side of the Sesan River. His post was at the mouth of the Palawng stream, on the south side of the Sesan River.

21. Stephen Heder, pers. comm., 2005.

22. Kham Sai, pers. comm., Banlung, 2009.

23. He remained in command until 1971, when he relocated to Beijing and Son Sen replaced him as military leader of the northeast zone (Colm 1996).

24. Kham Toeung interview by Ben Kiernan, Phnom Penh, January 15, 1986.

25. This was followed on May 5 with the establishment of the Royal Government of the National Unification of Kampuchea, with Sihanouk as head of state and Penn Nouth as prime minister.

26. Charles Keller, pers. comm., Banlung, 2006.

27. The largest concentrations are in Massachusetts and Rhode Island (Charles Keller, pers. comm., 2006).

28. Jyao Dawl, pers. comm., Bang Koet Village, Taveng District, 2017.

29. Yoep Vanson, pers. comm., Banlung, 2007.

30. Yoep Vanson, pers. comm., Banlung, 2007.

31. Known by his revolutionary name Kham.

32. Bui Yung, pers. comm., Kate 2 Village, O Yadao District, 2017.

33. Bou Thang, pers. comm., Phnom Penh, 2009.

34. Kham Toeung interview by Ben Kiernan, Phnom Penh, January 15, 1986.

35. Bui Yung, pers. comm., Kate 2 Village, O Yadao District, 2017.

36. Bou Thang, pers. comm., Phnom Penh, 2017.

37. Bou Thang, pers. comm., Banlung, 2017.

38. Soy Keo, pers. comm., Phnom Penh, 2009.
39. Soy Keo, pers. comm., Phnom Penh, 2009.
40. Soy Keo, pers. comm., Phnom Penh, 2009.
41. Bou Thang, pers. comm., Phnom Penh, 2017.
42. Soy Keo, pers. comm., Banlung, 2017.
43. Kham Phai, pers. comm., Banlung, 2017.
44. Bou Thang, pers. comm., Phnom Penh, 2009; Banlung, 2017.
45. *Nakor* in Lao.
46. Bou Thang, pers. comm., Banlung, 2017.
47. Buo Khav was also known as Buo Kaev. He was arrested in March 1977 (Stephen Heder, pers. comm., 2005) and sent to Sector 21, where he was subsequently killed for treason (see "Confessions" of Buo Kaev alias Bǒy Kaev alias Buo Khav "Responses of Buo Kaev alias Khav, secretary of Kok Lak District, Sector 101: On the History of His Own Traitorous Activities," 8 September 1977).
48. Bou Thang, pers. comm., Banlung, 2017.
49. Kham Toeung interview by Ben Kiernan, January 15, 1986.

Chapter 2

1. Kham Toeung, pers. comm., Taveng District Center, 2009.
2. Kham Toeung interview by Ben Kiernan, Phnom Penh, January 15, 1986.
3. Kham Toeung interview by Ben Kiernan, Phnom Penh, January 15, 1986.
4. Kham Toeung interview by Ben Kiernan, Phnom Penh, January 15, 1986.
5. Kreng Siengnoi pers. comm., Banlung, 2009.
6. Kham Khoeun, pers. comm., Phnom Penh, 2017.
7. Yoep Sat, pers. comm., Bong Village, Taveng District, 2012.
8. Veng Khoun, pers. comm., Bang Koet Village, Taveng District; Kham Sai, pers. comm., Banlung, 2009.
9. Bui Yung, pers. comm., Kate 2 Village, O Yadao District, 2017.
10. Veng Khoun, pers. comm., Bang Koet Village, Taveng District, 2002; Kham Sai, pers. comm., Banlung, 2009.
11. Veng Khoun, pers. comm., Taveng District, 2002; Kham Sai, pers. comm., Banlung, 2009.
12. Two of the medics were men and one was a woman. One of the male medics was Kham Khoeun, who would later become governor of Ratanakiri Province.
13. Veng Khoun, pers. comm., Taveng District, 2002; Kham Sai, pers. comm., Banlung, 2009.
14. Veng Khoun, pers. comm., Taveng District, 2002.
15. Veng Khoun, pers. comm., Taveng District, 2002; Kham Sai, pers. comm., Banlung, 2009.

16. Kham Khoeun, pers. comm., Phnom Penh, 2017.

17. Veng Khoun, pers. comm., Taveng District, 2002; Kham Sai, pers. comm., Banlung, 2009.

18. Veng Khoun, pers. comm., Taveng District, 2002; Kham Sai, pers. comm., Banlung, 2009.

19. Veng Khoun, pers. comm., Taveng District, 2002.

20. Kham Sai, pers. comm., Banlung, 2009.

21. Kham Sai, pers. comm., Banlung, 2009; Jyao Dawl, pers. comm., Bang Koet Village, Taveng District, 2017; Kham Toeung interview by Ben Kiernan, Phnom Penh, January 15, 1986.

22. According to Bou Thang (pers. comm., Banlung, 2013, 2017), Ya also used the revolutionary names Maen San, Venta, Kham, Khoeun, and Sen. He was married to an ethnic Lao woman named Voeun, who came from Keng Sanh Village in Lumphat. They had two children together.

23. Veng Khoun, pers. comm., Taveng District, 2002.

24. Veng Khoun, pers. comm., Taveng District, 2002; Kham Sai, pers. comm., Banlung, 2009.

25. Veng Khoun, pers. comm., Taveng District, 2002; Kham Sai, pers. comm., Banlung, 2009.

26. Veng Khoun, pers. comm., Taveng District, 2002.

27. Veng Khoun, pers. comm., Taveng District, 2002.

28. Veng Khoun, pers. comm., Taveng District, 2002.

29. Veng Khoun, pers. comm., Bang Koet Village, Taveng District, 2002.

30. Thang Bai was the younger brother of Bou Thang's mother (Bou Thang, pers. comm., Banlung, 2013).

31. Kham Sai, pers. comm., Banlung, 2009.

32. Bou Thang, pers. comm., Banlung, 2012.

33. Bou Thang, pers. comm., Banlung, 2017.

34. Bou Thang, pers. comm., Banlung, 2012.

35. Bou Thang, pers. comm., Banlung, 2013.

36. Bou Thang, pers. comm., Banlung, 2017.

37. Soy Keo, pers. comm., Phnom Penh, 2009.

38. Bou Thang, pers. comm., Banlung, 2017.

39. Soy Keo, pers. comm., Banlung, 2017.

40. The Vietnamese guarded a wide area in groups of 10–20 soldiers.

41. Bou Thang, pers. comm., Banlung, 2017.

42. Dop Khamchoeung, pers. comm., Bang Koet Village, Taveng District, 2017.

43. Bou Lam is presently the member of the National Assembly for Ratanakiri Province.

44. Bou Thang, pers. comm., Banlung, 2012.

45. Phuy Bunyok, pers. comm., Banlung, 2017.

46. Kham Sai, pers. comm., Banlung, 2009.

47. Phuy Bunyok, pers. comm., Banlung, 2017.

48. Phuy Bunyok, pers. comm., Banlung, 2017; Jampong Jari, pers. comm., Phak Nam Village, Voeunsai District, 2017.

49. Kham Sana, pers. comm., Phak Nam Village, Voeunsai District, 2017.

50. Phuy Bunyok, pers. comm., Banlung, 2017.

51. Kham Sai, pers. comm., Banlung, 2009; Soy Keo, pers. comm., Banlung, 2017.

52. Muan Poi, pers. comm., Banlung, 2017.

53. Jampong Jari, pers. comm., Phak Nam Village, Voeunsai District, 2017.

54. Kham Khoeun, pers. comm., Phnom Penh, 2017.

55. Bou Thang, pers. comm., Banlung, 2017.

56. Kham Phai, pers. comm., Banlung, 2017.

57. Kham Phai, pers. comm., Banlung, 2017.

58. Dam Jyun, pers. comm., Phak Nam Village, Voeunsai District, 2017.

59. Kham Phai, pers. comm., Banlung, 2017.

60. Kham Sai, pers. comm., Banlung, 2009; Soy Keo, pers. comm., Banlung, 2017.

61. The Vietnamese side of the border near Gia Gom is known as Heurl Mek.

62. Yao Than, pers. comm., Bang Koet Village, Taveng District, 2017.

63. Kham Khoeun, pers. comm., Phnom Penh, 2017.

64. Bou Thang, pers. comm., Banlung, 2009.

65. Bou Thang, pers. comm., Banlung, 2017.

66. Kham Toeung interview by Ben Kiernan, Phnom Penh, January 15, 1986.

67. Bou Thang, pers. comm., Banlung, 2012.

68. Bou Thang, pers. comm., Banlung, 2017.

69. Kham Sai, pers. comm., Banlung, 2009; Dop Khamchoeung, pers. comm., Bang Koet Village, Taveng District, 2017.

70. Kham Sai, pers. comm., Banlung, 2009.

71. Kham Toeung interview by Ben Kiernan, Phnom Penh, January 15, 1986.

72. Kham Sai, pers. comm., Banlung, 2009; Dop Khamchoeung, pers. comm., Bang Koet Village, Taveng District, 2017.

73. Kham Toeung interview by Ben Kiernan, Phnom Penh, January 15, 1986.

74. Kham Toeung, pers. comm., Banlung, 2009.

75. Kham Sai, pers. comm., Banlung, 2009.

76. Kham Sai, pers. comm., Banlung, 2009; Dop Khamchoeung, pers. comm., Bang Koet Village, Taveng District, 2017.

77. Phuy Bunyok, pers. comm., Banlung, 2017.

78. Kham Khoeun, pers. comm., Phnom Penh, 2017.

79. Kham Sai, pers. comm., Banlung, 2009; Bou Thang, pers. comm., Banlung,

2017; Dop Khamchoeung, pers. comm., Bang Koet Village, Taveng District, 2017.

80. Bui Yung, pers. comm., Banlung, 2017.

81. Bui Yung, pers. comm., Kate 2 Village, O Yadao District, 2017.

82. Bui Yung, pers. comm., Kate 2 Village, O Yadao District, 2017.

83. Bui Yung, pers. comm., Kate 2 Village, O Yadao District, 2017.

84. This area has since become part of Vietnam (Bui Yung, pers. comm., Kate 2 Village, O Yadao District; Bou Thang, pers. comm., Phnom Penh, 2017).

85. Bui Yung, pers. comm., Kate 2 Village, O Yadao District, 2017.

86. Somlit Chanthakaly, pers. comm., Attapeu town, 2017.

87. Channiang Gle, pers. comm., Bang Koet Village, Taveng District, 2017.

88. Somlit Chanthakaly, pers. comm., Attapeu town, 2017.

89. Channiang Gle, pers. comm., Bang Koet Village, Taveng District, 2017; Yak, pers. comm., Keng Makkheua Village, Xaysettha District, 2017.

90. Yao Thai, pers. comm., Bang Koet Village, Taveng District, 2017.

91. Jyao Dawl, pers. comm., Bang Koet Village, Taveng District, 2017.

92. Phoet Phoeua, pers. comm., Taveng District Center, 2017.

93. Ms. Min Sut, pers. comm., Banlung, 2017.

94. Somlit Chanthakaly, pers. comm., Attapeu town, 2017.

95. Kham Toeung interview by Ben Kiernan, Phnom Penh, January 15, 1986.

96. Somlit Chanthakaly, pers. comm., Attapeu town, 2017.

97. Lot, pers. comm., Done Nyieu Village, Xaysettha District, 2017.

98. Kham Sai, pers. comm., Banlung, 2009; Institute of Military History 2010.

99. Kham Sai, pers. comm., Banlung, 2009; Institute of Military History 2010.

100. Kham Sai, pers. comm., Banlung, 2009; Bou Thang, pers. comm., Banlung, 2017.

101. Phuy Bunyok, pers. comm., Banlung, 2017.

102. Yoep Vanson, pers. comm., Banlung, 2017; Dop Khamchoeung, pers. comm., Bang Koet Village, Taveng District, 2017.

103. Bou Thang, pers. comm., Banlung, 2012.

104. Bou Thang, pers. comm., Banlung, 2017.

105. Kham Phai, pers. comm., Banlung, 2017.

106. Dop Khamchoeung, pers. comm., Bang Koet Village, Taveng District, 2017.

107. Dop Khamchoeung, pers. comm., Bang Koet Village, Taveng District, 2017.

108. Dop Khamchoeung, pers. comm., Bang Koet Village, Taveng District, 2017.

109. Teng was later murdered at Gia Poc due to conflict with another Brao man over a woman they were both courting.

110. Dop Khamchoeung, pers. comm., Bang Koet Village, Taveng District, 2017.

111. Yoep Vanson, pers. comm., Banlung, 2017.

112. Dop Khamchoeung, pers. comm., Bang Koet Village, Taveng District, 2017.

113. Dop Khamchoeung, pers. comm., Bang Koet Village, Taveng District, 2017.

114. Dop Khamchoeung, pers. comm., Bang Koet Village, Taveng District, 2017.

115. Dop Khamchoeung, pers. comm., Bang Koet Village, Taveng District, 2017.

116. Phuy Bunyok, pers. comm., Banlung, 2017. When I worked with her in the early 2000s, she still was only literate in Vietnamese.

117. Ya was detained in September 1976 and sent to Sector 21 (Office of the Co-Investigating Judges 2010), where he was killed for treason. Um Neng, or Vong, Vy, his deputy, replaced him. Ya was reportedly accused of supporting the Brao who fled Cambodia (Kham Toeung interview by Ben Kiernan, Phnom Penh, January 15, 1986).

118. Lat Vansao, pers. comm., Banlung, 2012.

119. Kham Toeung interview by Ben Kiernan, Phnom Penh, January 15, 1986.

120. Stephen Heder, pers. comm., Phnom Penh, 2017.

121. However, in "Gumroo" cooperative in present-day O Chum, there were apparently about six hundred people.

Chapter 3

1. Stephen Heder, pers. comm., Phnom Penh, 2017.

2. Yoep Vanson, pers. comm., Banlung, 2017.

3. Kham Sai, pers. comm., Banlung, 2009.

4. Khang Sarin would later rise up to become the deputy chief of staff of UFNSK (Vũ 1979) and then from 1979 to 1980 he became the chairman of the People's Revolutionary Committee to Phnom Penh (Pen 2000). Later he became minister of interior in the PRK government (Gottesman 2002). However, at the time he started working with Lieutenant Colonel Cung, he had apparently retired and worked scrubbing out the insides of oil barrels (Huy Đức 2012a).

5. Bou Thang, pers. comm., Phnom Penh, 2017.

6. Yoep Vanson, pers. comm., Banlung, 2017.

7. Yoep Vanson, pers. comm., Banlung, 2009.

8. Yoep Vanson, pers. comm., Banlung, 2009.

9. Slocomb (2003) incorrectly reported that organizing began in October 1977. In fact, it began up to six months earlier.

10. Muan Poi, pers. comm., Banlung, 2017.

11. This is earlier than 1978, which was reported by Chanda (1986).

12. Bou Thang, pers. comm., Phnom Penh, 2009.

13. Kham Sana, pers. comm., Phak Nam Village, Voeunsai District, 2017.

14. Kham Phai, pers. comm., Banlung, 2017; Kham Sana, pers. comm., Phak Nam Village, Voeunsai District, 2017.

15. Bou Thang, pers. comm., Phnom Penh, 2012.

16. However, the Khmer Rouge leadership did not publicly admit to wanting to seize Kampuchea Kraom (Vickery 1984).

17. Stephen Heder, pers. comm., Phnom Penh, 2017.

18. Yoep Vanson, pers. comm., Banlung, 2017.

19. Soy Keo, pers. comm., Banlung, 2017.

20. Soy Keo, pers. comm., Banlung, 2017.

21. Yoep Vanson, pers. comm., Banlung, 2009, 2017.

22. Kham Phai, pers. comm., Banlung, 2017.

23. Yoep Vanson; Noi Hoeung, pers. comm., Banlung, 2009; Phoet Phoeua, pers. comm., Taveng District Center, 2017; Kham Phai, pers. comm., Banlung, 2017.

24. Kham Khoeun, pers. comm., Phnom Penh, 2017.

25. Kham Sai, pers. comm., Banlung, 2009.

26. Noi Hoeung, pers. comm., Banlung, 2009.

27. Khameng, pers. comm., Bang Koet Village, Taveng District, 2017.

28. Kham Phai, pers. comm., Banlung, 2017.

29. Yoep Vanson, pers. comm., Banlung, 2009.

30. Kham Khoeun, pers. comm., Phnom Penh, 2017.

31. Kham Sai, pers. comm., Banlung, 2009.

32. Yoep Vanson, pers. comm., Banlung, 2017.

33. Jarang, pers. comm., Keng Makkheua Village, Xaysettha District, 2017.

34. Yoep Vanson, pers. comm., Banlung, 2017.

35. Yoep Vanson, pers. comm., Banlung, 2017.

36. Dop Khamchoeung, pers. comm., Bang Koet Village, Taveng District, 2017.

37. Channiang Gle, pers. comm., Bang Koet Village, Taveng District, 2017.

38. Yao Than, pers. comm., Bang Koet Village, Taveng District, 2017.

39. Yak, pers. comm., Keng Makkheua Village, Xaysettha District, 2017.

40. Kro Ban, pers. comm., Leang Veng Village, Taveng District, 2017.

41. Kham Sana, pers. comm., Phak Nam Village, Voeunsai District, 2017.

42. Group 578 also operated further south with defectors from the eastern zone.

43. Bou Thang, pers. comm., Phnom Penh, 2017.

44. Later, Vietnam's Ministry of Defense Decision Order. No. 229/QD-QP disbanded Group 578 and formed in its place the Military Specialists Office

directly subordinate to Command Headquarters 579, which was subordinate to Military Region 5 (Trung Hoc Hoang Dao 2016).

45. Bou Thang, pers. comm., Banlung, 2017.

46. Kham Phai, pers. comm., Banlung, 2017.

47. Bou Thang, pers. comm., Phnom Penh, 2017.

48. Rao Nuong, pers. comm., Stung Treng, 2009.

49. Bou Thang, pers. comm., Phnom Penh, 2009.

50. Bou Thang, pers. comm., Phnom Penh, 2009.

51. Bou Thang, pers. comm., Phnom Penh, 2017.

52. Muan Poi, pers. comm., Banlung, 2017.

53. Muan Poi, pers. comm., Banlung, 2017.

54. Dop Khamchoeung, pers. comm., Bang Koet Village, Taveng District, 2017.

55. Yoep Vanson, pers. comm., Banlung, 2017.

56. Jampong Jari, pers. comm., Phak Nam Village, Voeunsai District, 2017.

57. Kham Phai, pers. comm., Stung Treng, 2009; Banlung 2017.

58. Ma Ranchai, pers. comm., Banlung, 2009.

59. Muan Hoi, pers. comm., Stung Treng, 2009.

60. Bou Thang, pers. comm., Phnom Penh, 2017.

61. Heng Khamvan, pers. comm., Stung Treng, 2009; Yoep Vanson (pers. comm., 2009) also thinks there were about six hundred soldiers at Gia Poc before the attack in late 1978.

62. Kham Sana, pers. comm., Phak Nam Village, Voeunsai District, 2017.

63. Dop Khamchoeung, pers. comm., Bang Koet Village, Taveng District, 2017; Kham Phai, pers. comm., Banlung, 2017.

64. Bui Yung, pers. comm., Kate 2 Village, O Yadao District, 2017.

65. Lê Đức Thọ, a founding member of the Indochinese Communist Party, is probably best known as the North Vietnamese negotiator who concluded the Paris Accord with Henry Kissinger in January 1973 (Kamm 1998; Gottesmen 2002).

66. Bou Thang, pers. comm., Phnom Penh, 2017.

67. Vickery (1984) reported that the Vietnamese did not enter Sector (*Tambon*) 505 near Snoul until November 1978.

68. Bou Thang, pers. comm., Phnom Penh, 2009.

69. Kham Suk, pers. comm., Stung Treng, 2009.

70. Heng Khamvan, pers. comm., Stung Treng, 2009.

71. Heng Khamvan, pers. comm., Stung Treng, 2009.

72. Bou Thang, pers. comm., Phnom Penh, 2009.

73. Dop Khamchoeung, pers. comm., Bang Koet Village, Taveng District, 2017.

74. Kham Phai and Kham Suk, pers. comm., Stung Treng, 2009.

75. Heng Khamvan, pers. comm., Stung Treng, 2009.

76. Dop Khamchoeung, pers. comm., Bang Koet Village, Taveng District, 2017.

77. Heng Khamvan, pers. comm., Stung Treng, 2009.

78. Bou Thang, pers. comm., Phnom Penh, 2017.

79. Soy Keo, pers. comm., Banlung, 2017.

80. Bou Thang, pers. comm., Phnom Penh, 2017.

81. Kham Phai, pers. comm., Stung Treng, 2009.

82. Kham Phai, pers. comm., Banlung, 2017.

83. Hangao Pat, pers. comm., Bong Village, Taveng District, 2012.

84. Khameng, pers. comm., Bang Koet Village, Taveng District, 2017.

85. Kham Phai, pers. comm., Banlung, 2017.

86. Ayk Chon, pers. comm., Banlung, 2009.

87. Kham Phai, pers. comm., Banlung, 2017.

88. Dop Khamchoeung, pers. comm., Bang Koet Village, Taveng District, 2017.

89. Heng Khamvan was initially expected to serve in the battalion assigned to Stung Treng, but because nobody in the Mondulkiri battalion could speak Vietnamese, Khmer, and Lao, he switched battalions. Kham Suk claimed that there were only 120 soldiers with Heng Khamvan (Kham Suk, pers. comm., Stung Treng, 2009).

90. Heng Khamvan, pers. comm., Stung Treng, 2009.

91. Heng Khamvan, pers. comm., Stung Treng, 2009.

92. Dop Khamchoeung, pers. comm., Bang Koet Village, Taveng District, 2017.

93. Kham Sana, pers. comm., Phak Nam Village, Voeunsai District, 2017.

94. Quyenkh, reply #445 of Vietnamese Military History website, May 17, 2009, http://www.quansuvn.net/index.php?topic=5972.440.

95. Heng Khamvan, pers. comm., Stung Treng, 2009.

96. Kham Sana, pers. comm., Phak Nam Village, Voeunsai District, 2017.

97. Heng Khamvan (pers. comm., Stung Treng, 2009) claimed that there were 220, not 120, soldiers, but the higher number seems likely to be incorrect.

98. Heng Khamvan, pers. comm., Stung Treng, 2009; Kham Sana, pers. comm., Phak Nam Village, Voeunsai District, 2017.

99. Quyenkh, reply #445 of Vietnamese Military History website.

100. Heng Khamvan and Kham Suk, pers. comm., Stung Treng, 2009; Kham Sana, pers. comm., Phak Nam Village, Voeunsai District, 2017.

101. Quyenkh, reply #451 of Vietnamese Military History website, May 18, 2009, http://www.quansuvn.net/index.php?topic=5972.450.

102. Heng Khamvan, pers. comm., Stung Treng, 2009; Bou 2011.

103. Quyenkh, reply #451 of Vietnamese Military History website.

104. Quyenkh, reply #451 of Vietnamese Military History website.

105. Supha Subin, pers. comm., Talao Village, Andong Meas District, 2015.

106. Nou Phit, pers. comm., Fang Village, Voeunsai District, 2017.

107. Supha Subin, pers. comm., Talao Village, Andong Meas District, 2015.

108. Ho Hong, pers. comm., Banlung, 2017.

109. Ho Hong, pers. comm., Banlung, 2017.

110. Bou Thang, pers. comm., Banlung, 2017.

111. Dop Khamchoeung, pers. comm., Bang Koet Village, Taveng District, 2017.

112. Jampong Jari, pers. comm., Phak Nam Village, Voeunsai District, 2017.

113. Kreng Siengnoi, pers. comm., Banlung, 2009.

114. In January 1976 there were apparently 72,248 regular soldiers in the Khmer Rouge armed forces, not including Regional and Militia forces (see http://www.yale.edu/cgp/army_v3.html, accessed March 23, 2013).

Chapter 4

1. Soy Keo, pers. comm., Banlung, 2017.

2. These sixty-two were apparently representing more than two hundred members (Slocomb 2003).

3. The eighteen included Kham Len, Bun Mi, Ma Ranchai, Lao Nyai, Thang Ngon, Ms. Phian (Lun, Taveng Village), Ms. Lang (Lun, Taveng), Ky, Jandrun (Brao, Kopong Commune), Bou Thang, Soy Keo, Khamphun (Tampuon, Kachoan Village), Kham Phuy (Tampuon, Kachoan Village), Keun (Lao, Pong Village), Doeun, and one other. There were also two Vietnamese in attendance, Voen and one other. Thang Bai and Nu Beng did not come in time for the meeting (Bou Thang, pers. comm., Banlung, 2017).

4. Bou Thang, pers. comm., Banlung, 2017.

5. Bou Thang, pers. comm., Banlung, 2017.

6. There were reportedly 7,500 members of the People's Revolutionary Party of Kampuchea at the Fifth Congress between October 13 and 16, 1985 (Slocomb 2003), 10,000 members by 1986 (Chanda 1986), and over 22,000 by 1988 (Slocomb 2003). In 1990, the party's name was changed to the Cambodia People's Party (CPP) (Kamm 1998).

7. In 2007, Bun Mi was still known to be alive but crazy in Dong Thap, Vietnam (Bou Thang, pers. comm., 2009).

8. Bou Thang, pers. comm., Phnom Penh, 2009. In March 1979, however, Chan Kary, who was a Khmer Kraom, and Van Son were removed from their positions by Pen Sovan, apparently without consulting with the Vietnamese, who were unhappy with the move (Dũng 1995).

9. Under the control of the Party of Democratic Kampuchea.

10. Stephen Heder, pers. comm., 2017.

11. This election cannot be considered to be fully democratic.

12. Bou Thang, pers. comm., Banlung, 2017.

13. Kreng Siengnoi, pers. comm., Banlung, 2009.

14. She had worked her way up from initially sewing clothes and cooking food for Vietnamese soldiers in Voeunsai beginning in February 1979. She had done a little teaching in villages during the Khmer Rouge period, so she had basic knowledge of the Khmer language (Dam Chanty, pers. comm., Banlung, 2017).

15. Dam Chanty, pers. comm., Banlung, 2017.

16. Bou Thang, pers. comm., Banlung, 2017.

17. In 1981, Bou Thang represented the four northeastern provinces of Ratanakiri, Stung Treng, Mondulkiri, and Preah Vihear. However, in 2003, National Assembly representation was divided into two positions. Therefore, Bou Thang was only able to become elected in Stung Treng and Ratanakiri, and in 2008 he was reelected to the position.

18. Bou Thang, pers. comm., Banlung, 2017.

19. Bou Thang, pers. comm., Phnom Penh 2012.

20. Later, in 1986, he left the Ministry of Health and became the deputy speaker in the National Assembly, under Chea Sim. He died in Banlung, Ratanakiri Province, in June 2008, at the age of 72.

21. He would later become a four-star general in the Cambodia army.

22. Bou Thang, pers. comm., Phnom Penh, 2017.

23. Bou Thang, pers. comm., Banlung, 2017.

24. Bou Thang, pers. comm., Banlung, 2017.

25. Bou Lam, pers. comm., Banlung, 2012.

26. Bou Thang, pers. comm., Banlung, 2017.

27. Bou Thang, pers. comm., Phnom Penh, 2017.

28. Bui Yung, pers. comm., Kate 2 Village, O Yadao District, 2017.

29. Bui Yung, pers. comm., Kate 2 Village, O Yadao District, 2017.

30. Kham Toeung, pers. comm., Banlung, 1996.

31. Kham Khoeun, pers. comm., Phnom Penh, 2017.

32. Nou Phit, pers. comm., Fang Village, Voeunsai District, 2017.

33. Bou Thang, pers. comm., Banlung, 2012.

34. Bou Thang, pers. comm., Banlung, 2017.

35. Kreng Siengnoi, pers. comm., Banlung, 2009.

36. Bou Thang, pers. comm., Phnom Penh, 2017.

37. Yoep Vanson, pers. comm., Banlung, 2017.

38. Kadam Kham was district chief of Voeunsai from 1980 to 1990 (Heng Bunthan, pers. comm., Banlung, 2017). Bang Jangao (Kreung, Khuan Village) was made district chief of Bokeo (Yoep Vanson, pers. comm., Banlung, 2009; Bou Thang, pers. comm., Banlung, 2017) although he was soon transferred to O Chum because he could not speak Tampuon, the dominant language of Bokeo. He was replaced by Sev Luo. Kham Khoeun was made district chief of Lumphat (Bou Thang, pers. comm., Phnom Penh, 2017).

39. Bou Thang, pers. comm., Banlung, 2017; Boua Keo, pers. comm., Voeunsai, 2019.

40. Kham Khoeun, pers. comm., Phnom Penh, 2017.

41. Yoep Vanson, pers. comm., Banlung, 2017. Bou Thang, pers. comm., Banlung, 2017.

42. Yoep Vanson held this position until 1989.

43. The Khmer Rouge had blown up the National Bank of Cambodia in Phnom Penh to symbolize Cambodia's total abolition of capitalism (Kamm 1998).

44. Lat Vansao, pers. comm., Banlung, 2013; Kham Khoeun and Yoep Vanson, pers. comm., Banlung, 2017; Bou Thang, pers. comm., Banlung, 2012.

45. Kham Sai, pers. comm., Banlung, 2009.

46. Yoep Vanson and Bou Thang, pers. comm., Banlung, 2017.

47. Yoep Vanson, pers. comm., Banlung, 2017.

48. Kreng Siengnoi, pers. comm., Banlung, 2009; Bou Thang, pers. comm., Banlung, 2017.

49. Kham Khoeun, pers. comm., Phnom Penh, 2017; Dam Chanty, pers. comm., Banlung, 2017.

50. Bou Thang, pers. comm., Phnom Penh, 2017.

51. Bou Thang, pers. comm., Phnom Penh, 2017.

52. Phuy Bunyok, pers. comm., Banlung 2017.

53. Bui Yung, pers. comm., Kate 2 Village, O Yadao District, 2017; Luon Vandy, pers. comm., Stung Treng, 2017.

54. Dop Khamchoeung, pers. comm., Bang Koet Village, Taveng District, 2017.

55. Dop Khamchoeung, pers. comm., Bang Koet Village, Taveng District, 2017.

56. A 500,000-riel house was built for Moi Choem in Banlung.

57. Tom Mout, pers. comm., Banlung, 2009.

58. Thang Ngon, pers. comm., Trabok Village, Taveng District, 2009.

59. Kavet La-In, pers. comm., Khuan Village, Voeunsai District, 2017.

60. Kavet La-In, pers. comm., Khuan Village, Voeunsai District, 2017.

61. Bou Thang, pers. comm., Phnom Penh, 2017.

62. Bou Thang, pers. comm., Banlung, 2017.

63. Phuy Bunyok, pers. comm., Banlung, 2017.

64. Bou Thang, pers. comm., Banlung, 2017.

65. Kham Phai, pers. comm., Banlung, 2017.

66. Kham Phai, pers. comm., Stung Treng, 2009.

67. Kham Phai, pers. comm., Banlung, 2017.

68. Kham Suk, pers. comm., Stung Treng, 2009.

69. Kham Phai, pers. comm., 2017.

70. Bou Thang, pers. comm., Banlung, 2017.

71. Kham Phai, pers. comm., Banlung, 2017.

72. Bun Chan, pers. comm., Taveng District, 2009.

73. Kham Toeung interview by Ben Kiernan, Phnom Penh, January 15, 1986.

74. Dop Khamchoeung, pers. comm., Bang Koet Village, Taveng District, 2017.

75. Nou Phit, pers. comm., Fang Village, Voeunsai District, 2017.

76. Nou Phit, pers. comm., Fang Village, Voeunsai District, 2017.

77. Bui Yung, pers. comm., Kate 2 Village, O Yadao District, 2017.

78. Nou Phit, pers. comm., Fang Village, Voeunsai District, 2017.

79. Bou Thang, pers. comm., Banlung, 2017.

80. Nou Phit, pers. comm., Fang Village, Voeunsai District, 2017; Van, pers. comm., Phnom Kok Lao Village, Voeunsai District, 2019.

81. Bui Yung, pers. comm., Kate 2 Village, O Yadao District, 2017.

82. There was not actually much reeducating done.

83. Dam Jyun, pers. comm., Phak Nam Village, Voeunsai District, 2017.

84. Bui Yung, pers. comm., Kate 2 Village, O Yadao District, 2017.

85. Bang Jangao was transferred to be the district chief of O Chum District after it was established in the early 1980s (Dam Chanty, pers. comm., Banlung, 2017).

86. Bui Yung, pers. comm., Kate 2 Village, O Yadao District, 2017.

87. Eung Saneuk, pers. comm., Trabok Village, Taveng District, 2009.

88. Bou Thang, pers. comm., Phnom Penh, 2009.

89. According to Kreng Siengnoi (pers. comm., Banlung, 2009), Bun Mi's younger brother was also mentally unstable.

90. Bou Thang, pers. comm., Phnom Penh, 2013.

91. Bou Thang, pers. comm., Phnom Penh, 2013.

92. Bou Thang, pers. comm., Phnom Penh, 2013.

93. Kham Toeung, pers. comm., Taveng District Center, 2009.

94. Bou Thang, pers. comm., Phnom Penh, 2013.

95. Kreng Siengnoi, pers. comm., Banlung, 2009.

96. Eung Saneuk, pers. comm., Trabok Village, Taveng District, 2009.

97. Few people from northeastern Cambodia had ever flown in an airplane at this time.

98. Yak, pers. comm., Keng Makkheua Village, Xaysettha District, Attapeu, 2017.

99. Yoep Vanson, pers. comm., Banlung, 2017; Yak, Keng Makkheua Village, Xaysettha District, 2017.

100. Eung Saneuk, pers. comm., Trabok Village, Taveng District, 2009.

101. Yoep Vanson, pers. comm., Banlung, 2017.

102. Kham Toeung, pers. comm., Taveng District Center, 2009; Yoep Vanson and Bou Thang, pers. comm., Banlung, 2017.

103. Yoep Vanson, pers. comm., Banlung, 2017.

104. Bou Thang, pers. comm., Banlung, 2017.

105. Bou Thang, pers. comm., Phnom Penh, 2013.

106. Kham Phai, pers. comm., Banlung, 2017.

107. Bou Thang, pers. comm., Banlung, 2013.

108. Bou Thang, pers. comm., Phnom Penh, 2013; Jyao Dawl, pers. comm., Bang Koet Village, Taveng District, 2017; Kham Phai, pers. comm., Banlung, 2017.

109. Jyao Dawl, pers. comm., Bang Koet Village, Taveng District, 2017.

110. Bou Thang, pers. comm., Phnom Penh, 2013.

111. Yoep Vanson, pers. comm., Banlung, 2017.

112. Kham Phai, pers. comm., Banlung, 2017.

113. Kham Toeung, pers. comm., Taveng District Center, 2009; Eung Saneuk, pers. comm., Trabok Village, Taveng District, 2009.

114. Kham Phai, pers. comm., Banlung, 2017.

115. Bou Thang, pers. comm., Phnom Penh, 2013.

116. Kreng Siengnoi, pers. comm., Banlung, 2009.

117. Bou Thang, pers. comm., Phnom Penh, 2009.

118. Bou Thang, pers. comm., Phnom Penh, 2009.

119. Bou Thang, pers. comm., Phnom Penh, 2017.

120. Dam Chanty, pers. comm., Banlung, 2017.

121. Bou Thang, pers. comm., Banlung, 2012.

122. Bui Yung, pers. comm., Kate 2 Village, O Yadao District, 2017.

Chapter 5

1. Bui Yung, pers. comm., Kate 2 Village, O Yadao District, 2017.

2. Bou Thang, pers. comm., Phnom Penh, 2017.

3. Although she was still young and did not have much power then.

4. Bou Thang, pers. comm., Banlung, 2012; Lat Vansao, pers. comm., Banlung, 2013; Bui Yung, pers. comm., Kate 2 Village, O Yadao District, 2017.

5. Kham Khoeun, pers. comm., Phnom Penh, 2017.

6. Yoep Vanson, pers. comm., Banlung, 2017.

7. Bou Thang, pers. comm., Banlung, 2012.

8. Bui Yung, pers. comm., Kate 2 Village, O Yadao District, 2017.

9. Lat Vansao, pers. comm., Banlung, 2013.

10. Bui Yung, pers. comm., Kate 2 Village, O Yadao District, 2017.

11. Lat Vansao, pers. comm., Banlung, 2013.

12. Phuy Bunyok, pers. comm., Banlung, 2017.

13. Bou Thang, pers. comm., Banlung, 2012.

14. Bou Thang, pers. comm., Banlung, 2017.

15. Lat Vansao, pers. comm., Banlung, 2013.

16. Bou Thang, pers. comm., Phnom Penh, 2017.

17. There were rumors that the Vietnamese wanted the dong to be used as the currency of Cambodia, but these seem to have been based on anti-Vietnamese propaganda, with no evidence that such a plan ever existed. Various other anti–Salvation Front accusations were also made but turned out to be inaccurate (Vickery 1984) or wildly exaggerated (Vickery 2010).

18. Kham Sana, pers. comm., Phak Nam Village, Voeunsai District, 2017.

19. Bou Thang, pers. comm., Banlung, 2012.

20. Tong Lieu, pers. comm., Banlung, 2009.

21. Dam Jyun, pers. comm., Phak Nam Village, Voeunsai District, 2017.

22. Lieu Thong, pers. comm., Banlung, 2009.

23. Jop Moer, pers. comm., Banlung, 2013.

24. Jop Moer, pers. comm., Banlung, 2013.

25. Kham Sana, pers. comm., Phak Nam Village, Voeunsai District, 2017.

26. Yoep Sat, pers. comm., Bong Village, Taveng District, 2012.

27. Phuy Bunyok, pers. comm., Banlung, 2017.

28. Sim Sonlai, pers. comm., Banlung, 2009.

29. Dop Khamchoeung, pers. comm., Bang Koet Village, Taveng District, 2017.

30. Phoet Phoeua, pers. comm., Taveng District Center, 2017.

31. A few who married Jarai people in Vietnam opted not to return to Cambodia (Phuy Bunyok, pers. comm., Banlung, 2017).

32. Phuy Bunyok, pers. comm., Banlung, 2017.

33. Jem Yen worked as the head of commerce in Ratanakiri Province until retiring in 1989.

34. Yoep Vanson, pers. comm., Banlung, 2009.

35. Yoep Vanson, pers. comm., Banlung, 2009.

36. Robert Cooper, pers. comm., Vientiane, 2012.

37. Jarang, pers. comm., Keng Makkheua Village, Xaysettha District, 2017.

38. Yoep Vanson, pers. comm., Banlung, 2009.

39. Channiang Gle and Yao Than, pers. comm., Bang Koet Village, Taveng District, 2017.

40. Somlit Chanthakaly, pers. comm., Attapeu town, 2017.

41. Jarang, pers. comm., Keng Makkheua Village, Xaysettha District, 2017.

42. Jarang, pers. comm., Keng Makkheua Village, Xaysettha District, 2017.

43. Yak, pers. comm., Keng Makkheua Village, Xaysettha District, 2017.

44. Kadawm, pers. comm., Keng Makkheua Village, Xaysettha District, 2017.

45. Jarang, pers. comm., Keng Makkheua Village, Xaysettha District, 2017.

46. Sot, pers. comm., Keng Makkheua Village, Xaysettha District, 2017.

47. Semrem, pers. comm., Keng Makkheua Village, Xaysettha District, 2017.

48. Bou Thang, pers. comm., Phnom Penh, 2017.

49. Hangao Pat, pers. comm., Bong Village, Taveng District, 2012; Channiang Gle, pers. comm., Bang Koet Village, Taveng District, 2017.

50. Kro Ban, pers. comm., Leang Veng Village, Taveng District, 2017.

51. Hangao Pat, pers. comm., Bong Village, Taveng District, 2012.

52. Yoep Vanson, pers. comm., Banlung, 2017.

53. Jyao Dawl, pers. comm., Bang Koet Village, Taveng District, 2017.

54. Khameng, pers. comm., Bang Koet Village, Taveng District, 2017.

55. Khameng, pers. comm., Bang Koet Village, Taveng District, 2017.

56. Jyao Dawl, pers. comm., Bang Koet Village, Taveng District, 2017.

57. Dop Khamchoeung, pers. comm., Bang Koet Village, Taveng District, 2017.

58. Prang Preul (Huak), pers. comm., Banlung, 2009.

59. Heng Bunthan, pers. comm., Banlung, 2017.

60. Bou Thang, pers. comm., Banlung, 2017.

61. Bou Thang, pers. comm., Banlung, 2017.

62. Kham Sai, pers. comm., Banlung, 2009.

63. Luon Vandy, pers. comm., Stung Treng, 2017.

64. Feuay Bunma, pers. comm., Banlung, 2009.

65. Thang Ngon, pers. comm., Trabok Village, Taveng District, 2012.

66. Dop Khamchoeung, pers. comm., Bang Koet Village, Taveng District, 2017.

67. Luon Vandy, pers. comm., Stung Treng, 2017.

68. Yoep Vanson, pers. comm., Banlung, 2017.

69. Bou Thang, pers. comm., Banlung, 2017.

70. Bou Thang, pers. comm., Banlung, 2012.

71. Nou Phit, pers. comm., Fang Village, Voeunsai District, 2017.

72. Kreng Siengnoi, pers. comm., Banlung, 2009.

73. In Pone, pers. comm., Banlung, 2009.

74. She was one of the first to move to Banlung with the provincial government in late 1979 (Dam Chanty, pers. comm., Banlung, 2017).

75. Dam Chanty, pers. comm., Banlung, 2017; Kham Khoeun, pers. comm., Phnom Penh, 2017.

76. Jop Moer, pers. comm., Banlung, 2013.

77. Bou Thang, pers. comm., Banlung, 2013.

78. Dam Chanty, pers. comm., Banlung, 2009.

79. Dam Chanty, pers. comm., Banlung, 2017.

80. BBC (1980) reported that three meters of cloth were given to each inhabitant in the province.

81. Prang Preul (Huak), pers. comm., Banlung, 2009.

82. Jampong Jari, pers. comm., Phak Nam Village, Voeunsai District, 2017.

83. Bou Thang, pers. comm., Phnom Penh, 2017.

84. Jampong Jari, pers. comm., Phak Nam Village, Voeunsai District, 2017.

85. Jampong Jari, pers. comm., Phak Nam Village, Voeunsai District, 2017.

86. Yoep Vanson, pers. comm., Banlung, 2017.

87. Heng Bunthan, pers. comm., Banlung, 2017; Jampong Jari, pers. comm., Phak Nam Village, Voeunsai District, 2017.

88. Muan Poi, pers. comm., Banlung, 2017.

89. Muan Poi, pers. comm., Banlung, 2017.

90. Heng Bunthan, pers. comm., Banlung, 2017.

91. Muan Poi, pers. comm., Banlung, 2017.

92. Muan Poi, pers. comm., Banlung, 2017.

93. Chan Khamkhoeua, pers. comm., Banlung, 2012.

94. Deth Sok Udom, pers. comm., Phnom Penh, 2017.

95. Heng Bunthan, pers. comm., Banlung, 2017.

96. Chan Khamkhoeua, pers. comm., Banlung, 2012.

97. Chan Khamkhoeua, pers. comm., Banlung, 2012.

98. Chan Khamkhoeua, pers. comm., Banlung, 2012.

99. Chan Khamkhoeua, pers. comm., Banlung, 2012.

100. In 2012, apparently 82 percent of children were studying elementary school (Chan Khamkhoeua, pers. comm., Banlung, 2012), but in reality many of those still do not study regularly.

101. Chan Khamkhoeua, pers. comm., Banlung, 2012.

102. Bou Thang, pers. comm., Banlung, 2012; Yoep Vanson, pers. comm., Banlung, 2017.

103. Yoep Vanson, pers. comm., Banlung, 2017.

104. In 1996, nongovernmental organizations (NGOs) began supporting nonformal education in parts of Ratanakiri Province, initially in Khmer and later with Indigenous language options.

105. Jop Moer, pers. comm., Banlung, 2013.

106. Bou Thang, pers. comm., Phnom Penh, 2017.

107. Bou Thang, pers. comm., Banlung, 2012.

108. He was probably thinking mainly of Vietnamese minorities.

109. Bou Thang, pers. comm., Banlung, 2012.

110. Yoep Vanson, pers. comm., Banlung, 2017.

111. Yoep Vanson, pers. comm., Banlung, 2017.

112. Dam Chanty, pers. comm., Banlung, 2017.

113. Yoep Vanson, pers. comm., Banlung, 2017.

114. Bou Thang, pers. comm., Phnom Penh, 2017.

115. By 1983 only 10 percent of the collectives in Cambodia were still reportedly functioning, and by 1984 all had been privatized (Slocomb 2003).

116. Yoep Vanson, pers. comm., Banlung, 2017.

117. Supha Subin, pers. comm., Talao Village, Andong Meas District, 2012.

118. Heng Bunthan, pers. comm., Banlung, 2017.

119. Dop Khamchoeung, pers. comm., Bang Koet Village, Taveng District, 2017.

120. Bui Yung, pers. comm., Kate 2 Village, O Yadao District, 2017.

121. He was also head of the Commerce Department at the time (Ho Hong, pers. comm., Banlung, 2017).

122. Bui Yung, pers. comm., Kate 2 Village, O Yadao District, 2017; Ho Hong, pers. comm., Banlung, 2017.

123. Bui Yung, pers. comm., Kate 2 Village, O Yadao District, 2017.

124. Bui Yung, pers. comm., Kate 2 Village, O Yadao District, 2017.

125. Bou Thang, pers. comm., Phnom Penh, 2017.

126. Bou Thang, pers. comm., Phnom Penh, 2017.

127. Bui Yung, pers. comm., Kate 2 Village, O Yadao District, 2017; Dam Chanty, pers. comm., Banlung, 2017.

128. Kham Khoeun, pers. comm., Banlung, 2017.

129. Bui Yung, pers. comm., Kate 2 Village, O Yadao District, 2017.

130. Bui Yung, pers. comm., Kate 2 Village, O Yadao District, 2017.

Chapter 6

1. Stephen Heder, pers. comm., 2017.

2. Eung Saneuk, pers. comm., Trabok Village, Taveng District, 2012.

3. Bou Thang, pers. comm., Phnom Penh, 2017.

4. Stephen Heder, pers. comm., 2017.

5. Bou Thang, pers. comm., Banlung, 2017.

6. Bou Thang, pers. comm., Banlung, 2017.

7. Bou Thang, pers. comm., Banlung, 2017.

8. Nou Phit, pers. comm., Fang Village, Voeunsai District, 2017.

9. Bou Thang, pers. comm., Phnom Penh, 2017.

10. Kham Sana, pers. comm., Phak Nam Village, Voeunsai District, 2017.

11. To Bioe, pers. comm., Soin Village, Taveng District, 2017.

12. Kham Phai, pers. comm., Banlung, 2017; Bou Thang, pers. comm., Banlung, 2017.

13. Kham Sana, pers. comm., Phak Nam Village, Voeunsai District, 2017.

14. Later, Leng stepped on a mine and was killed when he was working on the K5 project in Preah Vihear Province (Dam Jyun, pers. comm., Phak Nam Village, Voeunsai District, 2017).

15. Dam Jyun, pers. comm., Phak Nam Village, Voeunsai District, 2017.

16. Dam Jyun, pers. comm., Phak Nam Village, Voeunsai District, 2017.

17. Dop Khamchoeung, pers. comm., Bang Koet Village, Taveng District, 2017.

18. Dop Khamchoeung, pers. comm., Bang Koet Village, Taveng District, 2017.

19. Dop Khamchoeung, pers. comm., Bang Koet Village, Taveng District, 2017.

20. Dop Khamchoeung, pers. comm., Bang Koet Village, Taveng District, 2017.

21. Yoep Vanson, pers. comm., Banlung, 2017.

22. Dop Khamchoeung, pers. comm., Bang Koet Village, Taveng District, 2017.

23. Stephen Heder, pers. comm., 2017.

24. Stephen Heder, pers. comm., 2017.

25. Stephen Heder, pers. comm., 2017.

26. Stephen Heder, pers. comm., 2017.

27. Stephen Heder, pers. comm., 2005.

28. However, So Saroeun was apparently based along the Cambodian-Thai border between 1979 and 1981 (Ho Hong, pers. comm., Banlung, 2017). He was known as Roeun.

29. Stephen Heder, pers. comm., 2017.

30. Stephen Heder, pers. comm., 2017.

31. Stephen Heder, pers. comm., 2017.

32. Rao Nuong, pers. comm., Stung Treng, 2009.

33. Kreng Siengnoi, pers. comm., Banlung, 2009.

34. Tong Lieu, pers. comm., Banlung, 2009.

35. Stephen Heder, pers. comm., 2005.

36. Soy Keo, pers. comm., Banlung, 2017.

37. Soy Keo, pers. comm., Banlung, 2017.

38. Soy Keo, pers. comm., Banlung, 2017.

39. Stephen Heder, pers. comm., 2005.

40. Yoep Vanson, pers. comm., Banlung, 2009.

41. Kham Sana, pers. comm., Phak Nam Village, Voeunsai District, 2017.

42. Ho Hong, pers. comm., Banlung, 2017.

43. Dam Jyun, pers. comm., Phak Nam Village, Voeunsai District, 2017.

44. Bun Ma, pers. comm., Rok Village, Voeunsai District, 2001.

45. This is an area where three districts in Ratanakiri Province come together (Lumphat, Bokeo, and Koun Moum).

46. Kreng Siengnoi, pers. comm., Banlung, 2009.

47. Kham Khoeun, pers. comm., Phnom Penh, 2017.

48. Bou Thang, pers. comm., Banlung, 2012.

49. Kreng Siengnoi, pers. comm., Banlung, 2009.

50. Dam Kalang, pers. comm., Banlung, 2009.

51. Supha Subin, pers. comm., Talao Village, Andong Meas District, 2015.

52. Dam Kalang, pers. comm., Banlung, 2009.

53. Nou Phit, pers. comm., Fang Village, Voeunsai District, 2017.

54. Kreng Siengnoi, pers. comm., Banlung, 2009.

55. Bou Thang, pers. comm., Banlung, 2012.

56. Kouich Thoeun, a native of Ratanakiri Province, was the Commander of 709 Division (formed out of Divisions 108 and 800). It operated in Ratanakiri and Stung Treng (Stephen Heder, pers. comm., 2005).

57. Kreng, Siengnoi, pers. comm., Banlung, 2009.

58. Kreng Siengnoi, pers. comm., Banlung, 2009.

59. Kham Khoeun, pers. comm., Phnom Penh, 2017.

60. Kham Toeung, pers. comm., Taveng District Center, 2009; Tong Lieu, pers. comm., Banlung 2009.

61. In 1992, Kham Veang was recorded as a regiment commander in Division 105, which was operating in Mondulkiri.

62. Dam Kalang, pers. comm., Banlung, 2009. He also claimed that Chan died in the 3 *Srok* area in 1987. In 1987 and 1988 there were still a small number of Khmer Rouge in the 3 *Srok* area.

63. Kham Voen, pers. comm., Banlung, 2017.

64. Tom Mut, pers. comm., Banlung, 2009.

65. Thang Ngon, pers. comm., Trabok Village, 2012.

66. Phoet Phoeua, pers. comm., Taveng District Center, 2017.

67. Dop Khamchoeung, pers. comm., Bang Koet Village, Taveng District, 2017.

68. Dop Khamchoeung, pers. comm., Bang Koet Village, Taveng District, 2017.

69. Dop Khamchoeung, pers. comm., Bang Koet Village, Taveng District, 2017.

70. Thang Ngon, pers. comm., Trabok Village, Taveng District, 2012; Phoet Phoeua, pers. comm., Taveng District Center, 2017.

71. Kreng Siengnoi, pers. comm., Banlung, 2009.

72. Dop Khamchoeung, pers. comm., Bang Koet Village, Taveng District, 2017.

73. Yoep Vanson, pers. comm., Banlung, 2009.

74. Kham Toeung, pers. comm., 2009.

75. Bout Than, pers. comm., Phluk Village, Sesan District, 2017.

76. Phat Sounit, pers. comm., Khamphun Village, Sesan District, 2017.

77. Bout Than, pers. comm., Phluk Village, Sesan District, 2017.

78. Bout Than, pers. comm., Phluk Village, Sesan District, 2017.

79. Kham Toeung, pers. comm., Taveng District Center, 2009.

80. Kham Phai, pers. comm., Banlung, 2017.

81. Kham Toeung, pers. comm., Taveng District Center, 2009.

82. Bout Than, pers. comm., Phluk Village, Sesan District, 2017.

83. Stephen Heder, pers. comm., 2017.

84. Kham Toeung, pers. comm., Taveng District Center, 2009.

85. Kham Toeung, pers. comm., Taveng District Center, 2009.

86. Doeun, pers. comm., Taveng Village, Taveng District, 2009.

87. Stephen Heder, pers. comm., 2005.

88. He was apparently protected by his brother-in-law, Son Sen.

89. Kham Toeung, pers. comm., Taveng District Center, 2009.

90. Kham Phai, pers. comm., Banlung, 2017.

91. Nou Phit, pers. comm., Fang Village, Voeunsai District, 2017.

92. Lat Vansao, pers. comm., Banlung, 2013.

93. Dop Khamchoeung, pers. comm., Bang Koet Village, Taveng District, 2017.

94. Dam Jyun, pers. comm., Phak Nam Village, Voeunsai District, 2017.

95. Lat Vansao, pers. comm., Banlung, 2013. Later he was killed due to an electricity accident.

96. Yoep Sat, pers. comm., Bong Village, Taveng District, 2012.

97. Lat Vansao, pers. comm., Banlung, 2013.

98. Bou Thang, pers. comm., Phnom Penh, 2017.

99. Lat Vansao, pers. comm., Banlung, 2013.

100. Lat Vansao, pers. comm., Banlung, 2013.

101. Jop Moer, pers. comm., Banlung, 2013.

102. Dam Chanty, pers. comm., Banlung, 2017.

103. Lat Vansao, pers. comm., Banlung, 2013.

104. That was the year the PRK government declared a policy of national reconciliation. Hun Sen and Norodom Sihanouk met in France in December 1987 (Slocomb 2003).

105. Yoep Vanson, pers. comm., Banlung, 2017.

106. Doeun, pers. comm., Taveng Village, Taveng District, 2009.

107. Muan Hoi, pers. comm., Stung Treng, 2009.

108. Hangao Pat, pers. comm., Bong Village, Taveng District, 2012.

109. Kham Phai, pers. comm., Stung Treng, 2009.

110. Jum Bleo, pers. comm., Taveng District Center, 2012.

111. Bou Thang, pers. comm., Phnom Penh, 2017.

112. Kham Phai, pers. comm., Banlung, 2017.

113. Bou Thang, pers. comm., Phnom Penh, 2017.

114. Kham Phai, pers. comm., Banlung, 2017.

115. Another key player was Khanh Sean, an ethnic Khmer deputy of Bou Thang (Soy Keo., pers. comm., Banlung, 2017).

116. Bou Thang, pers. comm., Banlung, 2017.

117. Dam Chanty, pers. comm., Banlung, 2017.

118. Bou Thang, pers. comm., Phnom Penh, 2017.

119. Soy Keo, pers. comm., Phnom Penh, 2009.

120. Soy Keo, pers. comm., Phnom Penh, 2009.

121. Bou Thang, pers. comm., Banlung, 2017.

122. Deth Sok Udom, pers. comm., Phnom Penh, 2017.

123. Deth Sok Udom, pers. comm., Phnom Penh, 2017.

124. Stephen Heder, pers. comm., 2017.

125. Bou Thang, pers. comm., Phnom Penh, 2017.

126. Bou Thang, pers. comm., Banlung, 2017.

127. Bou Thang, pers. comm., Phnom Penh, 2017.

128. Bou Thang, pers. comm., Phnom Penh, 2017.

129. Kham Phai, pers. comm., Banlung, 2017.

130. Muan Hoi and Heng Khamvan, pers. comm., Stung Treng, 2009.

131. Kreng Siengnoi, pers. comm., 2009; Muan Hoi, pers. comm., 2009.

132. Soy Keo, pers. comm., Banlung, 2017.

133. Lat Vansao, pers. comm., Banlung, 2013.

134. Heng Khamvan, pers. comm., Stung Treng, 2009.

Chapter 7

1. Dop Khamchoeung, pers. comm., Bang Koet Village, Taveng District, 2017.

2. Tong Lieu, pers. comm., Banlung, 2009.

3. Sai Sopheap, pers. comm., Stung Treng, 2013.

4. Dam Chanty, pers. comm., Banlung, 2017.

5. Bou Thang, pers. comm., Banlung, 2017.

6. Nou Phit, pers. comm., Fang Village, Voeunsai District, 2017.

7. Dop Khamchoeung, pers. comm., Bang Koet Village, Taveng District, 2017.

8. Kreng Siengnoi, pers. comm., Banlung, 2009.

9. Nou Phit, pers. comm., Fang Village, Voeunsai District, 2017.

10. Jop Moer, pers. comm., Banlung, 2013.

11. Dop Khamchoeung, pers. comm., Bang Koet Village, Taveng District, 2017.

12. Nou Phit, pers. comm., Fang Village, Voeunsai District, 2017.

13. Nou Phit, pers. comm., Fang Village, Voeunsai District, 2017.

14. Bou Thang, pers. comm., Phnom Penh, 2009.

15. Bou Thang, pers. comm., Phnom Penh, 2012.

16. Yoep Vanson, pers. comm., Banlung, 2009.

17. Yoep Vanson, pers. comm., Banlung, 2017.

18. Bou Thang, pers. comm., Banlung, 2012.

19. Bou Thang, pers. comm., Phnom Penh, 2017.

20. Bou Thang, pers. comm., Banlung, 2012.

21. Bou Thang, pers. comm., Phnom Penh, 2017.

22. Yoep Vanson and Bou Thang, pers. comm., Banlung, 2017.

23. Sai Sopheap, pers. comm., Stung Treng, 2013.

24. Dam Chanty, pers. comm., Banlung, 2017.

25. Sai Sopheap, pers. comm., Stung Treng, 2013.

26. Kreng Siengnoi, pers. comm., Banlung, 2009.

27. Joeun Wel, pers. comm., Talao Village, Andong Meas District, 2015.

28. Lat Vansao, pers. comm., Banlung, 2013.

29. Bui Yung, pers. comm., Kate 2 Village, O Yadao District, 2017.

30. Kreng Siengnoi, pers. comm., Banlung, 2009.

31. Yoep Vanson, pers. comm., Banlung, 2009.

32. Jop Moer, pers. comm., Banlung, 2013.

33. Yoep Vanson, pers. comm., Banlung, 2017; Muan Poi, pers. comm., Banlung, 2017.

34. Yoep Vanson, pers. comm., Banlung, 2017.

35. Thang Ngon, pers. comm., Trabok Village, Taveng District, 2012.

36. Dam Chanty, pers. comm., Banlung, 2017.

37. Bou Thang, pers. comm., Phnom Penh, 2017.

38. Dam Chanty, pers. comm., Banlung, 2017.

39. Bou Thang, pers. comm., Phnom Penh, 2017.

40. Sai Sopheap, pers. comm., Stung Treng, 2013.

41. Sai Sopheap, pers. comm., Stung Treng, 2013.

42. Sai Sopheap, pers. comm., Stung Treng, 2013.

43. Sai Sopheap, pers. comm., Banlung, 2013.

44. Supha Subin, pers. comm., Talao Village, Andong Meas District, 2015.

45. Bou Thang, pers. comm., Banlung, 2012.

46. Sai Sopheap, pers. comm., Stung Treng, 2013.

47. Supha Subin (former policeman during Vietnamese period), pers. comm., Talao Village, Andong Meas District, 2016.

48. Dam Chanty, pers. comm., Banlung, 2017.

49. Dam Chanty, pers. comm., Banlung, 2017.

50. Soy Keo, pers. comm., Banlung, 2017.

51. Bou Thang and Yoep Vanson, pers. comm., Banlung, 2017.

52. Soy Keo, pers. comm., Banlung, 2017.

53. To Bioe, pers. comm., Soin Village, Taveng District, 2017.

54. Eung Saneuk, pers. comm., Trabok Village, Taveng District, 2012; Bou Thang, pers. comm., Banlung, 2017; Bui Yung, pers. comm., Kate 2 Village, O Yadao District, 2017.

55. To Bioe, pers. comm., Soin Village, Taveng District, 2017.

56. To Bioe, pers. comm., Soin Village, Taveng District, 2017.

57. Kham Toeung, pers. comm., Taveng District Center, 2009.

58. Doeun, pers. comm., Taveng Village, Taveng District, 2009.

59. Doeun, pers. comm., Taveng Village, Taveng District, 2009.

60. Kreng Siengnoi, pers. comm., Banlung, 2009.

61. Thang Ngon, pers. comm., Trabok Village, Taveng District, 2012.

62. Joeun Wel, pers. comm., Talao Village, Andong Meas District, Ratana-kiri Province, 2015.

63. Luon Vandy, pers. comm., Stung Treng, 2017.

64. Kham Sai and Yoep Vanson, pers. comm., Banlung, 2009.

65. Ma Ranchai, pers. comm., Banlung, 2009.

66. Nou Phit, pers. comm., Fang Village, Voeunsai District, 2017.

67. Bui Yung, pers. comm., Kate 2 Village, O Yadao District, 2017.

68. Supha Subin, pers. comm., Talao Village, Andong Meas District, 2016.

69. Bui Yung, pers. comm., Kate 2 Village, O Yadao District, 2017.

70. Yoep Vanson, pers. comm., Banlung, 2017.

71. Luon Vandy, pers. comm., Stung Treng, 2017.

72. Bui Yung, pers. comm., Kate 2 Village, O Yadao District, 2017.

73. Sai Sopheap, pers. comm., Stung Treng, 2017.

74. Lat Vansao, pers. comm., Banlung, 2013.

75. Kham Khoeun, pers. comm., Phnom Penh, 2017.

76. In Pone, pers. comm., Banlung, 2009.

77. Dam Chanty, pers. comm., Banlung, 2009.

78. Yoep Vanson, pers. comm., Banlung, 2017.

79. Kham Sana, pers. comm., Phak Nam Village, Voeunsai District, 2017.

80. Yoep Vanson, pers. comm., Banlung, 2009.

81. Yoep Vanson, pers. comm., Banlung, 2017.

82. Bou Thang, pers. comm., Banlung, 2017.

83. Yoep Vanson, pers. comm., Banlung, 2017.

84. Yoep Vanson, pers. comm., Banlung, 2017.

85. Yoep Vanson, pers. comm., Banlung, 2017.

86. Yoep Vanson, pers. comm., Banlung, 2017.

87. Bou Thang, pers. comm., Banlung, 2012.

88. Bou Thang, pers. comm., Banlung, 2017.

89. Bou Thang, pers. comm., Banlung, 2017.

90. Thang Ngon, pers. comm., Trabok Village, Taveng District, 2012.

91. Kham Sai, pers. comm., Banlung, 2009.

92. Feuay Bunma, pers. comm., Banlung, 2009.

93. Kham Khoeun, pers. comm., Phnom Penh, 2017.

94. Kreng Siengnoi, pers. comm., Banlung, 2009.

95. Kham Toeung, pers. comm., Taveng District Center, 2012.

96. Lat Vansao, pers. comm., Banlung, 2013.

97. Kham Phai, pers. comm., Banlung, 2017.

98. Kham Phai, pers. comm., Banlung, 2017.

99. Luon Vandy, pers. comm., Stung Treng, 2017.

100. Bou Thang, pers. comm., Phnom Penh, 2017.

Chapter 8

1. Heng Khamvan, pers. comm., Stung Treng, 2009.

2. Bou Thang, pers. comm., Banlung, 2012; Phnom Penh, 2017.

3. However, Dũng (1989) acknowledged that some Vietnamese troops were sent back into Cambodia to fight the NADK between October 1989 and early 1991.

4. Bou Thang, pers. comm., Banlung, 2012.

5. Yoep Vanson, pers. comm., Banlung, 2017; Channiang Gle, pers. comm., Bang Koet Village, Taveng District; Kro Ban, pers. comm., Leang Veng Village, Taveng District, 2017.

6. Kro Ban, pers. comm., Leang Veng Village, Taveng District, 2017.

7. http://www.ipu.org/parline-e/reports/arc/2051_93tm, accessed March 13, 2017.

8. Both had served on the Standing Committee of the Central Committee during the State of Cambodia period.

9. Bou Thang, pers. comm., Phnom Penh, 2017.

10. However, it was not until November 2004 that the last small isolated group of mainly Kreung and Tampuon peoples who had fled to the forests of northern Ratanakiri Province in 1979 finally gave themselves up in a small Brao village in Phouvong District, Attapeu Province, in southern Laos. They have since been relocated to their former villages in Ratanakiri Province (Purtill 2015; Baird 2008).

11. Jampong Jari, pers. comm., Phak Nam Village, Voeunsai District, 2017.

12. Sai Sopheap, pers. comm., Stung Treng, 2013.

13. Kham Voen, pers. comm., Banlung, 2017.

14. Yoep Vanson, pers. comm., Banlung, 2009.

15. Bou Thang, pers. comm., Phnom Penh, 2009.

16. Bou Thang, pers. comm., Banlung, 2012.

17. Bou Thang, pers. comm., Phnom Penh, 2017.

18. Bou Thang, pers. comm., Banlung, 2017.

19. Bou Thang, pers. comm., Banlung, 2012.

20. Jop Moer, pers. comm., Banlung, 2013.

21. Kham Voen, pers. comm., Banlung, 2017.

References

Ablin, David A., and Marlowe Hood, eds. 1990. *The Cambodian Agony*. New York and London: M. E. Sharpe.

AFP (Agence France-Presse). 1979. "Khmer Rouge Hit Hard by Lao-SRV Offensive." FBIS, April 15.

Ấm, Phụng Đình. 2002. *Một Thời Để Nhớ: Hồi Ký* [in Vietnamese]. Translated into English by Merle Pribbenow as *A Time to Remember: A Memoir*. Hanoi: People's Army Publishing House.

Anh, Lê Đức. 1986. *Quân đội nhân dân Việt Nam và nhiệm vụ quốc tế cao cả trên đất Bạn Campuchia* [in Vietnamese]. Translated into English by Merle Pribbenow as *The People's Army of Vietnam and Its Noble International Mission in Neighboring Cambodia*. Hanoi: People's Army Publishing House.

Anh, Lê Đức. 2015. *Cuộc đời và sự nghiệp cách mạng: Hồi ký* [in Vietnamese]. Translated into English by Merle Pribbenow as *My Life and My Revolutionary Cause: A Memoir*. Hanoi: National Political Publishing House [NXB Chính trị quốc gia].

ASEAN. 1979. "Statement by the Chairman of the ASEAN Standing Committee on the Vietnam-Kampuchea Conflict Source." *Contemporary Southeast Asia* 1 (3): 290.

Associated Press. 1990. "Vietnam Vows to Withdraw Advisers." *Hong Kong Standard*. September 30.

Ayres, David M. 2000. *Anatomy of a Crisis: Education, Development, and the State in Cambodia, 1953–1998*. Honolulu: University of Hawai'i Press.

Baird, Ian G. 2003. "*Dipterocarpus* Wood Resin Tenure, Management and Trade: Practices of the Brao in Northeast Cambodia." Master's thesis, Geography Department, University of Victoria, Victoria, Canada.

Baird, Ian G. 2008. "Various Forms of Colonialism: The Social and Spatial Reorganization of the Brao in Southern Laos and Northeastern Cambodia." PhD dissertation, Department of Geography, University of British Columbia, Vancouver, Canada.

Baird, Ian G. 2009a. "Best Practices in Compensation and Resettlement for Large Dams: The Case of the Planned Lower Sesan 2 Hydropower Project in Northeastern Cambodia." Report prepared for the Rivers Coalition in Cambodia (RCC), Phnom Penh, Cambodia.

Baird, Ian G. 2009b. "Controlling the Margins: Nature Conservation and State Power in Northeastern Cambodia." In *Development and Dominion: Indigenous*

Peoples of Cambodia, Vietnam and Laos, edited by Frédéric Bourdier, 215–248. Bangkok: White Lotus Press.

Baird, Ian G. 2009c. *"Dipterocarpus" Wood Resin Tenure, Management and Trade: Practices of the Brao in Northeast Cambodia.* Saarbrücken, Germany: Verlag Dr. Müller.

Baird, Ian G. 2009d. "From Champasak to Cambodia: *Chao Thammatheva,* a Wily and Influential Ethnic Lao Leader." *Aséanie* 23: 31–62.

Baird, Ian G. 2009e. "Identities and Space: The Geographies of Religious Change amongst the Brao in Northeastern Cambodia." *Anthropos Redaktion* 104 (2): 457–468.

Baird, Ian G. 2010a. "Different Views of History: Shades of Irredentism along the Laos-Cambodia Border." *Journal of Southeast Asian Studies* 41 (2): 187–213.

Baird, Ian G. 2010b. "Making Space: The Ethnic Brao and the International Border between Laos and Cambodia." *Geoforum* 41 (2): 271–281.

Baird, Ian G. 2010c. "Private, Small Groups or Communal: *Dipterocarpus* Wood Resin Tree Tenure and Management in Teun Commune, Kon Mum District, Ratanakiri Province, Northeastern Cambodia." *Society and Natural Resources* 23: 1–16.

Baird, Ian G. 2010d. "The US Central Intelligence Agency and the Brao: The Story of Kong My, a Non-Communist Space in Attapeu Province, Southern Laos." *Aséanie* 25: 23–51.

Baird, Ian G. 2011a. "The Construction of 'Indigenous Peoples' in Cambodia." In *Alterities in Asia: Reflections on Identity and Regionalism,* edited by Leong Yew, 155–176. London: Routledge.

Baird, Ian G. 2011b. "Turning Land into Capital, Turning People into Labour: Primitive Accumulation and the Arrival of Large-scale Economic Land Concessions in Laos." *New Proposals: Journal of Marxism and Interdisciplinary Inquiry* 5 (1): 10–26.

Baird, Ian G. 2013a. "'Indigenous Peoples' and Land: Comparing Communal Land Titling and Its Implications in Cambodia and Laos." *Asia Pacific Viewpoint* 54 (3): 269–281.

Baird, Ian G. 2013b. "Millenarian Movements in Southern Laos and Northeastern Siam (Thailand) at the Turn of the Twentieth Century: Reconsidering the Involvement of the Champassak Royal House." *South East Asia Research* 21 (2): 257–279.

Baird, Ian G. 2013c. "Shifting Contexts and Performances: The Brao-Kavet and Their Sacred Mountains in Northeast Cambodia." *Asian Highlands Perspectives* 28: 1–23.

Baird, Ian G. 2014. "Political Memories of Conflict, Economic Land Concessions, and Political Landscapes in the Lao People's Democratic Republic." *Geoforum* 52: 61–69.

Baird, Ian G. 2016a. "Non-government Organizations, Villagers, Political Culture and the Lower Sesan 2 Dam in Northeastern Cambodia." *Critical Asian Studies* 48 (2): 257–277.

Baird, Ian G. 2016b. "Should Ethnic Lao People Be Considered Indigenous to Cambodia? Ethnicity, Classification and the Politics of Indigeneity." *Asian Ethnicity* 17 (4): 506–526.

Baird, Ian G. 2017. "Resistance and Contingent Contestations to Large-scale Land Concessions in Southern Laos and Northeastern Cambodia." *Land* 6 (16): 1–19.

Baird, Ian G. 2019. "The Politics of Indigeneity in Southeast Asia and Cambodia: Opportunities, Challenges, and Some Reflections Related to Communal Land Titling in Cambodia." In *Indigenous Places and Colonial Spaces: The Politics of Intertwined Relations,* edited by Nicole Gombay and Marcela Palomino-Schalscha, 176–193. New York: Routledge.

Baird, Ian G., and Keith Barney. 2017. "The Political Ecology of Cross-sectoral Cumulative Impacts: Modern Landscapes, Large Hydropower Dams and Industrial Tree Plantations in Laos and Cambodia." *Journal of Peasant Studies* 44 (4): 769–795.

Baird, Ian G., and Jefferson Fox. 2015. "How Land Concessions Affect Places Elsewhere: Telecoupling, Political Ecology, and Large-Scale Plantations in Southern Laos and Northeastern Cambodia." *Land* 4 (2): 436–453.

Baird, Ian G., and Peter Hammer. 2013. "Contracting Illness: Reassessing International Donor-Initiated Health Service Experiments in Cambodia's Indigenous Periphery." *South East Asia Research* 21 (3): 457–473.

Baird, Ian G., and Philippe Le Billon. 2012. "Landscapes of Political Memories: War Legacies and Land Negotiations in Laos." *Political Geography* 31 (5): 290–300.

Baird, Ian G., and Bruce Shoemaker. 2008. *People, Livelihoods and Development in the Xekong River Basin of Laos.* Bangkok: White Lotus Press.

Baird, Ian G., Kaneungnit Tubtim, and Monsiri Baird. 1996. "The Kavet and the Kreung: Observations of Livelihoods and Natural Resources in Two Highlander Villages in the Districts of Veun Say and Ta Veng, Ratanakiri Province, Cambodia." Unpublished Livelihoods and Natural Resources Study Report, Oxfam (UK and Ireland) and Novib, Ban Lung, Ratanakiri, Cambodia.

BBC. 1980. "Development of Ratanakiri Province." October 22.

BBC. 1991. "Hydroelectric Power Project in Ratanakiri." February 27.

BBC. 1992. "Khmer Rouge Radio Says Vietnamese Battalions Are 'Concealed' in Ratanakiri." May 5.

BBC. 1998. "Former Khmer Rouge Commanders Appointed to Posts in Armed Forces." August 31.

Becker, Elizabeth. 1998 [1986]. *When the War Was Over: Cambodia and the Khmer Rouge Revolution.* Rev. ed. New York: Public Affairs.

Beijing in Cambodia to Kampuchea. 1983. "'Vietnamization' Policy under Way in Kampuchea." July 8.

Bekaert, Jacques. 1997. *Cambodian Diary: Tales of a Divided Nation, 1983–1986*. Bangkok: White Lotus Press.

Bekaert, Jacques. 1998. *Cambodian Diary: A Long Road to Peace, 1987–1993*. Bangkok: White Lotus Press.

Berman, Jennifer S. 1996. "No Place Like Home: Anti-Vietnamese Discrimination and Nationality in Cambodia." *California Law Review* 84 (3): 817–874.

Bitard, Pierre. 1952a. "Carte ethnolinguistique de la région de Voeunsai et les cultes agraires des Kha Braou (Cambodge)." *Bulletin de la Societé des Étude Indochinoises* 27 (1): 1–8.

Bitard, Pierre. 1952b. "Rites agraires des Kha Braou." *Bulletin de la Societé des Étude Indochinoises* 27 (1): 9–17.

Boliek, Brooks. 2007. "Cambodia's Hun Sen Rejects K5 Project Accusations." *Radio Free Asia*. February 2.

Bottomley, Ruth. 2002. "Contested Forests: An Analysis of the Highlander Response to Logging, Ratanakiri Province, Northeast Cambodia." *Critical Asian Studies* 34 (4): 587–606.

Bourdier, Frédéric. 2006. *The Mountain of Precious Stones. Ratanakiri, Cambodia*. Phnom Penh: Center for Khmer Studies.

Bou Thang. 1993. *Historical Travel That Cannot Be Forgotten* [in Khmer]. Phnom Penh: Self-published.

Bou Thang. 2011. *The Northeast: Traditions and Development* [in Khmer]. Phnom Penh: Self-published.

Bruel, Henri. 1916. *Monographie de la Circonscription de Stung Treng*. Saigon: C. Ardin et fils.

Burchett, Wilfred G. 1970. *The Second Indochina War: Cambodia and Laos*. New York: International Publishers.

Cang, Dao Trong, ed. 2005. *Van Kien Dang, Toan Tap, 38, 1977* [in Vietnamese]. Translated into English by Merle Pribbenow as *Collected Party Documents, Volume 38, 1977*. Hanoi: NXB Chính trị quốc gia [National Political Publishing House].

Carney, Timothy. 1986. "Heng Samrin's Armed Forces and the Military Balance in Cambodia." *International Journal of Politics* 16 (3): 150–185.

Chanda, Nayan. 1986. *Brother Enemy: The War after the War*. San Diego, New York and London: Harcourt Brace Jovanovich.

Chandler, David P. 1996 [1991]. *A History of Cambodia*. 2nd ed. Chiang Mai: Silkworm Books.

Chhak, Sarin. 1966. *Les Frontières du Cambodge*, tome 1. Paris: Dalloz.

Co, Tran Quang. 2003. *Hồi Ký Trần Quang Cơ* [in Vietnamese]. Translated into English by Merle Pribbenow as *Tran Quang Co: A Memoir*. Ebook posted at http://timsach.com.vn/viewEBOOK_38_7503_hoi-ky-Tran-Quang-Co.html.

Colm, Sara. 1996. "The Highland Minorities and the Khmer Rouge in North-eastern Cambodia 1968–1979." Unpublished report for the Cambodian Genocide Program of Yale University.

Colm, Sara. 2000. "Sacred Balance: Conserving the Ancestral Lands of Cambodia's Indigenous Communities." *Indigenous Affairs* 4: 30–39.

Colm, Sara, and Sorya Sim. 2008. "Khmer Rouge Purges in the Mondul Kiri Highlands." Unpublished manuscript.

Conboy, Kenneth, with James Morrison. 1995. *Shadow War: The CIA's Secret War in Laos*. Boulder, CO: Paladin.

Conboy, Kenneth. 2013. *The Cambodian Wars: Clashing Armies and CIA Covert Operations*. Lawrence: University Press of Kansas.

Conboy, Kenneth, and Kenneth Bowra. 1989. *The War in Cambodia 1970–75*. London: Osprey.

Condominas, Georges. 1977 [1957]. *We Have Eaten the Forest: The Story of a Montagnard Village in the Central Highlands of Vietnam*. New York: Hill and Wang.

Cung, Trần Tiến, with Nguyễn Sĩ Long. 2011. *Quê hương và đồng đội* [in Vietnamese]. Translated into English by Merle Pribbenow as *Home and Fellow Soldiers: A Memoir*. Hanoi: People's Army Publishing House.

Cupet, Captain P. 1998 [1891]. *Among the Tribes of Southern Vietnam and Laos "Wild" Tribes and French Politics on the Siamese Border*. Translated and with an introduction by Walter E. J. Tips. Bangkok: White Lotus Press.

Deth, Sok Udom. 2009. "The People's Republic of Kampuchea 1979–1989: A Draconian Savior?" Master's thesis, Center for International Studies, Ohio University, Athens.

Deth, Sok Udom. 2011. "Remembering January 7, 1979: A 33-Year Debate in Cambodian Political History." Conference paper presented at the fifth Thai-Malaysian International Conference on Southeast Asian Studies, Re-Making Historical Memory in Southeast Asia, December 1–2.

Deth, Sok Udom. 2014. "Factional Politics and Foreign Policy Choices in Cambodia-Thailand Diplomatic Relations, 1950–2014." Dissertation, der Philosophischen Fakultät III der Humboldt—Universität zu Berlin.

Dũng, Huỳnh Anh. 1995. *Ghi chép về Campuchia (1975–1991)* [in Vietnamese]. Translated into English by Merle Pribbenow as *Notes on Cambodia (1975–1991)*. Vietnam: Self-published.

Ea Meng-Try. 1981. "Kampuchea: A Country Adrift." *Population and Development Review* 7 (2): 209–228.

Edwards, Penny. 2007. *Cambodge: The Cultivation of a Nation (1860–1945)*. Honolulu: University of Hawai'i Press.

Ellen, Rosa. 2013. "From Russia, with Love to Cambodia: A Unique Friendship." *Phnom Penh Post*, July 19.

Emerson, Bridget, ed. 1997. "The Natural Resources and Livelihood Study,

Ratanakiri Province, Northeast Cambodia." The Non-Timber Forest Products (NTFP) Project, Ban Lung, Ratanakiri, Cambodia.

Encyclopedia of World Biography. 2004. "Heng Samrin." Accessed April 7, 2011, http://www.encyclopedia.com/topic/Heng_Samrin.aspx.

Engelbert, Thomas. 2004. "From Hunters to Revolutionaries: The Mobilisation of Ethnic Minorities in Southern Laos and North-Eastern Cambodia during the First Indochina War (1945–1954)." In *Ethnic Minorities and Politics in Southeast Asia*, edited by Thomas Engelbert and H. Dieter Kubitscheck, 225–270. Frankfurt: Peter Lang.

Evans, Grant, and Kelvin Rowley. 1984. *Red Brotherhood at War: Indochina since the Fall of Saigon*. London: Verso.

Fawthrop, Tom, and Helen Jarvis. 2004. *Getting Away with Genocide? Elusive Justice and the Khmer Rouge Tribunal*. London: Pluto Press.

Fentress, James J., and Chris Wickman. 1992. *Social Memory: New Perspectives on the Past*. Oxford: Blackwell Publishing.

Forest, Alain. 1980. *Le Cambodge et la Colonisation Francaise: Histoire d'une Colonisation sans Heurts (1897–1920)*. Paris: L'Harmattan.

Foucault, Michel. 1978. *The History of Sexuality. Volume I: An Introduction*. New York: Vintage Books.

Fox, Jefferson, Tuyen Nghiem, Ham Kimkong, Kaspar Hurni, and Ian G. Baird. 2018. "Large-Scale Land Concessions, Migration, and Land Use: Industrial Estates in the Red River Delta of Vietnam and Rubber Plantations of Northeast Cambodia." *Land* 7 (2): 77.

Frings, Viviane. 1993. "The Failure of Agricultural Collectivization in the People's Republic of Kampuchea (1979–1989)." Working Paper 80, Center of Southeast Asian Studies, Monash University.

Global Witness. 2009. "Country for Sale: How Cambodia's Elite Have Captured the Country's Extractive Industries." Accessed June 6, 2018, http://www.globalwitness.org/library/country-sale.

Global Witness. 2013. "Rubber Barons: How Vietnamese Companies and International Financiers Are Driving a Land Grabbing Crisis in Cambodia and Laos." Accessed June 6, 2019, https://www.globalwitness.org/en/campaigns/land-deals/rubberbarons/.

Goscha, Christopher E. 2005. "Vietnam and the World Outside: The Case of Vietnamese Communist Advisors in Laos (1948–1962)." *South East Asia Research* 12 (2): 141–185.

Gottesman, Evan. 2002. *Cambodia after the Khmer Rouge: Inside the Politics of Nation Building*. New Haven: Yale University Press.

Grabowsky, Volker. 1997. "Lao and Khmer Perceptions of National Survival: The Legacy of the Early Nineteenth Century." In *Nationalism and Cultural Revival in Southeast Asia: Perspectives from the Centre and the Region*, edited by Sri Kuhnt-Saptodewo, Volker Grabowsky, and Martin Grossheim, 145–65. Wiesbaden: Harrassowitz Verlag.

Guan, Ang Cheng. 2013. "Revisiting the Vietnamese Invasion of Kampuchea (December 1978) and the Sino-Vietnamese War (February 1979): An International History Perspective." Unpublished draft, April 12.

Guérin, Mathieu. 2003. "Des casques blancs sur le plateau des herbes. Les pacification des aborigènes des hautes terres du Sud-Indochinois (1858–1940)." PhD thesis, Université de Paris.

Guérin, Mathieu. 2008. *Paysans de la forêt à l'époque coloniale. La pacification des aborigènes des hautes terres du Cambodge (1863–1940)*. Rennes: Presses Universitaires de Rennes/HSR.

Gunn, Geoffrey C., and Jefferson Lee. 1991. *Cambodia Watching Down Under*. Bangkok: Institute of Asian Studies, Chulalongkorn University.

Hanoi Domestic Service. 1978. "PRC-Cambodia Story about Poison Gas Deceives No One." FBIS, November 14.

Hanoi Domestic Service. 1986. "Biographies of Honored PRK Leaders Reported." FBIS, February 17.

Hanoi Domestic Service. 1991. "Vietnam Helps to Build Hydroelectric Power Plant." FBIS, February 19.

Hanoi VNA. 1970. "FUNK Announces Liberation of Ratanakiri Province." FBIS, July 2.

Hanoi VNA. 1978. "Insurgents Forces' Leaflet Asks Cambodia to Rebel or Flee." FBIS, November 26.

Hanoi VNA. 1983. "Briefs." FBIS, May 3.

Hanoi VNA. 1985. "Army Volunteers Welcomed on Return from Cambodia." FBIS, April 5.

Hansen, Anne. 2007. *How to Behave: Buddhism and Modernity in Colonial Cambodia, 1860–1930*. Honolulu: University of Hawai'i Press.

Hardy, Andrew. 2003. *Red Hills: Migrants and the State in the Highlands of Vietnam*. Copenhagen: Nordic Institute of Asian Studies.

Harvey, David. 2003. *The New Imperialism*. Oxford: Oxford University Press.

Heder, Stephen. 1979. "Kampuchea's Armed Struggle: The Origins of an Independent Revolution." *Bulletin of Concerned Asian Scholars* 11 (1): 2–24.

Heder, Stephen. 1997. "Racism, Marxism, Labelling and Genocide in Ben Kiernan's *The Pol Pot Regime*." *South East Asia Research* 5 (2): 101–153.

Heder, Stephen. 2003. "Cambodia (1990–98): The Regime Didn't Change." In *Regime Change: It's Been Done Before*, edited by R. Gough, 66–75. London: Policy Exchange.

Heder, Stephen. 2004. *Cambodian Communism and the Vietnamese Model. Volume 1, Imitation and Independence, 1930–1975*. Bangkok: White Lotus Press.

Heder, Stephen, and Judy Ledgerwood. 1995. *Propaganda, Politics and Violence in Cambodia: Democratic Transition under United Nations Peace-Keeping*. London: Routledge.

Heng Samrin. 2018. *The People's Struggle: Cambodia Reborn*, edited by Peter Starr. Singapore: Editions Didier Millet.

Hickey, Gerald C. 1982a. *Free in the Forest: Ethnohistory of the Vietnamese Central Highlands 1954–1976*. New Haven: Yale University Press.

Hickey, Gerald C. 1982b. *Sons of the Mountains: Ethnohistory of the Vietnamese Central Highlands to 1954*. New Haven: Yale University Press.

Hirsch, Philip, and Andrew Wyatt. 2004. "Negotiating Local Livelihoods: Scales of Conflict in the Se San River Basin." *Asia Pacific Viewpoint* 45 (1): 51–68.

Hòa, Nguyễn Đức, and Nguyễn Duy Tường, eds. 2008. *Sư đoàn Bộ Binh 968 (1968–2008)* [in Vietnamese]. Translated into English by Merle Pribbenow as *968th Infantry Division (1968–2008)*. Hanoi: People's Army Publishing House.

Hồng, Nguyễn Văn. 2004. *Cuoc Chien Tranh Bat Buoc: Hoi Uc* [in Vietnamese]. Translated into English by Merle Pribbenow as *The Unwanted War: A Memoir*. Ho Chi Minh City: Nha Xuat Ban Tre [Tre (Youth) Publishing House].

Hughes, Caroline. 2009. "Constructing Legitimate Political Authority through Election." In *Beyond Democracy in Cambodia: Political Reconstruction in a Post-Conflict Society*, edited by Joakim Ojendal and Mona Lilja, 31–69. Copenhagen: NIAS Press.

Hun Sen. 2012. Speech in Khmer, translated into Vietnamese. Translated into English by Merle Pribbenow as "An Unforgettable Part of History." *Quan Doi Nhan Dan*, January 2.

Huy Đức. 2012a. *Bên thắng cuộc: I. Giải phóng* [in Vietnamese]. Translated into English by Merle Pribbenow as *The Winning Side. Volume I, Liberation*. Los Angeles: Self-published, Osinbook.

Huy Đức. 2012b. *Bên thắng cuộc: II. Quyền bính* [in Vietnamese]. Translated into English by Merle Pribbenow as *The Winning Side. Volume II, Power*. Los Angeles: Self-published, Osinbook.

Institute of Military History (of the Ministry of Defense). 2010. *Lich Su Quan Tinh Nguyen va Chuyen Gia Quan Su Viet Nam Giup Cach Mang Campuchia (1978–1989)* [in Vietnamese]. Translated into English by Merle Pribbenow as *History of Vietnamese Volunteer Army Forces and Vietnamese Military Specialists in Cambodia, 1978–1989*. Hanoi: Nhan Xuat Ban Quan Doi [Army Publishing House].

Ironside, Jeremy. 2009. "Poverty Reduction or Poverty Creation? A Study on Achieving the MDGS in Indigenous Communities in Cambodia." In *Development and Dominion: Indigenous Peoples in Laos, Vietnam and Cambodia*, edited by Frédéric Bourdier, 79–113. Bangkok: White Lotus Press.

Ironside, Jeremy W., and Ian G. Baird. 2003. "Wilderness and Cultural Landscape: Settlement, Agriculture, and Land and Resource Tenure in an Adjacent to Virachey National Park, Northeast Cambodia." Report prepared for Biodiversity and Protected Area Management Project (BPAMP), Ban Lung, Cambodia.

Izvestiya (Moscow). 1978. "Growing Khmer Army Mutiny against Phnom Penh Reported." FBIS, October 26.

Jacobson, Trude. 2008. *Lost Goddesses: The Denial of Female Power in Cambodian History*. Copenhagen: NIAS Press.

Jennar, Raoul M. 1998. *Cambodian Chronicles 1989–1996. Volume 1, Bungling a Peace Plan 1989–1991*. Bangkok: White Lotus Press.

Joint Task Force. 1994a. "Cambodia Oral History Program Report: Interview of BG Kham Chhanh." Phnom Penh, September 5.

Joint Task Force. 1994b. "Cambodia Oral History Program Report: Interview of MG Soy Keo." Phnom Penh, August 27.

Jones, Martin. 2009. "Phase Space: Geography, Relational Thinking, and Beyond." *Progress in Human Geography* 33 (4): 487–506.

Jonsson, Hjorleifur. 2010. "Above and Beyond: Zomia and the Ethnographic Challenge of/for Regional History." *History and Anthropology* 21 (2): 191–212.

Jonsson, Hjorleifur. 2012. "Paths to Freedom: Political Prospecting in the Ethnographic Record." *Critique in Anthropology* 32: 158–172.

Kamm, Henry. 1998. *Cambodia: Report from a Stricken Land*. New York: Arcade Publishing.

Keating, Neal B. 2003. "Kuy Alterities: The Struggle to Conceptualise and Claim Indigenous Land Rights in Neoliberal Cambodia." *Asia Pacific Viewpoint* 54 (3): 309–322.

Keller, Charles E. 1976. "A Grammatical Sketch of Brao, a Mon-Khmer Language." Master's thesis, Summer Institute of Linguistics, University of North Dakota, Grand Forks.

Keller, Charles E. 2001. "Brao-Krung Phonology." *Mon-Khmer Studies* 31: 1–13.

Keller, Charles, Jacqueline Jordi, Kenneth Gregerson, and Ian G. Baird. 2008. "The Brao Dialects of Cambodia: Lexical and Phonological Variations." *Revue de l'Institut de la Langue Nationale de l'Académie Royale du Cambodge*. Institute of Language, Phnom Penh, Special Issue, July: 87–152.

Kenney-Lazar, Miles. 2012. "Plantation Rubber, Land Grabbing and Social-Property Transformation in Southern Laos." *The Journal of Peasant Studies* 39 (3–4): 1017–1037.

Ker, Munthit. 1993. "Chakrapong-led Secession Collapses." *Phnom Penh Post*, June 18.

Ker, Munthit. 1996. "Funcinpec MPs Rally against Jan. 7 Holiday." *Phnom Penh Post*, January 12.

Khin, Sok. 2002. *L'Annexion du Cambodge par les Vietnamiens au XIXèm siècle. D'après les deux poèmes du vénérable Bâtum Baramey Pich*. Paris: Editions You-Feng.

Kiernan, Ben. 1986. Review essay: "William Shawcross, Declining Cambodia." *Bulletin of Concerned Asian Scholars* 18 (1): 56–63.

Kiernan, Ben. 2008. *The Pol Pot Regime: Race, Power, and Genocide in Cambodia under the Khmer Rouge, 1975–79*. 3rd ed. New Haven: Yale University Press.

Kiernan, Ben, and Chanthou Boua, eds. 1982. *Peasants and Politics in Kampuchea, 1942–1981*. London: Zed Press.

Kimkong Heng, and Sovinda Po. 2017. "Cambodian Youth: Shaping Relations with Vietnam." Accessed June 6, 2019, *New Mandala* blog, April 14.

Klein, Henri. 1912. "Monographie du Khet de Moulapoumok." *Revue Indochinoise* 2: 124–142.

La Depeche. 1959. "New Province" [in French]. FBIS, February 25.

Lebar, Frank M., Gerald C. Hickey, and John K. Musgrave. 1964. *Ethnic Groups of Mainland Southeast Asia*. New Haven: Human Relations Area Files Press.

Lee, Mai Na. 2015. *Dreams of the Hmong Kingdom: The Quest for Legitimation in French Indochina, 1850–1960*. Madison: University of Wisconsin Press.

Leighton, Marian Kirsch. 1978. "Perspectives on the Vietnam-Cambodia Border Conflict." *Asian Survey* 18 (5): 448–457.

Leonard, Christine. 1996. "Racism against Vietnamese Thriving." *Phnom Penh Post*, January 26.

Liên, Lê. 2013. Translated into English by Merle Pribbenow as "Installment 1: The Traitors"; "Installment 2: The Dam Breaks"; "Installment 3: Shoulder to Shoulder in Adversity"; "Installment 4: The Decisive Campaign (Conclusion)." *Quan Doi Nhan Dan*, December 23–28.

Loschmann, Heike. 2006–2007. "Buddhism and Social Development in Cambodia since the Overthrow of the Pol Pot regime in 1979." *Siksacakr* 8–9: 98–110.

Maître, Henri. 1912. *Mission Henri Maître (1909–1911) Indochine Sud-Centrale. Les Jungles Moi*. Paris: Emile Larose, Libraire-Editeur.

Mallow, Kreg P. 2002. "Perceptions of Social Change among the Krung Hilltribe of Northeast Cambodia." Master's thesis, Department of Interdisciplinary Studies, Wheaton College Graduate School, Wheaton, Illinois.

Marx, Karl. 1976. *Capital: A Critique of Political Economy*, vol 1. London: Penguin Books.

Masis, Julie. 2010. "Why Some Cambodians Speak Russian." *Christian Science Monitor*, March 4.

Matras-Troubetzkoy, Jacqueline. 1975. "Eléments pour l'étude du village et de l'habitation Brou." *Asie du Sud-est et Monde Insulindien* 6 (2–3): 201–228.

Matras-Troubetzkoy, Jacqueline. 1983. *Un Village en Forêt. L'essartage chez les Brou du Cambodge*. Paris: SELAF.

McAndrew, John P. 2000. "Indigenous Adaptation to a Rapidly Changing Economy: The Experience of Two Tampuan Villages in Northeast Cambodia." *Bulletin of Concerned Asian Scholars* 32 (4): 39–51.

Meas, Sokchea. 2012. "Opposition Party President Puts Blame on China, Vietnam for Khmer Rouge." *Phnom Penh Post*, April 18.

Mertha, Andrew. 2014. *Brothers in Arms: Chinese Aid to the Khmer Rouge, 1975–1979*. Ithaca: Cornell University Press.

Meyer, Charles. 1979. "Les nouvelles provinces: Ratanakiri—Mondolkiri." *Revue Monde en Développement* 28: 682–690.

Milne, Sarah. 2013. "Under the Leopard's Skin: Land Commodification and the Dilemmas of Indigenous Communal Title in Upland Cambodia." *Asia Pacific Viewpoint* 54 (3): 323–339.

Minh Nam. 2012. "Genocidal Khmer Rouge Regime Was Backed by the US in 'Shameful Foreign Policy Episode.'" *Thanh Nien News*, January 5.

Mysliwiec, Eva. 1988. *Punishing the Poor: The International Isolation of Kampuchea*. Oxford: Oxfam.

Natural History Institute and National University of Laos. 2017. "Sustainable Hydropower Master Plan for the Xe Kong Basin in Lao PDR." Report prepared for the Natural History Institute and National University of Laos, San Francisco and Vientiane.

NCNA (Peking). 1978. "Cambodians Deal Telling Blows to SRV Aggressors." FBIS, December 29.

Neef, Andreas, Siphat Touch, and Jamaree Chiengthong. 2013. "The Politics and Ethics of Land Concessions in Rural Cambodia." *Journal of Agricultural and Environmental Ethics* 26 (6): 1085–1103.

Neth, Baromey, Sam Rith, and Makoto Yokohari. 2013. "Development without Conformity: Impacts of Large-Scale Economic Development on Indigenous Community Livelihoods in Northeastern Cambodia." *Environmental and Rural Development* 4 (2): 82–87.

NGO Forum on Cambodia. 2004. "Land Alienation from Indigenous Minority Communities in Ratanakiri." NGO Forum on Cambodia, Phnom Penh, Cambodia.

NGO Forum on Cambodia. 2005. "Down River: The Consequences of Vietnam's Se San River Dams on Life in Cambodia and Their Meaning in International Law." NGO Forum on Cambodia, Phnom Penh, Cambodia.

NGO Forum on Cambodia. 2006. "Land Alienation from Indigenous Minority Communities, Ratanakiri Province, Cambodia." NGO Forum on Cambodia, Phnom Penh, Cambodia.

Nguyễn-vo, Thu-huong. 1992. *Khmer-Viet Relations and the Third Indochina Conflict*. Jefferson, NC: McFarland.

Nhan, Nguyễn Thi, ed. 2005. *Van Kien Dang, Toan Tap, 40, 1979* [in Vietnamese]. Translated into English by Merle Pribbenow as *Collected Party Documents, Volume 40, 1979*. Hanoi: NXB Chính trị quốc gia [National Political Publishing House].

Office of the Co-Investigating Judges. 2010. "Closing Order. Extraordinary Chambers in the Courts of Cambodia." Case File No. 002/19-09-2007-ECCC-OCIJ.

Ong, Aiwha. 1999. *Flexible Citizenship: The Cultural Logics of Transnationality.* Durham: Duke University Press.

Osborne, Milton. 1973. *Politics and Power in Cambodia: The Sihanouk Years.* London: Longman.

Ovesen Jan, and Ingrid Trankell. 2004. "Foreigners and Honorary Khmer: Ethnic Minorities in Cambodia." In *Civilizing the Margins: Southeast Asian Government Policies for the Development of Minorities,* edited by Christopher R. Duncan, 241–270. Ithaca: Cornell University Press.

Paasi, Anssi. 2011. "The Region, Identity and Power." *Procedia Social and Behavioral Sciences* 14: 9–16.

Padwe, Jonathan. 2013. "Highlands of History: Indigenous Identity and Its Antecedents in Cambodia." *Asia Pacific Viewpoint* 54 (3): 282–295.

Padwe, Jonathan. Forthcoming. *Written on the Land: Violence and Social Formation on a Cambodian Frontier.* Seattle: University of Washington Press.

Pao-Min, Chang. 1985. *Kampuchea between China and Vietnam.* Singapore: Singapore University Press.

Pen, Khon. 2000. *Phnom Penh before and after 1997.* Phnom Penh: Self-published.

Phnom Penh Domestic Service. 1968a. "Sihanouk Warns Montagnard Red Plotters." FBIS, February 1.

Phnom Penh Domestic Service. 1968b. "Sihanouk: Situation Grave in Many Provinces." FBIS, April 13.

Phnom Penh Domestic Service. 1970. "Lon Nol Goes to Ratanakiri to Study Situation." FBIS, March 9.

Phnom Penh Domestic Service. 1978a. "25–28 December Battle Report." FBIS, December 28.

Phnom Penh Domestic Service. 1978b. "Cambodian Position on Vietnam Conflict Further Detailed." FBIS, January 6.

Phnom Penh Domestic Service. 1978c. "Pol Pot Holds Interview on Cambodia-SRV Conflict." FBIS, April 12.

Phnom Penh Domestic Service. 1978d. "Revolutionary Army's Role in Northeast Praised." FBIS, May 20.

Phnom Penh Domestic Service. 1979a. "Propaganda Chairman Bou Thang Visits Stung Treng." FBIS, Ratanakiri, October 30.

Phnom Penh Domestic Service. 1979b. "Thousands Join Armed Forces to Fight Pol Pot Remnants." FBIS, August 8.

Phnom Penh Domestic Service. 1980a. "Knufns Delegation Distributes Goods in Ratanakiri Province." FBIS, March 13.

Phnom Penh Domestic Service. 1980b. "Pen Sovan Speech." FBIS, June 19.

Phnom Penh Domestic Service. 1980c. "Ratanakiri." FBIS, November 15.

Phnom Penh Domestic Service. 1980d. "Ratanakiri Received Aid from SRV; Life Returning to Normal." FBIS, February 9.

Phnom Penh Domestic Service. 1981a. "National Assembly Candidates' List." FBIS, May 1.

Phnom Penh Domestic Service. 1981b. "Results of National Assembly Elections Announced." FBIS, May 9.

Phnom Penh Domestic Service. 1983a. "Military Delegation Returns from E. Europe, USSR." FBIS, May 26.

Phnom Penh Domestic Service. 1983b. "PRK Ceremony Marks Return of Reeducated to Families." FBIS, April 14.

Phnom Penh Domestic Service. 1983c. "SRV's Vo Van Kiet Visits Ratanakiri Province." FBIS, August 5.

Phnom Penh Domestic Service. 1984a. "Circular on LPRP, Lao Treaties Anniversaries." FBIS, March 16.

Phnom Penh Domestic Service. 1984b. "Kampuchea Calls for Greater Effort in Education." FBIS, September 27.

Phnom Penh Domestic Service. 1985. "Further Delegate Speeches to KPRP Congress." FBIS, October 20.

Phnom Penh Domestic Service. 1987. "Soviet-Aided Airline Development Described." FBIS, October 29.

Phnom Penh Domestic Service. 1989a. "Bou Thang-Led Delegation Returns from Vietnam." FBIS, August 10.

Phnom Penh Domestic Service. 1989b. "Party Paper on Troop Recruitment Efforts in 1989." FBIS, March 12.

Phnom Penh Domestic Service. 1990. "Bou Thang Opens Hydropower Station Building Site." FBIS, December 20.

Phnom Penh SPK. 1980. "Details Aids from Vietnamese Provinces." FBIS, February 16.

Phnom Penh SPK. 1981a. "Minority Praise for Congress." FBIS, May 25.

Phnom Penh SPK. 1981b. "River Transportation System." FBIS, July 24.

Phnom Penh SPK. 1982. "Provincial Leader Meets with Lao Counterpart." FBIS, September 28.

Phnom Penh SPK. 1984a. "Bou Thang Leaves for VPA Anniversary Celebration." FBIS, December 18.

Phnom Penh SPK. 1984b. "Report on Opening of National Assembly Session." FBIS, August 15.

Phnom Penh SPK. 1985a. "Bou Thang Led Delegation Leaves for Moscow." FBIS, May 6.

Phnom Penh SPK. 1985b. "Provincial Meetings Mark SRV Troop Withdrawal." FBIS, April 4.

Phnom Penh SPK. 1989. "1st Military Region Commander Interviewed." FBIS, August 21.

Phnom Penh SPK. 1990. "Economic Cooperation with Laos Reviewed." FBIS, December 5.

Phnom Penh SPK. 1991. "Construction of Hydroelectric Plant Progressing." FBIS, June 27.

Pouvatchy, Joseph R. 1986. "Cambodian-Vietnamese Relations." *Asian Survey* 26 (4): 440–451.

Pribbenow, Merle. 2006. "A Tale of Five Generals: Vietnam's Invasion of Cambodia." *The Journal of Military History* 70: 259–286.

PRK Foreign Ministry. 1985. "PRK White Book: 'Undeclared War against the PRK.'" BBC, December 31.

Puangthong Rungswasdisab. 2004. "Thailand's Response to the Cambodian Genocide." Working Paper No. 12, Genocide Studies Program, 79–126.

Purtill, Corinne. 2015. *Ghosts in the Forest.* Kindle Single.

Rathie, Martin. 2006. "Laos-Cambodia Relations: 'The Revolutionary Dimension.'" PhD thesis (draft), School of History, Philosophy, Religion and Classics, University of Queensland, Brisbane, Australia.

Rathie, Martin. 2019. "The Lao Long of Cambodia: Ethnic Lao in the Cambodian Revolutions." In *Engaging Asia: Essays on Laos and Beyond in Honour of Martin Stuart-Fox*, edited by Desley Goldston, 190–229. Copenhagen: NIAS Press.

Ruohomaki, Olli. 2003. "Encounters in Borderlands: Social and Economic Transformations in Ratanakiri, Northeast Cambodia." *Moussons* 7: 71–94.

Salemink, Oscar. 2018. "The Regional Centrality of Vietnam's Central Highlands." In *Oxford Research Encyclopedia of Asian History*, edited by David Ludden. Oxford: Oxford University Press.

Schliesinger, Joachim. 1998. *Hill Tribes of Vietnam: Profiles of Existing Tribe Groups*, vol. 2. Bangkok: White Lotus Press.

Scott, James C. 1985. *Weapons of the Weak: Everyday Forms of Peasant Resistance.* New Haven: Yale University Press.

Scott, James C. 2009. *The Art of Not Being Governed: An Anarchist History of Upland Southeast Asia.* New Haven: Yale University Press.

Shawcross, William. 1979. *Side-show: Kissinger, Nixon and the Destruction of Cambodia.* New York: Pocket Books.

Shawcross, William. 1984. *The Quality of Mercy: Cambodia, Holocaust and Modern Conscious.* London: Andre Deutsch, and Simon and Schuster.

Short, Philip. 2004. *Pol Pot: Anatomy of a Nightmare.* New York: Henry Holt.

Slocomb, Margaret. 2001. "The K5 Gamble: National Defence and Nation Building under the People's Republic of Kampuchea." *Journal of Southeast Asian Studies* 32 (2): 195–210.

Slocomb, Margaret. 2003. *The People's Republic of Kampuchea 1979–1989. The Revolution after Pol Pot.* Chiang Mai: Silkworm Books.

Smith, Frank. 1989. "Khmer Rouge Years: Personal Experience in Cambodian

Peasant World View." Wisconsin Papers on Southeast Asia, Center for Southeast Asian Studies, University of Wisconsin–Madison.

Son, Hong. 2016. "Campuchia—chuyện chưa kể về Ủy ban khởi nghĩa Đông bắc" [three installments in Vietnamese]. Translated into English by Merle Pribbenow as "Cambodia—Untold Story about the Northeastern Insurrection Committee." *Tuoi Tre News*, January 4–6.

Sorpong, Peou. 2000. *Intervention and Change in Cambodia: Toward Democracy?* Singapore: Institute of Southeast Asian Studies.

Sutsakhan, Lt. Gen. Sak. 1978. *The Khmer Republic at War and the Final Collapse.* Indochina Monographs. Reprinted by Dalley Book Service, Christiansburg, VA.

Swift, Peter. 2006. "Livelihoods in the Srepok River Basin in Cambodia." Phnom Penh: NGO Forum on Cambodia.

Swift, Peter. 2013. "Changing Ethnic Identities Among the Kuy in Cambodia: Assimilation, Reassertion, and the Making of Indigenous Identity." *Asia Pacific Viewpoint* 54 (3): 296–308.

Tan, Le Minh. n.d. *LỊCH SỬ Sư ĐOÀN BỘBINH 2—TẬP 2 (1975–2005)* [in Vietnamese]. Translated into English by Merle Pribbenow as *History of the 2nd Infantry Division, Volume 2 (1975–2005).* Hanoi: People's Army Publishing House.

TASS. 1978. "Operations against Pol Pot–Ieng Sary Clique Reported." FBIS, December 17.

Thet Sambath and E. Kinetz. 2006. "KR Built Love Homes to Boost Regime Ranks." *Cambodia Daily*, December 25.

Tomoda, Seki. 1997. "Detaching from Cambodia." In *Vietnam Joins the World*, edited by James W. Morley and Masashi Nishihara, 134–153. Armonk: M. E. Sharpe.

Tran Dinh Tho, Brig. Gen. 1979. "The Cambodian Incursion." *Indochina Monograph.* Washington, DC: US Army Center of Military History.

Trung Hoc Hoang Dao [Hoang Dao High School]. 2016. "On the Commanders of Group 578." Blog site (in Australia). Accessed September 6, 2016, http:// trunghochoangdao.blogspot.com.au/2016/06/ve-nhung-chi-huy-oan-578 .html, June 7.

Tully, John. 2005. *A Short History of Cambodia: From Empire to Survival.* Crows Nest, NSW: Allen & Unwin.

Tuoi Tre News. 2015. "Vietnamese, Cambodians Owe Debt of Gratitude to One Another." July 30.

Tyner, James A. 2009. "Imagining Genocide: Anti-Geographies of the Erasure of Space in Democratic Kampuchea." *Space and Polity* 13 (1): 9–20.

Uk, Krisna. 2016. *Salvage: Cultural Resilience among the Jorai of Northeast Cambodia.* Ithaca: Cornell University Press.

United Nations. 1990. *World Population Monitoring 1989: Special Report, the Population Situation in the Least Developed Countries.* New York: United Nations.

US Library of Congress. 2006. *The Khmer Loeu*. Washington, DC: US Library of Congress.

Vachon, Michelle. 2017. "Healing a Nation." *Cambodia Daily*, April 21.

Vickery, Michael. 1984. *Cambodia 1975–1982*. Chiang Mai: Silkworm Books.

Vickery, Michael. 1989. "Cambodia (Kampuchea): History, Tragedy, and Uncertain Future." *Bulletin of Concerned Asian Scholars* 21 (2–4): 35–58.

Vickery, Michael. 2007. *Cambodia: A Political Survey*. Phnom Penh: Editions Funan.

Vickery, Michael. 2010. *Kicking the Vietnam Syndrome in Cambodia; Collected Writings 1975–2010*. Accessed March 20, 2013, http://michaelvickery.org/.

Vientiane Domestic Service. 1983. "PRK Military Delegation Ends Visit 27 Jan." FBIS, January 27.

Vientiane KPL. 1989. "Cambodian Delegations Ends Visit to Attopeu." FBIS, December 9.

VODK. 1979a. "Kok Lak Clashes." FBIS, February 7.

VODK. 1979b. "Kra Claims Nearly 300 Killed 2–4 February." FBIS, February 4.

VODK. 1979c. "Ratanakiri Villagers' Retaliation." FBIS, November 10.

VODK. 1979d. "VODK Airs Battle Reports, Notes Victories." FBIS, April 14.

VODK. 1979e. "VODK Cites Ingenious Tactics of Ratanakiri Guerillas." FBIS, May 30.

VODK. 1980. "Over 2,000 Vietnamese Killed, Wounded in Northeast." FBIS, March 24.

VODK. 1982. "VODK Condemns SRV 'Genocide' in Ratanakiri." FBIS, January 13.

VODK. 1983a. "190 SRV Soldiers Desert, Return to SRV." FBIS, June 19.

VODK. 1983b. "VODK Condemns Chemical Attack in Ratanakiri." FBIS, August 13.

VODK. 1984a. "Ratanakiri Communes Liberated." FBIS, March 19.

VODK. 1984b. "VODK Claims 5 Ratanakiri Villages 'Liberated.'" FBIS, August 8.

VODK. 1984c. "VODK Commentary Attacks Lao Offer to Fight." FBIS, January 13.

VODK. 1985a. "Attack on Ratanakiri Airport." FBIS, February 23.

VODK. 1985b. "SRV Regiment Commander Killed in Ratanakiri." FBIS, July 14.

VODK. 1985c. "VONADK: District Seat of Ratanakiri 'Liberated.'" FBIS, August 11.

VODK. 1985d. "VONADK: SRV Regiment Ambushed in Ratanakiri." FBIS, October 18.

VODK. 1986. "VONADK Raps 'Vietnamization' of Education by SRV." FBIS, January 9.

VODK. 1987. "Truck Ambushed on Kratie-Stung Treng Road." FBIS, November 22.

VODK. 1989a. "More Vietnamese Families Said Sent to Settle." FBIS, February 11.

VODK. 1989b. "SRV Envoy's Statement on Pullout Questioned." FBIS, September 17.

VODK. 1989c. "Vietnamese Said to Settle in Ratanakiri." FBIS, February 8.

VODK. 1991. "700 SRV Troops Reportedly Hidden in Ratanakiri." FBIS, January 7.

VODK. 1992. "400 SRV Troops to Ratanakiri Province." FBIS, February 9.

Voice of the Cambodian People. 1978. "Insurgents Battle Government Troops 25 Nov–8 Dec." FBIS, December 15.

Voice of the Khmer. 1989. "SRV Troops Reportedly Left Behind in Jungles." FBIS, November 14.

Vong Sokheng. 2012. "Premier Hails 'Liberation Day.'" *Phnom Penh Post*, January 6.

Vũ, Bùi Cát. 1979. Đuường *vào Phnom-Pênh* [in Vietnamese]. Translated into English by Merle Pribbenow as *The Road to Phnom Penh*. Vietnamese Military History website, topic box for posting of books and memoirs. Accessed September 11, 2016, http://www.vnmilitaryhistory.net/index.php?topic= 13646.0.

Vu, Hoang Minh. 2014. "Facing the Inevitable? Vietnam's Decision to Invade Cambodia, 1977–78." Undergraduate dissertation, International Relations and History, London School of Economics and Political Science, London.

Whitaker, Donald P., Judith M. Heimann, John E. MacDonald, K. W. Martindale, R-S. Shinn, and C. Townsend. 1973. *Area Handbook for the Khmer Republic (Cambodia)*. Washington, DC: Government Printing Office.

White, Joanna. 1995. "Of Spirits and Services: Health and Healing among the Hill Tribes of Ratanakiri Province, Cambodia." Report prepared for Health Unlimited, Ban Lung, Ratanakiri, Cambodia.

Wyatt, Andrew B., and Ian G. Baird. 2007. "Transboundary Impact Assessment in the Sesan River Basin: The Case of the Yali Falls Dam." *International Journal of Water Resources Development* 23 (3): 427–442.

Xinhua (Beijing). 1979a. "Ieng Sary Appeals to UN on SRV Aggression." FBIS, January 3.

Xinhua (Beijing). 1979b. "Revolutionary Army Surprise Attacks Wipe Out More Invaders." FBIS, March 28.

Yen, Hoang Bach, ed. 2005. *Van Kien Dang, Toan Tap, 39, 1978* [in Vietnamese]. Translated into English by Merle Pribbenow as *Collected Party Documents, Volume 39, 1978*. Hanoi: NXB Chính trị quốc gia [National Political Publishing House].

Yun Shui. 2002. "The Collapse of the Phnom Penh Regime." Translated by Paul Marks. *Critical Asian Studies* 34 (4): 497–500.

Ziv, Guy, Eric Baran, So Nam, Ignacio Rodriguez-Iturbe, and Simon Levin. 2012. "Trading-Off Fish Biodiversity, Food Security, and Hydropower in the Mekong River Basin." *Proceedings of the National Academy of Sciences* 109 (15): 5609.

Zweers, J., and Sok Mary. 2002. "'The Spirits Are Leaving': Changing Beliefs and Attitudes among the Krueng, Jarrai and Tompuen regarding Their Natural Resources." Report prepared for IDRC, Banlung, Ratanakiri, Cambodia.

Index

New Perspectives
in Southeast Asian Studies